THE FIRST HUMANS

Human Origins and History to 10,000 BC

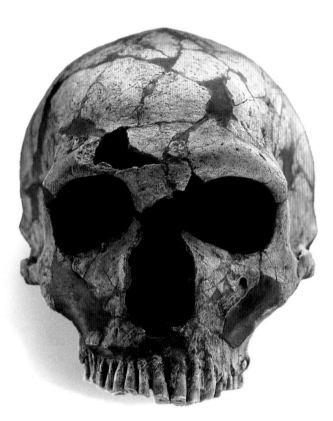

AMERICAN MUSEUM OF NATURAL HISTORY

The Illustrated History of Humankind

THE FIRST HUMANS

Human Origins and History to 10,000 BC

General Editor
GÖRAN BURENHULT

Foreword by DONALD C. JOHANSON

HarperSanFrancisco
A Division of HarperCollinsPublishers

FIRST EDITION
Reprinted 1994, 1995

Conceived and produced by
Weldon Owen Pty Limited
43 Victoria Street, McMahons Point NSW 2060, Australia
Fax 61 2 929 8352

and

Bra Böcker AB
S–263 80 Höganäs
Sweden
Fax 46 42 330504

The Illustrated History of Humankind
Publisher: Sheena Coupe
Series Coordinator: Annette Carter
Copy Editors: Roderic Campbell, Carson Creagh,
Glenda Downing, Jacqueline Kent, Margaret McPhee
Editorial Assistants: Julia Burke and Vesna Radojcic
Picture Editor: Anne Burke
Illustrations Editor: Joanna Collard
Index: Dianne Regtop
Art Director: Sue Burk
Computer layout: Sylvie Abecassis and Paul Geros
Production Director: Mick Bagnato
Production Coordinator: Simone Perryman

Weldon Owen Pty Limited
Chairman: Kevin Weldon
President: John Owen
General Manager: Stuart Laurence
Coeditions Director: Derek Barton

Bra Böcker AB
Publisher and Vice-President: Kari Marklund
Editorial Director: Claes Göran Green
Editor: Christina Christoffersson

Library of Congress Cataloging-in-Publication Data

The First humans / Göran Burenhult, general editor.
        p.   cm. -- (The Illustrated history of humankind : v. 1)
     Includes index.
     ISBN 0-06-250265-4
     1. Man--Origin. 2. Man, Prehistoric. I. Burenhult, Göran.
     II. Series.
     GN281.I365   1993 vol. 1
     573.2--dc20   92-56108
                              CIP

95 96 97 WOHK 10 9 8 7 6 5 4 3

Manufactured by Mandarin Offset
Printed in Hong Kong

A WELDON OWEN PRODUCTION

C O N T E N T S

9 Foreword • **11** Preface • **13** Introduction

PAGE **17**

WHAT IS HUMANKIND?

Roland Fletcher

F e a t u r e s

20 Olduvai Gorge: the cradle of humanity — Roland Fletcher
22 From sounds to speech: a human discovery — William Noble and Iain Davidson
26 Aggression and war: are they part of being human? — Irenäus Eibl-Eibesfeldt
30 Sex roles in prehistory — Michelle Lampl

PAGE **33**

HUMAN ORIGINS

Colin Groves

F e a t u r e s

41 Sexual dimorphism: comparative and evolutionary perspectives — Walter Leutenegger
42 Our earliest ancestors — Colin Groves
46 When did language begin? — Iain Davidson and William Noble
53 So similar and still so different: the Great Apes and ourselves — Wulf Schiefenhövel

PAGE **55**

TOWARDS *HOMO SAPIENS*

Göran Burenhult

F e a t u r e s

60 Mighty hunter or marginal scavenger? — Peter Rowley-Conwy
65 What do the Zhoukoudian finds tell us? — Peter Rowley-Conwy
68 The Neanderthals — Colin Groves
70 Was there a Neanderthal religion? — Peter Rowley-Conwy
74 Dating the past — Colin Groves

PAGE **77**

MODERN PEOPLE IN AFRICA AND EUROPE

Göran Burenhult

F e a t u r e s

82 Ice through the ages — Björn E. Berglund and Svante Björck
86 Animals of Ice Age Europe — Ronnie Liljegren
94 Radiocarbon: a key to the past — Göran Burenhult

PAGE **97**

THE RISE OF ART

Göran Burenhult

F e a t u r e s

102 The Venus figurines — Göran Burenhult
112 Pech-Merle: a 20,000-year-old sanctuary — Göran Burenhult
118 Cosquer Cave: an ancient sunken gallery — Jean Clottes and Jean Courtin

PAGE **123**

SPREADING THROUGHOUT THE GLOBE
Göran Burenhult

F e a t u r e s

128 Tools and cultures in Late Paleolithic Southeast Asia   *Ian C. Glover*
134 Mammoth bone huts   *Roland Fletcher*
138 Sungir: a Stone Age burial site   *Olga Soffer*
144 Genes, languages, and archaeology   *Peter Rowley-Conwy*

PAGE **147**

THE SETTLEMENT OF ANCIENT AUSTRALIA
J. Peter White

F e a t u r e s

152 Thermoluminescence dating   *Richard G. Roberts*
158 Art of the land   *Paul Tacon*
162 Hunters on the edge of the Tasmanian ice   *Richard Cosgrove*
168 The lost animals of Australia   *Timothy Flannery*

PAGE **171**

THE FIRST PACIFIC ISLANDERS
J. Peter White

F e a t u r e s

175 Moving animals from place to place   *Timothy Flannery*
176 Heat treatment: a 50,000-year-old technology   *J. Peter White*
178 From stone to tools: residue analysis   *Tom Loy*
183 Relics of the first New Ireland settlers   *Christopher Gosden*

PAGE **185**

MODERN PEOPLE IN THE NEW WORLD
George C. Frison

F e a t u r e s

190 Who were the first Americans?   *David Hurst Thomas*
194 Clovis weapons: a modern experiment   *George C. Frison*
200 The Paleoindian bison hunters   *George C. Frison*
206 The fate of North America's early animals   *Donald K. Grayson*

PAGE **209**

PIONEERS OF THE ARCTIC
Moreau Maxwell

F e a t u r e s

214 Arctic animals
220 Early Arctic cultures   *Moreau Maxwell*
227 A Dorset camp   *Moreau Maxwell*

228 Glossary   •   **232** Notes on contributors   •   **235** Index

8

THE STUDY OF PALEOANTHROPOLOGY concerns the origins of humankind—a very personal investigation of how we came to be *Homo sapiens*. The broad outlines of the last four million years of human evolution are fairly well known to paleoanthropologists. Every year, with each new discovery, with each novel interpretation, we are slowly beginning to fill in the details. Because of the vagaries of the archaeological and paleontological record, however, vital clues may never be found.

One overriding observation is certain: Africa has played a critical role at every stage of the human career. Hominids arose in Africa from an as yet unidentified ape-like ancestor some time between 4 and 10 million years ago, during the Miocene period. By 4 million years ago, a primitive, but erect, walking hominid known as *Australopithecus afarensis* made an appearance in the geological record of East Africa. This species apparently gave rise to two distinct branches of hominid evolution. One branch consisted of robust vegetarians, which became extinct about a million years ago. The other lineage was characterized by increasing brain size; the first known species is called *Homo habilis*. Current evidence suggests that 1.5 million years ago, *Homo erectus* arose and became the first hominid to leave Africa and begin to populate Eurasia. Although still very controversial, recent work suggests that anatomically modern humans first appeared in Africa more than 100,000 years ago. Anthropologists cannot agree on how many branches sprouted from the "mother" of us all, "Lucy", but today only one hominid survives—ourselves.

I am a fossil hunter, but I am not interested just in finding more fossil remains of our ancestors, but also in trying to understand what these finds tell us about our origins and about ourselves. The science of paleoanthropology has grown into a respectable discipline incorporating developments from the fields of behavior, molecular biology, ecology, the Earth sciences, evolutionary biology, and many other fields into a powerful investigation that addresses a series of intriguing questions. Who are we? Where did we come from? What does it mean to be human? Where are we going? These questions do not have simple answers, but in order to comprehend our own nature, we must strive to find answers.

Paleoanthropology is really still in its infancy, and the puzzle of our origins is far from complete. The puzzle is an especially difficult one, since we have no picture on the box top to guide us. It is not always easy to find the correct place in the puzzle for a new discovery. It may take considerable study before the true importance of a fossil find is unraveled. This is why the field of paleoanthropology is constantly changing. Interpretations are frequently modified, and we must all be receptive to altering our personally held views of human origins. For some, this is a disturbing aspect, but for me, I find it stimulating to be at the cutting edge of such a dynamic science. It is often said that space is the last frontier, but I believe that time is also one of the last frontiers—the distant past when our ancestors initiated the long evolutionary journey that led to *Homo sapiens*. This was a tortuous and unpredictable path. There was no grand plan that ensured that modern humans would evolve. At any point along the way, as was the case for the robust vegetarians, our ancestors could have become extinct. So far, we have survived the evolutionary journey, and today we have became the introspective species, a species that has the capacity to plan for the future while retaining the curiosity to ponder its past. Let us hope that we will use the enlightenment of the past to carefully and thoughtfully prepare the road for the future.

Donald C. Johanson, PhD
President, Institute of Human Origins
Berkeley, California

◄ Excavation at the Upper Paleolithic site of Kostenki, near Voronesh, in Russia.

HELPING TO TRAILBLAZE *The Illustrated History of Humankind* has been both a professional and a personal pleasure. From the outset, the publishers demonstrated beyond all doubt their ability to produce a final product tuned to the very highest scholarly and graphic standards. Convinced that the publication would justify a long-term commitment, those of us on the Editorial Board set out to round up a truly distinguished consortium of archaeologists and other scientists.

The text is brisk and unambiguous. But readers should know that the authors are much more than professional writers. They are dedicated scientists, those literally working in the trenches. We have drawn together the leaders in their respective fields, more than 150 participants from diverse branches of science—archaeology, anthropology, paleontology, classics, ethology, geology, and biology. Never before has such a prominent group of archaeologists joined forces with their colleagues in related disciplines on such a grand scale.

High-quality scholarship like this is usually restricted to specialized international congresses, whose results rarely reach the interested public. In effect, *The Illustrated History of Humankind* offers those on the scientific front lines a unique opportunity to "take their findings public".

The Illustrated History of Humankind transcends mere historical narrative. These pages set out the ongoing story of how humans are unshrouding their own past. The format is multivolume, yet highly integrated, defining an unequaled breadth of coverage. Ranging across the first four million years of humanity, the *History* details events long forgotten. But these volumes go beyond the products of science, delving into the very process by which scientists learn about our human past. In these pages, we can see modern humans coming to grips with themselves, their origins, their diversity, their common experience. This is how science addresses our very being.

The Illustrated History of Humankind makes no attempt to downplay the controversies that must arise when humans explore humanity. The philosophy undergirding this project is to preserve the flavor of science in action, to present the controversies and the disagreements, the skirmishes and the disputes. *The Illustrated History of Humankind* should debunk, once and for all, the myth of a scientific consensus about the human past. This is not homogenized science.

The volumes are visually stunning, lavish in their use of color photography and illustrated maps. The graphic standards are high indeed, and I'm particularly delighted with the archaeological reconstructions, created from scratch by scientists working with talented artists to present sometimes radically new perspectives on the human past. *The Illustrated History of Humankind* provides a unique visual glimpse of the human past.

I derive a personal sense of gratification from this project because it promises to take the lessons of today's archaeology to new audiences. The archaeological record is one of the world's precious resources—nonrenewable and irreplaceable. Not only will the *History* provide the public with a better grasp of what archaeologists do, but we can also hope that it will inspire a sense of urgency to protect archaeological sites around the world, which are increasingly coming under threat.

◄● Magnificent weapons of flint and bone, about 11,000 years old, found in Montana, in the United States.

David Hurst Thomas

IN THE LAST FEW DECADES, research into our prehistoric past has undergone explosive developments. The biological and cultural evolution of humankind is being seen in a new light. Traditional and stereotyped ideas about different "cultures" and lines of evolution, and one-sided explanations of changes resulting from the spread of people, ideas, and other cultural elements, have been replaced by a deeper understanding of the fact that human cultural manifestations are the result of regional adaptations to the surrounding environment and its resources, to the continuously changing ecology of planet Earth. New findings and a greater degree of inter-disciplinary cooperation have provided a better insight into environmental development and into the social and economic conditions our ancestors would have experienced. New and more accurate dating methods have in many cases revolutionized our thinking about considerable parts of our prehistoric past.

Archaeology is about facts: the unearthed remains of human activities in the past. But archaeological finds don't speak for themselves—they have to be interpreted. And often there are many ways of interpreting the data. The aim of archaeological research is to link the silent, static find materials to the living, dynamic society that once created them. Archaeology thus becomes the study of the social processes that lie behind the visible remains of prehistoric activities. All archaeological interpretation, therefore, must be based on known facts. The only facts known to archaeologists are the archaeological source materials, most often represented by the remains we excavate.

Compared to the vast span of time that human evolution embraces, our own individual lifetime is little more than the twinkling of an eye. Tool-making humans have existed on Earth for more than two million years. As a comparison, historic time comprises only some two or three thousand years—that is, about 0.2 percent of the time that humans have existed. The heyday of the Vikings, for instance, is only 30 generations away.

During this long period, humans have adapted to—and evolved in—a variety of different ecological systems: from tropical rainforests and deserts to high mountains and icy tundras. The highly specialized economy of the Paleolithic big-game hunters, the rich subsistence of Europe's Mesolithic hunter-gatherers, and the appearance of farming cultures are all examples of this process of adaptation.

It was not until this century that, as a result of the industrialization process, the majority of the world's population was no longer actively involved in producing food. In just a few generations, this alienation from our natural surroundings has created a profound and alarming ignorance of the vital natural balance. Short-term economic interests and employment policies destroy irreplaceable parts of the ecosystem, and we are often overconfident of modern technology's ability to artificially replace this natural balance.

One of the primary aims of prehistorians must be to spread knowledge of how the conditions of human life have changed over the millennia as a result of our remarkable ability to adapt to our surroundings. A more profound knowledge of human evolution paves the way for a better understanding of humans' role in the ecosystem and can in this way help to arrest the overexploitation of natural resources and the destruction of the environment.

At the same time, prehistory—and history—tells us that social structures and religious concepts, as well as different kinds of prejudice, emanate directly from a given society's accumulated needs and are influenced by the subsistence and ecological systems prevailing in particular cases. This knowledge is vital if we are to master our own problems of supply and overpopulation, and to be able to understand the background to, and counteract, the cultural and racial antagonisms that so greatly influence our daily lives. With a better insight into the ways in which humans have adapted to their natural surroundings in the past, we are better equipped to tackle our future in an ever-shrinking world. Without a perspective backwards in time, we can't look into the future—indeed, the very existence of succeeding generations is at risk.

The first volume of *The Illustrated History of Humankind* describes the evolution of humans, which began in Africa some five million years ago. It also tells the story of how modern humans expanded throughout the world—to Europe, Asia, Australia, the Pacific, the Americas, and the Arctic.

The first three chapters overlap in time and deal with three different aspects of early human prehistory. "What Is Humankind?" describes the development of human behavior, some of the ways in which it has changed, and its relation to the visible cultural manifestations left behind in the archaeological record. "Human Origins" analyzes human evolution from a biological and anatomical point of view, from the first hominids to the appearance of anatomically modern humans. "Towards *Homo sapiens*" gives an account of our knowledge of cultural development and tool technologies as revealed by the archaeological find material, as well as by what we know of social and economic conditions.

"Modern People in Africa and Europe" embraces the period between 200,000 and 12,000 years ago, and covers the development of modern humans in Africa and their subsequent spread into Southwest Asia and Europe. "The Rise of Art" deals with the appearance of the first examples of human artistic expression and the development of Upper Paleolithic cave art in Europe between 30,000 and 12,000 years ago. "Spreading Throughout the Globe" describes the background to the expansion of modern humans across Asia and towards Australia and the Americas between 50,000 and 10,000 years ago. "The Settlement of Ancient Australia" and "The First Pacific Islanders" give details about the first humans to set foot in Australia and settle the Pacific. "Modern People in the New World" deals with the first humans in the New World, between 15,000 and 12,000 years ago. And finally, "Pioneers of the Arctic" tells the story of the people who first settled the frozen north, some 4,500 years ago—the ancestors of today's Eskimos, the last surviving representatives of the Upper Paleolithic way of life.

Göran Burenhult

◄● Carved Venus figure from Laussel, in France, dating from the Upper Paleolithic period.

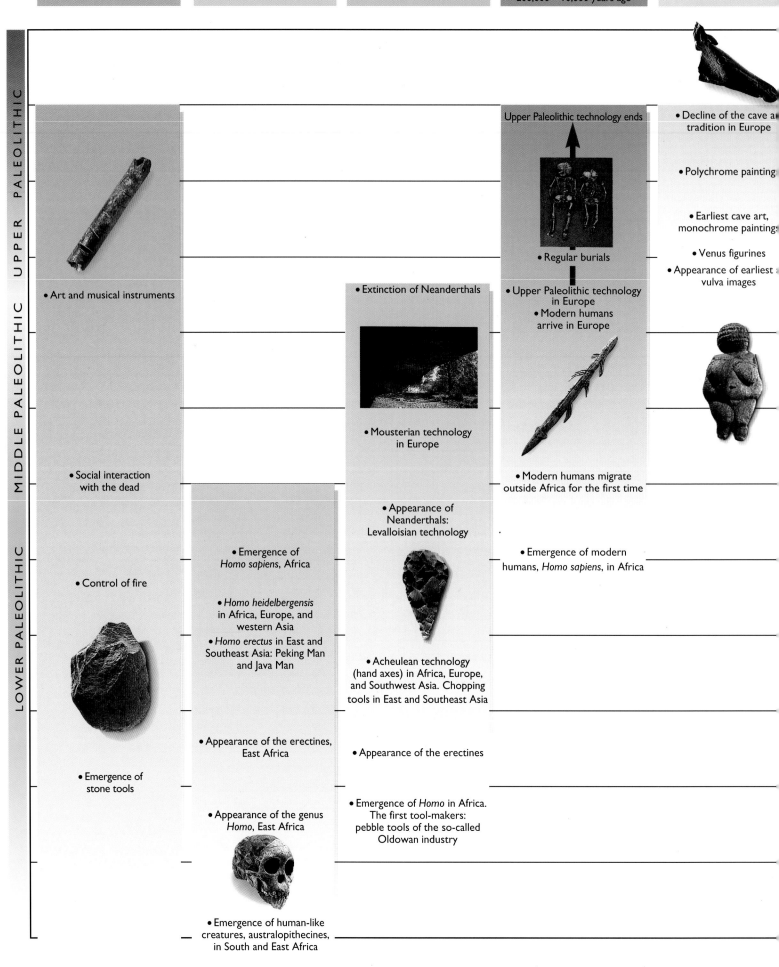

WHAT IS HUMANKIND?
5 million – 10,000 years ago

HUMAN ORIGINS
20 million – 100,000 years ago

TOWARDS *HOMO SAPIENS*
2.5 million – 35,000 years ago

MODERN PEOPLE IN AFRICA AND EUROPE
200,000 – 10,000 years ago

THE RISE OF ART
35,000 – 10,000 years ago

UPPER PALEOLITHIC

MIDDLE PALEOLITHIC

LOWER PALEOLITHIC

Upper Paleolithic technology ends

- Decline of the cave a⸱ tradition in Europe

- Polychrome painting⸱

- Earliest cave art, monochrome painting⸱

- Venus figurines

- Appearance of earliest ⸱ vulva images

- Art and musical instruments

- Extinction of Neanderthals

- Regular burials

- Upper Paleolithic technology in Europe
- Modern humans arrive in Europe

- Mousterian technology in Europe

- Social interaction with the dead

- Modern humans migrate outside Africa for the first time

- Appearance of Neanderthals: Levalloisian technology

- Control of fire

- Emergence of *Homo sapiens*, Africa

- *Homo heidelbergensis* in Africa, Europe, and western Asia
- *Homo erectus* in East and Southeast Asia: Peking Man and Java Man

- Emergence of modern humans, *Homo sapiens*, in Africa

- Acheulean technology (hand axes) in Africa, Europe, and Southwest Asia. Chopping tools in East and Southeast Asia

- Emergence of stone tools

- Appearance of the erectines, East Africa

- Appearance of the erectines

- Emergence of *Homo* in Africa. The first tool-makers: pebble tools of the so-called Oldowan industry

- Emergence of the genus *Homo*, East Africa

- Emergence of human-like creatures, australopithecines, in South and East Africa

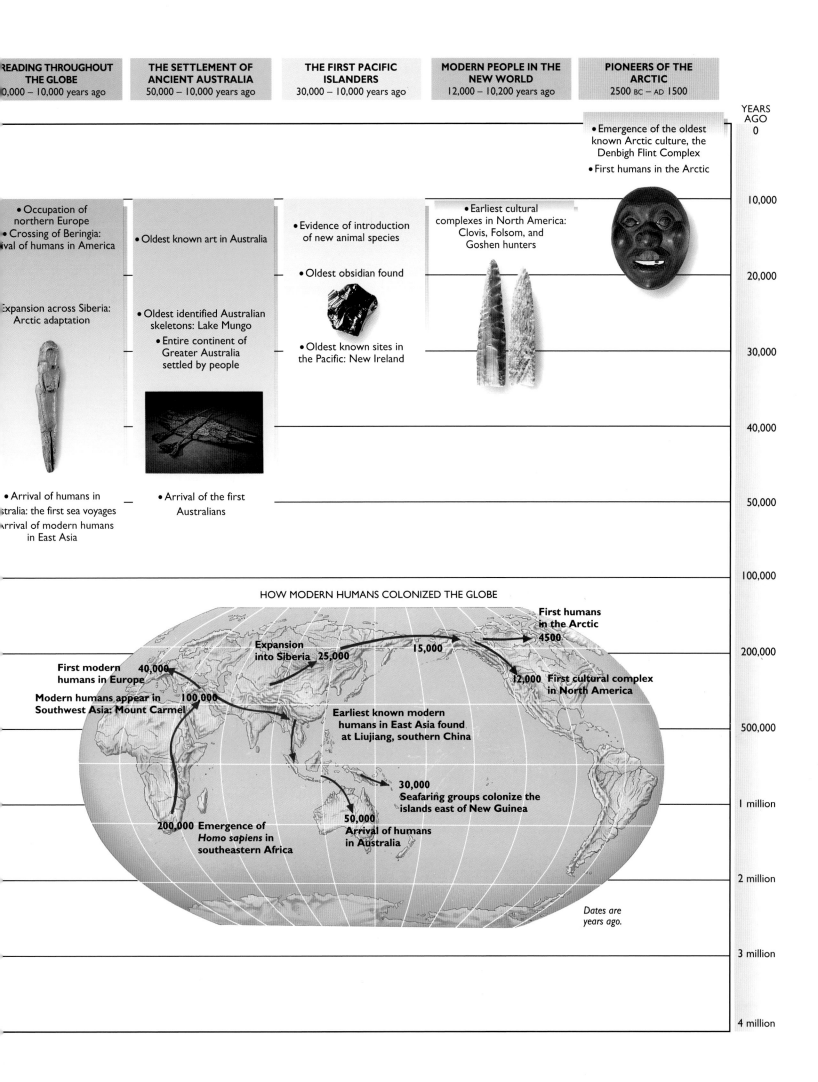

YEARS AGO

• Emergence of the oldest known Arctic culture, the Denbigh Flint Complex

• First humans in the Arctic

0

• Occupation of northern Europe
• Crossing of Beringia: ival of humans in America

• Oldest known art in Australia

• Evidence of introduction of new animal species

• Earliest cultural complexes in North America: Clovis, Folsom, and Goshen hunters

10,000

• Oldest obsidian found

20,000

Expansion across Siberia: Arctic adaptation

• Oldest identified Australian skeletons: Lake Mungo
• Entire continent of Greater Australia settled by people

• Oldest known sites in the Pacific: New Ireland

30,000

40,000

• Arrival of humans in stralia: the first sea voyages
rrival of modern humans in East Asia

• Arrival of the first Australians

50,000

100,000

HOW MODERN HUMANS COLONIZED THE GLOBE

First humans in the Arctic
4500

Expansion into Siberia 25,000

15,000

First modern humans in Europe 40,000

12,000 First cultural complex in North America

200,000

Modern humans appear in Southwest Asia: Mount Carmel 100,000

Earliest known modern humans in East Asia found at Liujiang, southern China

500,000

30,000
Seafaring groups colonize the islands east of New Guinea

200,000 Emergence of *Homo sapiens* in southeastern Africa

50,000
Arrival of humans in Australia

1 million

Dates are years ago.

2 million

3 million

4 million

15

WHAT IS HUMANKIND?

The Evolution of Human Behavior

ROLAND FLETCHER

HUMAN BEHAVIOR HAS EVOLVED over the past three to four million years. Beginning with walking upright, in combination with the usual camping and tool-using behavior of the higher primates, successive generations of hominids have developed the capacity to control fire, to interact socially with their dead, and to represent the universe in art. We are a unique species because we have these characteristics. They are readily visible in the archaeological record, and this has allowed us to date their appearance as habitual features of our behavior.

We also have less tangible characteristics, such as our distinctive sexual behavior, a remarkable capacity for persistence, the power of speech, our elaborate moral beliefs, and, combined with a ready tendency to kill other humans, an extraordinary ability to care for the helpless and the aged. Quite when these aspects of our nature evolved is less obvious, and is subject to considerable dispute.

⬅ The early hominids were rare and scarcely visible on the East African savanna, which teemed with herbivores such as zebras and buffaloes. A remnant of those great herds can still be seen in the Ngorongoro Crater, in Tanzania.

⬆ Oldowan "chopper", 1.5 to 2 million years old.

DAVID L. BRILL, © 1985

↪ Humans and other primates have a very similar skeletal structure. The key difference is that humans (right) habitually walk with the upper body held upright above the pelvis. By contrast, gorillas (left) occasionally walk upright but do not maintain an upright posture for very long.

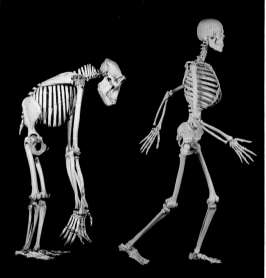

Primates have a general, though not universal, pattern of periodic sexual accessibility (the estrus cycle). However, like the tree-climbing, solitary orang-utan, we can be sexually active at any time, regardless of whether conception is possible. Nor is our tendency to kill each other unique. Lions, for example, sometimes kill other lions. But we are unique in lacking the behavioral controls found among many other species that would normally prevent such incidents. Caring for each other is not unique, either. Reciprocal altruism is not uncommon among animals, playing a straight-forward evolutionary role by helping closely related individuals with similar genes to survive. True, humans attach moral values to caring for each other, but morals are probably a very recent development.

To transmit moral values, we need language, and there is no evidence that our current form of language is much more than 50,000 years old. We were becoming human long before that, and our humanness is founded in our distant past, not uniquely created by our most recent forms of behavior.

Creating tools requires the ability to remember actions. Humans have long made simple tools and continue to do so, but we have developed the ability to carry out the increasingly complex sequences of actions required to make more and more elaborate stone tools. Similarly, while we made only the simplest windbreaks a million or more years ago, by the end of the most recent Ice Age, about 15,000 years ago, we were able to build elaborate huts from hundreds of interlocked mammoth bones. Within the last half-million years, the action sequences became complex enough for us to make and sustain fires. By remembering actions, we began, within the last 100,000 years, to recall the movements and gestures associated with our dead, turning meaningless corpses into remembered relatives. And within the last 50,000 years, our capacity to make such associations and to retain mental images has led to the ability to represent the outside world and the content of our minds in art. What we must strive to understand is how long all these things took. Our evolution began very slowly, and the majority of the changes and elaborations we recognize as distinctly human are, in archaeological terms, very recent.

↥ The earliest stone tool assemblages, between about 2.6 and 1.5 million years old, consisted of numerous small flakes of varied shapes and a few larger pieces usually referred to as "choppers", although they were probably the cores from which flakes were struck to make tools. The production of stone tools results in large amounts of debris.

Towards a Human Culture

Over the past two to three million years, human cultural behavior has become considerably more complex. As our ability to make things, using progressively longer sequences of actions, has evolved, we have also developed a much greater range of distinctively human behavior. The capacity to retain information in our mind and to retrieve this information has increased enormously over this time, and at some point allowed us to consciously know who we are. Our evolving culture creates new opportunities but also complex problems.

Stand Up and Be Human

Once we stood up and began to walk on two legs (or, in other words, became bipedal), important physical changes began to occur. Our new stance altered the position of our sexual organs and made the frontal surface of the body conspicuously visible. Sexual signaling had to change as a result. In ground-dwelling primates, the onset of estrus is marked by a distinctly visible alteration to the external genitalia. But when humans stood up, the female genitalia were concealed between the legs, and a variety of different adaptations may have resulted. Estrus disappeared, a distinctly female form evolved, and females became capable of sexual activity at any time. As humans became bipedal very early in their evolution, our distinctly human sexuality probably evolved at an early stage, too.

Durable Tools

We did not have to walk upright in order to be able to make and use tools, but it did free the hands to carry and manipulate objects much more readily. Primates are very dexterous. They are also playful and inquisitive. The making and use of tools by early hominids is not in itself surprising, since our nearest primate relatives possess this ability. What is different with hominids is that they began to manipulate durable materials. We might expect this from a creature living in less wooded country and camping on open ground by streams and lakes. The search for food in shallow water, scrabbling among pebbles for lizards and insects, or pushing aside dead branches and bits of rock to define a camping space brought hominids into habitual contact with durable materials. This ability is what sets us apart. Inevitably, the camp sites became marked by fragments of stone and food debris as hominids began to use naturally fractured rock, and then started to smash rocks to obtain sharp pieces. Eventually, the ability to repeatedly produce tools of similar form evolved. The earliest known tools of this kind have been found at Hadar, in Ethiopia. But we should not assume that stone tools gave us an immediate adaptive advantage. For a million years, hominids were no more successful as a species than monkeys or apes had been.

This relationship with durable materials, whether in the form of tools or debris on camp sites, began a profound transformation of our behavior. Several new factors were introduced into our social life. Significantly, territorial control could be signaled by inanimate objects, such as abandoned camp sites. These not only indicated the location of hominid groups throughout the landscape, they also served as a warning to newcomers that they might be trespassing. An inanimate, durable, cultural geography appeared, signaling the way in which hominids were spread across the landscape even when the individuals were no longer present. While this signaling was not at first deliberate, it would gradually have become so under selective pressure. Here, too, our behavior sets us apart from the higher primates, who mark territory primarily by active confrontation between individuals.

➌ At Laetoli, in Tanzania, Mary Leakey found the footprints of a hominid adult and child preserved in volcanic ash. This is the earliest evidence for bipedalism. About 3.5 million years ago, they walked northwards across the ash fall from a nearby volcano, the child walking in the footsteps of the adult. Small antelope passed by, and a brief rainstorm splattered across the landscape, before further eruptions buried the footprints.

OLDUVAI GORGE: A WINDOW ON THE PAST

R OLAND F LETCHER

O LDUVAI G ORGE cuts across the Serengeti Plain, in Tanzania, close to the Ngorongoro Crater. Long before the gorge began to develop, the area was occupied by a lake, which periodically expanded and contracted. Hominids lived around the shore and near the small rivers that flowed into it. When the lake flooded, layers of mud buried these sites, along with any skeletal remains that lay there.

From time to time, great deposits of volcanic ash covered the region. These are especially valuable to archaeologists, because they create a natural sequence of layers within a site, and the sequence can be dated. The gorge exposes a sequence of layers nearly 90 meters (300 feet) deep. At the bottom, in Bed I, are layers dated to 1.8 to 1.6 million years ago. The upper layers, in Bed IV, date to 200,000 to 100,000 years ago. Because of its depth, the gorge provides an extraordinary opportunity to study human evolution.

♠ An Acheulean hand axe made about 400,000 years ago by *Homo erectus*. Each tool was made in at least two stages and required about 50 actions. Such tools are more elaborate than those of the earlier Oldowan type.
MARY JELLIFFE/ANCIENT ART & ARCHITECTURE COLLECTION

♀ View over Olduvai Gorge and the Serengeti Plain to Ngorongoro Crater.

R.I.M. CAMPBELL/BRUCE COLEMAN LTD

☝ Looking into the gorge.

↩ Oldowan tools were found in Bed I and may be associated with *Homo habilis*. The assemblage included small flakes of stone as well as large cores, or "choppers".
MARY JELLIFFE/ANCIENT ART & ARCHITECTURE COLLECTION

↪ Louis and Mary Leakey began work at Olduvai in the 1930s. They soon found stone tools made from basalt and other kinds of volcanic rock, associated with concentrations of animal bone. Only after 30 years' work, however, did they discover the hominid fossils for which they and Olduvai are famous.

Mary Leakey is shown here meticulously excavating a hominid site. When *Australopithecus boisei* was found in 1959, it took 19 days of excavation just to free the face and teeth.

R.I.M. CAMPBELL/BRUCE COLEMAN LTD

↪ The Leakeys' research involved the whole family, especially one of their sons, Richard, seen here measuring hominid fossils. Richard Leakey later became Director of the Kenya National Museum.

↩ *Australopithecus boisei* (top), found in 1959, and *Homo habilis* (bottom), found in 1961, both from Bed I.
TOP: R.I.M. CAMPBELL/BRUCE COLEMAN LTD
BOTTOM: MARY JELLIFFE/ANCIENT ART & ARCHITECTURE COLLECTION

R.I.M. CAMPBELL/BRUCE COLEMAN LTD

FROM SOUNDS TO SPEECH: A HUMAN DISCOVERY

WILLIAM NOBLE AND IAIN DAVIDSON

LANGUAGE IS A SYSTEM of symbols, consisting of either visible patterns (such as written or sign language) or audible sounds (such as speech), which represent things other than themselves. Not all visible patterns or audible signs, of course, amount to language. Those who make and perceive these signs must know what they represent, so the signs must be both consistent and easily recognizable. For example, all people who understand and recognize the English word *cat* can relate it to the domestic animal. But, while language must be used consistently, in another sense it is arbitrary: the written or spoken word *cat* bears no resemblance to the animal it refers to.

⊕ Statuette of a mammoth from Vogelherd, southwest Germany, dated to about 32,000 years ago.
STAATLICHE MUSEEN ZU BERLIN/PREUSSISCHER KULTURBESITZ, MUSEUM FÜR VOR- UND FRÜHGESCHICHTE

⊷ This statuette with human body and feline head from Hohlensteinstadel, southwest Germany, is about 32,000 years old. Statuettes with similar parallel markings on the shoulders have been found in neighboring sites.
K.H. AUGUSTIN/ULMER MUSEUM

From Signaling to Signs

Animals cannot be said to use language, although they do respond to visible and audible signals. Vervet monkeys in eastern Africa make different sounds in response to the presence of different kinds of predators, such as snakes, leopards, and eagles. Other monkeys in the area respond immediately and appropriately when they hear these calls. They look up when an "eagle" call is made, around when they hear a "leopard call", and down in response to a "snake" call. These animals, however, show no sign of realizing that the sounds they make and the postures they adopt signify the predators in question. They utter these signals only in the presence of predators. For these vocal calls to be considered linguistic, the monkeys would need to use and respond to them when predators were not present.

We believe that language emerged when our ancestors realized that the sounds or signals they made were a means of referring to features of the environment. Once this happened, then and only then could these sounds or signals be used, altered, and multiplied to refer to more and more such features. In this way, early humans discovered the symbolic possibilities of gestures used for communication. As a result, their behavior became more complex. They could remark upon their current behavior, conceive of other ways of behaving, recite past events, and plan future ones—and were thus able to bring their environment, including their social environment, under increasing control.

Hominid evolution is said to have involved an increasing capacity for visual control of the arms and hands, and thus improvement in one-handed, aimed throwing. This, of course, would have enabled hominids to point in order to indicate features of the environment—such as prey or predators. In turn, this could have led to tracking the movements of animals, and characteristic features of the animal being tracked could

also have been signaled by hand and arm movements tracing or mimicking the animal's gait or outline. These silent maneuvers would have communicated the necessary information to other group members without alerting the prey to the group's presence.

From Signs to Symbols

The next step in the emergence of language-like behavior could have occurred when, in the act of making such signs, our ancestors left marks in mud or sand. The marks would have become visible as objects in the external world. The gesture as a visible record could then be seen as an independent entity, conveying information by itself. When this happened, the way was open for signs, both visible and audible, to be seen and exploited as symbols. In Europe, evidence of such symbols is not found earlier than about 36,000 to 32,000 years ago, in the form of three-dimensional figures which were clearly created using common conventions of representation and reference.

The arrival of humans in Australia, which has been reliably dated to at least 50,000 years ago, is our earliest evidence for the use of language. The people who came to Australia would have to have crossed open seas, and to do this they obviously had to build seagoing craft. To have conceived, planned, and carried out such activity without the use of language would clearly have been impossible.

⊕ A python approaches a group of vervets. The monkeys show alarm when they hear one of the group calling in response to the approach. The call is specific to this source of danger.

RICHARD WRANGHAM/ANTHROPHOTO

Aggression at a Distance

Stone tools would also have become a part of the signaling behavior within each group. Some primate signaling is very aggressive. Chimpanzees and gorillas, for example, recognize status hierarchies among both males and females. A dominant male, the most powerful in the group, may be challenged by another male in a contest for control of sexual access to females. These fights usually involve a great deal of face-to-face posturing, noise, and the displaying of teeth, but rarely cause serious injury. When one of the contestants acknowledges defeat, the contest stops. Chimpanzees also throw sticks during fights, and when they are tense or insecure. Because the contestants are usually very close to each other, facial and bodily gestures of submission are easy to see, serving to switch off the victor's aggressive drive.

But throwing or hitting with lumps of stone or other hard objects is much more drastic than bodily posturing. Hominids who kept their distance from their opponents and aimed straight would have been at a distinct advantage. This, in turn, would have made facial and bodily gestures less necessary and less effective. The most useful defense was the ability to predict a competitor's next move and to pre-empt it. Individuals who could do this were more likely to avoid injury and therefore more likely to produce offspring with the same aptitude. The advent of hard tools may help to explain why human aggression is not tied to overt display and why gestures of submission do not necessarily control violence among humans.

The Persistent Human

Being able to remember and to predict actions would have led to the development of the characteristic human trait of persistence. Clearly, the more information a hominid could remember as a basis for its actions—whether in making tools, social competition, or the search for food— the more advantaged it would be. For instance, between one and two million years ago, we may

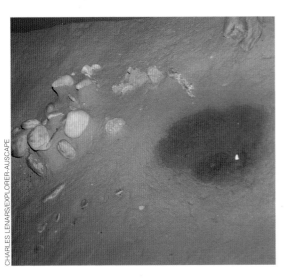

have hunted, but we were certainly opportunistic scavengers. At least 100,000 to 50,000 years ago, we were successfully hunting big game, perhaps even in a coordinated way. Modern humans continue to hunt even when the prey is out of sight for many hours. The more information we have stored in our brains, the more persistent we are likely to be in order to achieve our end.

Fire Power

Alone among the animals, humans are attracted to fire and can control it. But we should not suppose that savanna animals are unfamiliar with fire or always avoid it. Grassland fires are frequent and extensive. Numerous insects and small animals die. Scavengers move in behind the fires to obtain food, and early hominids would presumably have sought food in the same way, picking through the ashes and moving charred sticks to get at food. They might well have carried a smouldering stick as a tool. But actually maintaining fires and having the capacity to create fire require quite elaborate

J-P VARIN/JACANA-AUSCAPE

♦ When chimpanzees are frightened or become aggressive, they sometimes run bipedally and can carry a stick to threaten an intruder or a predator. Vigorous facial gestures and vocal signaling are a feature of attacks and status fights, which take place at close range.

◄● Traces of fire and occupation debris dating back to between 300,000 and 200,000 years ago have been found at Terra Amata, in France, at camp sites on the sand near the former shore of the Mediterranean. Some of the hearths are in shallow pits, while others are on patches of pebbles.

CHARLES LENARS/EXPLORER-AUSCAPE

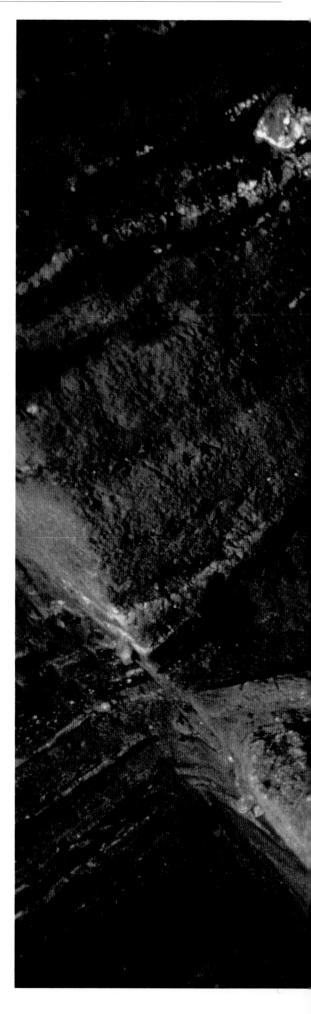

☝ In the Gombe Reserve, in Tanzania, Jane Goodall and Hugo van Lawick saw a chimpanzee mother carrying her dead baby around for a day or so. After a while, she began to hold the corpse negligently. Eventually, she put it down, went for a drink, and did not pick the dead baby up again.

HUGO VAN LAWICK/REPRINTED BY PERMISSION OF THE PUBLISHERS FROM *THE CHIMPANZEES OF GOMBE* BY JANE GOODALL, CAMBRIDGE, MASSACHUSETTS: THE BELKNAP PRESS OF HARVARD UNIVERSITY PRESS, COPYRIGHT © 1986 BY THE PRESIDENT AND FELLOWS OF HARVARD COLLEGE.

↪ There is intense debate as to whether the Neanderthals buried their dead—and if so, why they did. The recent discovery of a Neanderthal at Kebara Cave, in Israel, dated to 60,000 years ago, has added a further example for discussion. Part of the reason for the debate is the new claim for an African origin for modern humans that would exclude the Neanderthals from our direct ancestry. But we need not envisage a simple continuity of behavior. Neanderthal bodies are found in very varied contexts and in a variety of positions, and we should not assume that this behavior can be explained in terms familiar to us.

sequences of actions. Near the underground lake of Escale, in France, possible remains of fires have been found, along with the debris of human occupation, dating back as far as 700,000 years ago. Most evidence of hearths, however, is found within the last 300,000 years.

The control of fire has several consequences. Food can be cooked, and wooden tools shaped and hardened. Controlled burning of grassland helps to drive animals toward hunters. Accidental, repeated fires in woodland increase the extent of open pasture, encouraging larger populations of herbivores, such as deer. Fires also signal the presence of humans. When Captain James Cook first approached the eastern seaboard of Australia, he knew the country was inhabited because he could see plumes of smoke from numerous camp fires. At night especially, a fire can indicate where people are living. By using fire, humans inadvertently provided additional signals, visible over considerable distances, about their location in the landscape. Meetings no longer depended entirely on chance, and the social world became more complex. Just as stone tools gave humans a new means of signaling, so too did fire, adding to their capacity to predict and control their world.

Remembrance of Things Past

The next major change in human behavior was the ability to recognize that the dead body was once human. Up to 100,000 years ago, there is no evidence that hominids perceived their dead any differently from other kinds of dead meat. Hominid bones have been found scattered and broken among the rubbish of camp sites. This is consistent with the way other primates neglect the dead. A chimpanzee mother will carry her dead baby around for a day or two, but becomes increasingly less aware of it. At first she cuddles the corpse, but she is then likely to carry it by one leg or drag it along, until eventually she puts it down and forgets it. The body no longer emits signals indicating that it is a chimpanzee, and the mother does not have the conceptual capacity to remember the actions once associated with her offspring.

After about 100,000 years ago, the Neanderthals began to interact with their dead, which they treated in many different ways. But we should beware of inferring that they thought as we do. The Neanderthals may be fascinating precisely because they perceived their dead in ways entirely beyond our experience. What if memory span varied among Neanderthals, as intelligence does among modern humans? The Neanderthal bodies found at Krapina, in the Balkans, were elaborately defleshed and burned, yet in the cave of Hortus, in the Pyrenees, they were just dumped in with the rubbish. In the cave of La Chapelle-aux-Saints, in southern France, an old man was buried in a deep pit.

◄◉ Threat display of a male chimpanzee: characteristics of this expressive behavior are the bristled hair, which enlarges the silhouette, the exposed teeth, and the threatening stare. Staring and displaying the teeth as though in readiness to bite are also basic to human expressions of anger. The bristling of the fur exists in vestigial form in the "shiver" we experience when the hair erector muscles contract—and, as we say, our hair stands on end.

AGGRESSION AND WAR: ARE THEY PART OF BEING HUMAN?

IRENÄUS EIBL-EIBESFELDT

AGGRESSION OCCURS WHENEVER a person or a group of people attempts to dominate another by the use of physical force or threat. It is very common among animals, arising out of competition for limited resources such as food, mates, and territory. It may also be used as a means of defense—for example, when mothers protect their young. Within species, aggressive behavior is often ritualized, so that the opponents reduce the risk of physical harm. The loser can end the fight by assuming a submissive posture, which switches off the victor's aggressive drive.

Individual aggression needs to be distinguished from aggression between groups. The sort of intergroup aggression we could consider to be a precursor of war occurs only among nonhuman and human primates and some species of rodents, such as the Norwegian rat. Jane Goodall observed intergroup aggression among chimpanzees who live in fairly close proximity to other groups. The males of such groups patrol the borders of their territory and attack members of other groups, mauling and often killing them. Humans, too, exhibit aggression individually and collectively— for example, in disputes over rank, territory, and rivalry for mates.

◉➤ Bushmen fighting: rock painting from South Africa copied by D. F. Bleek, 1930.

The basic expressions of threat, in the form of facial expressions and posturing, are universal among humans, and similar behavior is found among chimpanzees and other nonhuman primates. Humans have also evolved other patterns of behavior that serve, among other things, to dampen aggression. Crying, for example, generally elicits a sympathetic reaction. It is significant that newborn babies respond to tapes of crying by themselves crying in sympathy, but not to tapes with different human sounds. Another effective strategy is to threaten to cut off social contact with the aggressor (see the sequence of photographs).

External and Internal Triggers

Contrary to what some of the more romantic anthropologists think, human beings do not necessarily grow up to be peaceful when raised in a warm family environment with affection and body contact. Nor do they necessarily become aggressive when these are lacking. In contemporary warrior cultures, both mothers and fathers treat their children with great affection and love, yet the children grow up to become fierce fighters. This is because children who grow up in a loving environment identify with their parents and their group and are prepared to accept their values, whether warrior-like or pacifist. Until the late 1960s, it was believed that hunter-gatherers were nonterritorial and peaceful, living in open societies. Investigations carried out over the last decades, however, have revealed this to be a myth. Warriors in combat have been a theme of rock paintings from the Stone Age to the present day—as evidenced by contemporary paintings of the Bushmen of southern Africa.

Aggressive behavior is not just a response to external stimuli. It can result from a number of internal factors. One of these is male hormones. Success in real or symbolic fights (such as sports or examinations) leads to an increase of testosterone in men, but this is not automatically switched off when the goal is reached, as is the case with such consummatory acts as eating and sex. This may explain why the drive for power and military superiority runs wild in some men. The spontaneous activity of certain neurons in the brain can also trigger aggression, but cultural factors can override this, of course.

Negative and Positive Aggression

Aggression in humans, as in animals, serves several different purposes. It can lead to destructive behavior and cause enormous difficulties, but sometimes it has a positive aspect. For example, we overcome physical and mental problems—any goal-directed activities blocked by an obstacle—by taking an aggressive approach to them. This point needs to be emphasized, for aggression is often considered solely as a negative force. Some people have even proposed that children should be brought up in such a way that they would lack any aggressive tendency at all. This would do great harm to the individuals concerned, rendering them defenseless. Among other things, aggression is necessary if people are to rebel against injustice and dictatorship.

War as Organized Aggression

War is, of course, an organized form of human aggression. Despite the biological precursors to be found in chimpanzee behavior, it must be considered as a product of cultural evolution, as it involves strategically planned and concerted effort, is carried out with weapons that kill at a distance (thereby reducing the likelihood of personal contact), and is aimed at destroying a common enemy. Apart from aggression, war depends on feelings of group loyalty, which are often promoted by propaganda that dehumanizes the enemy. In this way, conflict is shifted to a moral plane, where killing becomes sportive and virtuous, if not positively heroic—a tactic that has worked fairly well throughout history.

To understand group aggression in human beings, it is important to realize that people have fundamentally ambivalent feelings toward their fellow humans. They respond with friendly behavior (particularly towards acquaintances), but also with fear. They fear domination, but often attempt to dominate when they perceive weakness.

War, as such, is certainly not in our genetic make-up, but it has always been a very efficient way of acquiring and defending limited resources. As increasingly destructive weapons have been developed, it has become a very much riskier undertaking, although certain conventions and rituals have arisen to lessen this risk. Clearly, we must strive to resolve the large-scale problems that confront our species not by aggression and war but by social and political contracts that respect others' rights.

⊖ Threatening to cut off social contact is one of the ways in which humans ward off aggression. A Yanomami boy is threatened by another boy, who attempts to push him aside. The attacked boy initially smiles appeasingly, but this tactic is ineffective. After being hit, he averts his gaze (contact avoidance), lowers his head, and pouts— a very effective way of counteracting aggression from another individual. The aggressor then leaves.

1

2

3

4

5

6

7

8

IRENÄUS EIBL-EIBESFELDT

⊕ *Opposite page:* Some of the earliest art in Europe, about 25,000 to 30,000 years ago, consists of simple engravings on the walls of caves in France. The engravings on this boulder at La Ferrassie have been interpreted as vulvas—roughly triangular shapes with a line bisecting the narrowest angle.

⊕ This smoothed plaque of ivory from Tata, in Hungary, colored with ocher, is about 50,000 years old. Opinions are sharply divided as to whether it is a product of natural processes or was made by humans.
HUNGARIAN NATIONAL MUSEUM/ANDRAS DABASI

⊕ Dated to the Upper Paleolithic period, this bone plaque from Abri Blanchard, in France, has been studied in great detail by Alexander Marshack. It is marked with rows of gouged holes arranged in groups. Each group was usually made by the same tool and may represent some form of tallying procedure.
JEAN VERTUT/MUSEE DES ANTIQUITES NATIONALES, ST GERMAIN-EN-LAYE

When hominids began to bury their dead, we have the first indication that they were able to connect past actions with an inert body. No great memory capacity was required, probably no more than a few weeks. The Neanderthals usually interred complete bodies, presumably within a few days of death. We should not conclude from this that these early burials are evidence of a belief in an afterlife. That surely requires the combination of a developed capacity for memory and the ability to envisage a future stretching beyond one's own lifetime.

The Meaning of Art

Once humans could consciously link past actions with an object, they possessed the basic capacity needed for artistic behavior. Linking an observed object with remembered characteristics leads to the ability to recall the characteristics of a person or animal without direct observation. Instead of seeing an object and merely remembering the past, humans could remember versions of the past and represent them as objective shapes, or see an object and shortly after immediately recall it to produce an image. This was probably an unusual aptitude— even today many people cannot do it well.

At first these shapes and images were vague, uncertain, or simple. There is much dispute as to what constitutes the earliest recognizable art, such as a few pieces of polished and scratched ivory from Tata, in Hungary, and some scratches on a bone from La Ferrassie, in southern France, dating back to 50,000 years ago. By 30,000 years ago, we find small carvings of horses and simple engraved shapes which have generally been interpreted as

images of vulvas. Over the next 10,000 to 15,000 years, art became more elaborate, both in technique and content. Among the cave art discovered at Lascaux, also in southern France, there are even images of fictitious creatures combining features of several animals.

As well as trying to understand what the art meant, we can ask what purpose it served. Just as fire signaled location over great distances, so art allowed detailed messages to be transmitted through time. We no longer needed to remember all we had learned—we simply needed to know where to find the required information in the material records we could create.

The Rhythms of Life

Art also provided us with the means to represent periodicity. In paintings and carvings, this took the form of repeated rows of marks. It also appeared in the first known musical instruments, which consisted of bone tubes with holes drilled in them to produce different sounds. Both the signs and the musical instruments take a continuum and divide it up. This is the essential logical device for imposing human order on the natural phenomena of time and sound. Simple though they are, each represents a fundamental development of human thought. Once humans had the concept of periodicity, time could be divided up and patterns of change,

⊕ This flute made from bird bone, from Grotte de Placard, France, is about 10,000 to 15,000 years old.
MUSEE DE L'HOMME, PARIS/ M. DELAPLANCHE/COLLECTION MUSEE DES BEAUX ARTS D'ANGOULEME

such as lunar cycles and the breeding habits of herd animals, could be recognized. Prediction no longer depended upon our capacity to remember. Instead, we gained a material means of understanding and managing our otherwise unpredictable world.

What our ancestors did two to three million years ago was to commit us to a complex relationship with artifacts made of hard materials. In a myriad ways, these objects created social stresses and new signals and have successively affected the way we interact with other human beings in our communities, across space and time. Not only did these artifacts help to shape our behavior, developing our ability to predict and persist, they eventually gave our finite brains the material means to store, organize, and analyze potentially unlimited knowledge.

SEX ROLES IN PREHISTORY

Michelle Lampl

Sex roles refer to the prescribed ways in which men and women relate to each other and behave in their daily life. All human societies have defined roles for men and women that are both overt or active roles and passive roles that are learned by imitation and instruction as children. Scientists continue to debate the nature of biological and cultural contributions to sex roles, and often turn to the study of human evolution for insights into the origins of modern sex roles.

Our knowledge of our prehistoric ancestors comes from the archaeological record, which reveals details of settlement patterns, food habits, and other aspects of our ancestors' way of life. The fossil record provides information on physical features, health status, and life span. Unfortunately, neither form of evidence can provide us with definitive answers as to how and why modern human sex roles evolved.

Males and females differ in their reproductive biology. Women have larger amounts of body fat in proportion to the rest of their body mass, broader hips to permit the passage of the infant at birth, and mammary glands to nurture the young after birth. Men, in contrast, tend to have more muscle in proportion to their body mass. Together with body size differences, these differences between the sexes are known as sexual dimorphism.

Although in many human populations men are usually somewhat bigger than women, modern humans are not especially sexually dimorphic, in contrast to some of our closest primate relatives. Sexual dimorphism is an often debated characteristic in the human fossil record, because primate researchers have noted that few primates living in social groups where males and females are highly dimorphic live in male–female, monogamous units.

The earliest fossil evidence of creatures directly ancestral to humans belongs to the genus *Australopithecus*, who lived in East and South Africa two to four million years ago. Although this continues to be debated, some scientists studying these fossil bones note a marked difference in the body size of males and females. An adult female individual (named "Lucy" by her discoverers) has been reconstructed as about 1.1 meters (3 feet, 7 inches)

tall and some 27 kilograms (59 pounds) in weight. A presumed male individual was reconstructed to perhaps 1.6 meters (5 feet, 3 inches) tall and about 50 kilograms (110 pounds) in weight.

On the basis of this evidence, it has been suggested that early in our evolutionary history, the pair-bonded, monogamous nuclear family common to many modern human societies, and the sex roles associated with it, had not yet evolved. During subsequent human evolution, the fossil evidence shows a gradual reduction in dimorphism, so that by the time individuals who looked like modern humans appear on the scene, some 100,000 years ago, dimorphism is similar to that in living humans. None of this tells us precise details about sex roles; but if our understanding of skeletal and social relationships is accurate, it implies that male–female relationships were different in our earliest prehistory. What the situation was, we do not know.

The second kind of evidence, archaeology, does not tell us much, either. The oldest information, the stone tool record from some 2.5 million years ago, does not provide information about sex roles. Personal ornaments are found about 30,000 years ago in Europe: shells with holes drilled in them, probably to be strung as bracelets and body

◄● In contrast to modern humans, some of our closest primate relatives are very sexually dimorphic. The gorilla female (left) is only some 60 percent of the size of the male. Sexual dimorphism appears to be greatest where males compete for sexual access to females, and least in those species whose males and females often pair-bond for life.

YANN ARTHUS-BERTRAND/JACANA-AUSCAPE

ornaments, found in the graves of both sexes. Not long after, also in Europe, are found some of the remarkable remains of the plastic art of the time: incised or, sometimes, sculptured images of women on bone and ivory, and clay sculptures such as the well-known Venus of Willendorf. While some images of males are found in the famous cave art paintings or engraved on rock faces, most images are of women with exaggerated anatomical features in the form of pronounced breasts and buttocks. Scholars debate the significance of these objects. Were they simply accurate images of local women? Did they represent fertility images? Or were they intentionally erotic? By the time agriculture appeared, some 10,000 years ago, humans were living in organized groups that we would not find unusual.

Lacking specific evidence, scholars speculate about the ways by which male–female sex roles evolved in our evolutionary history. These conjectures have often projected modern notions onto the past and have followed our own social trends. For example, many scholars believed until recently that the evolutionary history of human social groups involved male and female division of labor, whereby males hunted and brought back the spoils to so-called home places, where they shared this food with the females, who waited for them, nurturing and caring for infants and young. A modification of this view proposed that males and females initially had separate feeding strategies and that a monogamous pair bond was not only a way of sharing resources and maximizing the survival potential of each sex but also had the benefit of ensuring paternity. The dietary preferences and concerns of many modern societies can be identified in these scenarios.

By contrast, recent researchers have pointed to the importance of women in modern, egalitarian hunting and gathering societies and have suggested this as a model for our prehistoric past. Here, men and women have overlapping activities and spheres of influence, in which the basic food items (vegetables,

seeds, nuts, insects, small animals) are supplied by women, with men supplying much less material of daily importance. Other contemporary accounts not only focus on gender roles but also look at aspects of sexual behavior and emotion. Recognizing nonmonogamous lifestyles and reconsidering the nature of male and female sexuality, some investigators have suggested multiple sexual partners for both sexes, in the form of mild polygyny or serial pair-bonding, as a pattern accompanying our

evolutionary history.

Thus, the concerns of modern American and European society as to the place of monogamy and the nuclear family, and division of labor in terms of power relations, sharing, and cooperation in daily life, have all contributed to reconstructions of prehistoric sex roles. The accuracy of these notions when applied to prehistory is unclear. It may be that instead of looking down the long corridor of the past, we have been looking in the mirror.

J.M. LABAT/AUSCAPE

⚲ Female figures appear in the Upper Paleolithic period across Europe. Both the figurines emphasizing sexual anatomy, with indistinct heads and legs, and the detailed, graceful head from Brassempouy, France (bottom, right), reflect an image of female form we can only aspire to see through the eyes of that time.

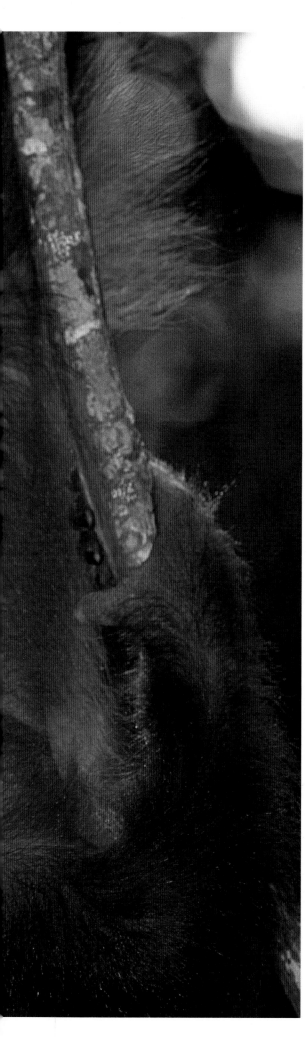

HUMAN ORIGINS

20 MILLION YEARS AGO – 100,000 YEARS AGO

Our Earliest Ancestors

COLIN GROVES

During the eighteenth century, European intellectuals became fascinated by apes. What kind of creatures were they? Monkeys were already a familiar sight: Madame de Pompadour owned a pet marmoset from Brazil; two centuries earlier, Dürer had painted a pair of mangabeys from West Africa; while the Barbary macaque from North Africa (often mistakenly called an ape) had been well known since Roman times. But real apes—at that time called "orang-utans"—were different: tailless, upright creatures, almost human in form but covered in hair, their eyes shining with intelligence, their faces so expressive that they seemed to need no speech to make themselves understood. Indeed, many wondered whether, with a little training, they might actually learn to speak. Others were convinced that they had their own language, and that it was only a matter of time before they would be able to communicate in fashionable society.

It is rather surprising that so much speculation was based on so little careful observation. It was not until near the end of the eighteenth century that it dawned on such naturalists as Johann Friedrich Blumenbach, in Germany, and Georges Cuvier, in France, that the young apes that had been brought to Europe from time to time (and soon died for want of proper care) were of two kinds. The big red ones—the real orang-utans—as well as the little gibbons came from the East Indies, while the big black ones, which came to be called chimpanzees, were from Africa.

◄❍ Orang-utans were the first of the Great Apes to become well known to scientists. This Southeast Asian ape is our third closest relative, after the chimpanzee and the gorilla.

⛎ This skull from Sterkfontein has usually been classified as *Australopithecus africanus*, but it has recently been suggested that it may in fact be a very primitive specimen of *Paranthropus*.
DAVID L. BRILL, 1985

↪ The intelligence that seems to shine out of the eyes of this chimpanzee is no illusion. Chimpanzees are our closest living relatives: they make and use tools in the wild, have a complex social organization, and even have a rudimentary self-awareness.

By the time that a third ape, the gorilla, was made known to science, in 1847, the differences between chimpanzees and orang-utans were becoming better known. But it was that conceptual bombshell of 1859, Charles Darwin's *The Origin of Species*, that finally put them into perspective. The apes are like us because they are related to us.

As early as 1863, in an essay entitled "Man's Place in Nature", Thomas Huxley had concluded that the African apes—the chimpanzee and the gorilla—are more closely related to us than is the orang-utan. In his *Descent of Man*, published in 1872, Darwin argued that if the African apes are

and, eventually, analysis of the DNA itself. The answer was always the same. Chimpanzees, gorillas, and humans are very closely related indeed, orang-utans are more distantly related to us, gibbons are further away, and monkeys still further off. There is still disagreement as to whether chimpanzees are closer to humans or to gorillas (or whether all three are equally closely related), but there is no longer any doubt about the closeness of all three.

Many now believe that, taken overall, changes in the protein structure and DNA of living organisms occur fairly regularly over long periods of time. If it is known how different two species are in terms of one of their proteins, or in parts of their genome (the complete genetic material for any cell, which determines heredity), it is possible to calculate how long ago they shared a common ancestor. This concept is known as the molecular clock, and although it does not keep perfect time, it does set limits—and it tells us that our evolutionary line must have separated from the chimpanzee's between about seven and five million years ago.

The Early Apes

The taxonomic group that includes humans and apes—the superfamily known as Hominoidea, or the hominoids—was established by about 20 million years ago. In the Early Miocene period (19 to 18 million years ago), there were at least 10 different species of apes in East Africa, large and small. The best-known belong to the genus *Proconsul* (named after a popular zoo chimpanzee of the 1890s called Consul), discovered in 1933 and now known from a nearly complete skeleton (and several partial ones) and dozens of jaws, teeth, and skull fragments. Studies of the remains have shown that *Proconsul* lived in trees, walked on all fours, lived on fruit, was probably tailless, and had large canine teeth. One species was smaller than a modern chimpanzee, another nearly as big as a gorilla.

Many authorities considered *Proconsul* a good candidate for the common ancestor of the Hominidae, the family comprising humans, chimpanzees, gorillas, and orang-utans (but not gibbons, whose evolutionary line was already separate). Others were unsure, pointing to features of the teeth, the jaw, and the limb bones that were not what we would expect to see in such a common ancestor. In the mid-1980s, a new fossil ape was discovered, contemporary with *Proconsul*. Named *Afropithecus*, it is still less well known than *Proconsul* but seems much more like what we would expect the common ancestor to have looked like. In a sense, it is a fossil that had to be invented before it was discovered.

Another large ape, *Kenyapithecus*, has been identified from the Middle Miocene period (14 million years ago). Like its probable ancestor,

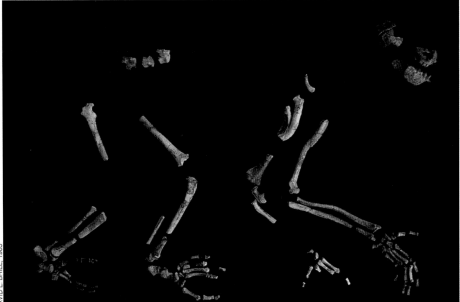

DAVID L. BRILL, 1985

⬥ An almost complete skeleton of *Proconsul nyanzae*, a hominid that lived in East Africa 18 million years ago. Medium-sized apes like this flourished in rainforests at that time, amid a primitive primate fauna that included the ancestors of monkeys as well as of apes.

indeed more closely related to us than the Asian ones, our own origins are likely to have been in Africa. Though a number of authorities have from time to time argued otherwise, since the 1940s the consensus has been that Huxley and Darwin were right: the chimpanzee and gorilla are closer to us than is the orang-utan, and it is in Africa, not in Asia or elsewhere, that we should look for remains of our earliest ancestors.

Traditionally, apes have been classified as belonging to a zoological family, Pongidae, separate from our own family, Hominidae. Increasingly, however, specialists have been inclined to include the Great Apes as well among the Hominidae, putting the orang-utan in one subfamily and humans, chimpanzees, and gorillas in another.

Tracing Our Family Tree

By the early 1960s, analytical techniques were available that allowed us to compare different primate groups in terms of their biochemistry. Immunological techniques were used at first, but these were gradually superseded by the more sophisticated techniques of protein sequencing

COLIN GROVES

⬥ A skull of *Afropithecus turkanensis*, a recently discovered contemporary of *Proconsul*, and probably closer to the ancestry of humans and apes.

↩ Despite appearances, the giant ape, the gorilla, is usually a gentle, family-oriented, near-human ape. Males weigh about 150 kilograms (330 pounds) on average, females only 70 kilograms (154 pounds). Today, deforestation, hunting, and human population pressures threaten the continued existence of this remarkable creature.

D. PARER AND E. PARER-COOK/AUSCAPE

LÁSZLÓ KORDOS

⚭ *Dryopithecus* has been known since the mid-nineteenth century, but a skull found recently in Hungary gave us new information about it. One specialist has recently proposed that it is close to the direct ancestor of the Great Apes and humans.

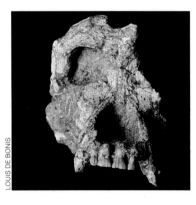

LOUIS DE BONIS

⚭ *Ouranopithecus macedoniensis* is known by many skull, jaw, and skeleton specimens from 10 million-year-old sites in Greece. It is likely to be on the common ancestral line of humans, chimpanzees, and gorillas.

↩ Until comparatively recently, almost nothing was known of the evolution of the Great Apes. But in 1980, this magnificent fossil of a proto-orang-utan was discovered in Pakistan. Known as *Sivapithecus indicus*, it is about 10 million years old.

Afropithecus, it had large canine teeth, but the face was shorter, and in other respects, too, it was more "advanced" in evolutionary terms towards the living Hominidae, whose last common ancestor it may well have been.

The earliest fossils of other hominoid species so far found outside Africa date from about the same time: *Dryopithecus* in Europe and, a little later, *Sivapithecus* in South and West Asia and *Lufengpithecus* in China. Well-preserved fossils, mainly skulls,

DAVID L. BRILL, 1985

from the Siwalik Hills, in Pakistan, and Sinap, in Turkey, have shown that *Sivapithecus* is almost certainly the ancestor of the orang-utan. (Some fragmentary remains from the Siwaliks were at one time thought to be human ancestors and dignified with the name *Ramapithecus*, but it is now clear that they belong to a small species of *Sivapithecus*.) Fossils of later representatives of the orang lineage have been found in China and Indonesia.

But if we have now traced the orang-utan's ancestors, the same cannot be said of the chimpanzee or the gorilla. We know nothing of their evolution after their ancestors separated from ours, and very little of what happened to the common stock between the time the orang line split off, between 12 and 10 million years ago, and the time the gorilla, chimpanzee, and human lines separated, between 7 and 5 million years ago.

There are, in fact, only two serious candidates for this intermediate phase: a maxilla (upper jaw) from the Samburu Hills, in Kenya, dating to 9 million years ago; and a series of fossils from Rain Ravine, in northern Greece, dating to about 10 million years ago, which have been named *Ouranopithecus*. Parts of a facial skeleton of *Ouranopithecus* discovered recently at another Greek site, Xirochori, strongly suggest that this fossil is part of the non-orang lineage. If it is, it is clear that this line ranged outside Africa from time to time.

Enter the Australopithecines

From about four million years ago, it is as if a curtain has suddenly been lifted. Instead of a few frustrating scraps of bone, we are confronted with an abundance of fossils. Key sites are Laetoli, in Tanzania, dating to between 3.75 and 3.5 million years ago; Hadar, in Ethiopia, dating to between 3.3 and 2.9 million years ago; and two sites in South Africa, Sterkfontein and Makapansgat, both between 3 and 2.5 million years old.

The fossils found at these sites belong to the genus *Australopithecus* (meaning "southern ape"). Like apes, they had a small cranial capacity and a protruding jaw (a feature known as prognathism), but their canine teeth were much shorter and they walked upright. The first specimen was an infant, discovered by Raymond Dart in 1924 at Taung, in Cape Province, South Africa. Robert Broom discovered the rich site of Sterkfontein, while Dart himself excavated Makapansgat, and Mary Leakey, Tim White, Don Johanson, and others were involved in the discoveries further north.

The earliest of these fossils, from Laetoli, have been given the name *Australopithecus afarensis*. They consist of the jaws and teeth of some 24 individuals, the partial skeleton of a juvenile, and some fossil

footprints. The jaws show canine teeth much smaller than those of apes, but rather larger and more pointed than our own, and the dental arcades are neither parabolic like those of modern humans nor rectangular like those of apes. The footprints are contentious, but they seem, on most assessments, to indicate creatures that walked on two legs, but had slightly divergent great toes and lateral toes that are long relative to humans but somewhat shortened relative to apes.

◄● The famous Taung child, discovered by Raymond Dart in 1924, was the first known specimen of *Australopithecus*. It is a tribute to Dart's anatomical expertise that, from this very young skull and brain endocast, he was able to recognize its status as an intermediate between ape and human—an insight abundantly confirmed by later discoveries.
DAVID L. BRILL, 1985

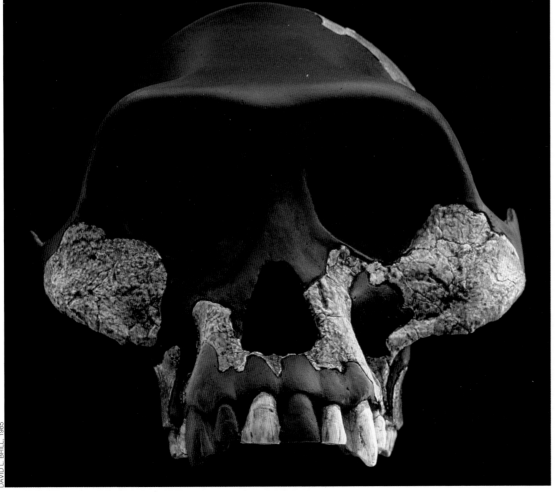

JOHN READER/SCIENCE PHOTO LIBRARY/THE PHOTO LIBRARY

⚲ An australopithecine footprint from Laetoli, 3.75 to 3.5 million years old, shows that bipedal walking—if not of a fully modern type—had developed by that time.

DAVID L. BRILL, 1985

◄● The reconstructed skull of a male from the "First Family", at Hadar, is generally classified as *Australopithecus afarensis*, although controversy persists. But there is no controversy about its position on or close to the human lineage, and all agree that it is more primitive than *Australopithecus africanus*, *Paranthropus*, or any species of *Homo*.

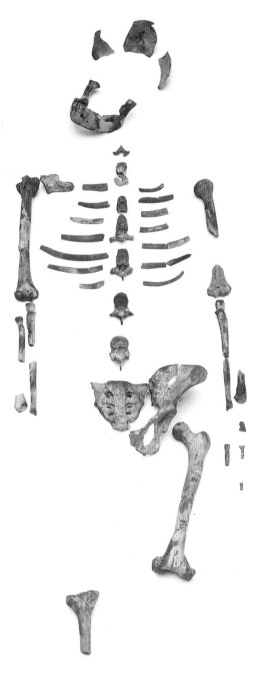

↩ Here at Hadar, a joint United States–French team discovered australopithecine remains in the 1970s, including the famous "Lucy" skeleton and the "First Family". Since that date, further finds have been made here by Berhane Asfaw, an Ethiopian anthropologist.

↩ Lucy, the two-thirds-complete skeleton from Hadar, is 3.2 million years old. Should it be included in the same species, *Australopithecus afarensis*, as other Hadar and Laetoli remains? There is no agreement on this question.

The abundant fossil remains from Hadar include a two-thirds-complete skeleton nicknamed "Lucy"; a group of fossils that, from their context, most likely represent a single social group (known as the "First Family"); and sundry other specimens. Lucy is only about a meter (3 feet, 7 inches) tall and has long arms and short legs, a funnel-shaped (ape-like) chest, and a V-shaped jaw, but a pelvis that indicates an upright (but not fully human) gait. The members of the First Family are mostly larger than Lucy, and it is claimed that their limb bones indicate a more human-like gait than Lucy's. Are they two different species? One school of thought thinks so. Others think that they are all the one species, *Australopithecus afarensis*, the same as that from Laetoli.

↥ There is no doubt that "Lucy" stood and walked upright, but she did not have the long legs of modern humans.

OUR EARLIEST ANCESTORS

COLIN GROVES

THE EARLIEST KNOWN primate lived in Africa 60 million years ago. Known as *Purgatorius,* it had a long, slender snout and four premolar teeth—more than any living primate. Other undisputed primates from this period include the Petrolemuridae (members of the suborder Strepsirrhini, to which living lemurs and lorises belong), from China, and a few, difficult to classify, fossils of Haplorrhini, the suborder to which modern tarsiers, monkeys, apes, and humans belong.

The Adapiformes and Omomyiformes, which include most of the earliest strepsirrhines and haplorrhines, were abundant during the Eocene period, and many skulls and partial skeletons are known. The Omomyiformes lingered on in North America until the Early Miocene period, while Adapiformes survived in India until the Middle Miocene.

The earliest known platyrrhine, or New World monkey, *Branisella*, lived 26 million years ago in Bolivia, while the catarrhines—the group that includes Old World monkeys, apes, and humans—are known from about 40 million years ago in Egypt and perhaps 50 to 40 million years ago in Algeria. Fossil catarrhines are easy to recognize, having only two premolars in each half of each of their jaws, and long canine teeth that hone against the first lower premolar.

Early Old World monkeys, Hylobatidae (ancestral gibbons), and Hominidae (ancestors and cousins of humans and Great Apes) are known from several East African sites dated to 20 to 17 million years ago. *Kenyapithecus,* from East Africa, and *Dryopithecus,* from Eurasia, represent a stage before modern hominid lines had begun to separate from other Great Apes. *Sivapithecus*, from India, Pakistan, and Turkey, is, at 8 to 12 million years old, the earliest member of the orang-utan lineage. *Ouranopithecus,* a contemporary species from Greece, may be on the human–chimpanzee–gorilla line.

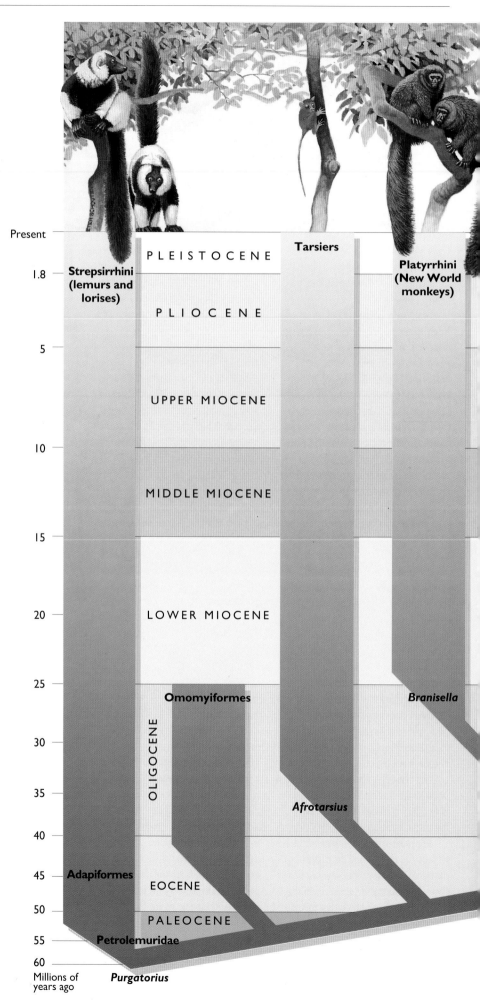

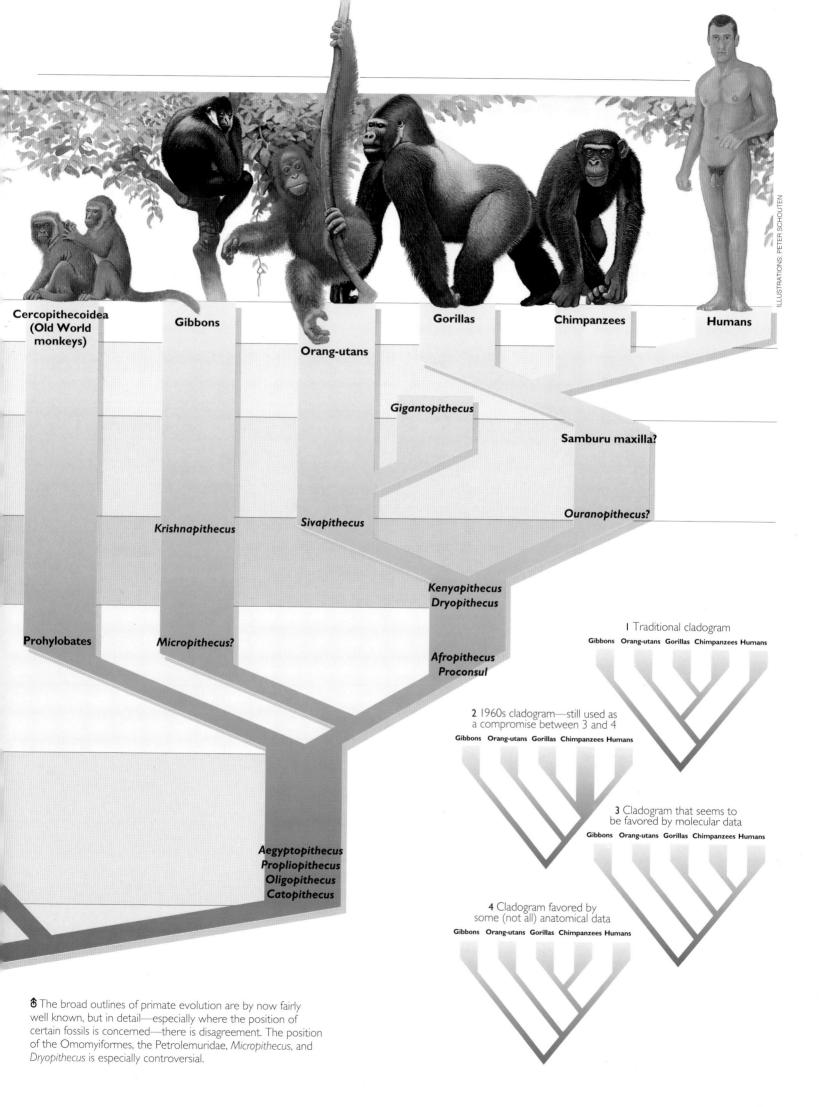

Cercopithecoidea
(Old World
monkeys)

Gibbons

Orang-utans

Gorillas

Chimpanzees

Humans

Gigantopithecus

Samburu maxilla?

Ouranopithecus?

Krishnapithecus

Sivapithecus

Kenyapithecus
Dryopithecus

Prohylobates

Micropithecus?

Afropithecus
Proconsul

Aegyptopithecus
Propliopithecus
Oligopithecus
Catopithecus

1 Traditional cladogram

Gibbons   Orang-utans   Gorillas   Chimpanzees   Humans

2 1960s cladogram—still used as
a compromise between 3 and 4

Gibbons   Orang-utans   Gorillas   Chimpanzees   Humans

3 Cladogram that seems to
be favored by molecular data

Gibbons   Orang-utans   Gorillas   Chimpanzees   Humans

4 Cladogram favored by
some (not all) anatomical data

Gibbons   Orang-utans   Gorillas   Chimpanzees   Humans

♌ The broad outlines of primate evolution are by now fairly
well known, but in detail—especially where the position of
certain fossils is concerned—there is disagreement. The position
of the Omomyiformes, the Petrolemuridae, *Micropithecus*, and
Dryopithecus is especially controversial.

ILLUSTRATIONS: PETER SCHOUTEN

Olduvai Gorge, in present-day Tanzania, cleaves the Serengeti Plain. In the Early Pleistocene period, it was the site of a lake.

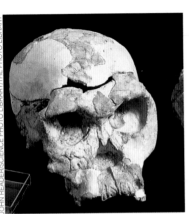

A skull of *Homo habilis* from Olduvai—nicknamed "Twiggy". Despite its general resemblance to *Australopithecus*, anatomical details show that it is more "advanced" in the human direction.

A skull of *Paranthropus boisei* from Olduvai. This grotesque, herbivorous hominid coexisted in East Africa with the small, protohuman *Homo habilis* about 2 to 1.7 million years ago.

Ancestors and Cousins

After *Australopithecus africanus* disappears from the archaeological record about 2.5 million years ago, there is a gap in the record of half a million years broken only by a few rather uninformative scraps of fossils recovered from deposits in the Omo Valley of southern Ethiopia. The next important fossils we have date from two million years ago and come mainly from two Rift Valley sites: Olduvai Gorge, in Tanzania, and Koobi Fora, in Kenya. The thick deposits accumulated at these two sites in the course of at least a million years have yielded abundant remains of skulls, jaws, teeth, and parts of skeletons, giving us a picture of the changes that occurred over this period. Unexpectedly, the picture is one of diversity. At

both sites, two different prehuman species lived side by side from at least 2 to about 1.5 million years ago, and at the lower levels of Koobi Fora (known as the Upper Burgi Member), there is a third contemporary species as well.

The two Olduvai species are quite distinct. There is a small, lightly built one and a larger one with enormous premolar and molar teeth. The small one has a higher, more rounded braincase, with an average cranial capacity of 650 cubic centimeters (40 cubic inches), ranging in four specimens from 590 to about 700 cubic centimeters (36 to 43 cubic inches); a lightly built face with smaller, narrower cheekteeth; and the beginnings of a protruding nose. The large one has a smaller braincase—the average cranial capacity is 515 cubic centimeters (31 cubic inches), ranging in five specimens from 500 to 530 cubic centimeters (30 to 32 cubic inches)—and a foreshortened but heavily buttressed face, with tiny front teeth but huge cheekteeth and enormously developed chewing muscles, commonly giving rise to a crest on top of the head where they attached (known as the sagittal crest). Both walked upright, with the foramen magnum even further forward than in *Australopithecus*—as far forward as in modern humans—but both still had short legs and long arms.

There is no doubt that the small, lightly built one is *Homo*. In every respect it is more "modern" than *Australopithecus*, more like ourselves. The very earliest specimen of *Homo* is a scrap of skull from Chemeron, near Lake Baringo, dated as being 2.5 million years old. The Olduvai species is known as *Homo habilis*. The large, robustly built type has traditionally been considered to be a late survival of *Australopithecus*, but most authorities now recognize it as something rather different and call it *Paranthropus* (sometimes, affectionately, "the Nutcracker"). The Olduvai species is called *Paranthropus boisei*.

There are abundant remains of *Paranthropus boisei* at Koobi Fora, and they are accompanied by not one but two species of *Homo*. One is small and short-faced, the cranial capacity of the two specimens found being 510 and 582 cubic centimeters (31 and 36 cubic inches). The other is larger, with a muzzle-like face, one specimen having a cranial capacity of 770 cubic centimeters (47 cubic inches) and two others a slightly larger capacity.

Opinion is divided over their relationship to each other and to *Homo habilis*. The large species is generally thought to be a distinct species, called *Homo rudolfensis*. Some think the small one is *Homo habilis*, while others think it is a different species. They are in some respects rather like each other, though only because they are both very primitive representatives of the human lineage. To avoid arguments over taxonomy, we can lump them together informally as "the habilines". As to which habiline is ancestral to later forms of *Homo*—that is another controversy!

Remains of *Homo habilis* have been discovered further south in Africa, at Sterkfontein, in more recent deposits than those in which *Australopithecus* was found. The nearby sites of Swartkrans and Kromdraai have yielded remains of the Nutcrackers, though of a different species (*Paranthropus robustus*) from the East African one. Some authorities consider that only the Kromdraai species is *Paranthropus robustus*, and that the Swartkrans species is different, calling it *Paranthropus crassidens*.

Where did these new species, the habilines and the Nutcrackers, come from? We still do not know where the habilines came from. Many anthropologists think they are directly descended from creatures like the "First Family" of Hadar, while others think they derived from *Australopithecus africanus*. The scrappy fragments that have survived from intervening time periods simply do not allow us to decide. But a magnificent skull from West Turkana, Kenya, dated to 2.5 million years ago, solves the problem of the Nutcrackers. Very like *Paranthropus boisei* in its general features, it has a long, muzzle-like face and large front teeth like *Australopithecus*. This early, primitive species has been named *Paranthropus walkeri*, after the famous paleoanthropologist Alan Walker.

There seems little doubt that the habilines made simple stone tools. The earliest stone tools were found at Hadar and are 2.6 million years old. From two million years ago, artifacts are found in the archaeological record in their thousands, and wherever we find traces of their makers, they are members of the genus *Homo*—beginning with the habilines.

The Road to Homo sapiens

Where did our own direct ancestors come from? Many people believe that a key fossil is a well-preserved skull from Koobi Fora known as ER-1813, one of the habilines. It has a very small braincase—

the cranial capacity is only 510 cubic centimeters (31 cubic inches)—but its facial modeling and other aspects of the skull are just what we would expect in a direct ancestor of later human beings. It is certainly more "modern" in this respect than the other habilines, *Homo habilis* and *Homo rudolfensis*, which have larger cranial capacities. If this is so, it means that different species evolved large brains independently. Parallel evolution is well known among animals and plants, but somehow it is unexpected in the brain—the very feature we regard as making us superior to all other animals!

⬧ Skull 1470 from Koobi Fora, northern Kenya. Formerly considered to represent *Homo habilis*, this specimen and others like it have recently been shown to belong to a separate species, *Homo rudolfensis*. There were probably several closely related species of early *Homo* living in Africa at this time, about two million years ago.

⬧ The Black Skull, from West Turkana, 2.5 million years old, is the earliest, most primitive representative of *Paranthropus*.

◀⬥ *Paranthropus crassidens*, from Swartkrans, South Africa, was a smaller but closely related contemporary of the East African *Paranthropus boisei*.

WHEN DID LANGUAGE BEGIN?

IAIN DAVIDSON AND WILLIAM NOBLE

We find it almost impossible to imagine what it would be like to "think" about the world without language—either spoken or signed. As language is one of the things that distinguishes the behavior of humans from that of other animals, however, it clearly must have emerged at some time during the course of our evolution. The question is when.

Some scientists believe that language evolved at a very early stage in human development, basing their view on two pieces of evidence: our ancestors' brain size and the shape of stone tools.

Language and the Brain

Over the course of the last two million years, the hominid brain has become bigger. Although the brain does not fossilize, it leaves some blurred indications of the convolutions of the cortex on the inside of the skull. By making a latex endocast, it is possible to study something of the shape of the cortex. It has been suggested that the cortex of australopithecines was very similar to that of chimpanzees, while the earliest habiline skull, known as KNM ER-1470, which is at least 1.8 million years old, already shows signs of some of the distinctive features of the human brain, particularly in the regions said to be associated with speech. But this theory does not attempt to explain how or why spoken language became distinct from the noises made by other apes. The suggestion is simply that language appeared as a result of the human brain becoming bigger.

Did We Need Language to Make Tools?

A second theory that has been put forward is that language was necessary for early hominids to have organized their actions sufficiently to make stone tools. But others have pointed out that the earliest tools that have been found,

from the Oldowan period, did not require any more organization or technical skills than tools made by modern chimpanzees.

Still another theory is that the symmetrical and apparently standard dimensions of Acheulean hand axes, dating back to between 1.5 million years ago and 150,000 years ago, indicate that early hominids had a mental image of the desired end product, which must have been communicated through language. But the dimensions of the axes found in Africa that were cited in support of this theory were

similar to those of axes found in Europe and Asia, so it is unlikely that they result from any deliberate attempt to produce an object of a particular shape. Even if hominids did have mental images of ideal axe shapes, these are unlikely to have been the same over such widespread areas. The similarities could have resulted from similar physical limitations in early hominids' ability to manipulate objects of particular sizes and shapes, and from their learning by imitation to make flakes from standard cores by using a restricted set of hand and arm movements.

Human Behavior?

Shelter, the use of fire, and meat-eating are often considered fundamental to early hominids' ability to move out of Africa and successfully colonize new territory in more temperate and seasonal parts of the world. But much of the claimed evidence for these aspects of behavior has recently been brought into question. For instance, a stone circle dated to about 1.8 million years ago at Olduvai Gorge, in present-day Tanzania, said to be the remains of a human shelter, was in an area

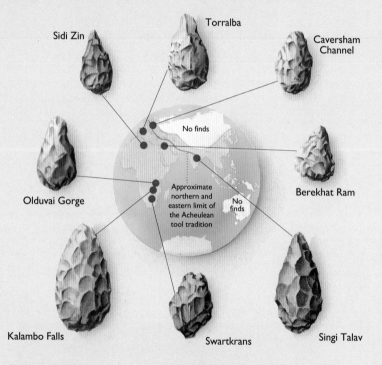

Torralba
Sidi Zin
Caversham Channel
No finds
Olduvai Gorge
Approximate northern and eastern limit of the Acheulean tool tradition
Berekhat Ram
No finds
Kalambo Falls
Swartkrans
Singi Talav

⚒ The shape of Acheulean hand axes around the world suggests species-specific behavior rather than individual planning.

where crocodiles would most likely have eaten any hominids who rested there. Similarly, claims for the existence of a bough hut at Terra Amata, in southern France, 230,000 years ago rest on the evidence of nothing more than four stains in the sand. And although evidence of fire has been claimed from sites such as Chesowanja, dating back to 1.4 million years ago, and Zhoukoudian, dating back to 500,000 years ago, a recent

assessment suggests that none of the claims earlier than Terra Amata is reliable—and even 230,000 years ago, it is doubtful whether hominids could regularly make fire. Furthermore, although meat has probably been an important part of the hominid diet since the genus *Homo* began to emerge, it is not clear how early hominids obtained meat. Early sites such as Torralba and Ambrona, in Spain, where large deposits of animal bones have been found, seem more likely to have been scavenging areas than places where hunted animals were butchered. There seems to be no good evidence that hominids built shelters, regularly made and used fire, or hunted systematically earlier than 125,000 years ago.

Claims for "modern"-seeming behavior among Neanderthals are exaggerated. The cave bear cult has been dismissed as wishful thinking inspired by nothing more than the accidental survival of a few bones of the many bears that died while hibernating in caves. The romantic story of the burial of a Neanderthal with flowers at Shanidar, in modern-day Iraq, does not stand up in the light of evidence that the Shanidar hominids died in, and were buried by, rock falls. In fact, most of the objects that have been interpreted as indicating that Neanderthals were capable of symbolic behavior prove to have simpler explanations in the physical world.

It seems, then, that language is not necessary to account for a number of early features of the archaeological record. It is necessary, however, to account for events that occurred around the world from about 60,000 years ago: the colonization of Australia and later of the Arctic and the Americas; the beginnings of art; the fact that ritual and convention became regionalized and localized; the beginnings of gender roles and power structure; and the start of agriculture. More than this we cannot say at present.

The Turkana Newcomer

About 1.6 million years ago, a new species appeared in East Africa. The first specimen discovered was a complete skull, ER-3733, from Koobi Fora (KBS Member). Other, less complete skulls, as well as other bones, have been found there since. In the mid-1980s, a nearly complete skeleton, WT-15000, was discovered at Nariokotome, on the other side of Lake Turkana from Koobi Fora. So we now know a good deal about this new species, which for the moment we can call simply the Turkana Newcomer. Bernard Wood has proposed that the species should be called *Homo ergaster*, and this is probably correct.

The two measurable specimens found had a cranial capacity of 848 and 908 cubic centimeters (52 and 55 cubic inches): bigger than ER-1813, but not bigger than some of the other fossils similar to *Homo habilis*. They had projecting brow ridges, a short face, a rather angular skull, and the merest

beginnings of a projecting nose. They also had long legs and a much more modern skeleton than the australopithecines or habilines. The skeleton known as WT-15000 was that of a boy about 12 years old. If he had survived into adulthood, he would have been 180 centimeters (6 feet) tall. Very clearly, the Turkana Newcomers were directly ancestral to later members of the human stock. Equally clearly, they were descended from the habilines—in fact, there is one habiline specimen, ER-1805, that some authorities prefer to place along with the Newcomers.

These people made stone tools, at first not very different from those made by *Homo habilis*. Did they make fire, hunt big game, speak? We do not know—the evidence is equivocal. What they did do is replace the habilines. In some way, they were just that much better at—what? At being human, or "nearly human", we suppose.

A new phase in human evolution: *Homo ergaster*, the Turkana Newcomer. The brain was only a little larger than in the habilines, but the shape of the skull is more like *Homo erectus*, as which it was classified until very recently.

SITES WHERE OUR FOSSIL FOREBEARS HAVE BEEN FOUND

Earlier members of the human group have been found only in Africa. About a million years ago, *Homo* spilled out of Africa and populated the entire Old World. They did not reach Australia until about 50,000 years ago, and arrived in the Americas later still.

1   Laetoli, Olduvai, Ndutu, Natron, Eyasi
2   Hadar, Bodo, Belohdelie, Maka
3   Koobi Fora, Omo, Nariokotome, Lothagam, Tabarin, Baringo
4   Sterkfontein, Swartkrans, Kromdraai, Taung, Makapansgat
5   Sangiran, Trinil, Mojokerto, Ngandong, Kedung Brubus, Sambungmacan, Wajak
6   Gongwangling, Jenjiawo
7   Zhoukoudian, Jinniushan
8   Hexian, Dali, Maba, Liujiang
9   Hathnora
10 Petralona
11 Mauer, Steinheim, Bilzingsleben, Neanderthal, Hahnöfersand, Ehringsdorf
12 Montmaurin, Arago, La Ferrassie, Biache, Cro-Magnon, Dordogne sites, St Césaire
13 Swanscombe
14 Gibraltar, Atapuerca
15 Monte Circeo, Saccopastore
16 Jebel Irhoud, Casablanca, Rabat, Salé
17 Tighenif
18 Yayo
19 Zuttiyeh, Tabun, Skhul, Qafzeh, Amud
20 Shanidar
21 Teshik-Tash
22 Klasies, Saldanha
23 Kabwe

CARTOGRAPHY: RAY SIM

JOHN READER/SCIENCE PHOTO LIBRARY/THE PHOTO LIBRARY

↪ Exactly which Lower and Middle Pleistocene fossils should be classed as *Homo erectus* is controversial, but the Zhoukoudian fossils belong to this species. So-called "Peking Man" lived in North China 450,000 to 250,000 years ago.

From Homo erectus . . .

The earliest traces of humans found outside Africa appear a little more than a million years ago. The best-known fossils of this period belong to a species called *Homo erectus*. In Java, the earliest specimens are about a million years old, the youngest only 100,000 years old. In China, they range from at least 800,000 to 230,000 years old.

Like the Turkana Newcomers, *Homo erectus* have large brow ridges, but they are different in form: straight and thick, flaring out to the sides. The cranial capacity is larger, ranging from 750 to 1300 cubic centimeters (46 to 79 cubic inches), with some evidence from both Java and China that it increased over time. The braincase was low, flat, and angular, with thickened bone along the midline and at the back. There are some differences between fossils found in Java and China: the Java skulls have a flat, receding forehead, while the Chinese skulls have a convex forehead, and there are other slight differences. They are generally considered to be two different subspecies: *Homo erectus erectus* (Java) and *Homo erectus pekinensis* (China). The forehead shape of the Java fossils is the more primitive type, and the earliest of the China fossils, from Gongwangling, is, in fact, similar to the Java type.

The earliest subspecies of all was excavated

from levels at Olduvai dating to about 1.2 million years ago, and this primitive race, *Homo erectus olduvaiensis*, is held by some to be the only record of *Homo erectus* in Africa. If so, it evolved in Africa, then migrated elsewhere, and died out in its homeland. Others consider the Turkana Newcomers to be early representatives of *Homo erectus*, and others again include later African fossils in the same species.

Fossils from the same period have been found in Africa, and even Europe. Specimens from Tighenif (Ternifine), in Algeria, may be 900,000 years old. The most recent of these "contemporaries" with an agreed date is from Bilzingsleben, in Germany, and is more than 300,000 years old. Both the African and European fossils differ from the *Homo erectus* fossils found in Java and China in characteristic ways: the brow ridges are more curved and do not flare out at the sides; the braincase is less flattened and angular, without the thickening along the midline and at the back; and there are differences in other features, including the shape of the mandible and the ear region.

Should these, then, be classified as *Homo erectus* or as a different species? Those who believe they are a different species call them *Homo heidelbergensis*, after the earliest discovered specimen, a jaw found in 1908 near Heidelberg, in Germany. Those who believe they are a subspecies of the same species call them *Homo erectus heidelbergensis*. This may seem to be nothing more than a question of semantics, but it is important. If they were all one species, they could all have been in some way ancestral to modern humans—a view known as the regional continuity hypothesis (or, sometimes, the

"candelabra" model). If they were two different species, because by definition different species do not interbreed to any significant extent, only one of them could have been our ancestor, and it or its descendants must have replaced the other—a view known as the replacement hypothesis (or the "Noah's Ark" model).

. . . *to* **Homo sapiens**

The earliest representatives of our own species, *Homo sapiens*, are known from two sites in Israel. Fossils found at Qafzeh have been dated by the thermoluminescence technique to 91,000 years ago, although a technique known as electron spin resonance analysis (ESR) suggests an even earlier date. Those found at Skhul are dated by ESR to 80,000 years ago. However, two sites in South Africa, Border Cave and Klasies River Mouth, may be equally old. Like modern humans, they have a high, rounded, shortened braincase, a rounded forehead, and a straight face with a chin. The brow ridges are smaller than in more primitive species, and the limb bones are long and straight.

Even older fossils found in Africa seem to indicate that *Homo sapiens* developed from *Homo heidelbergensis*. Two specimens from the Kibish Formation on the Omo River, in Ethiopia, as well as one from Ngaloba, in Tanzania, have been dated by the uranium–thorium method to 130,000 years ago; two from Jebel Irhoud, in Morocco, are about 120,000 years old; and there are a few others. They are all intermediate between *Homo heidelbergensis* and modern humans, but the two Omo skulls are particularly interesting. One, of which only the braincase has survived, resembles *Homo heidelbergensis* but has a higher braincase and

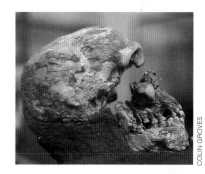

COLIN GROVES

In Skhul Cave, at the foot of Mount Carmel, in Israel, 10 human skeletons were found in the 1930s. It is now known that they are 80,000 years old—older than many fossils of Neanderthals found in the same region.

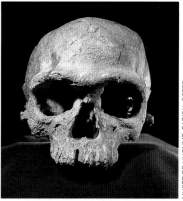

MUSEE DE L'HOMME, PARIS/J. OSTER

Jebel Irhoud I is one of a group of fossils from various parts of Africa, some 120,000 to 130,000 years old, that document the transition between an ancestral, primitive species, often called *Homo heidelbergensis*, and its descendant species, *Homo sapiens*.

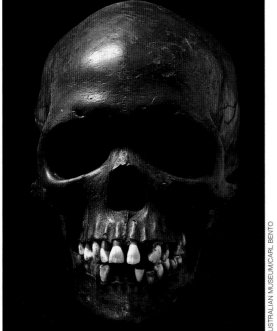

AUSTRALIAN MUSEUM/CARL BENTO

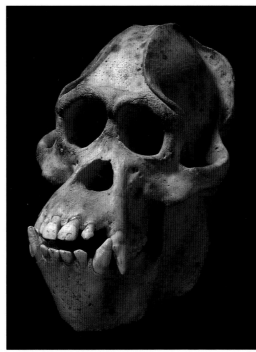

AUSTRALIAN MUSEUM/CARL BENTO

The skull of the orang-utan (right) has tall, narrow orbits (eye sockets), with no brow ridges above them, unlike that of the chimpanzee and the gorilla. Despite this superficial similarity, the fossil evidence shows that our ancestors are descended from quite different-looking apes, with large, projecting brow ridges.

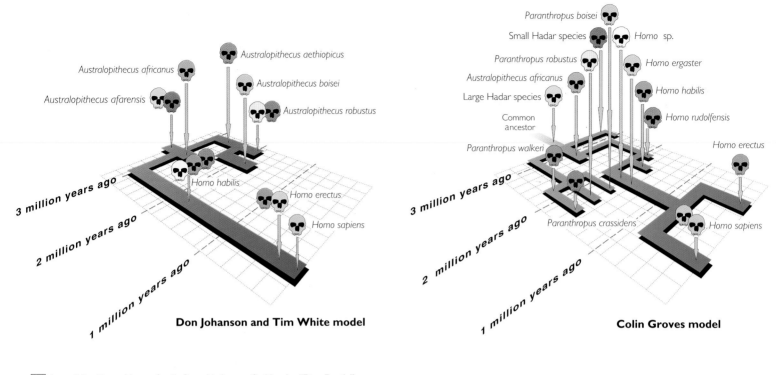

Don Johanson and Tim White model

Colin Groves model

Labels on left diagram: Australopithecus africanus, Australopithecus aethiopicus, Australopithecus afarensis, Australopithecus boisei, Australopithecus robustus, Homo habilis, Homo erectus, Homo sapiens; 3 million years ago, 2 million years ago, 1 million years ago.

Labels on right diagram: Paranthropus boisei, Small Hadar species, Homo sp., Paranthropus robustus, Homo ergaster, Australopithecus africanus, Large Hadar species, Homo habilis, Common ancestor, Homo rudolfensis, Paranthropus walkeri, Homo erectus, Paranthropus crassidens, Homo sapiens; 3 million years ago, 2 million years ago, 1 million years ago.

- Laetoli fossils, and larger fossils from Hadar, typified by the "First Family"
- Smaller fossils from Hadar, typified by "Lucy"
- The Black Skull from Lomekwi, West Turkana
- Swartkrans fossils of "robust australopithecines"
- Kromdraai fossils of "robust australopithecines"
- East African "robust australopithecines"
- *Australopithecus africanus* from Sterkfontein, Makapansgat, and Taung
- Large-brained Turkana *Homo*, typified by ER-1470
- Olduvai *Homo habilis*
- Small-brained Turkana *Homo*, typified by ER-1813
- "Turkana Newcomer" fossils
- *Homo erectus* from Java and China
- Middle and Upper Pleistocene fossils from Africa and Europe—Kabwe, Bodo, Arago, Petralona, Steinheim, Neanderthal—and people of modern type

smaller brow ridges. The other, more complete, is much more modern and resembles one of the Skhul skulls. These transitional populations evidently varied a good deal.

If *Homo sapiens* evolved in Africa between 130,000 and 120,000 years ago, they had probably begun to spread out into Eurasia by about 90,000 years ago, or a little earlier. By 68,000 years ago,

our species was in China. By 50,000 years ago, they were in Australia (which they had to reach by crossing open water, as Australia was never connected to Asia by dry land). And by 36,000 years ago, they were in western Europe, where we know them as the Cro-Magnon. It seems, however, that they did not reach the Americas until 15,000 to 12,000 years ago, although there is much controversy about this. If the regional continuity model, rather than the replacement model, is correct, then these dates simply record when modern humans evolved independently in different areas.

Wherever *Homo sapiens* were found—in Africa, Europe, East or Southeast Asia, or Australia—the earliest people tended to resemble present-day peoples of the same region, but with one difference: they were bigger and more "robust". At the end of the Pleistocene period, people everywhere rapidly became slightly smaller-boned, with smaller teeth. This is puzzling. It was at one time suggested that once people began to practice agriculture, they did not need such big teeth, but the same development took place even in people who remained hunter-gatherers, as in Australia. Perhaps, as the climate became warmer, more succulent foods became available, and it was simply easier to exist with smaller teeth and less chewing effort. The changes were small, but we simply do not know why they occurred.

What Makes Us Human?

The Great Apes are not only closely related to us anatomically, they also have very similar biochemistry to ours. A study carried out in the 1970s showed that humans and chimpanzees have nearly

---

HOMO SAPIENS SAPIENS ?

You will often see the term *Homo sapiens sapiens* used for modern humans, and the Upper Pleistocene fossils that look more or less like us. What does it mean, and why do some of our contributors not use it ?

A biological species is denoted by a two-word name. When there are subspecies (that is, geographical segments of a species that differ a little from one another), we simply add a third word to the name. So, to call us *Homo sapiens sapiens* means that we are all one subspecies, and that there are other subspecies of *Homo sapiens* that are now extinct (such as *Homo sapiens neanderthalensis*, the Neanderthal people of Upper Pleistocene Europe and Southwest Asia).

Are we all one subspecies? We do differ from one another in different parts of the world: we have "races", and these, in a way, are like subspecies. But our geographic variation is very complex, and we do not know how many modern subspecies there are, or what they would be. Moreover, our fossil relatives such as Neanderthals may actually be distinct *species*—there is no evidence that we and they ever interbred. Some experts therefore restrict the species *Homo sapiens* just to us and our forebears up to, say, 120,000 years ago, choosing not to imply a degree of knowledge that we simply do not have by using what they regard as the cumbersome and misleading "*Homo sapiens sapiens*".

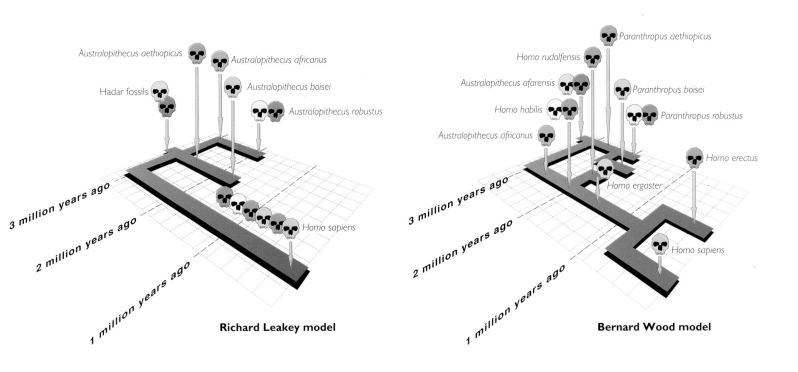

Richard Leakey model

Australopithecus aethiopicus
Australopithecus africanus
Hadar fossils
Australopithecus boisei
Australopithecus robustus
3 million years ago
2 million years ago
Homo sapiens
1 million years ago

Bernard Wood model

Paranthropus aethiopicus
Homo rudolfensis
Australopithecus afarensis
Paranthropus boisei
Homo habilis
Paranthropus robustus
Australopithecus africanus
Homo erectus
Homo ergaster
3 million years ago
2 million years ago
Homo sapiens
1 million years ago

99 percent of their DNA (the material of heredity) in common—a pretty amazing statistic. Given that they are so similar to us in terms of both anatomy and genetics, might we not expect them to be similar psychologically as well—particularly in terms of those features we think of as being uniquely human, such as tool-making, intelligence, self-awareness, and even language? Should we not expect to find these qualities at least in a rudimentary form?

The use of stone tools has characterized human (or, at first, protohuman) activity from 2.6 million years ago. It has been known for a long time that Great Apes in zoos and laboratories show a certain inventive flair in regard to mechanical aids. During the First World War, Wolfgang Koehler found that the chimpanzees in his laboratory on the Canary Islands could not only use sticks to get food that was out of reach, but could join different-sized sticks together, and pile boxes on top of each other, to reach food that was high up. Though gorillas are less dexterous, some orang-utans have developed extraordinary tool-making skills. In the London Zoo, an orang-utan manufactured a wooden replica of the key to its cage and let itself out. Another, in the 1960s, was shown how to work stone, and made itself a sharp-edged flake to cut the string around a box containing food.

In the 1970s, the intriguing discovery was made that chimpanzees learn to recognize themselves in mirrors. Monkeys, in contrast (like dogs and even elephants), react to their reflection as if it were another individual, even though they can come to understand the general concept of a mirror and use it to find hidden objects, as well as recognizing cage mates in it. Like chimpanzees, orang-utans and gorillas can also learn to recognize their own reflection. Does this mean that, like humans and unlike other animals, the Great Apes have a concept of self?

The first language experiments were performed in the 1950s, when a home-reared chimpanzee was taught, with extraordinary time and effort, to say "Mama", "Papa", "cup", and "up". Watching a film of this laborious experiment, psychologists Allen and Beatrice Gardiner noticed that the chimpanzee seemed to be using its hands to express itself, and they decided to try and repeat the language experiment using hand signs instead of words. The success of this sign-language experiment with a young female chimpanzee named Washoe encouraged a number of other researchers to do similar work with orang-utans and gorillas and to use other linguistic modes such as computer language.

But too much was claimed for much of this early work—even, at one point, that the apes were using elementary syntax. When Herbert Terrace analyzed videotaped ape-language sessions in 1979, he found that the hand signs the apes made were often not spontaneous, but depended on inadvertent cues from their trainers. He also found that multiword utterances were not like sentences but consisted mostly of important words repeated, and that most of the apes' signs were techniques for requesting food or other things. There was little evidence that they understood words or signs as symbols. As a result, language researchers reconsidered their methods as well as their earlier findings.

The most significant language work with apes since then has been done by Sue Savage-Rumbaugh

♘ Why do the specialists disagree? There are many reasons. One is that it is difficult to recognize what are different species in the fossil record. Another is differences of opinion as to the meaning of some anatomical features. But the outlines of the evolutionary story remain the same.
ILLUSTRATIONS: COLIN BARDILL

♘ Kanzi, a young bonobo (pygmy chimpanzee), learned simply by watching how to interpret "lexigrams" as symbols—a very crude approach to language. He and his trainers take the lexigram board with them on their visits to the woods near Atlanta, and he indicates where he intends to go and what he will do.

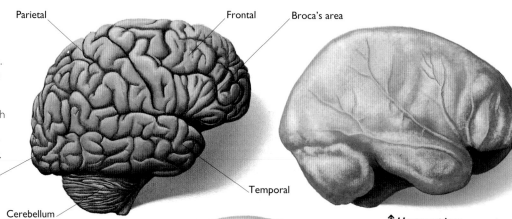

Parietal | Frontal | Broca's area
Occipital | Temporal
Cerebellum

⊕ Brains increased in size stage by stage along the path from australopithecine to modern human. What is more difficult is to read the bumps and folds on the surface, as they are very poorly reproduced on the inside of the skull, from which these endocasts are made. So it is not clear whether, for example, any of our ancestor species could speak.

ILLUSTRATIONS: OLIVER RENNERT

♂ *Homo sapiens*
130,000 years ago to the present
1,040–1,595 cubic centimeters
(63–97 cubic inches)
(normal range: 90 percent of individuals)

900–2,000 cubic centimeters
(55–122 cubic inches)
(extreme range)

⊕ ***Homo erectus erectus*** (early)
1 million to 700,000 years ago
815–1,059 cubic centimeters
(50–65 cubic inches)

Homo erectus erectus (late)
100,000 years ago
1,055–1,300 cubic centimeters
(64–79 cubic inches)

♀ ***Paranthropus robustus***
1.8 million years ago
500–530 cubic centimeters
(31–32 cubic inches)

♂ ***Homo habilis***
2 to 1.6 million years ago
590–700 cubic centimeters
(36–43 cubic inches)

⟺ ***Australopithecus africanus***
3.3 to 2.9 million years ago
420–500 cubic centimeters
(26–31 cubic inches)

♂ **Chimpanzee**
305–485 cubic centimeters
(19–30 cubic inches)

and her colleagues, who taught a sort of computer language to chimpanzees. Using a special technique, they managed to teach apes to name objects, and not merely request them; to "converse" with each other using computerized symbols; and to announce by this means what they were going to do next. Most recently, a young pygmy chimpanzee spontaneously learned the computer "language" just by watching—without having to be taught.

All this work on the mentality and intelligence of apes reminds us that we, as members of the human species, are part of the natural world. Even our special abilities (those we think of as being uniquely human) are not qualitatively but quantitatively different from those of our nearest nonhuman relatives. When we start speculating on the origin of various characteristically human forms of behavior, we have to remember that we did not evolve directly from animals that acted purely by instinct and lacked all traces of a human-like intellect.

And Our Big Brains?

Did life on the savanna become so complex that we developed big brains to cope with it? Did early humans' way of life—the cooperation needed to hunt big game, or the need to outsmart lions to scavenge their prey, or the need to calculate where the most productive plants were likely to be ripening, or the requirements of food sharing, or the need to make tools—require us to have greater intelligence?

Before speculating on such things, it is as well to recall that the Great Apes are already more intelligent than other primates, including gibbons and monkeys, and to ask ourselves why this should be so. Chimpanzees and orang-utans, and some populations of gorillas, live on fruit, and because they are all very large, they have an energy conservation problem. They certainly make calculations, both about the likelihood of fruiting in particular parts of the forest and about each other's motives. Their high intelligence also seems to enable them to be physically lazy. Is this what brainpower is really all about?

Perhaps, then, the question is not why are we so intelligent, but what is it that apes do that our ancestors did more of? In addition, there is certainly a great deal of serendipity involved, different aspects of our ancestors' anatomy and psychology seeming to pre-adapt us for full humanity. By the evolutionary process known as neoteny, the head remains juvenile in appearance (small jaws, large brain) but continues to grow. Upright posture: the hands are freed for tool use. Head balance: the larynx is repositioned, as if ready for articulate speech. Mobile shoulder: the arm is already adapted for throwing. Intelligence and sociability: social traditions develop into culture. Humans could not have evolved from any creatures other than apes.

SO SIMILAR AND STILL SO DIFFERENT: THE GREAT APES AND OURSELVES

WULF SCHIEFENHÖVEL

His mother had been ailing before she died. The child, old enough to be cared for by his relatives, became more and more depressed. It was obvious that he had lost the will to live. Three and a half weeks later, he, too, died.

This and similar cases were documented by Jane Goodall in her ground-breaking studies of mother–child relationships among chimpanzees (*Pan troglodytes*)—with their cousins, the bonobos (*Pan paniscus*), most probably our closest relatives. In the last decades, clinical research has confirmed that traumatic events in our lives, such as the loss of a beloved person, can trigger our own death. This is an extreme example of the psychosomatic effects that can result from emotions such as deep depression. If chimpanzees react to such events with the same grief, the same loss of joy and will to live, as we do, where do we draw the line between these creatures and ourselves?

The Great Apes are surprising in many ways. Bonobos engage in sexual acts for various apparently non-reproductive purposes, as Frans de Waal has demonstrated. This behavior acts as a kind of social lubricant—for example, to console, to appease, or to achieve goals. The biggest of all the Great Apes, gorillas (*Gorilla gorilla*), sometimes display astoundingly human-like behavior in the films Dian Fossey made during the time she spent with them. In one case, a powerful male can be seen watching her intensely while she writes notes in her scientific diary. She holds her pen in his direction, he slowly takes it, looks and sniffs at it, and hands it quietly back to her. He seems to respect the principle of ownership, returning to her what he recognizes as her property.

Neurobiologists have compared the brains of humans and chimpanzees and have found no structural differences between the two species. There seem to be no nuclei (the foci where neuroelectric impulses are generated), no tracts connecting the various brain parts with each other, and no areas (the sections responsible for specific perceptions or actions) in a chimpanzee's brain that cannot be found in our own brain. So why do we speak, count, calculate, write, travel to the moon, and wear business suits? Not all these things are typical of our species, of course. Sophisticated counting, calculating, writing, and all the achievements of our impressive technology are quite recent events in the time scale of our evolution.

It was thought for a long time that the real difference between the "animals" and us was the fact that we have developed culture and they have not. However, we now believe that monkeys and apes are able to "teach" things to their young, which they, in turn, pass on to their own young, or which are imitated by the whole group: one animal picks up a technique or habit from the next. For instance, in studying a group of Japanese monkeys (*Macaca fuscata*, which do not belong to the Great Apes), Michael Huffman and other primatologists

♂ Members of a group of *Macaca fuscata*, living in semi-wild conditions near Kyoto, Japan, have developed the habit of playing with small stones. As this behavior has been passed on through a number of generations, many scientists view it as a precursor of "culture".

♀ A young chimpanzee catching termites with a specially modified twig—another example of behavior passed on from mother to children.

discovered that they have developed the custom of playing with stones in a specific way. Other Japanese monkeys, for many generations now, have been carefully washing sweet potatoes in a stream before eating them. Certain groups of chimpanzees use stone hammers to open hard nuts, while others do not. Clearly, these achievements are at least equivalents or precursors of culture, forms of behavior passed on by tradition.

Chimpanzees, bonobos, and gorillas live in groups and have social hierarchies. The orang-utan (*Pongo pygmaeus*), on the other hand, seems to be mostly solitary, except at mating time. In gorilla harems, the females are not related to each other and must therefore have migrated into the group. The same pattern seems to operate among chimpanzees: young females may leave the group to find partners outside. In most human societies, young women are required by custom (which may be genetically based) to leave their parents' family and to live with their husband.

We cannot, of course, conclude from such single behavioral and social traits that human beings are shaped after the model of a particular species of Great Apes. In so many ways, the apes are very different from each other and from us in their preferences, their characteristics, their behavior, and their social structure. But by studying the Great Apes and the other nonhuman primates, scientists can trace probable evolutionary connections between such variables as habitat, social structure, behavior, cognitive abilities, and capacity for culture. By continued study of these creatures, preferably in the wild in groups, we will not only learn more about their own fascinating lives, but will also come to a better understanding of our own species' history. But this will only be possible if we, as a species, stop encroaching on their habitat and threatening their very survival as a species.

54

TOWARDS *HOMO SAPIENS*

2.5 MILLION YEARS AGO – 35,000 YEARS AGO

Habilines, Erectines, and Neanderthals

GÖRAN BURENHULT

ABOUT 2.5 MILLION YEARS AGO, a series of crucial events were to influence the human family tree. In Africa, different species of *Australopithecus* and *Paranthropus* lived side by side, and recently, at Chesowanja, in Kenya, the existence of very early *Homo* has been confirmed at this age. This early *Homo* was named *Homo habilis* ("clever human"), but many now believe that more than one species is represented in this phase.

These events resulted in a number of anatomical changes that mainly occurred during the period that preceded the erectines—that is, about 1.5 million years ago. Brain size increased, hips and thigh bones became more and more adapted to bipedalism, and there was a reduction in sexual dimorphism—that is, size difference due to sex. The oldest fossils of *Homo* have a brain size of little more than 500 cubic centimeters (30 cubic inches), but apart from that the difference between the new genus and *Australopithecus* was not particularly striking. They all grew to roughly the same height, 1 to 1.3 meters (3 to 4 feet), and weighed 40 kilograms (88 pounds) on average. All of them were bipedal and thus moved freely on two legs. Early *Homo* had a slightly more rounded skull and were probably less ape-like than other hominids. The greatest anatomical difference was the appearance of the teeth, especially the reduced premolar and molar width, but the signs of wear on preserved teeth show that all species fed mainly on seeds and plants, especially fruits. Moreover, anatomical studies indicate that early *Homo* probably spent a great deal of time in the trees and for this reason was less "human" than previously assumed. It has turned out that the greatest difference was the mental capacity. Habilines were the first hominids to make stone tools.

◄○ The erectines were the first humans to leave the African homeland. By 700,000 years ago, they had occupied much of the Old World and had spread as far east as China and Southeast Asia. The volcanic soils of East and central Java, in Indonesia, have produced a number of *Homo erectus* fossils.

↥ A hand axe—the typical tool of the Acheulean phase.

Defining the use of tools is not a simple matter. Californian sea otters fetch mussels on the seabed and, swimming on their back, crush the shell against their chest with a suitable stone to be able to reach the food. This behavior is remarkable but does not mean that a stone tool has been manufactured, or that the sea otter becomes a human. Chimpanzees, our closest relatives among the apes, not only use tools such as stones, branches, or slips of wood, but, by using their teeth and hands, they often also improve objects of wood or fibers to make them more efficient. Although an obvious manufacturing process, not even this kind of tool can be ranked in the same category as the tools made by habilines. The greatest difference lies in the mental functions—in the decision-making process. The chimpanzee is manufacturing a suitable slip of wood as a result of an instantaneous, intelligent idea, whereas the human action was characterized by a more advanced foresight, a deliberate manufacturing of an object with a particular appearance and for a certain purpose. A picture of the final product and its range of uses was already projected in the brain before the individual started to collect the raw material in the form of stones of suitable kinds and sizes. Furthermore, the knowledge of the manufacturing process could be transmitted to other members of the group as well as to succeeding generations.

The Habilines: The First Tool-makers

The first tool-making technique—which, as far as we know at present, is entirely linked to early *Homo*—existed between 2.5 and 1.5 million years ago and is distinguished by the use of pebbles from riverbeds as raw material. By means of another, smaller stone, flakes were struck off from both sides of the core. This bifacial flaking procedure is usually called the chopping-tool technique and was named the Oldowan industry after the site of its first discovery—Olduvai. Even though this technique sometimes has been considered simple, it nevertheless reveals a sound knowledge of the nature of the raw material, how to strike the stone to get a suitable flake, and, not least, the final result after a long series of strokes in a given succession.

For a long time, the general opinion was that the shaped core in itself represented the final product—the tool—and that the flakes were to be regarded as waste or leftovers from the manufacturing procedure. Close examination has shown, however, that much of the variation among chopping tools was the result of a deliberate production of flakes, which then could be used as knives, scrapers, or other tools for cutting meat, woodwork, and gathering plants. Many of the chopping tools found have probably been used for rough jobs, such as crushing animal bones, to be able to reach the much sought-after marrow, or digging up edible tubers and bulbs.

The chimpanzee may begin to gather materials for tools while still not in sight of the objective;

⚲ More than two million years ago, early *Homo* began to make stone tools from pebbles collected from riverbeds. The chopping-tool technique used by these early tool-makers is called the Oldowan industry, after Olduvai, in Tanzania, the site where such tools were first discovered.

ILLUSTRATION: JOHN RICHARDS

in Gombe National Park, for example, where chimpanzees modify grass stems and thin twigs to "fish" for termites in their mounds, they collect stems and take them to the termite mounds, where they are modified as and when necessary. If Richard Potts is right, that the accumulations of pebbles found at Olduvai represent "caches" of stone placed conveniently for future use by *Homo habilis*, then we can attribute to our early ancestors, of two million years ago, a degree of foresight considerably greater than that shown by modern chimpanzees. But we must not make the mistake of thinking of these primitive forebears as already human. Thomas Wynn has analyzed samples of their pebble tools and found no evidence that they modified them in anything but an ad hoc manner, striking off one flake after another until a usable tool resulted.

However, the findings from Koobi Fora and Olduvai also show that stone tools were carried considerable distances. This is yet another piece of evidence that habilines planned a future use for their tools, that they were able to think in the future tense. "Culture" was born.

Any Time but Not with Anybody

Why, then, did this new branch on the human family tree suddenly evolve some 2.5 million years ago? Today, most experts agree that human evolution resulted from the same sorts of pressures as the evolution of other animal species, and very often it is obvious that these processes of evolution occurred at the same time. Clearly, global climatic alterations, and the ecological changes that followed, played a crucial part in these processes.

About five million years ago, the Antarctic ice sheet started to grow substantially, whereas the corresponding glacial period of the Arctic did not begin until about 2.5 million years ago. During these two Ice Ages, the average temperature on Earth dropped markedly. In Africa, as in other parts of the world, this meant great changes in both flora and fauna. Vast tropical rainforest regions disappeared and were replaced by savanna, and parts of the fauna became extinct or changed owing to the adaptation to the new environment. These great ecological changes can be traced back to both of the glacial periods. The first one resulted in the development of the australopithecines— perhaps the separation of the human line itself— and it was surely not an accidental occurrence that the latter Ice Age coincided with the appearance of the genus *Homo* and the rise of tool use.

As we have seen, a number of different proto-human species lived side by side during this period, but, as far as we know at present, australo-pithecines never manufactured or used stone tools. While australopithecines in the course of time became extinct, the *Homo* groups survived and evolved into modern humans. But what was the biological difference between nonhuman

JOHN READER/SCIENCE PHOTO LIBRARY/THE PHOTO LIBRARY

hominids and early humans? This is a controversial issue, but one of the basic differences is human females' total lack of estrus periods—that is, mating seasons. They are, unlike many other mammals, always sexually receptive, almost independently of the menstrual cycle, although chimpanzees, especially pygmy chimpanzees (bonobos), also have very little sexual cyclicity. This evolution of human sexuality can perhaps be linked to a gradual reduction of body hair, resulting in increased skin sensitivity and a strengthening of female sexual signals. For example, the growth of the breasts is not necessary for the production of mother's milk or for breastfeeding, but is instead related to a visual, sexual stimulation for males. A change in the food composition, with a changeover to a diet consisting of more meat, and accompanying changes in the social organization, has been suggested as one reason for this evolution.

Far-reaching studies of baboons and chimpanzees show these considerable differences between different mammal species, and the interpretations can, with caution, be transferred to the study of early hominids. Among baboons, old males possess absolute dominance over food and mating, and they defend this position with extremely aggressive behavior. Sexual dimorphism is con-siderable—for example, males are twice as big as females. The dominant males and females lay their hands on most, and the best, of the food, and apart from the fact that a mother and her young sometimes share food, a systematic distribution never occurs among the different members of the group.

This habiline skull discovered at Koobi Fora, on the eastern shores of Lake Turkana, in Kenya, in 1972 is believed to be about 1.9 million years old. Known as no. 1470, it has a relatively large braincase—nearly 800 cubic centimeters (49 cubic inches)— and was reconstructed from 150 pieces of fossil bone found scattered over a large area.

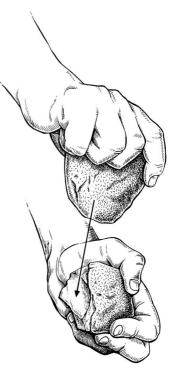

The Oldowan industry represents the simplest form of tool-making. The raw material consisted of pebbles collected from riverbeds at Koobi Fora and Olduvai. By means of a small stone, flakes were struck off from both sides of the core. Each core could yield a large number of flakes, and probably both the flakes and the remaining core were used as tools.

ILLUSTRATIONS: KEN RINKEL

The reverse is the case among chimpanzees. These lack a hierarchic division, and all males have free access to the receptive females—any time and with anybody. There are no mating seasons, but female receptivity varies. Furthermore, chimpanzees have a much less strict organization in terms of territorial control. Ethologist and primatologist Pierre van den Berghe described the agreeable life of chimpanzees in the following way: "Chimpanzees, it seems, successfully achieve what *Homo sapiens* radicals only dream of: peaceful, non-competitive, non-coercive, non-possessive, egalitarian, jealousy-free, promiscuous, non-tyrannical communes."

Of course, this must not be taken too far. Dominant males often do monopolize fertile

⚲ Olduvai Gorge, in northern Tanzania, is one of the world's most important archaeological sites. Its many fossil finds of australopithecines, habilines, and erectines, as well as modern humans, have added immensely to our knowledge of our distant prehistoric past.

females, although free consortships are often formed as well; and the males of a community patrol the territory boundaries, and one case is known where the males in one community apparently set out (successfully) to exterminate the small neighboring community. Maybe, after all, we are being a bit romantic: chimpanzees may be more like us than we care to admit.

It seems clear, then, that hunting behavior, the lack of mating seasons, the distribution of food within the group, as well as family structure, are factors that are intimately associated with each other and that probably were of crucial importance in the subsequent evolution of humans. An increasingly marked disposition toward living in couples, or perhaps small polygamous groups, which also created a basis for a more rigid distribution of work between the sexes, may have helped to reduce conflict within groups. Any time but not with anybody became typically human behavior.

Hunters or Scavengers?

The use of stone tools made possible the exploitation of foodstuffs previously inaccessible to hominids. When taking care of meat, entrails, and hides, sharp-edged flakes were a great advantage, especially in competition with predators such as hyenas and lions. Large amounts of meat could be cut loose from a dead animal in a short time, something that would have been impossible if only hands, teeth, and wooden objects were used. But detailed knowledge of the eating habits of early *Homo* is still very limited. (See the feature *Mighty Hunter or Marginal Scavenger?*)

Inevitably, the archaeological record gives us a very incidental and selective picture of prehistoric reality. Preserved food remnants are rare, and, when found, they almost always consist of animal bones. This means that stone tools, which are always well preserved, represent the most important source of information in our attempt to establish the modes of subsistence and the preparation of food of early humans. These tools thus become overrepresented in the interpretation of what once took place on the site in question. Scattered remnants of animal bones are often found together with large numbers of chopping tools and flakes, and these concentrations have usually been interpreted as sites of activity or even occasional home bases where animals were brought in, quartered, and eaten.

The problem is, however, that we do not know to what extent habilines made use of meat in their diet, nor if they, in that case, only grabbed the prey of predators by scaring off the true hunters, or were themselves actively engaged in big-game hunting. The use of stone tools has often been associated with big-game hunting and

thereby with a rapidly changing economic and social organization, but modern analyses have shown that early *Homo* may never actually have hunted big game and may to a very small extent only have depended upon any form of hunting. Still, great numbers of stone tools are found together with the bones of large animals such as hippopotamuses, buffaloes, or gnus, and unquestionably the tools have been transported there over considerable distances. The facts indicate that these kinds of sites represent locations where quartering and possibly scavenging took place, and where predators were frightened away after having brought down their prey. These sites can by no means be looked upon as more or less permanent settlements or home bases where humans stayed for some time, but in some cases it cannot be excluded that pieces of meat were carried to safe spots and consumed out of reach of wild beasts. Without fire and advanced weapons such as spears or bows and arrows, this kind of subsistence must have been a risky business in an open savanna environment with few or no possibilities to seek shelter or take flight. Many of the examined animal bones show traces

of both stone tools and teeth of predatory animals, clear evidence of the prevailing competitive situation. Marks of animal teeth that superimpose those of stone tools may, of course, indicate that animals consumed leftovers from habiline meals, but in many cases marks of tools superimpose those of animal teeth, and this surely indicates scavenging on predator kills.

Finds of bones of many different animal species on these sites have, however, led many experts to believe that early *Homo* actually, to some extent, used hunting as part of the subsistence—a part that certainly became more important as time went on—and that a combination of hunting and scavenging is the most probable explanation. Yet most experts agree that vegetable foodstuffs such as plants, bulbs, roots, and fruits formed an overwhelming part of the diet, and that animal products such as birds' eggs, larvae, lizards, and small game played a much more important role than big game. This is the case among chimpanzees, and the same kind of food constitutes an important part of the diet of present-day hunter-gatherers. Nothing in the find material indicates that early *Homo* differed from this pattern.

MAJOR ERECTINE SITES

It is generally believed that the erectines migrated outside Africa more than 700,000 years ago and settled southern Asia and much of Europe. Coastlines and ice sheets are shown as they are assumed to have been during the peak of one of the extensive glacials that preceded the last Ice Age. European sites are shown in the detail map at left.

CARTOGRAPHY: RAY SIM

MIGHTY HUNTER OR MARGINAL SCAVENGER?

PETER ROWLEY-CONWY

What was life like for our earliest hominid relatives? How did they live? Archaeologists have been seeking to answer these questions ever since 1924, when Raymond Dart identified the Taung skull as that of a hominid he named *Australopithecus africanus*. In the process, they have produced some of the most interesting archaeological work of recent years.

The Australopithecines of South Africa

The australopithecine group known as the Nutcrackers has been studied in detail in South Africa, where several important fossil sites have been excavated, including Makapansgat. As well as hominid remains, these sites have yielded numerous bones of other large mammals, including buffalo and various species of antelopes and carnivores. Should we conclude that these bones are the remains of animals hunted and eaten by the australopithecines? Dart's answer was a decided "Yes", for several reasons.

No stone tools were found in these sites, but Dart believed that the australopithecines at Makapansgat used tools made of bone, teeth, and horn instead. He argued that evidence of pitting and breakage on some of the animal bones showed that they had been used for hammering or pounding, and that some pieces of bone had been sharpened to a point for use as weapons. In other words, Dart claimed that these hominids were using a whole range of bone tools in their daily lives, some of them intended to hunt and kill their prey, and perhaps other hominids, too.

Recent work by C.K. Brain and others has largely demolished this theory. In a book entitled *The Hunters or the Hunted?*, published in 1981, Brain argues that all the bones at these sites, including those of hominids, result from the hunting behavior of large carnivores, especially leopards. Hominids

SHAH ANÚP/JACANA-AUSCAPE

would have been one of the animals leopards preyed upon, and after a leopard had eaten its fill, hyenas would have moved in to scavenge the remains of the carcass. This explains the bone finds much better than Dart's theory did. Bones collected from present-day hyena dens are pitted and broken in very much the same way as those from the South African sites, and the same sharp points are also found.

In fact, there is no evidence that the South African australopithecines used bone for any purpose at all. And as their own bones were gnawed and broken like those of the other animals, they must have suffered the same fate—they were

the hunted rather than the hunters.

This theory has been given further support by recent geological work showing that the sites where these bones have accumulated were not caves but vertical cracks or fissures in the ground. These would have retained water in the otherwise dry landscape, leading to the growth of isolated groups of trees. Leopards today can be seen to carry their prey up into trees in order to escape the hyenas attracted by a fresh kill. As the leopard eats, parts of the carcass fall to the ground. The hyenas set upon these, and the discarded bones are likely to end up in any natural fissures in the vicinity. This is the best explanation of

Leopards often carry their prey into trees. As they consume their victims, bones fall to the ground, where some are gnawed by scavenging hyenas. Sites such as Swartkrans were deep fissures that trapped and preserved such bones, including those of early hominids.

the South African sites: they are natural fossil traps. No one ever lived there, and they have preserved the evidence of leopard kills made as far back as two or three million years ago.

Early Homo in East Africa

By the time *Homo habilis* appears in the archaeological record in East Africa, some two million years ago, many differences are immediately apparent. Accumulations of animal bones are still found, but there are two crucial differences. First, they are found scattered in horizontal layers, not down deep fissures; and second, they are found together with stone tools. They look, in fact, very like habiline camp sites.

But are they? In such key areas as Olduvai Gorge and Koobi Fora, collections of stones and bones have often been found on the shores of ancient rivers or lakes. It is therefore possible that floods washed the various items together by chance. Just because the bones and stones are found together now, it does not necessarily mean that they started that way. Sometimes, however, various fragments of stone found within a short distance of each other have been able to be fitted back together again. This must mean that someone made a tool on that very spot, because the various pieces would have become separated if the area had later been flooded. Similarly, several pieces of animal bone have sometimes been able to be fitted back together.

The animal bones provide a vital clue to habiline behavior. Many leg bones bear impact marks, where they were struck with stone

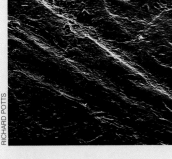

RICHARD POTTS

RICHARD POTTS

☝Cut marks on prehistoric bones (top) can look similar to gnaw marks made by carnivores (bottom) to the naked eye, but can usually be distinguished by microscopic examination.

tools to break them open for marrow, and some have cut marks, indicating that flesh was cut from them with sharp stone flakes. The inference is clear: habilines brought animal bones to these sites, using stone tools to get at the flesh and marrow.

It would be tempting to conclude that these sites were regular home bases, to which hunters brought back their kill, but it would also be premature. Archaeologist Glynn Isaac came to this conclusion some years ago, and it is instructive to see what followed from this. If animals were hunted, Isaac postulated, there would have been a division of labor. Males would have been the hunters, while females, encumbered by children, would more likely have gathered plant foods and small animals in the vicinity of the camp site. This would mean that food was shared between the sexes, implying a reasonably complex social structure.

This scenario is instantly recognizable—it is a simplfied version of the behavior of modern hunter-gatherers at their base camps. What the theory does is to project a form of modern behavior two million

years back into the past, all on the basis of the division of labor implied by hunting. The hunting hypothesis has a lot to answer for.

So how well founded is it? More recently, archaeologists including Lewis Binford and Richard Potts have re-examined the evidence. Clearly, the origin of modern forms of behavior is of key importance for our understanding of ourselves. It is something we should try to discover, not something we should have preconceived ideas about.

Interest has focused on the evidence of the animal bones. Some, as mentioned, have cut marks. Others, however, have gnaw marks made by carnivores, and where cuts and gnaw marks are found on the same bone, the gnaw marks were usually made first. This shows that, in some cases at least, the habilines were getting their hands on these bones only after the carnivores had finished with them. There is only one way to explain this: the habilines were in such instances demonstrably

scavenging from carnivore kills, not killing their own prey.

This casts a new light on many things. First, scavenging requires no division of labor and does not imply sharing or any other social behavior approaching our own modern forms of behavior. Second, this may explain the early use of sharp stone tools. Habiline scavengers would have been competing with other scavengers such as hyenas, which are biologically much better equipped for the job and, indeed, could easily have killed and eaten the habilines if the opportunity had arisen. For the habiline scavengers, the crucial thing was probably to get away from a carcass as quickly as possible. Lacking their competitors' sharp teeth, they may have used sharp stone tools to cut quickly through the tough skin and sinew, fleeing with edible portions before the hyenas arrived.

According to this theory, the "home bases" would have been places to which the habiline scavengers

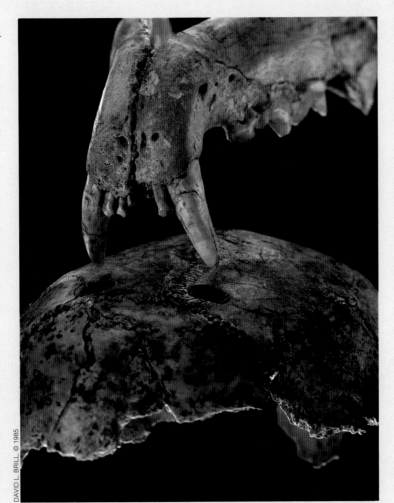

DAVID L. BRILL, © 1985

took their food to eat it in safety. Paleoecological work has provided further information about such sites. As mentioned, they have often been found on the banks of former streams or lakes, under what would once have been stands of trees. This might seem to be a perfectly reasonable place to live—but not for early habilines, and not in tropical Africa. Even modern hunter-gatherers do not camp under trees along waterways, because at night lions prowl these locations, killing animals that come down to drink.

This is a crucial point, because it suggests that habilines did not sleep at the sites that have yielded evidence of their presence. We do not know where they slept. If they were similar to other primates, they might have done so on cliffs or rocks some distance from the water. The so-called "home bases" were therefore no such thing, but rather places visited during the daytime to eat food scavenged from the kills of large carnivores. Habilines do not appear to have operated from bases as modern humans do. It is more likely that they ranged over considerable areas during the daytime, much as baboons do.

The evidence now suggests a pattern of movement from the sleeping site across the open savanna, via abandoned carnivore kills, sources of plant foods, and caches of stone suitable for making tools, to a daytime waterside site under the trees—and back again before nightfall. This is hardly recognizable as specifically human behavior. As Lewis Binford puts it, our earliest ancestors were really not very like us.

◄● Two injuries on the skull of an australopithecine child from Swartkrans were formerly thought to have been inflicted with a pointed club. However, the injuries exactly match up with the canine teeth of a leopard, suggesting that the child was a hunting victim.

⟳ The Great Rift Valley—the cradle of humanity—is the most extensive rift in the Earth's surface. It extends from southwestern Asia southwards through East Africa to Mozambique. The section of the valley shown here is in Kenya.

The period between 2.5 and 1.5 million years ago was a crucial and formative phase in the evolution of humans—mentally, technologically, and economically, as well as socially. The pressure from the ecological competition enforced early human characteristics in early *Homo* and at the same time led to the extinction of other proto-hominid species. The number of hominids in central East Africa may have been equivalent to the number of baboons living in the same region today—in other words, a very large number of individuals in mutual competition. The ever-increasing brain size led to considerably smaller brains in infants than in adults, which facilitated childbirth. This in turn resulted in a considerable prolongation of the period in which children were dependent on their mothers, which involved important changes in the social organization and the division of work between the sexes.

Habilines probably lived in small groups or bands, much like present-day hunter-gatherers, but the social organization was more similar to that of chimpanzees. Only with the appearance of *Homo erectus* some 1.6 million years ago did a more human social structure develop.

The Homo erectus *Phase: "Apeman Who Walks Upright"*

When the erectines came on the scene, entirely new characters in human evolution appeared, with abilities and driving forces that made our ancestors spread outside Africa for the first time. This demanded totally different ways of ecological adaptation. The cold climate and trying environment further north implied that humans used fire and wore well-adapted clothing to be able to keep warm during the winter. Above all, the migration of *Homo erectus* into northern regions shows that people now were able to adjust themselves to considerably harsher ecological situations, where the supply of food varied markedly during the different seasons and where hunting became increasingly important, especially during the winter. Many of the edible plants withered in the autumn, and it was necessary to store nonperishable foodstuffs such as nuts, bulbs, and tubers.

Physically, the erectines were more similar to modern humans than to habilines. The greatest difference was probably the shape of the head and face, which still had strikingly primitive features— a sloping forehead, very heavy brow ridges, and a receding chin. The muscles at the nape of the neck were extremely well developed. Brain size increased over time from 775 to 1,300 cubic centimeters (47 to 79 cubic inches), which on average is equivalent to 70 percent of that of modern humans. Fully adapted to an upright gait and equipped with a muscular and stocky body of between 1.5 and 1.8 meters (about 5 and 6 feet) in height, *Homo erectus* must have made the impression of being very strong and powerful.

MICHAEL DENIS HUOT/JACANA-AUSCAPE

Today, most experts agree that the erectines slowly evolved from the habilines in central East Africa, from where they spread north across the Old World. The oldest fossils have been found in East Turkana, in Kenya—sometimes referred to as the "Turkana Newcomers"—and date back some 1.6 million years. A million years later, *Homo erectus* and its sister species, *Homo heidelbergensis*, occupied all of Eurasia, from the Atlantic coast in the west to China and Java in the east.

It was never really a matter of migration. Hunter-gatherers move across vast areas in search of food, and an increasing population implied that groups split up and new territories were occupied. At a pace of 20 kilometers (12 miles) per generation, a distance of 14,000 kilometers (9,000 miles), or roughly the distance between Nairobi and Beijing, was covered in 20,000 years. Even with much shorter movements, this natural, successive spread was enough for the erectines to occupy these vast areas in just a few hundreds of thousands of years. As colder and darker regions of Europe and Asia became populated, skin color became lighter to allow the rays of the sun to penetrate the skin to produce vitamin D, and the protecting fat layer, as well as the sweat glands, adapted to the new climatic situation. The big question is why these groups of people were forced to leave the always well-laid African table.

As we have seen, *Homo* itself, and, later, the erectines, evolved on the savannas of tropical Africa. The great climatic fluctuations that prevailed

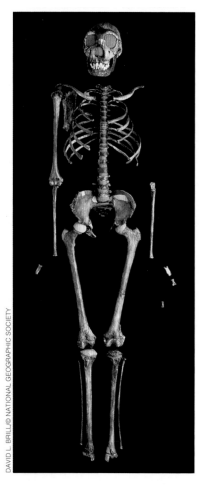

DAVID L. BRILL/© NATIONAL GEOGRAPHIC SOCIETY

⟳ A well-preserved, 1.6 million-year-old erectine skeleton discovered near Lake Turkana, in Kenya, in 1984 is believed to be that of a 12-year-old boy. The skeleton measures almost 1.7 meters (5 feet, 6 inches) in length, suggesting that adult erectines grew as tall as 1.8 meters (about 6 feet)

oldest date in Southwest Asia has been obtained at Ubeidiya, in modern-day Israel, at an age of 700,000 years, although there are no diagnostic human remains from there, while the oldest known find in western Europe has been uncovered in Italy, at Isernia La Pineta, southeast of Rome; stone tool finds show that humans lived there some 730,000 years ago. However, on the basis of a recent find of a lower jaw beneath the city of Dmanisi, southwest of Tblisi, in the former Soviet republic of Georgia, it has been claimed that humans had already spread outside Africa 1.8 million years ago.

◄○ This *Homo erectus* skull found at Sangiran, in central Java, Indonesia, is believed to be about 800,000 years old.

♀ The famous Zhoukoudian Cave, outside Beijing, in China, was first excavated by Davidson Black in the early 1920s. So far, the remains of some 40 *Homo erectus* individuals have been uncovered here, together with more than 100,000 stone tools such as scrapers and chopping tools, making it one of the most important erectine sites in the world. Its layers date back to between 460,000 and 230,000 years ago.

between five and one million years ago intensified about 900,000 years ago, and the global climate was influenced by glacial periods alternating with warmer interglacials. Consequently, the African vegetation was characterized by savanna alternating with rainforest. To be able to survive these freaks of nature, humans had to adapt in different ways, either by moving or by occupying new climatic zones. The latter implied, among other things, the ability to alternate vegetable foodstuffs with a meat diet.

Obviously, the Sahara Desert played an important role in this process. During periods with higher rainfall, populations from the south entered the virgin soils in the north, and during drier periods they were forced to leave. In some cases, the retreat southwards may have been cut off, and for that reason a northward expansion toward the Mediterranean coast and southwestern Asia was necessary. Demonstrably, a heavy increase in the number of big land animals took place in Europe about 700,000 years ago, when elephants, hoofed animals, hippopotamuses, and a series of predators such as lions and leopards migrated north from Africa. It is probable that the causes that lie behind these migrations are also behind the contemporary appearance of humans outside Africa.

To sum up, the erectines—of which *Homo erectus* is the best known species—first appeared in Africa, and a number of finds from Lake Turkana, Chesowanja, and Olduvai date back to between 1.6 and one million years ago. The Asian finds, on the other hand, are all of a later date. Ban Mae Tha, in Thailand, is one of the oldest known sites in Southeast Asia, at an age of 700,000 years, whereas the *erectus* finds from Zhoukoudian, in China, date back to between 460,000 and 230,000 years ago. Other Chinese finds from Lantian, Jenjiawo, and Gongwangling have proved to be somewhat older than the earliest layers of Zhoukoudian, and have been dated to 600,000 years ago. For the Java humans, there are potassium–argon dates of between 900,000 and 600,000 years ago, and these are supported by fission-track dates which go back to a little over a million years ago.

Erectine groups, it seems, entered Europe at roughly the same time as they entered Asia. The

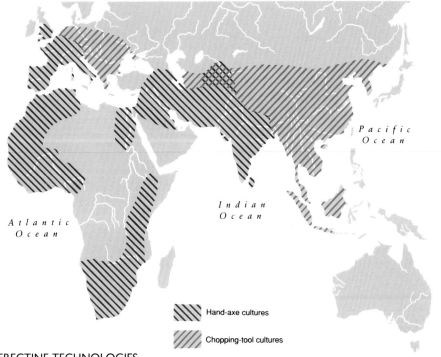

Hand-axe cultures

Chopping-tool cultures

CARTOGRAPHY: RAY SIM

ERECTINE TECHNOLOGIES

During the erectine phase, two technologically distinct regions can be distinguished in the Old World. The technology of the populations in Africa, western Europe, and Southwest Asia was characterized by the hand axe, and is usually called the Acheulean tradition. In East and Southeast Asia, as well as in eastern Europe, however, chopping tools dominated.

This magnificent hand axe, the characteristic tool of the Acheulean period, was found at the site that gave the period its name—St Acheul, in northern France.

GÖRAN BURENHULT

Acheulean: Period of Hand Axes

During the erectine era, bifacially worked hand axes became the dominant tool type in many parts of the Old World. This tool tradition is called the Acheulean and was named after the site of its first documentation—St Acheul, in France. The subtriangular hand axe probably had a wide range of uses, such as cutting, digging, and scraping, and was often shaped into a neat but very efficient tool. Wynn's analysis of Oldowan pebble tools has shown clearly that the makers of hand axes must have had, before they started, a clear mental picture of the finished object, and worked towards achieving it as they flaked. Presumably, hand axes were never hafted, but were instead used by hand, and some experts have even suggested that they were used during hunting as a kind of missile or discus. The extent of big-game hunting at this period is, however, a most controversial issue.

During the long erectine period, the Old World gradually split up into two technologically distinct regions. The reason for this split is still unclear. The tool assemblage of one region, which embraced Africa, Europe, and parts of western and southern Asia, was dominated by the hand axe, whereas that of East and Southeast Asia lacked hand axes and was dominated by local chopping-tool industries. It is interesting that the East/Southeast Asian area was the domain of *Homo erectus* itself, while many specialists consider that the western region was occupied by the species *Homo heidelbergensis*.

Acheulean technology was extremely long-lived. In Africa, it existed from 1.5 million until between 200,000 and 150,000 years ago, when it was replaced by the more complex stone technology of the so-called Middle Stone Age. This was characterized by scrapers and points manufactured out of flakes. In Europe, the hand-axe tradition survived much longer, until more modern humans appeared some 100,000 years ago.

The appearance of hand axes has led most experts to believe that big-game hunting constituted an important part of the erectine subsistence, and a number of sites have been pointed out as evidence of this. At Olorgesailie, southwest of Nairobi, in Kenya, Glynn and Barbara Isaac have excavated a kill site with the remains of large mammals such as hippopotamuses, but, above all, also the remains of 63 giant baboons, a now extinct species, which were found together with more than 10,000 beautiful hand axes. The area was no bigger than 12 meters by 20 meters (40 feet by 65 feet). The excavators interpreted the spot as a kill site where the baboons had been hemmed in, probably at night, frightened, and then clubbed to death when they tried to escape; others are more convinced that the site represents a longer time span, over which giant baboons were favored prey.

American anthropologist Lewis Binford has, however, called not only Olorgesailie in question, but even the whole idea that the erectines were big-game hunters. In his opinion, there is presently no way of determining whether a site is the result of butchering or if there are other explanations of the accumulated find material. The deposits of animal remains may very well be leftovers from scavenging on predator kills. According to Binford, the same applies to other classic sites that have been pointed out as "proof" of big-game hunting in Europe and Asia in Middle Pleistocene times—Torralba, in Spain, and Zhoukoudian, in China.

Terra Amata, in Nice, on the French Riviera, is another important European site from this period that has been under intense discussion. The site contained the remains of 10 large, oval-shaped huts 8 to 10 meters (26 to 33 feet) long and equipped with centrally situated hearths and longitudinal stone arrangements along the postholes and walls. The excavator, Henry de Lumley, considered the 300,000-year-old find to be a seasonal settlement, where its inhabitants during parts of the year supported themselves on fishing and gathering, particularly sea mussels, oysters, and limpets. Terra Amata, too, has been questioned by many experts, but the claimed remains of postholes and stone tools are not easily explained away. Although the original layer may have been disturbed—by landslides and freezing, for example—it is still very likely that the site was used in some way by human groups. Pollen analyses show that the settlement in that case was used especially during late spring.

WHAT DO THE ZHOUKOUDIAN FINDS TELL US?

PETER ROWLEY-CONWY

Imagine a huge cavern. Imagine it existing for hundreds of thousands of years, and consider a few of the things that would take place there through this colossal span of time. From time to time, hyenas inhabit the cave. They bring in their prey and gnaw the bones, they rear their young, they defecate, and they die. At other times, wolves live there. Huge cave bears occasionally hibernate in the cave, some of which die and add their bones to the debris inside. Owls roost in suitable crannies, regurgitating pellets of indigestible fur and bones, the remnants of the small animals they prey upon. Sand, dust, and mud are continually blown and washed inside by wind and rain, gradually building up into thick layers.

From time to time, pieces of rock break loose from the roof, crushing anything beneath, to lie on the cave floor until covered by the rising deposits. Sometimes a roof fall blocks an existing entrance or creates a new one, changing the appearance of the cavern. Plants grow near the entrances. Their seeds are blown inside or are carried in by the rodents that live in rock crevices round about. These rodents sometimes perish inside the cave, or fall victim to owls or wolves. All the while, the various deposits and objects inside the cave are being worked upon by the unceasing processes of nature that erode, break, move, redeposit, change, and destroy. And finally, people sometimes enter the cavern —to do what?

This is the archaeological problem in such caves—disentangling all the agents of accumulation to find out what the humans did. And let us build in a few additional problems. The cave is not excavated as part of a single coherent campaign, but in a series of excavations led by many directors over many years. Some of these excavations do not meet modern archaeological standards, not because of any shortcomings on the part of the various

PETER ROWLEY-CONWY

directors, but simply because the science of excavation was less advanced than it is today. The vicissitudes of civil war, world war, and revolution also pass over the site during the various excavations. In the confusion, many of the most important finds go missing in mysterious circumstances which many international experts still consider to be highly suspicious.

All this describes the situation at one of the most famous archaeological sites in Asia: Zhoukoudian (formerly spelt Choukoutien), where the richest fossil finds of a local group of *Homo erectus* known as Peking Man have been made. More bones of these people have been found here than anywhere else in Asia, along with many quartz tools.

But working out how Peking Man lived is extremely difficult. We certainly cannot assume that everything in the cave was brought in by people just because stone tools have been found there. Clearly, caves act as traps for all kinds of materials and bear witness to many different activities. Many early researchers—notably the great Chinese excavator Pei Wenzhong— were aware of this, but others have published accounts of Peking Man's life that go far beyond the evidence.

The Cannibalism Theory

All the *Homo erectus* skulls found at Zhoukoudian have the faces and undersides missing. This has excited much discussion of cannibalism, some people claiming that the brains were extracted and eaten by other humans. Moreover, many more skulls have been found than other human bones, leading to the suggestion that corpses were ritually dismembered outside the cave and that only the heads were brought inside—in other words, that some kind of religious ceremony took place there. If true, this would be of enormous significance, because it would be by far the earliest indication of such ritual behavior.

However, there is a less dramatic explanation of these finds. The parts of the skulls that are missing are the weakest parts, those most likely to be destroyed by natural means, so not too much can be concluded from this. Furthermore, we know that hyenas often carry the head of their prey to their den and break into the skull through the weakest parts. Human brains may well have been eaten at Zhoukoudian—but by hyenas. Most of the other animal bones were probably carried in by hyenas as well. Many are complete (whereas humans would have

⬤ *Homo erectus* skullcaps from Zhoukoudian all have missing faces and undersides. Formerly thought to indicate cannibalism, this is now believed to have resulted from gnawing by hyenas or natural breakage.

broken them for marrow), and there are also numerous skulls of other species. The fact that hyena feces are commonly found in the excavation layers also points to this explanation.

The Evidence for Fire

Black layers several meters deep and many meters long have been interpreted by some as evidence that humans built fires here, but this, too, is unlikely. These areas are far too extensive to have been fireplaces. Many tiny groups of rodent bones were found throughout these layers, indicating that owls had roosted above and regurgitated pellets. The black deposits could, in fact, be thousands of years' worth of owl droppings, which may even have ignited spontaneously. But while no regular fireplaces have been found, people probably did use fire. The upper teeth and skulls of some animals are burned, and this must have been done by people, presumably to cook the brains. Whether people hunted the animals is doubtful. No spearheads or arrowheads were found among the stone tools, and animal heads are at least as likely to have been scavenged from the kills of other carnivores.

What, then, does Zhoukoudian tell us? It tells us that people entered the cave, left some bones and tools there, and used fire—but that is about all it tells us. Humans used the cave much less frequently than hyenas did, and the various complexities should make us cautious in drawing any conclusions. This is not to diminish the importance of the site. As a source of hominid fossils, it is immensely important, and the problems it poses have given rise to new analytical methods that have revolutionized our approach to such sites.

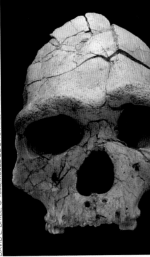

☝ This skull from Arago, in the eastern Pyrenees, in France, is considered by many to represent a transitory stage between erectines and Neanderthals.

NEANDERTHAL SITES

The major Neanderthal sites in Europe and Southwest Asia. The Neanderthals evolved during a warm phase and persisted in Europe well into the last glacial, eventually disappearing about 33,000 years ago. Coastlines and ice sheets are shown as they were during the peak of the last glacial.

Homo sapiens *in the Making*

The period between 300,000 and 40,000 years ago was an important transitional period between erectine and sapient stages and was characterized by a series of physical and technological changes. Brain size increased from 1,100 to about 1,400 cubic centimeters (67 to 85 cubic inches), and at the same time, face and bodily constitution more and more resembled those of modern humans. The tool technology was refined, and during the Neanderthal era the first signs of ritual life and religious beliefs appeared. In addition to the hand-axe technology of the Acheulean tradition, a typical flake technology arose, which is named the Clactonian, after the site of its first discovery—Clacton-on-Sea, east of London.

The finds of fossil humans from this important transitional period are still few, but in Europe some remains have been found that seem to document the emergence of Neanderthal features. A young adult woman found at Swanscombe, in England, lived about 225,000 years ago and had a brain volume of 1,325 cubic centimeters (80 cubic inches). Another woman, found at Steinheim, in Germany, is slightly older. However, the most important finds from this period so far discovered are from Arago, in the French Pyrenees, and date back at least 200,000 years. Undoubtedly, these were precursors of the classic European Neanderthals, who appeared for the first time about 130,000 years ago. Similar fossils have been uncovered at Bilzingsleben, in eastern Germany (more than 300,000 years old), and at Petralona, close to Thessaloniki, in Greece.

The finds from Swanscombe, Steinheim, and Arago show that people with an almost modern brain capacity lived in Europe and probably also in large parts of Asia and Africa between 300,000 and 200,000 years ago. In South and East Asia, populations of the same type replaced *Homo erectus* at about the same time: remains from Dali and Jinniushan, in China, and Hathnora, in India, are clearly like Steinheim or Petralona. But *Homo erectus* lingered on in Southeast Asia until 100,000 years ago. Their European/West Asian descendants, the enigmatic Neanderthals, were just round the corner.

The Neanderthal Enigma

Ever since the first fossil was found in 1856 at Neanderthal, close to Düsseldorf, in Germany, the relationship between Neanderthals and modern humans has been under constant discussion. New finds of Neanderthal fossils have resulted in recurring changes of opinion as to which role they actually played in the evolution of *Homo sapiens sapiens*. Recently, results from a series of African sites have once more overthrown established and universally recognized theories on the course of events. The Neanderthals are once again in the limelight.

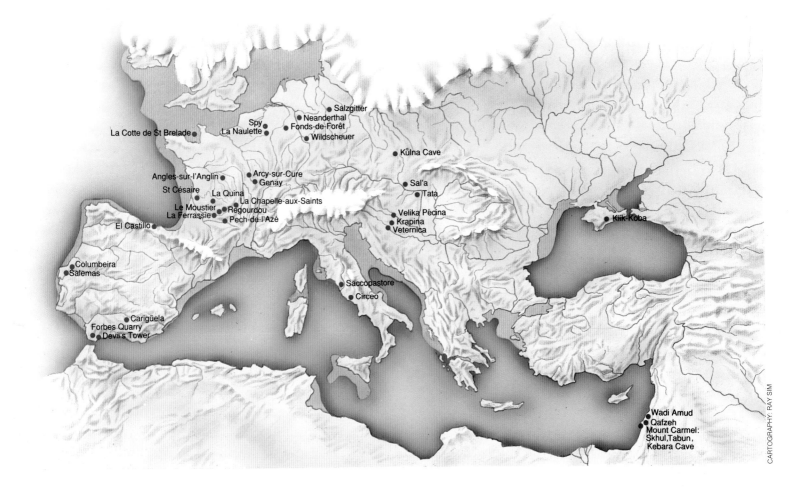

La Cotte de St Brelade
Spy
La Naulette
Salzgitter
Neanderthal
Fonds-de-Forêt
Wildscheuer
Kůlna Cave
Angles-sur-l'Anglin
Arcy-sur-Cure
Genay
St Césaire
La Quina
La Chapelle-aux-Saints
Sal'a
Tata
Le Moustier
Régourdou
La Ferrassie
Pech-de-l'Azé
Velika Pećina
Krapina
Veternica
El Castillo
Kiik-Koba
Columbeira
Salemas
Saccopastore
Circeo
Cariguela
Forbes Quarry
Devil's Tower
Wadi Amud
Qafzeh
Mount Carmel:
Skhul, Tabun,
Kebara Cave

For a long time it has been clear that the physical appearance of European Neanderthals in particular strongly differed from that of anatomically modern humans. Their brain was actually larger than ours on average. They had a considerably bigger face, with a heavy brow ridge and a remarkably robust nose. Their lower jaw was massive, and they had a receding chin. Even the teeth were considerably larger and were placed in a U-shaped curve, not in a parabola shape, like ours. Their head was supported by short and very robust muscles at the nape of the neck. The Neanderthals reached only about 1.6 meters (5 feet, 3 inches) in height, but were extremely muscular. (See the feature *The Neanderthals*.)

In spite of the physical differences, modern humans were for a long period of time considered to be lineal descendants of the Neanderthals. Only with the work of French paleontologist Marcellin Boule at the beginning of the twentieth century was it suggested that these differences were too great for the Neanderthals to be the ancestors of modern humans.

The Neanderthals evolved between 200,000 and 100,000 years ago and are usually associated with the so-called Mousterian culture, named after a site at Le Moustier, in the Dordogne, in France. Since anatomically modern humans made their appearance in Europe about 40,000 years ago, there clearly was no time for a transition from *Homo neanderthalensis* to *Homo sapiens sapiens*. Boule, instead, suggested that the Neanderthals became extinct during the last Ice Age and were replaced by the new immigrants. We now know that the last of the Neanderthals lingered on until 35,000 years ago, so that there was a brief period of coexistence.

However, a series of new discoveries led to conclusive reinterpretations of the relationship between Neanderthals and *Homo sapiens sapiens*. On Mount Carmel, close to Haifa, in Israel, and situated on the Mediterranean coast, several caves have been known for some time to contain important finds of fossil humans—for example, Mugharet es-Skhul, Mugharet et-Tabun, Kebara, and Jebel Qafzeh. In Qafzeh, a primitive form of modern humans has been found which already lived in the area some 92,000 years ago, whereas Tabun contained the remains of a Neanderthal form from about 120,000 years ago, and Neanderthals at Kebara lived only about 60,000 years ago—in other words, spanning the period of the modern people at Qafzeh. In Skhul, remains at an age of about 80,000 years have been found. All of these Levantine humans can be linked to the Mousterian tradition of the Middle Paleolithic, even those with modern traits.

If Neanderthals and people of modern type actually coexisted in the Middle East for some 60,000 years, and overlapped for about 5,000 years in Europe, then, obviously, one cannot be descended from the other. Most likely they both evolved from *Homo heidelbergensis*: the Neanderthals in the temperate zone of Europe and/or the Middle East, from ancestors such as Petralona or Arago; *Homo sapiens* in Africa, from precursors such as Kabwe or Bodo. In fact, a whole series of transitional remains from *Homo heidelbergensis* to *Homo sapiens* is now known, in the range of (approximately) 130,000 to 120,000 years ago: Omo, Ngaloba, Jebel Irhoud, and Eliye Springs. The earliest representatives of our species emerged from Africa about 100,000 years ago and coexisted with Neanderthals for many millennia, until something—perhaps the chance invention of the Upper Paleolithic stone technology—gave them an advantage and they were able to spread further and replace the unfortunate Neanderthals altogether.

Thinking about the Neanderthals has gone through several phases. In the 1860s, they were regarded as our ancestors. Boule then exaggerated the differences between them and us, not realizing that the skeleton he studied, known as the "Old Man of La Chapelle-aux-Saints", was deformed with arthritis. William Straus and A.J.E. Cave pointed this out in 1952, and once again the Neanderthals were given a place in our family tree, though perhaps as ancestors of modern Caucasians (Europeans, Middle Easterners, and Indians) only. Now, with new dating methods such as thermoluminesence and electron spin resonance, we have a fresh perspective, and they are preferably seen as our cousins rather than our ancestors, though very like us in many features. (See the feature *Dating the Past*.) The discussion is once again directly linked to the original home of humans—Africa.

◄○ The skull of one of the 11 individuals found in Skhul, one of the caves on Mount Carmel, near Haifa, in Israel. Formerly considered to be Neanderthals, they are now regarded as modern humans.
DAVID L. BRILL, © 1985/PEABODY MUSEUM, HARVARD UNIVERSITY

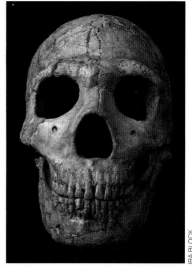

IRA BLOCK

⚲ This Neanderthal skull found in Amud Cave, near the Sea of Galilee, in Israel, had a brain volume of 1,800 cubic centimeters (110 cubic inches).

IRA BLOCK

⚲ The skull of one of the individuals found in Qafzeh Cave, Israel. Like those in Skhul Cave, the humans found at this site are regarded as archaic forms of *Homo sapiens*.

THE NEANDERTHALS

COLIN GROVES

IF THERE IS ONE FOSSIL human type everyone has heard of, it is the Neanderthals. For tens of thousands of years, scattered groups of these people roamed the tundras and forests of western Eurasia. European specimens are known from as early as about 60,000 years ago, at Saccopastore, in Italy, and as late as 35,000 years ago, at St Césaire, in France. In Southwest Asia, the earliest specimen, from Tabun Cave, in Israel, is 120,000 years old; the latest, from Shanidar, in Iraq, is about 45,000 years old. The Neanderthals are sometimes regarded as just a race of *Homo sapiens* that happens to be extinct, sometimes as a distinct human species, *Homo neanderthalensis*. In Southwest Asia, they overlapped for tens of thousands of years with modern humans, while in Europe, they coexisted for only a few thousand years. We do not know what the two peoples thought of each other, whether they normally traded or were at war, or even occasionally interbred. At any rate, the Neanderthals are no longer with us. Their disappearance remains a mystery, but it is generally thought that our own species gained some advantage, maybe technological or cultural or both, and the Neanderthals, unable to compete, died out.

ILLUSTRATION: JOHN RICHARDS

WAS THERE A NEANDERTHAL RELIGION?

PETER ROWLEY-CONWY

It is a common archaeological joke that any finding that cannot be explained in practical terms is labelled "ritual"—and the joke contains more than a grain of truth. The main text of this chapter refers to a number of finds that have often been thought to reflect ritual behavior of some kind among Neanderthals. Recently, these finds have come under renewed scrutiny. Here is a brief summary of three of the best-known claims, with the case against accepting them as fact.

The Cave Bear Cult

Popularized by Jean Auel's novel *The Clan of the Cave Bear* some years ago, this theory now has few, if any, supporters. It was based on the fact that quite a large number of caves have been found containing Neanderthal artifacts and thousands of bear bones. All this shows is that these early people occasionally visited a cave in which the huge bears hibernated and sometimes died. It does not show that Neanderthal people killed any of these bears, and still less that any ritual was involved.

There was also a reported finding from Drachenloch cave, in Switzerland, of several bear skulls set inside an arrangement of stone slabs—clear proof, it was claimed, of ritual behavior. But two mutually contradictory drawings of this were published at different times, no photographs exist, and it was recently established that the excavator was not even present on the day that the find was made. The whole thing, in fact, was reconstructed from the descriptions of the unskilled workmen who had carried out the excavation. Slabs of stone often fall from cave roofs and lie at unusual angles on the floor below, where the bones of dead cave bears would also lie. Verdict: a chance arrangement magnified by wishful thinking.

Cannibalism

Even if Neanderthals did eat each other, this of itself need indicate nothing more than hunger or greed.

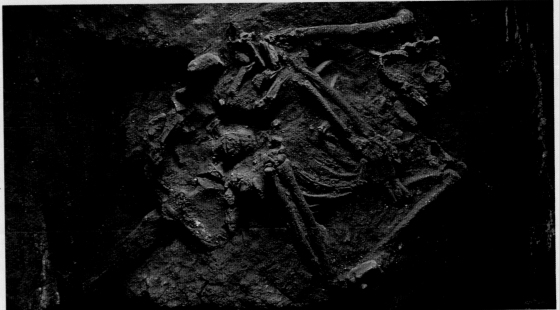

DAVID L. BRILL, © 1985

In a cave at Monte Circeo, in Italy, a Neanderthal skull was found in what was said to be a circle of stones, but, again, no photographs were taken before the skull was removed. Drawings made later by the person who found (and removed) the skull show a rough heap of stones rather than a regular circle, and nothing to suggest that the stones were deliberately arranged. The skull has no marks made by cutting tools, but appears to have been gnawed by a carnivore. Hyenas commonly carry animal skulls into their dens, and this is a more likely, if more prosaic, explanation of the presence of the skull. Verdict: a hyena settled on top of a rock fall to eat a grisly meal.

Neanderthal Burials

These are less easily dismissed. Certainly, some are doubtful, including the often quoted burial of a boy inside a circle of ibex horns at Teshik-Tash, in Uzbekistan. This in fact comprises a few bones (not the whole skeleton) of a 12-year-old Neanderthal boy found in close proximity to a few ibex horns. There is no evidence that the horns were ever in a circle, there is no sign of a grave pit, and we have already seen that hyenas commonly take skulls into their dens. Verdict: another hyena meal.

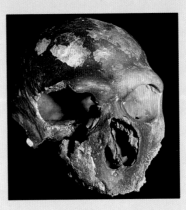

⚱ Kebara Cave, in Israel, has provided definite evidence of a Neanderthal burial. The grave pit is clearly visible, and must have been deliberately excavated, implying planned disposal of the corpse. However, most other finds of Neanderthals do not appear to result from deliberate burial.

⊷ The hole in this Neanderthal skull found at Monte Circeo was probably caused by a hyena breaking into the skull and eating the brain.

CHRIS STRINGER/MUSEO NAZIONALE PREHISTORICO EO ETNOGRAFICO "L. PIGORINI", ROME

There are also strong doubts about the famous "flower burial" from Shanidar, in Iraq. Not only is no grave pit visible, but the cause of death was a large roof slab that fell and crushed the Neanderthal man beneath it. Only a concentration of flower pollen suggests ritual activity: the heaping of flowers on the corpse, a scene reconstructed in many textbooks and films. Given the complexities of cave deposits, however, the pollen could have got there in various ways—indeed, even during the archaeological excavation. Verdict: an unfortunate Neanderthal who stood in the wrong place at the wrong time.

But at least two burials do seem to stand up to scrutiny. A skeleton from La Chapelle-aux-Saints, in France, was found in a steep-sided pit, and the findings were published in 1908. The pit seems too regular to be a natural depression into which the Neanderthal man simply crawled and died. It has been suggested that the hole may have been formed by floodwater, but it looks so square-cut that it appears to be a regular grave pit. The clearest grave pit found from this period is that in which a Neanderthal skeleton from Kebara, in Israel, was buried. This must have been deliberately dug. Verdict: these two Neanderthal men were buried, certainly, but does this prove that the Neanderthals had a religion or believed in an afterlife? It is not impossible that what we see is the simple disposal of dead bodies, and that nothing more complex than this was ever involved.

The Mousterian: Time of the Neanderthals

The Neanderthals were the first humans to really adapt to the cold northern climate. On the whole, their evolution took place during a warm period, the last interglacial. However, the classic tool technology of the Neanderthals—the Mousterian, named after the legendary rock shelter at Le Moustier, in the Dordogne—did not appear in Europe until the last Ice Age, about 70,000 years ago, although Mousterian-like industries were being used in the Middle East as early as about 120,000 years ago. They became an Ice Age people with all that this implied in terms of arctic survival and economic flexibility.

Like their predecessors, the Neanderthals roamed over extensive territories and used seasonal settlements during different times of the year. Presumably, big-game hunting (mainly deer and reindeer) played an increasingly important part in their subsistence. But above all, the cold climate forced people to adapt their diet to the cycle of the seasons, and the increasingly rich assemblages of different kinds of stone tools with different functions may be looked upon as a result of this. Storage of food was a vital necessity during parts of the year. Cave openings and rock shelters, so-called *abri*, were commonly used as dwellings, and although open-air settlements are known in many places, it is not unfounded to apply the term "cave people" to the Neanderthals.

About 130,000 years ago, the tool technology developed with great strides. For the first time, cores were preshaped in order to give the planned flake a certain look and size. This manufacturing process is called Levalloisian technology, after a site outside Paris. Furthermore, it was easier to make better use of the raw material, and several more flakes could be struck off from the same core. The top surface of the core was trimmed and shaped into a striking platform from which flakes were struck off. Owing to their appearance, the prepared cores have been named tortoise cores.

The new technique made possible the production of a series of new tool types with varying ranges of uses—particularly, different kinds of scrapers and points. During the Mousterian period, the technique was further refined and the new tools were equipped with effective and durable edges. The objects were sharpened by fine trimming, which created a toothed edge.

The Mousterian technology had a series of regional differences, where sets of tools varied greatly. Some experts have suggested that this shows that different European "Neanderthal cultures" lived side by side, whereas others suggest that the function of the tools had created the differences or simply that they were the result of a gradual, time-related change. In any case, the new tool technology of the Neanderthals was more varied and functionally adapted than ever before. The Mousterian technique was a result of the Neanderthals' vital ability to meet and adjust to the demands of the environment.

As we have seen, there was great anatomical variation within the Neanderthal population. Remains of classic Neanderthals are limited to western Europe, while those of Southwest Asia show less extreme features. It is believed that this physical diversity was the result of climatic adaptations, since the European Neanderthals really were the only ones living in typically Ice Age surroundings. Supposed Neanderthal-like humans in Africa and Southeast Asia were very different, and the sites of Kabwe (formerly Broken Hill), in Zambia (the so-called "Rhodesian Man"), Hopefield (Saldanha), near Cape Town, in South Africa, and Ngandong, by the Solo River, in Java, have provided some of the fossils that were formerly thought to represent Afro-Asian parallels to the European Neanderthals. Kabwe and Saldanha, however, are now recognized as belonging to *Homo heidelbergensis*, while the Ngandong fossils are late survivors (100,000 years ago) of *Homo erectus*.

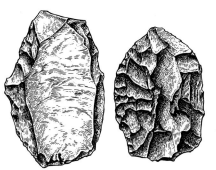

Making a Levalloisian flake: a suitable stone is trimmed on the edges and top surface, and a striking platform is then made in one end of the core. A large flake (right), the final product, is then struck off from the core (left).
ILLUSTRATIONS: KEN RINKEL

The classic Neanderthal rock shelter at Le Moustier, by the Vézère River, in the Dordogne, France, has given its name to the Mousterian period. A skeleton of a Neanderthal boy was unearthed here in 1908.

GÖRAN BURENHULT

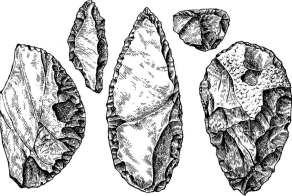

Examples of Mousterian points and scrapers. The Mousterian tool tradition is closely linked to the Neanderthals, being found at Neanderthal sites across Europe, western Asia, and northern Africa. Related technologies are found in Africa and in South and East Asia.
ILLUSTRATIONS: KEN RINKEL

It was thought for a long time that the Quaternary period was dominated by three or four distinct Ice Ages. Research in recent decades, however, has revealed a much more complex picture of climatic fluctuations through time. The left-hand side of the diagram shows global climatic change as revealed by deep-sea cores from the equatorial Pacific. By establishing the ratio between oxygen isotopes at different depths of such cores, it is possible to record the fluctuating global temperature. The traditional terminology used for the different glacials and interglacials is shown at right.

The remarkable circumstances surrounding the findings of the Ngandong, or Solo, humans have led to speculations about possible cannibalism. The 11 skulls found consisted only of braincases, with the rest of the head and face missing. As all the material was found within a limited area, the remains have been interpreted as leftovers from ritual feasting on human flesh. Also, the remains of some 20 individuals at Krapina, in Croatia—men, women, and children with their heads and bones smashed and split—have been interpreted as evidence that Neanderthals engaged in cannibalism, but other experts have called this evidence into question. If so, is there any other evidence that may strengthen the theory that Neanderthals were the first humans to perform rituals and have religious beliefs? The appearance of the first burials seems to point in that direction.

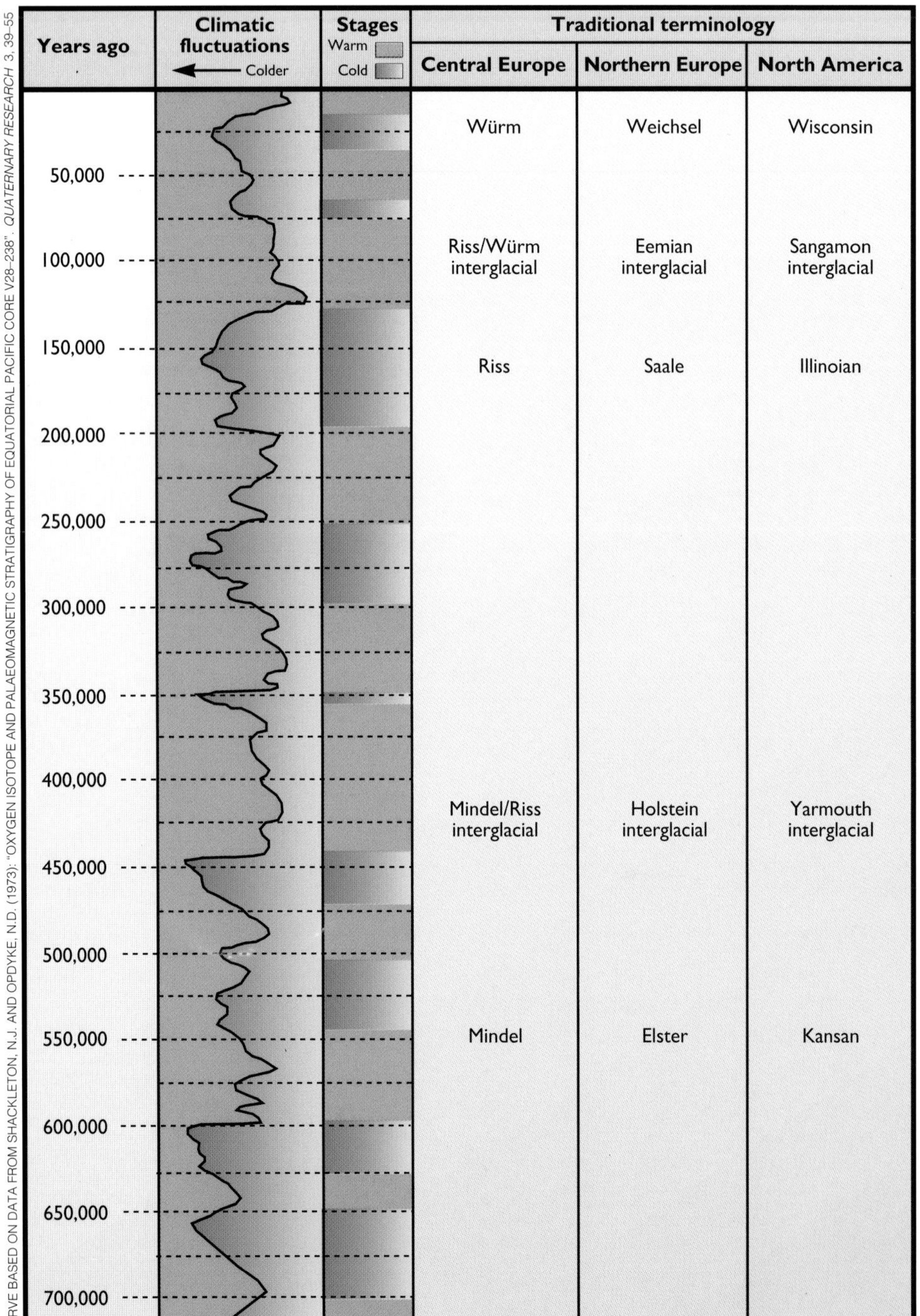

The Origins of Burial and Religious Belief?

Death is inescapable for all of us. The deposition of the mortal remains, in some way or another, is thus an action that is common to all human beings, in prehistory as well as in recent times. The appearance of the first burials shows that humans' ability to think in the abstract and to communicate orally had reached an advanced level. Whether a burial reflected notions of a "kingdom" of the dead or whether it was just a way to show regret at the loss of a family member, the burial ceremony reveals the presence of ritual conceptions and long-term thinking that previously had been impossible. Burial customs, such as sprinkling the dead with red ocher or depositing grave goods, bear witness to a world of magic thinking that lies behind the most definite of manifestations—that of dying. (See the feature *Was There a Neanderthal Religion?*)

It has long been accepted that Neanderthals buried their dead, and several important sites are known in Europe and Southwest Asia, most of them in caves. A teenage boy has been found in a pit at Le Moustier, in the Dordogne. His head rested on a collection of flint flakes and one arm was placed under his head, as if he were in a reclining position. Similar finds have been made in several other Neanderthal settlements in France—for example, at La Ferrassie and La Chapelle-aux-Saints. A small burial ground has been uncovered at La Ferrassie, where two grown-up individuals and four children had been buried in tightly placed pits. Many of the French burials had been sprinkled with red ocher, and large amounts of animal bones have been found in or nearby all of the graves.

On the western slopes of the Himalayas, a remarkable Neanderthal burial has been unearthed. At Teshik-Tash, in Uzbekistan, a young child had been buried together with the horns of six wild goats, which had been placed in a ring around the grave. Marks on the skeleton indicate that the flesh had been cut off before the body was buried, perhaps for ritual reasons. Other conspicuous burials have been found at Shanidar, in the Iraqi Zagros Mountains, where, according to the excavators, a 30-year-old man had been placed on a bed of flowers. Pollen analyses have shown the presence of yarrow (milfoil), horsetail, thistle, cornflower, grape hyacinth, and hollyhock, among other plants.

Lately, however, many experts have questioned the Neanderthal burials and the validity of the evidence. Excavations of Paleolithic sites are difficult enterprises, and the stratigraphy is generally hard to interpret. Later activities at the site, as well as falling debris, often make

CURVE BASED ON DATA FROM SHACKLETON, N.J. AND OPDYKE, N.D. (1973): "OXYGEN ISOTOPE AND PALAEOMAGNETIC STRATIGRAPHY OF EQUATORIAL PACIFIC CORE V28-238". QUATERNARY RESEARCH 3, 39-55

Years ago	Climatic fluctuations ← Colder	Stages Warm / Cold	Traditional terminology		
			Central Europe	Northern Europe	North America
50,000			Würm	Weichsel	Wisconsin
100,000			Riss/Würm interglacial	Eemian interglacial	Sangamon interglacial
150,000			Riss	Saale	Illinoian
200,000					
250,000					
300,000					
350,000					
400,000					
450,000			Mindel/Riss interglacial	Holstein interglacial	Yarmouth interglacial
500,000					
550,000			Mindel	Elster	Kansan
600,000					
650,000					
700,000					

it impossible to determine what actually took place at the time of the depositing of the body. Some have even stated that there is, in fact, no evidence whatsoever that Neanderthals buried their dead and that the finds are the result of coincidences and later disturbances. Contrary to this, it may be said that there is no evidence that they didn't.

In all scientific debate it is necessary to question and to present new hypotheses to, in that way, be able to force new and even more critical examining of the materials in question and, as far as archaeology is concerned, in which context they were found. Obviously, archaeologists previously accepted uncritically many of the finds of Neanderthal skeletons as true burials, and these must therefore be re-examined. But it is also important to point out that we at present cannot dismiss the majority of them as nothing but coincidences. Perhaps the recently excavated Neanderthal burial in Kebara Cave on the slopes of Mount Carmel, in Israel, can bring this issue to

Clusters of pollen found by the skeleton of this 30-year-old Neanderthal man in Shanidar Cave, in northern Iraq, have been interpreted by some as suggesting that he had been buried on a bed of flowers. Recently, however, others have questioned the validity of the evidence for a deliberate burial.

The huge Shanidar Cave, in Kurdistan, in northernmost Iraq, has yielded Neanderthal finds dating from between 60,000 and 44,000 years ago. Nihe Neanderthal individuals have been uncovered, among them the much debated burial of the 30-year-old man shown above, as well as bones of such animals as wild goats and boars.

a conclusion. It seems as if the burial structures, which are more distinct here than in any other Neanderthal site so far excavated, clearly indicate a deliberate burial.

Similar doubts about the ritual life of Neanderthals have been raised concerning findings from two other classic European sites: Regourdou, in the Dordogne, and Monte Circeo, south of Rome, in Italy. At Regourdou, a rectangular pit covered with a large stone slab was found which contained the skulls of at least 20 cave bears. A complete bear skeleton as well as an incomplete Neanderthal one was found nearby. This find has been

considered an example of a Neanderthal bear cult, a form of cult that has been practiced until recently by many arctic peoples. The circumstances surrounding the find are unclear, though, and today many experts feel dubious about this interpretation.

As far as the archaeological material is concerned, it is extremely difficult to interpret notions of the supernatural or the presence of magical or religious systems. In any case, however, it is no exaggeration to say that all these finds indicate that the Neanderthals developed complex ideological and social behavior which later on was also to become characteristic of modern humans.

DATING THE PAST

COLIN GROVES

Fossils that are more than a few tens of thousands of years old contain no material that can be dated directly. It is the deposits that contain them that are dated, not the fossils themselves. Dating methods can be broadly divided into absolute and relative methods.

Absolute Methods
URANIUM–LEAD DATING

Uranium is radioactive, which means that it decays, changing its atomic nucleus into other elements at a regular rate through a series (known as the U-series) and ending up as lead. The two main atomic forms (isotopes) of uranium, U_{235} and U_{238}, decay at different rates, through different intermediate stages, into different isotopes of lead. As we know what these rates of decay are (they do not change under conditions normally occurring on Earth), we can calculate how long ago it was since the decay began and thus the age of the deposit containing the uranium—including any fossils the deposit contains. The fact that the two isotopes have different decay series acts as an internal check on the date obtained, to make sure nothing has been lost or gained in the deposit since it was laid down. Uranium dating can be used to measure deposits as old as the Earth itself—4.5 billion years.

Particular parts of the decay series, such as that from uranium to thorium, can be used to date much shorter periods of time.

POTASSIUM–ARGON DATING

Many minerals in the Earth's crust contain the element potassium (K). A tiny proportion of all potassium consists of its radioisotope, potassium-40 (K_{40}). Like uranium, this decays at a known rate and becomes the gas argon (Ar).

When a volcano erupts, it spews forth molten lava, which includes potassium-containing minerals, and the argon that has

DAVID L. BRILL/© NATIONAL GEOGRAPHIC SOCIETY

been forming by decay of K_{40} is released into the atmosphere. As the lava cools, crystals are formed, and the argon that is formed subsequently is trapped in them. By measuring the relative proportions of K_{40} and argon in the crystals, we can work out how long ago the lava cooled—that is, when the volcanic eruption occurred. (There are ways of checking whether any argon has been lost from the crystals.) Lava flows are easy to date by this method.

Within a short time, volcanic lava and ash deposits start to erode. They are swept away by running water and deposited as sediments elsewhere, mixed in with sediments of different origin. Sediments containing material of recent volcanic origin are called tuffs. In a tectonically active area such as the East African

Rift Valley, the fossil-containing sediments are interspersed as layers with tuffs, and so we can calculate a series of dates at intervals throughout the formation. Like uranium-series dating, potassium–argon dating can be used for extremely ancient deposits as well as for some surprisingly young ones—provided that there has been volcanic activity in the region concerned.

RADIOCARBON DATING

This is one of the few methods based on the fossils themselves, but it can only be used over the past 50,000 years or so (70,000 years with the use of special techniques). Plants take in carbon from the atmosphere, and this carbon contains a tiny proportion of a radioisotope, C_{14} (formed in the atmosphere by cosmic radiation).

↩ Potassium–argon dating is still the most important method used to date the rock in which fossil hominids are found. Here, a geophysicist analyzes a rock sample to calculate the amount of radioactive potassium that has decayed into argon, and so the length of time that has elapsed since the volcanic eruption that produced the rock occurred.

Once the plant dies, it no longer takes in carbon, and so C_{14} is progressively lost from the remains. (It decays into nitrogen.) We can calculate the amount of C_{14} remaining, and thus the time that has elapsed since the plant died, but the decay rate is so rapid that all the C_{14} will be gone in a few tens of thousands of years.

The animals that eat the plants take in the plants' carbon, too, so their remains can also be dated in this way.

We now know that the amount of C_{14} in the atmosphere fluctuates, presumably in relation to the amount of cosmic radiation, so radiocarbon dates have to be calibrated against some known standard, such as annual growth rings in trees.

THERMOLUMINESCENCE DATING

When certain types of sediments are exposed to sunlight, or heated in some other way, they become bleached, and electrons are trapped. When the sediments are buried, the trapped electrons are progressively released. We can measure the light emitted by residual electrons, and so, when we have ascertained the original light dose, we can calculate the length of time that has elapsed since the sediments were first buried. Thermoluminescence (TL) dating covers the same time span as C_{14} dating (and more, as it can be used to date deposits more than 100,000 years old), so the two methods can be used to check each other. This method is now increasingly being used to date deposits in the formerly undatable range of 50,000 to 100,000 years.

A recently developed method, electron spin resonance (ESR), measures trapped electrons directly, and can be used to date biological materials such as tooth enamel.

FISSION-TRACK DATING

As well as undergoing radioactive decay, U_{235} sometimes undergoes spontaneous fission, and the subatomic particles emitted leave tracks through the mineral. These tracks can be revealed by etching with hydrofluoric acid and counted. As we know the rate at which fission occurs, we can calculate the time that has elapsed since the mineral was cooled and laid down. Volcanic glass yields excellent fission tracks, so this method can be used to cross-check potassium–argon dating.

Relative Methods
FAUNAL DATING

As new dating methods are discovered, relatively few sites remain that cannot be dated by one of the absolute methods. As far as human evolution is concerned, the only important sites that are still not directly datable are those on the highveldt in South Africa: Taung, Sterkfontein, Makapansgat, Swartkrans, and Kromdraai (although there has been a preliminary trial of ESR in the case of Sterkfontein). Here, faunal dating is used.

Long-lived species—for example, certain types of pigs, monkeys, and antelopes—have evolved in distinct stages. At some sites, such as Koobi Fora and Olduvai, in the East African Rift Valley, potassium–argon and fission-track methods can be used to date their remains, so that we know these species to have had characteristic shapes and measurements at certain dates. The animal fossils in sites such as Sterkfontein are then compared with fossils of the same species in the dated East African sites to determine their evolutionary stage. The limitation is, of course, that a more archaic stage in a species' evolution might have survived in South Africa when a more advanced form was already present in East Africa.

PALEOMAGNETISM

Another method is based on the fact that the Earth's magnetic field has swung back and forth during geological time. At present, it is centered on magnetic north, but before 700,000 years ago it was centered near the South Pole. A few hundred thousand years before that, it was north-centered again, and so on. A remnant magnetic orientation often remains in deposits, so a paleomagnetic column, showing the alternation between "normal" (north-pointing) and "reversed" (south-pointing), can be built up for some sites. This can then be compared with the standard column (based on the results of hundreds of magnetic determinations of levels of known date throughout the world); and other evidence—the presence of key fossils, or any stray absolute dates that have been made somewhere in the sequence—may help to line up, or "position", the magnetic reversals on the standard.

CHEMICAL METHODS

Chemical methods are sometimes used, as well. In many areas, the chemical composition of fossils changes; for example, the older a fossil is, the more fluorine it may contain. This method can only be used across very limited regions, where soil conditions do not vary much. Another method is based on the fact that a living organism's amino acids, the building blocks of proteins, rotate polarized light to the left. When the organism dies, polarization slowly alters until there are equal proportions of left-rotating and right-rotating amino acids. But the rate at which this occurs varies with temperature and, especially, humidity, so the method, which is known as amino acid racemization, can only be used under certain strict conditions (such as in sealed cave deposits).

↪ Over geologic time, the Earth's magnetic field has reversed itself many times. During long periods (chrons), the prevailing magnetism would be either normal or reversed, with shorter periods (subchrons) of the opposite magnetism. This chart shows in detail the paleomagnetic column for the last five million years.

Paleomagnetic time scale	Time (millions of years)	Epoch	Series
Subchrons	0.1		UPPER
BRUNHES	0.2–0.7	Pleistocene	MIDDLE
Jaramillo	0.8–0.9		LOWER
MATUYAMA	1.0–1.6		
Olduvai	1.7–1.8		
Reunion I	1.9–2.0		
Reunion II	2.1		
GAUSS	2.2–2.9	Pliocene	
Kaena	3.0		
Mammoth	3.1–3.3		
Cochiti	3.4–3.9		
Nunivak	4.0–4.2		
GILBERT	4.3		
Sidufjall	4.4–4.5		
Thvera	4.6–5.0		

MODERN PEOPLE IN AFRICA AND EUROPE

Out of Africa: Adapting to the Cold

GÖRAN BURENHULT

WHATEVER VIEW WE TAKE of the relationship between modern humans and Neanderthals, it is clear that *Homo sapiens sapiens* migrated into Europe about 40,000 years ago, carrying with them new technological and intellectual skills. There are significant differences between the tool technology of the Neanderthals in Europe during the Middle Paleolithic period, known as the Mousterian tradition, and that of the Upper Paleolithic period, known as the Aurignacian tradition. These changes can be directly linked to the arrival of modern humans in Europe.

One of the fundamental changes was that from flake tools to blade tools. Neanderthal scrapers are sidescrapers, having a retouched edge on one side of the flake, whereas the blade-scrapers that appeared in Europe during the Upper Paleolithic period are endscrapers. In addition, many new types of tools appeared, including burins and points of different kinds.

◄● Situated on the border between South Africa and Swaziland, Border Cave is one of a number of South African sites that have recently thrown new light on the origin of our species. Its oldest occupation layers date back to about 200,000 years ago.

⬥ An Aurignacian split-base spear-point from Gorge d'Enfer, in the Dordogne, France.

J. M. LABAT/AUSCAPE

77

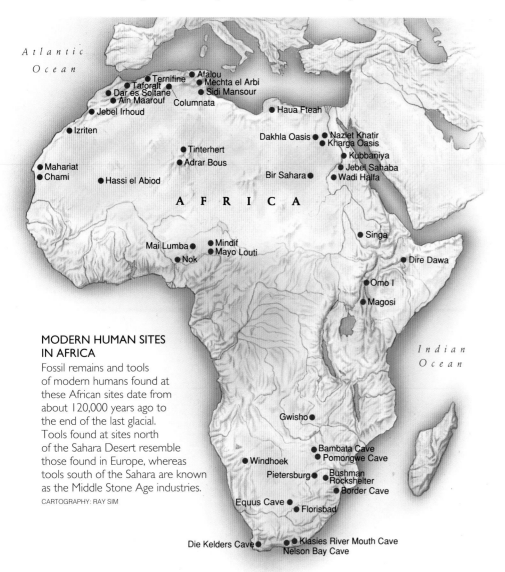

MODERN HUMAN SITES
IN AFRICA

Fossil remains and tools
of modern humans found at
these African sites date from
about 120,000 years ago to
the end of the last glacial.
Tools found at sites north
of the Sahara Desert resemble
those found in Europe, whereas
tools south of the Sahara are known
as the Middle Stone Age industries.

CARTOGRAPHY: RAY SIM

G⟩ Klasies River Mouth Cave, situated
at the southernmost tip of Africa, has
proved to be of immense importance
to our understanding of the evolution
of *Homo sapiens*. Fossil remains of
modern humans found here date to
between 115,000 and 80,000 years
ago, and from the fossil evidence of
mussels, limpets, and seals, we know
that marine foods were important to
the early modern humans at this site.

⌀ Ocean view at the mouth of the
Klasies River. Evidently, the sea provided
a considerable part of the food supply
for the early modern humans at this site.

While the Neanderthals almost never fashioned their tools from antler, bone, or ivory, these new raw materials formed an important part of the tool traditions during this period. They were shaped and polished into valuable articles for everyday use, as well as beautifully decorated works of art and adornments. And soon after these new types of tools were introduced, regional differences developed in the way they were used and decorated, in sharp contrast to the conservative and homogeneous tool technology of the Neanderthals.

But the most obvious differences between modern humans and Neanderthals are much more profound than the way they made and used tools. American anthropologist Richard Klein summarizes them as follows: "Initially, their behavioral capabilities differed little from those of the Neanderthals, but eventually, perhaps because of a neurological change that is not detectable in the fossil record, they developed a capacity for culture that gave them a clear adaptive advantage over the Neanderthals and all other nonmodern people." In other words,

they developed new, more flexible forms of social organization. They built new types of settlements, developed a rich ceremonial and ritual life, and began to express themselves through the medium of art. Richard Klein adds: "The result was that they spread throughout the world, physically replacing the nonmoderns, of whom the last to succumb were perhaps the Neanderthals of western Europe." The fact that these people simultaneously and rapidly replaced the Neanderthals all over Europe indicates, according to Klein, that we are dealing with a rapidly expanding population that can only be explained if modern humans migrated to Europe from elsewhere.

This theory is strongly supported by new finds in South Africa. Five notable sites—Klasies River Mouth Cave, Border Cave, Equus Cave, Florisbad, and Die Kelders Cave—have yielded evidence that is vital to our understanding of the origins of modern humans. Richard Klein considers Klasies River Mouth Cave, about 160 kilometers (100 miles) east of Cape Town, to be the most significant of these sites. Large numbers of fossilized human bones have been found there, some between 115,000 and 80,000 years old, and they have a strikingly modern appearance. These relatively modern humans, therefore, lived in Africa at the same time as the Neanderthals flourished in Europe. Although the differences in tool technology between the Middle and Upper Paleolithic periods were as great in Africa as they were in Europe, the humans who inhabited South Africa during the Middle Paleolithic period looked much more like modern humans than the European Neanderthals did.

The South African finds indicate that modern humans evolved in Africa over a very long period of time, perhaps more than 200,000 years. To the older and more archaic stage of this course of events belongs, for example, the find of "Rhodesia Man" (*Homo heidelbergensis*) from Kabwe (formerly Broken Hill), in Zambia, while the above-mentioned South African fossils represent a more advanced stage of human evolution. But if the cradle of *Homo sapiens* is to be found in Africa, who was the ancestor? *Homo erectus*? Many experts don't think so, suggesting that another, as yet unclassified, human species existed in Africa. Others are of the view that this species was the 1.5 million-year-old Turkana Newcomer, *Homo ergaster*.

The evolutionary process was probably slow and steady. The African savanna landscape probably provided ideal conditions for humans, and the tropical environment offered plentiful supplies of good-quality food. This might have brought humans together to live in larger groups, with a more selective diet.

These modern human beings, according to Richard Klein, did not migrate outside Africa until fairly late, and they subsequently replaced other,

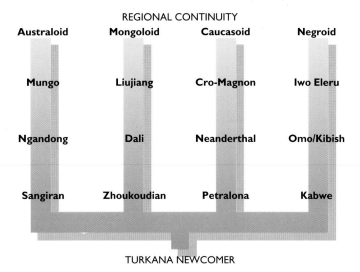

REGIONAL CONTINUITY

Australoid	Mongoloid	Caucasoid	Negroid
Mungo	Liujiang	Cro-Magnon	Iwo Eleru
Ngandong	Dali	Neanderthal	Omo/Kibish
Sangiran	Zhoukoudian	Petralona	Kabwe

TURKANA NEWCOMER

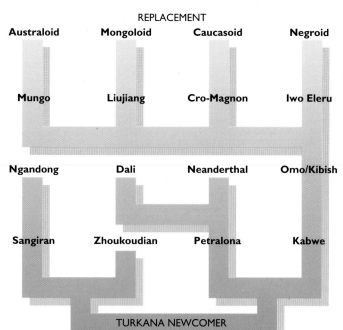

REPLACEMENT

Australoid	Mongoloid	Caucasoid	Negroid
Mungo	Liujiang	Cro-Magnon	Iwo Eleru
Ngandong	Dali	Neanderthal	Omo/Kibish
Sangiran	Zhoukoudian	Petralona	Kabwe

TURKANA NEWCOMER

☝ Two main theories have been put forward to explain the origin of our own species: regional continuity (the candelabra model) and replacement (the Noah's Ark model). The latter is supported by the finds from Klasies River and other sites in southern Africa, as well as recent DNA studies.

N. PETIT-MAIRE

☝ Burial found at the site of Hassi el Abiod, in Mali. This and several other North African sites have yielded remains of Cro-Magnon-like humans, and it has been suggested that the first modern Europeans originated here.

more archaic human types all over the so-called Old World. Anthropologist William Howells has named this the "Noah's Ark" hypothesis, because it implies that *Homo sapiens sapiens* originated in one single area of Africa. The opposing, more traditional view of human development is called the "candelabra" model. (These models are also known as the replacement theory and the regional continuity theory, respectively.)

Recently, the replacement theory has been strongly supported by modern genetic research, which has been able to tell us for how long the various human races have been separated from each other and how they are mutually related. Using the mitochondrial DNA technique (mt DNA), Allan Wilson and Mark Stoneking, of the University of California, at Berkeley, and Rebecca Cann, of the University of Hawaii, have concluded that all now-living humans are descended from a common first mother in South Africa who lived about 200,000 years ago. This is known as the "Eve" theory. It has been calculated that the descendants in the female line of all other mothers became extinct over the course of 50,000 generations, leaving only one set of matrilineal descendants. These results are consistent with the archaeological finds at such sites as Klasies River Mouth Cave. The same DNA technique shows that as modern humans spread across the globe, they rarely interbred with existing, but more archaic, human beings, such as the Neanderthals.

The "Eve" theory has not remained unchallenged, of course, but most evidence does indicate that modern humans spread rapidly from Africa to the rest of the world. If Africa is indeed the original home of modern humans, how and why did they spread into Europe and Asia? Finds from the caves of Mount Carmel, in present-day Israel, indicate that this migration occurred somewhat before 100,000 years ago. The only previous obstacle had been the Sahara Desert, but higher rainfall during this period transformed it into an area of verdant plains, with lakes and streams. A plentiful supply

of game and edible plants would have made northern migration not just possible but very attractive. Southwest Asia was a natural first stopping place, and this explains the Mount Carmel finds. But during the last Ice Age, which began about 75,000 years ago, this Levantine area became much drier. Food would have become scarce, and this may well have forced the humans who had settled there further north, towards the richer tundra and steppe regions of Europe. At the same time, modern humans were also spreading across Asia.

During the Middle and Upper Paleolithic periods, two tool traditions that are quite different in a number of important respects developed in North Africa and the part of Africa south of the Sahara Desert. That of the North African region, logically enough, had much in common with the tool tradition of Europe and Southwest Asia and developed about the same time. For example, excavations in Haua Fteah Cave, in Cyrenaica, northern Libya, show that the tool technology characteristic of the Upper Paleolithic period began there, as in Europe, about 40,000 years ago. This North African culture is known as the Aterian culture, after the site of Bir el Ater, in Tunisia. The Aterian culture extended from Libya in the east to the Atlantic coast in the west and as far south as the Lake Chad basin. A number of important sites in the region, including Mechta el Arbi, in Algeria, and Dar es Soltan, in Morocco, have yielded bones of Cro-Magnon-like humans.

Paleobotanical research at Tihodaine, in Algeria, among other places, has shown that at this time the North African region was steppe-like, with patches of forest near lakes. The area teemed with such animals as elephants, buffaloes, rhinoceroses,

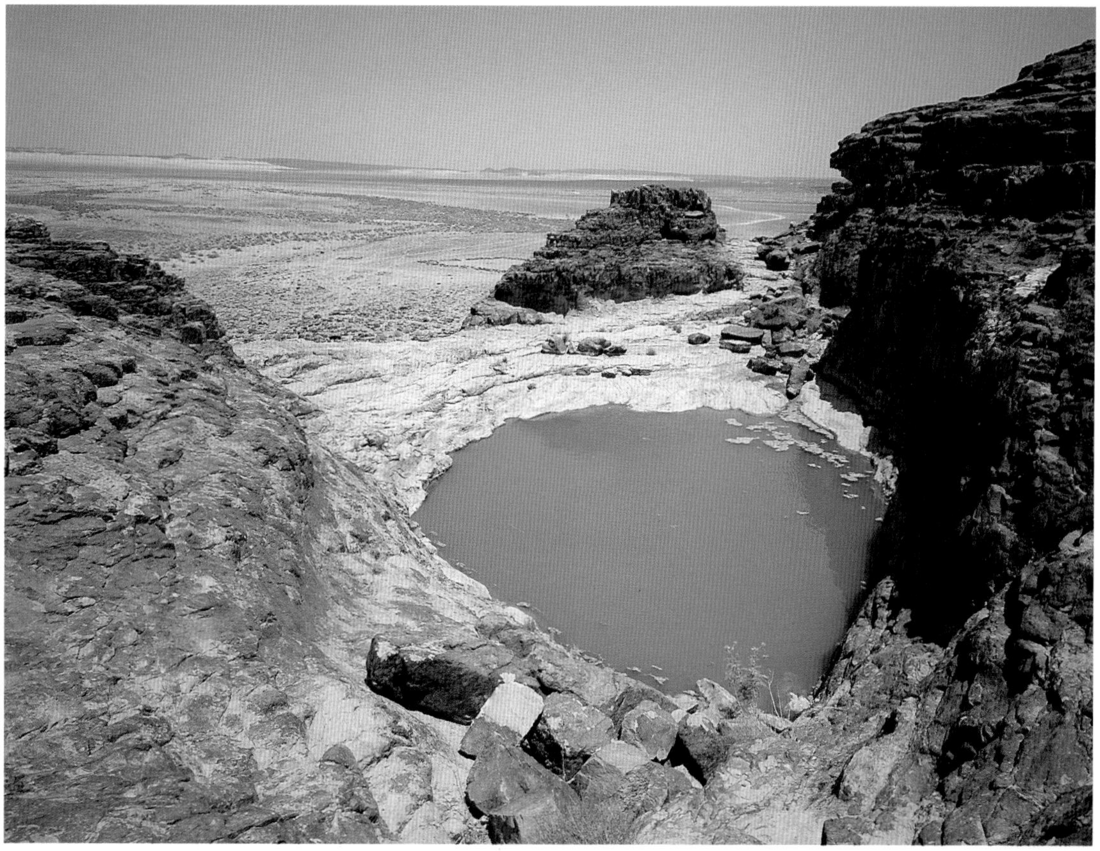

GÖRAN BURENHULT

Lakes, streams, and verdant plains once characterized what is now the Sahara Desert, making it an ideal area for human habitation. What is not generally known is that the Sahara still has large amounts of subsoil water, which sometimes reaches the surface in the form of so-called gueltas, like this one at Tinterhert, in Tassili n'Ajjer, southern Algeria.

This huge carving showing the North African aurochs (*Bubalus antiquus*) at Tinterhert, at the foot of Jebel Efehi, in Tassili n'Ajjer, southern Algeria, measures about 5 meters (16 feet) in length and is filled with carved lines, spirals, and circles. Belonging to the so-called "Bubalus period", it represents the earliest art in the Sahara. It may be as old as 12,000 years.

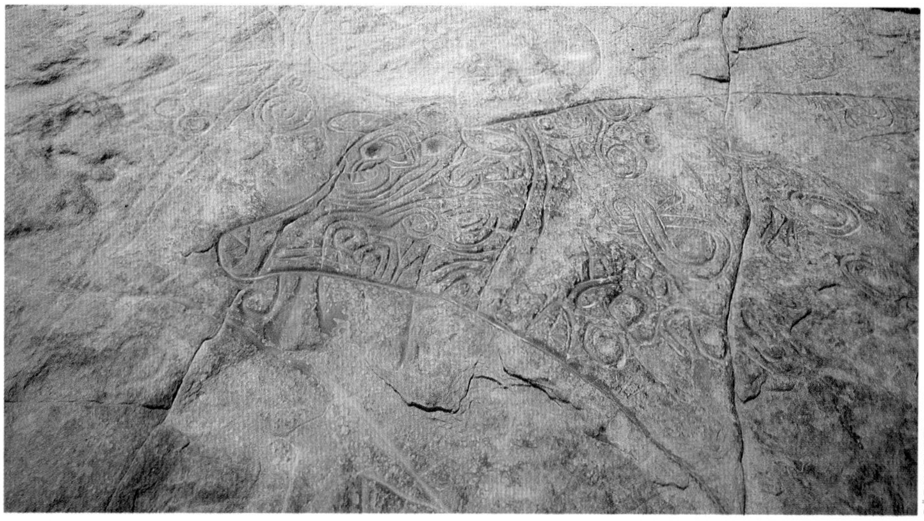

GÖRAN BURENHULT

and antelopes. Aterian people were the first to make points with tangs—that is, a retouched area at the base of the point to which a handle could be attached. These spear-like weapons were an important technological innovation, making it possible to bring down animals from a distance.

For natural reasons, the climatic and environmental changes that occurred at the end of the last Ice Age were much less dramatic in North Africa than in Europe. About 20,000 years ago, the Aterian tradition was replaced by a series of so-called epipaleolithic cultures (which means simply that they were related to Paleolithic cultures and existed around the same time). Finds of microliths—that is, very small points, edges, and barbs of flint—indicate that these people developed the bow and arrow. This was their only technological innovation of note, but it was a major one. Among the most important of these groups were the Quadan people of Upper Egypt, who existed between about 13,000 and 11,000 BC. They lived by hunting and fishing and also gathered seeds from wild grasses and other plants, and were among the few peoples of the Upper Paleolithic period who used grinding stones.

In the part of Africa south of the Sahara Desert, people were using much the same tools between 200,000 and 40,000 years ago, at much the same periods, as they were in Europe. In other words, the Middle Paleolithic period—in Africa, the Middle Stone Age—corresponds fairly closely in both these parts of the world. The Upper Paleolithic, or Late Stone Age, differs markedly from the previous period, but finds from 40,000 to 20,000 years ago are few. More recent finds, dating from 20,000 years ago or less, are much more common, and these show that people were hunting big game, especially buffalo and wild pig, to a greater extent than in earlier times and that scavenging had become much less important. Fishing had also become very important, which it had not been during the Middle Paleolithic. The appearance of microliths indicates that bows and arrows were in use, and from finds of microliths suitable for mounting in rows on sickles made of bone, antler, or wood, we know that plant gathering was also becoming more important.

ICE THROUGH THE AGES

BJÖRN E. BERGLUND AND SVANTE BJÖRCK

SVANTE BJÖRCK

LONGER OR SHORTER PERIODS of glaciation are a natural part of our planet's history. The most recent Ice Age epoch, called the Pleistocene, began about 2.5 million years ago. During the Pleistocene, there was a fluctuating pattern of cold, glacial periods, known as glacials, interrupted by warm periods, known as interglacials. The impetus behind these ice-sheet rhythms appears to have been the three solar insolation cycles, governed by the Earth's tilting and its orbit around the sun.

This East Greenland landscape shows an arctic environment with inland ice in the background much as we would imagine the situation to have been in mid-latitude and high-latitude parts of the world 18,000 years ago.

Paleotemperatures and paleo-ice volumes, deduced from oxygen isotope records in deep-sea cores, reveal that the first 1.8 million years of the Pleistocene were characterized by glacial–interglacial cycles of about 41,000 years. During the last 700,000 years, the dominant cycle has been about 100,000 years, including interglacials lasting 10,000 to 15,000 years. The most recent Ice Age began about 115,000 years ago and ended about 10,000 years ago, when the present interglacial was initiated. It was in this period that *Homo sapiens*, or modern human beings, developed. They had to adapt to quite rapid climatic changes which had a huge impact on the geological and other features of this planet.

Forty thousand years ago, we were in a milder part of the last glacial period. But Europe had already experienced three cold spells since the last interglacial, and the world looked very different from today. The sea level was 50 meters (nearly 200 feet) lower, the mountainous parts of North America and Eurasia were glaciated and surrounded by windswept tundras, and the vegetation and climate zones were much farther south than they now are. And the Big Chill was still to come!

The Big Chill

Twenty-five thousand years ago, the ice caps started to accumulate so much snow that large parts of northwest Europe, North America, and alpine areas such as the Andes, the Alps, and parts of central Asia gradually disappeared under huge sheets of ice. These continental ice sheets reached their greatest extent 20,000 years ago, when the sea level dropped to 120 meters (400 feet) below the present level and parts of today's continental shelf areas were dry land. Land bridges were formed in many areas where today there are sounds, including the English Channel, Bering Strait, and some of the sounds between Southeast Asia and Australia.

Most of Europe that was not actually under ice was virtually barren, with only tundra or steppe vegetation, and exposed to wind and cold. The average temperature was about 8 degrees Celsius (14 degrees Fahrenheit) lower than today. Trees

Global climate curves for the last 30,000, 150,000, and 900,000 years. Curves **a** and **b** are based on changes in oxygen isotopes in deep-sea sediments (the dotted line indicating where information is uncertain), and curve **c** on pollen data and alpine glacier variations.

FROM WEBB, T. III 1990: "THE SPECTRUM OF TEMPORAL CLIMATIC VARIABILITY: CURRENT ESTIMATES AND THE NEED FOR GLOBAL AND REGIONAL TIME SERIES". IN BRADLEY, R.S. (ED.): *GLOBAL CHANGES OF THE PAST*. UCAR/OIES, BOULDER, COLORADO, 61–81.

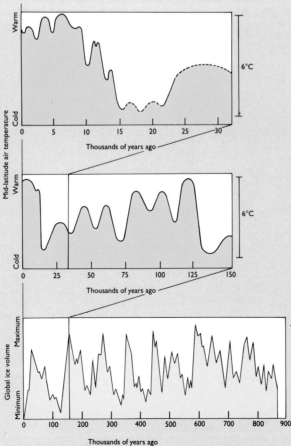

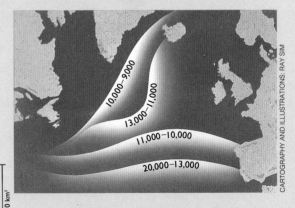

Changes in the position of the oceanic polar front between 20,000 and 9,000 years ago.

FROM RUDDIMAN, W.F. AND MCINTYRE, A. 1981: "THE NORTH ATLANTIC OCEAN DURING THE LAST DEGLACIATION". *PALAEOGEOGRAPHY* 35, 145–214.

CARTOGRAPHY AND ILLUSTRATIONS: RAY SIM

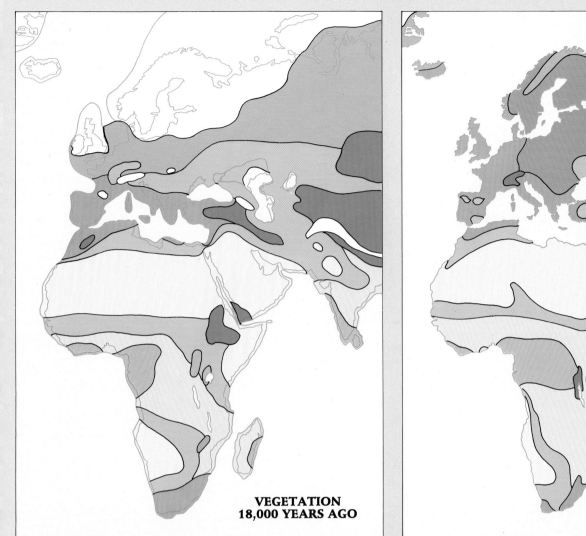

**VEGETATION
18,000 YEARS AGO**

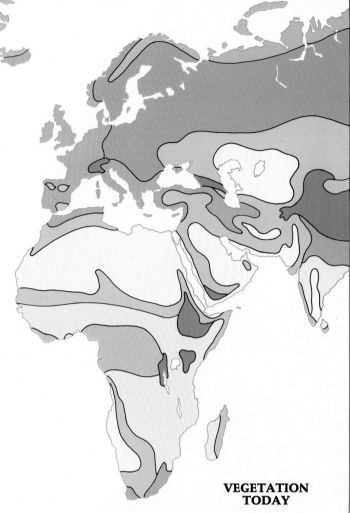

**VEGETATION
TODAY**

and woods were restricted to the Mediterranean peninsulas and some sheltered mountain areas. The tundra zone, however, was much narrower on the North American continent than in Europe, and from low lake levels and fossil sand dunes we know that low-latitude and mid-latitude areas were much drier than they now are. With no Indian monsoon, Southeast Asia was generally drier. In tropical regions, lower temperatures meant that mountain tree-belts grew between 1,000 and 2,000 meters (3,000 and 7,000 feet) lower than they do today.

The Start of the Thaw

About 15,000 years ago, temperatures began to rise throughout the globe. The melting ice caused the oceans to expand, drowning former land bridges. Forests grew in areas that had been tundra—earlier in North America than in Europe—and the highly productive grasslands and half-open woodlands that developed supported a wide range of animals. In low latitudes, such as in North Africa, the climate became moister. Here, former deserts changed into savannas and woodlands, not only supporting a diverse range of plants and animals but also being very favorable for humans.

A Mini Ice Age

About 11,000 years ago, the solar insolation reached a peak in the temperate regions, and a new interglacial was in sight. But in Europe and parts of North America, a glacial climate suddenly took hold. During this so-called Younger Dryas event, which lasted about 500 years, the North Atlantic polar front migrated from Iceland to the Bay of Biscay; summer temperatures dropped by 5 to 10 degrees Celsius (9 to 18 degrees Fahrenheit); the ice sheets that had started to melt began to increase and advance; the tundra and permafrost extended once again; and many animals and plants were forced southward.

This rather enigmatic period ended almost as abruptly as it began, about 10,000 years ago. Its ending marks the division between the Pleistocene and Holocene eras. With the start of this new interglacial, vegetation once again spread to the north. At high latitudes, this meant a change from glacial and periglacial tundra to temperate woodlands, while at low latitudes, it meant a change from arid desert steppe to humid, tropical woodlands. It was a period of dramatic environmental changes to which humans had to adapt.

 Vegetation and climate zones in Europe and Africa 18,000 years ago (left) and today (right).

BASED ON LILJEQUIST, G.H. 1970: *KLIMATOLOGI* (GENERALSTABENS LITOGRAFISKA ANSTALT, STOCKHOLM), AND MCINTYRE ET AL. 1976, IN *GEOLOGICAL SOCIETY OF AMERICA MEMOIR* 145 (BOULDER, COLORADO).

- Humid tropical: rainforests
- Tropical wet-dry: savannas
- Arid: deserts
- Semi-arid and dry-continental: steppes
- Humid, warm temperature: evergreen and deciduous forests
- Humid, cold temperature: coniferous forests
- Mountains
- Polar: tundra
- Polar: inland ice

- Settlement sites
- Burial sites

UPPER PALEOLITHIC BURIALS AND SETTLEMENTS IN EUROPE

Major Upper Paleolithic settlement and burial sites in Europe. The Dordogne region in France is shown in the detail. Coastlines and the extent of the ice sheet as they were at the peak of the last glacial, some 18,000 years ago, are indicated.

Europe—The Backwater Country

These new theories about the origins of modern humans have changed the way we look at Europe in the context of evolution. Once considered a center of physical and cultural development, it must now be regarded as a backwater, a marginal, stagnating region without further importance.

The classic finds of human fossils dating from the interglacial period that occurred between 300,000 and 200,000 years ago, at Swanscombe, in England, and Steinheim, in Germany, have recently been supplemented by new finds. These include the Petralona skull from Greece, dated to between 400,000 and 300,000 years ago, and the Arago skull from the French Pyrenees, which is about 200,000 years old. All are now classified, along with their African contemporaries, as *Homo heidelbergensis*. Although the earlier finds were considered to be the ancestors of modern humans and were called "pre-*sapiens*", these new finds indicate that they are most likely the ancestors of the European Neanderthals. It was these "pre-*sapiens*" finds that provided the framework of the traditional "candelabra" model of human evolution.

When *Homo sapiens sapiens* appeared in Europe about 40,000 years ago, during the last glacial,

they did so in the form of the Cro-Magnon people, who were named after a site in Les Eyzies, in the Dordogne, in France. They found the climate considerably harsher than the North African one they had come from, but, gradually, they adapted. Little by little their skin color became lighter to facilitate the absorption of the necessary vitamin D from the weak sunshine of the north. The arctic climate meant totally different requirements for human survival.

At that time, Europe was very different from the continent of today. The whole Scandinavian peninsula, as well as large parts of northern Germany, England, and Ireland, was covered with ice sheets a kilometer (3,000 feet) thick. As a result, the sea level was much lower than it is today. South of the ice edge lay widespread tundra plains with a rich variety of animals, including reindeer, horses, aurochs, bison, deer, mammoths, and rhinoceroses. Lions, leopards, and wolves competed with humans for the game. England and Ireland were part of the continental landmass, and large parts of the Bay of Biscay and the North Sea were drained. The climate was more hospitable in southern France and the Iberian

peninsula, with summer temperatures close to 15 degrees Celsius (59 degrees Fahrenheit). Here, food was more varied and plentiful, with a range of plant foods as well as fish and other marine foods.

The remains of Neanderthal-like individuals excavated at Hahnöfersand, near Hamburg, in Germany, and St Césaire, in France, may indicate that surviving Neanderthals lived side by side with the new immigrants. The fossils at both these sites have been dated to 36,000 years ago, and thus postdate the appearance of *Homo sapiens sapiens* in Europe. Neanderthals and modern humans may have interbred in some places, and so the original population may have been assimilated to some extent. But basically the newcomers took over completely. Time simply did not allow for any evolution from Neanderthals to *Homo sapiens sapiens*, since the physical differences were too great. As Richard Klein says, "compared to their antecedents, Upper Paleolithic people were remarkably innovative and inventive, and it is this characteristic more than any other that is their hallmark".

Tools and Traditions

The Upper Paleolithic period was a time of intense development and innovation. The Cro-Magnon people made many new tools, with a wide range of quite specialized uses. In contrast to the Neanderthals, the Cro-Magnon had a clear concept of style, of what the "ideal tool" should look like. A wide range of scrapers, burins, spear-points, and knives appeared, all made of flint, using the new blade technology. Styles varied according to function, region, period, and, presumably, social conditions.

For the first time, bone, antler, and ivory were widely used to make everyday articles as well as ceremonial objects and symbols of status. The latter were often decorated with elegantly carved patterns or shaped like animals. Many specialized kinds of burins have been found, indicating that these people enjoyed working with these new plastic, organic raw materials. By carving a deep incision on each side

of an animal bone, they split it into two halves to provide the raw material for beautifully worked bone tools such as harpoons, fish spears, points, and adornments. Needles have also been discovered, indicating that the Cro-Magnon people were the first to sew clothes and tents of animal hides. Stag antlers were shaped into efficient spear-throwers, the advanced weapon of the age.

When the Paleolithic period was first studied, all these new tools were grouped chronologically and geographically within a series of archaeological periods. We still use these classifications to identify stages within the Upper Paleolithic period. Because most of the research was carried out in France, these phases were named after important French sites. Their relationship, however, is only partly understood. Some coexisted, and it is reasonable to assume that different styles resulted as much from different regional traditions as from time-bound evolution.

The first appearance of Upper Paleolithic technology in Europe can be linked to two cultural phases, the Aurignacian and Chatelperronian, named after the sites of Aurignac and Châtelperron. Both existed in different regions between 35,000 and 30,000 years ago. The Aurignacian tradition dominated much of western and southern Europe.

⬅ Neanderthal skull from La Ferrassie, in the Dordogne, France (left), compared to the skull of an anatomically modern human found at Cro-Magnon, in the same area. Neanderthal skulls are characterized by a receding forehead, a long, low braincase, and heavy brow ridges.
JOHN READER/SCIENCE PHOTO LIBRARY/THE PHOTO LIBRARY

⬅ Barbed harpoons of bone became one of the characteristic tools of the Magdalenian phase, towards the end of the Upper Paleolithic period. A series of different types indicates that they were developed for highly specialized purposes.
DAVID L. BRILL, © 1985

⬆ Typical of the Solutrean phase, this beautifully worked spear-point of flint, in the shape of a laurel leaf, was found in the cave of Placard, at Vilhonneur, in Charente, France.
J. M. LABAT/AUSCAPE

ANIMALS OF ICE AGE EUROPE

Ronnie Liljegren

During the last glaciation, middle Europe—from the Atlantic coastal fringes to the Urals—formed part of an extensive steppe tundra commonly known as the mammoth steppe. This steppe stretched across Asia to the Pacific, and was at times even connected with the North American steppes via the land bridge of Beringia. The boundaries of the steppe shifted periodically with climatic changes, but its central area remained the same throughout the last glacial. The steppe had a cold, dry climate, often with strong winds, and a maximum summer temperature of 15 degrees Celsius (59 degrees Fahrenheit).

Different soils and varying exposure to wind, sun, and water produced a range of local environments, which supported many species of animals. Grasses, sedges, wormwoods, and other resistant species

The woolly mammoth (*Mammuthus primigenius*), once perhaps the commonest animal of the steppe, could stand as high as 3 meters (10 feet) at the shoulder but was usually a little smaller. It disappeared from Europe at the end of the last glacial, although it may have survived for another thousand years in arctic Asia.

The cave bear (*Ursus spelaeus*) was common during the early phase of the last glacial but disappeared towards the final phase. About the size of the present-day brown bear of Alaska, it was almost exclusively vegetarian. The remains of thousands of these bears have been found in European caves.

The wild horse (*Equus ferus*) was quite small, having a shoulder height of 115 to 145 centimeters (47 to 57 inches). A common inhabitant of the steppe, especially during the later part of the last glacial, it was heavily hunted by humans. Despite this, it survived in eastern Europe and Asia until quite recently.

The wolf (*Canis lupus*) is a successful survivor and can still be found in some of the wilder parts of Europe, as well as in Asia and North America.

The cave lion (*Panthera leo spelaea*) was about a third bigger than African lions but was probably closely related to them. Its relationship to more recent lions in Asia and the Balkans, however, is unknown. It disappeared from Europe at the end of the last glacial.

The wolverine (*Gulo gulo*) was considerably larger than present-day specimens and was found only in small numbers on the steppe. Today it inhabits the northern parts of Europe, Asia, and North America.

The willow grouse (*Lagopus lagopus*) is known from Pleistocene deposits and still exists. Fossil bird bones are rare but include many species.

Wild horse

Wolf

Cave lion

Woolly mammoth

Wolverine

Cave bear

Willow grouse

PETER SCHOUTEN 92

provided irregular cover. There were few trees, but woods of pine, spruce, juniper, and birch grew in sheltered areas.

With the end of the glacial, about 10,000 years ago, the climate rapidly became warmer and wooded areas increased. Some animals adapted to the new conditions or migrated to other areas, but many others died out. Many species disappeared earlier, in the later stages of the glacial. Such extinctions were even more marked elsewhere, notably in the Americas.

No evidence exists for a similar pattern of extinctions from previous glacials, and no one theory has yet emerged that satisfactorily explains it. Humans alone could not have caused these extinctions on such a vast scale. Nor is it likely that so many species simply failed to adapt to the new conditions, given that they appear to have survived similar changes following previous glacials. Many other theories founder on misinterpretations of fossil evidence.

The reasons for these extinctions remain mysterious. We can only speculate that they were caused by some as yet unknown combination of factors, including climatic change and human activity.

The steppe bison (*Bison priscus*), once common, became extinct at the end of the last glacial. A powerful animal, it was about 3 meters (10 feet) long and stood more than 2 meters (6 feet) at the shoulder. Its relationship to the modern European bison is unclear.

The reindeer (*Rangifer tarandus*) was one of the commonest animals of the steppe, especially during the later phase of the last glacial. It is today found in northern Europe and Asia.

The musk ox (*Ovibos moscatus*) was another characteristic inhabitant of the steppe. It disappeared from Europe at the end of the last glacial and is today found only in Canada and Greenland.

The woolly rhinoceros (*Coelodonta antiquitatis*) disappeared about 12,000 years ago. It had two very prominent nose horns.

The cave hyena (*Crocuta crocuta spelaea*) was probably the same species as the present-day spotted hyena of Africa but was considerably larger. It disappeared from Europe towards the end of the last glacial.

The Irish elk (*Megaloceros giganteus*), also known as the giant deer, was almost the size of the American moose. Its huge antlers probably served both to signal dominance to males and to attract females. It disappeared at the end of the last glacial.

The suslik (*Citellus citellus*), a type of ground squirrel, favored loess areas of the steppe. It is now found in eastern central Europe.

The saiga antelope (*Saiga tartarica*) was another characteristic animal of the steppe. It now inhabits southern Russia and the Asian steppes.

ILLUSTRATION: PETER SCHOUTEN

BOHUSLAV KLIMA

This was the culture of the Cro-Magnon people, and most finds of human fossils, including burials, date from this phase. The more local Chatelperronian tradition is also linked with modern humans, with the exception of one Neanderthal skull dating from the early Chatelperronian phase found at St Césaire. As noted previously, this shows that Neanderthals lived side by side with the Cro-Magnon for a time. It also shows that, at least to some extent, they adopted their technology.

About 27,000 years ago, the Gravettian tradition appeared (named after the site of La Gravette), followed by the Solutrean (named after the site of Solutré). The Gravettian is characterized above all by the emergence of artistic expression, particularly in the form of small, stylized female figures known as Venus figurines. When they arrived in Europe, the people of the Aurignacian culture had already developed the ability to express themselves symbolically through the medium of art. Sexual symbolism was dominant, in the form of images of vulvas, but the elegant Venus figurines, with their exaggeratedly swelling breasts and buttocks, strongly indicate that ritual and ceremonial systems were becoming established over vast distances. Very similar figurines appear south of the ice edge throughout a continuous area extending from the Atlantic coast in the west to Siberia in the east. For the first time, we can see that people had a need to be in regular contact with other groups over extensive areas. Exotic raw materials were transported and interchanged all over Europe, particularly shells from the Mediterranean and the Atlantic, as well as amber. Everything indicates that recurrent meetings with other groups played an increasingly important role in the social system.

In this connection, a series of important sites stands out as being particularly interesting. At Dolní Věstonice, in the Czech Republic, a couple

↑ Well-preserved burials unearthed at Dolní Věstonice, in Moravia, in the Czech Republic. Two of the skulls were adorned with ivory beads as well as teeth of wolf and arctic fox. The left-hand skeleton reaches toward red ocher on the ground.

BOHUSLAV KLIMA

→ Dolní Věstonice, in Moravia, in the Czech Republic, is one of the most famous and important Upper Paleolithic sites. Excavations have revealed the remains of several huts dating back to about 28,000 years ago, one of which contained an oven in which clay figurines had been fired.

Reconstruction of a mammoth bone dwelling excavated at Pushkari, in Ukraine. It measured 12 by 4.5 meters (40 by 15 feet), and consisted of three circular huts joined together.
ILLUSTRATION: STEVE TREVASKIS

of extensive open-air settlements dated to about 27,000 years ago have been excavated. People of this area lived in pit houses, the floor countersunk a meter (about 3 feet) into the ground to facilitate sealing between the roof and the floor against the winter storms. The walls were built of wooden posts and covered with animal hides. The constant need of fire required large amounts of solid fuel, and since wood was scarce, mammoth bones were used instead. It has been estimated that at least 100 to 125 people lived in one of these settlements.

A similar series of settlements and gathering places dating from about 25,000 years ago has been excavated at Kostenki, in Russia, on the shores of the River Don. With no wood available, the houses were built entirely of mammoth bones—a spectacular sight indeed. The ground plan is difficult to interpret but seems to indicate that the houses were longhouses about 12 meters (40 feet) long.

The most important region during the Upper Paleolithic period was, however, southern France. Although traces of open-air settlements have been found in this region, most people lived under the protection of the natural rock shelters, or *abri*, that are so characteristic of this limestone area.

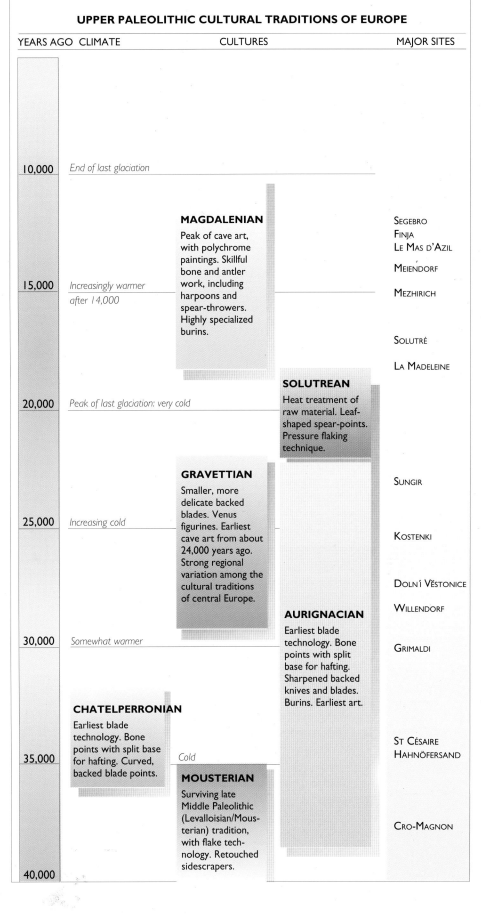

UPPER PALEOLITHIC CULTURAL TRADITIONS OF EUROPE

YEARS AGO	CLIMATE	CULTURES	MAJOR SITES
10,000	End of last glaciation		
15,000	Increasingly warmer after 14,000	**MAGDALENIAN** Peak of cave art, with polychrome paintings. Skillful bone and antler work, including harpoons and spear-throwers. Highly specialized burins.	SEGEBRO FINJA LE MAS D'AZIL MEIENDORF MEZHIRICH SOLUTRÉ LA MADELEINE
20,000	Peak of last glaciation: very cold	**SOLUTREAN** Heat treatment of raw material. Leaf-shaped spear-points. Pressure flaking technique.	
25,000	Increasing cold	**GRAVETTIAN** Smaller, more delicate backed blades. Venus figurines. Earliest cave art from about 24,000 years ago. Strong regional variation among the cultural traditions of central Europe.	SUNGIR KOSTENKI DOLNÍ VĚSTONICE WILLENDORF
30,000	Somewhat warmer	**AURIGNACIAN** Earliest blade technology. Bone points with split base for hafting. Sharpened backed knives and blades. Burins. Earliest art.	GRIMALDI
35,000	Cold	**CHATELPERRONIAN** Earliest blade technology. Bone points with split base for hafting. Curved, backed blade points.	ST CÉSAIRE HAHNÖFERSAND
40,000		**MOUSTERIAN** Surviving late Middle Paleolithic (Levalloisian/Mousterian) tradition, with flake technology. Retouched sidescrapers.	CRO-MAGNON

IRA BLOCK 1989

Unearthing mammoth bones at Kostenki, near Voronesh, in Russia. About 20 Upper Paleolithic sites have been discovered in this area, and several huts, as well as numerous art objects, have been found. Kostenki has yielded more Venus figurines than any other site in Europe.

Hunters of the North: The Magdalenian Period

About 18,000 years ago, the Solutrean tradition was swept away by the wave of technological, intellectual, and cultural developments that characterize the Magdalenian tradition. Named after the famous *abri* settlement of La Madeleine, on the shores of the Vézère River, close to Les Eyzies, in the Dordogne, the Magdalenian is the most intense period of change in the whole of the Upper Paleolithic period. It was to last until about 10,000 years ago.

The people who ushered in this new phase had adapted perfectly to their Ice Age environment. Over a period of 8,000 years, both craftsmanship, in the form of artifacts made of bone, antler, and flint, and art, in the form of portable art objects and cave art, reached a peak. More than 80 percent of known cave art was created between 15,000 and 12,000 years ago—during the latter part of the Magdalenian phase.

The fact that gathering places were becoming more important is also very evident in this region. Four settlements in the Dordogne, including La Madeleine, have yielded about 80 percent of all the known portable art from the Magdalenian phase in this region. Many of the large caves containing paintings and carvings, such as Lascaux, Pech-Merle, and Niaux, in France, and Altamira, in Spain, were probably used as communal ceremonial places.

The site that has most to tell us about social organization at the end of the last Ice Age is the enormous cave of Le Mas d'Azil, in the Pyrenees. It was used seasonally as a meeting place for neighboring groups of people from a very wide area. As deep as a 20-storied building, the thick occupation layers inside the cave have yielded thousands of examples of portable art and other decorated objects, including beautifully carved spear-throwers. The cave was important as a dwelling, gathering, and ceremonial place well beyond the end of the Paleolithic period, in recognition of which the name Azilian has been given to the transitional period between the end of the Paleolithic period and the rise of the hunter-gatherer cultures that developed in the postglacial period known as the Mesolithic.

The Earliest Herders?

The people of the Magdalenian phase were predominantly big-game hunters. They mostly hunted horned animals, especially reindeer, which became the most important game animal—to the extent that 99 percent of all animal bones found on many sites of this period are those of reindeer. Reindeer migrate seasonally in search of pasture over very large areas, sometimes thousands of kilometers (many hundreds of miles). Hunters who rely on reindeer all year round obviously have to follow these migrating herds.

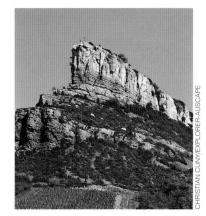

CHRISTIAN CUNY/EXPLORER-AUSCAPE

Beneath these cliffs at Solutré, near Lyon, in France, huge quantities of horse bones have been found, indicating that this was a major kill site during the Upper Paleolithic period.

Aerial view of the Vézère River at La Madeleine, in the Dordogne, France. This site was a major gathering place for the nomadic groups of big-game hunters that roamed the surrounding area during the last glacial.

The halter-like engravings on this horse's head of bone, found at St Michel d'Arudy, Basses-Pyrénées, France, have been interpreted by some as evidence that horses were domesticated during the Upper Paleolithic period.

MUSEE DES ANTIQUITES NATIONALES, ST-GERMAIN-EN-LAYE/R.M.N.

The wild horses of Ice Age Europe were similar to Przewalski horses, a species that until recently roamed the steppes of central Asia. Horses were an important source of food at this time and may also have been domesticated to some extent.

GERARD LACZ/NHPA

British archaeologist Paul Bahn has suggested that the way of life of the Upper Paleolithic people in southern France and the Pyrenees was probably very similar to that of present-day reindeer hunters and herders in Siberia. These people are seasonally nomadic, and as well as hunting, they keep domesticated animals to provide milk and to use as beasts of burden. Bahn suggests that the reindeer would have moved to pastures in several different directions during their seasonal migrations from the Dordogne: toward the Atlantic coast on the Bay of Biscay, the Pyrenees, and perhaps also the Alps. Analysis of the bone material from the *abri* settlement of Abri Pataud, in Les Eyzies, has shown that this settlement was occupied exclusively during late autumn, winter, and early spring. Abundant finds of cockle and mussel shells in almost every inland settlement lend support to the theory that humans followed the herds as they headed for the Atlantic coast.

Bahn is therefore open to the suggestion that Magdalenian hunters may have tamed part of the reindeer herds. It has long been wondered whether they may have tamed another important herd animal—the horse.

At the end of the nineteenth century, French researcher Edouard Piette suggested that the big-game hunters of the Upper Paleolithic period controlled or even domesticated some animals, in particular reindeer and horses. In support of this, he drew attention to carvings and paintings depicting animals apparently equipped with halters or harnesses of some kind—for example, a reindeer bull at the *abri* site of Laugerie-Basse and a horse in the cave of La Pasiega. The most striking example, however, was found in 1893 in the cave of St Michel d'Arudy—a carved horse's head equipped with something that could only have been a halter made of twisted rope. Piette's theories were heavily criticized, notably by the legendary and very influential Abbé Breuil, and after his death in 1906 the matter was more or less forgotten.

Sixty years after Piette's death, two French researchers found a carving of a horse's head wearing a halter at La Marche, in southwestern France. According to Paul Bahn, the halter was added after the head had been completed. This may indicate that horses were used for riding or as beasts of burden. Researchers who have studied finds of horses' teeth dating back to 30,000 years ago have claimed that many show distinct signs of so-called crib-biting—the wear pattern that results when a horse develops a habit of biting its stall—which was thought not to occur among wild horses. Recently, however, other researchers have strongly disputed this, claiming that it is more likely to be a natural wear pattern.

Notwithstanding this, there is some evidence to suggest that the big-game hunters of the Upper Paleolithic period did exercise some degree of control over horse and reindeer herds, and

perhaps also mountain goats. How is this to be reconciled with the large-scale drives and mass killings considered so characteristic of the period? These hunting methods would have required a joint effort by a very large number of hunters, who would have had to force the herds over a precipice or into a narrow gorge where the animals could be easily brought down. But to drive a galloping herd of horses on foot is clearly no easy task. Perhaps these Upper Paleolithic hunters were indeed the first horsemen.

One of the sites often cited as evidence of this large-scale hunting strategy is a precipice at Solutré, in the Rhône Valley. Excavations at the foot of the cliffs have uncovered the remains of tens of thousands of horses, dated to 17,000 years ago—that is, the early Magdalenian phase. More recently, it has been pointed out that the site is not particularly suitable for drives but ideally suited to a strategy of encirclement. The precipice was more likely used as a barrier to hedge the animals in, allowing them to be separated and slaughtered—or possibly, in the case of young animals, to be kept for future use, thereby ensuring a continuing food supply.

Whatever future research may tell us about Ice Age humans' control over animals, there was clearly great variation in living conditions and the availability of food across Eurasia. While big-game hunting was crucially important across the extensive tundra along the ice edge, the milder climate of southwestern Europe produced a plentiful and reliable supply of a variety of foods. As noted earlier, cockle and mussel shells have been found in most settlement sites in this area,

BRYAN AND CHERRY ALEXANDER/NHPA

indicating that marine foods were eaten, at least during some parts of the year. The numerous images of salmon, sole, and other saltwater species found among cave art would seem to suggest that fishing was an important means of subsistence. In some areas, fish may even have been the staple food, encouraging people to adopt a more settled way of life. Plant foods were readily available in western Europe, though lacking further east. All these factors were vitally important in promoting population growth, which, in turn, led to new forms of social organization and ceremonial life.

The Birth of Inequality

In southern France in particular, the rich food resources led to a substantial increase in population during the Magdalenian period. It has been estimated that between 2,000 and 3,000 people lived in this area 20,000 years ago. Ten thousand years later, at the end of the Ice Age, this figure must have tripled. During the later stages of the Magdalenian period, *abri* settlements were becoming much larger. Some of them, such as Laugerie-Haute, Laugerie-Basse, and St Christophe, by the Vézère River, close to Les Eyzies, may have sheltered several hundred people at the same time for part of the year. Some groups, or parts of groups, probably lived in this region all year round.

How was society organized within and between different groups of people during this period? Within modern traditional societies, the two main factors determining group size are the ability to survive and the ability to live in peace. The ability to survive is drastically reduced if the group is too small. A lone individual rarely survives for more

than a year, whereas a group of five can continue for up to a generation (about 30 years). A group of about 25 has a good chance of surviving for perhaps 500 years, assuming it is in regular contact with other groups, not least for intermarriage.

On the other hand, the risk of conflict within groups increases with the number of people. Again, it turns out that 25 is a reasonable average number, and ethnographic studies among present-day hunter-gatherers have shown that most of them live in groups of between 20 and 70. This is true of the Australian Aborigines, the Kalahari Bushmen, and the Andamanese, as well as the Birhor of northern India. American anthropologist Robert Carneiro has observed that when the Yanomami Indians of South America form a group of more than 100 people, aggressive tendencies become so great that the group has to split into two halves.

For survival, a number of groups or bands must be organized in larger units or tribes, and here there are always certain limits. To avoid the problem of inbreeding, there must be at least 475 in the larger group. In fact, most known tribes of hunter-gatherers have about 500 people, with a maximum of about 800. It seems likely that similar conditions prevailed in southwestern Europe during the Magdalenian phase.

By studying the food supply within present-day areas that have the same climatic conditions as the various ecological zones of the Paleolithic Ice Age, we can estimate the likely productivity of each area in terms of hunting, fishing, and food-gathering—in other words, we can estimate its carrying capacity. The poorest regions, such as the tundra zone close to the ice edge, could have

🔾 Judging by the quantities of bones found at settlements, reindeer were one of the main sources of food for the Ice Age hunters, who followed the seasonal migrations of the herds.

GÖRAN BURENHULT

🔾 This life-size reconstruction of a mammoth bone hut is on display at the Thot Museum, near Montignac, in the Dordogne. The original was excavated at Mezhirich, in the Ukraine.

RADIOCARBON : A KEY TO THE PAST

Göran Burenhult

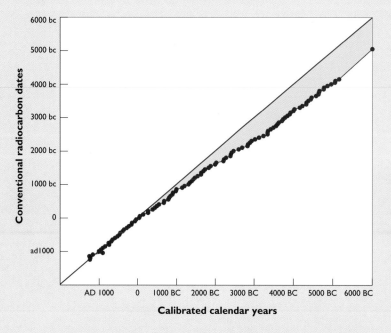

Diagram showing the deviation between conventional radiocarbon dates (bc/ad) and calibrated calendar years (BC/AD). The latter are based on C_{14} samples of tree-rings.
AFTER HANS E. SUESS

No other method has had such a revolutionary influence on modern archaeology's possibilities to establish absolute chronology as the radiocarbon or Carbon-14 method—the dating of radioactive carbon. This dating technique has been constantly refined, and a new revolution came about when the obtained C_{14} values could be calibrated into calendar years—that is, historically comparable dates. And right now we are in the middle of a third radiocarbon revolution—accelerator dating.

In 1949, an American physical chemist, Willard Libby, discovered that organic materials could be dated by measuring the amount of radioactive charcoal they contained. All living plants absorb small amounts of radioactive C_{14} from the atmosphere when they build up organic matter by photosynthesis and by using atmospheric carbon dioxide. There are three main isotopes of carbon, $C1_2$, C_{13}, and C_{14}. C_{12} and C_{13} are stable; C_{14} is radioactive and decays at a known rate. C_{14} is also continuously being produced in the upper atmosphere. Constant decay of C_{14} is balanced by constant production, which means that this radioactive isotope is in constant proportion to the common stable isotope C_{12}, the same as in carbon dioxide in the air. By consuming plants or herbivorous animals, all other animals and humans ingest and accumulate the radioactivity. When a human dies, or a tree is felled, the accumulation of radioactivity ceases and the measurable amount disintegrates at a known rate. The term "half-life" denotes the time it takes for radioactive matter to halve its number of atoms. For C_{14}, the half-life is 5,568 years. By measuring the remaining amount of C_{14}, it is thus possible to determine the time that has elapsed since the accumulation of radioactivity ceased. The obtained values are given in radiocarbon years BP (Before Present = before AD 1950), and can then easily be converted into radiocarbon years BC or AD. Deviation is given as a plus or minus factor—for example, 4,600 ± 100 years, which means with a possible deviation of plus or minus 100 years. The sample in this example can thus be dated in between the span of 4700 and 4500 BP. More exactly, there are 2 chances in 3 that this is the correct time span, but 19 chances in 20 that 4800 to 4400 BP is correct.

As the content of radioactivity constantly decreases over the years, the radiocarbon method has its limitations and is restricted to materials younger than about 70,000 years. The method is most effective on materials between 50,000 and 500 years old. Radiocarbon datings can be carried out on most organic materials, such as wood, charcoal, resin, hair, skin, bone, or peat. The margins of error vary, depending on material and quantity, and, as a rule, resin, wood, or charcoal provide more reliable dates than bone or peat, owing to their resistance to secondary influence.

When the radiocarbon method came into use, it was generally assumed that the absorption of atmospheric radioactivity had been relatively invariable over the millennia, and that radiocarbon years therefore on the whole corresponded with calendar years in the historical sense. However, during the 1960s, two scientists, Hans E. Suess and H.L. de Vries, showed independently of each other that this was not at all the case. Fluctuations as a result of variations in the Earth's magnetic field and alterations in solar activity and in the balance between atmosphere and oceans were proved to exist. Recently, too, exhaust fumes from cars, power stations, and the like, as well as nuclear tests, have influenced the C_{14} curve. By radiocarbon-dating the tree-rings of very old trees in the western United States—primarily giant sequoia (*Sequoiadendron giganteum*) and bristlecone pine (*Pinus longaeva*), which reach an age of more than 4,000 years—it was possible to check the C_{14} values and calibrate them into calendar years. By means of dendrochronology (the study of the annual growth rings on trees), it was possible to extend the sequence back to about 5300 BC, and today we can give very accurate archaeological dates in calendar years. In other words, these correspond exactly to historically known dates, such as the building of Cheops' pyramid in the Old Kingdom of Egypt, or later events in the classical world, in Greece and Rome.

To avoid confusion, and as the calibrated dates are still subject to adjustment, experts have agreed to give all C_{14} values in conventional radiocarbon years as well in the future, and to clearly state calibrations into calendar years.

The established deviation is at its greatest between about 4000 and 3000 BC. The calibrated C_{14} dates therefore greatly influenced the understanding of, for example, the important and complex cultural situation of Neolithic Europe. The timing of the appearance of agriculture was particularly important in this respect, as it was backdated nearly a thousand years. The Stone Age peoples of Europe could no longer be looked upon as passive recipients of cultural advances from the Mediterranean area and Southwest Asia.

The C_{14} method took a great leap forward when the accelerator mass spectrometric (AMS) technique was introduced, both in terms of exactness and applicability. The amount of material needed for a radiocarbon dating has been drastically reduced, and nowadays only a few milligrams will suffice to obtain reliable datings. In future, the method will become an extraordinarily important dating instrument to archaeologists, and a number of spectacular datings have already been carried out on, for example, the domestication of plants and the first appearance of humans in the New World. Moreover, the famous Shroud of Turin has been dated with the AMS technique: on no account can it be the authentic shroud of Jesus Christ—the linen was made about AD 1300.

supported only one person per 200 square kilometers (77 square miles), but in southern France and Spain, this might well have been one person per 20 square kilometers (8 square miles). A tribe of about 500 people would have had to use more than 100,000 square kilometers (39,000 square miles) in the former area, but only 10,000 square kilometers (3,900 square miles) in the latter. This great variation in population density explains the differences in social and ceremonial systems among Paleolithic peoples, clearly indicating the need for extensive networks over large areas. In southern France, where so much activity was centered in this period, regular, communal ceremonies were held in several important gathering places—for example, in connection with mating.

A study of 76 skeletons from the Upper Paleolithic period in Europe and Asia has shown that less than half the people reached the age of 21, only 12 percent were more than 40, and not one single woman reached 30 years of age. Many skeletons showed signs of malnutrition, rickets, and other deficiency diseases. Significantly, many bore traces of injury resulting from physical violence. Life during the Ice Age was undoubtedly a relentless struggle for survival, and the evidence of social organization and ceremonial life that has survived from this period reflects a society under heavy pressure as people competed for limited resources.

During the later part of the Upper Paleolithic period, large settlements became gathering places for people from surrounding areas, where goods were exchanged and rituals observed. The many examples of portable art that have been found from this period may have served as personal status symbols on such occasions. One of the most remarkable examples has been excavated at Mezhirich, on the Dnepr River, southeast of Kiev, in the Ukraine. Five houses were found here, built of about 70 tonnes (just under 70 tons) of mammoth bones.

There is a good deal of evidence to show that certain people had higher status than others, and these people—possibly in the form of shamans—probably conducted rituals and ceremonies. Finds of a number of magnificently ornate burials provide, perhaps, the most persuasive evidence of status in this period. At Sungir, near Moscow, remains have been found of two adults and two children, the man and children buried in clothes decorated with thousands of beads of ivory and animal teeth and accompanied by ornately carved weapons and other objects suggesting a high status. The remains of magnificently adorned children have also been excavated from a site known as Grotte des Enfants, on the Italian Riviera.

Because these children were aged between 7 and 13, they cannot have attained high rank in their society by their own efforts. Their elaborate adornments have been interpreted as the first

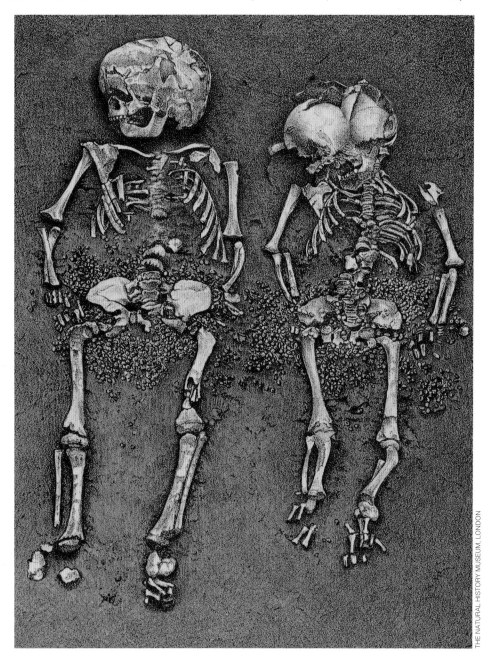

THE NATURAL HISTORY MUSEUM, LONDON

examples of hereditary status, evidence that some families in Paleolithic society were ranked higher than others. American writer John Pfeiffer summarizes: "A great deal of effort went into these burials, and into the appropriately elaborate ceremonies that must have accompanied them. Such honors are not for everyone, only for special people, indicating the beginnings of formal social distinctions. The burying of young children suggests further developments. A leader who earns his position by actual deeds needs time to win recognition as hunter or shaman. He must keep proving himself and when he can no longer do so he is replaced by someone else who can. But the existence of children buried with high honors before they are old enough to do anything outstanding raises the possibility of status by heredity rather than achievement."

♙ Richly adorned child burials excavated in Grotte des Enfants—one of the Grimaldi caves—at Balzi Rossi, Italy. Their elaborate adornments, in the form of clusters of perforated shells, are one of the earliest examples of what may be hereditary status symbols.

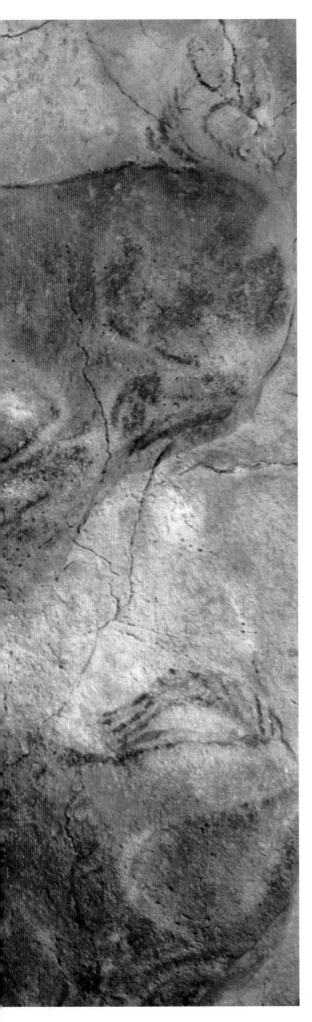

THE RISE OF ART

Image-making in Europe during the Ice Age

GÖRAN BURENHULT

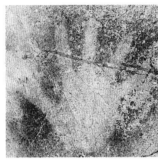

EVER SINCE A DAY in 1879 when Don Marcelino de Sautuola's five-year-old daughter happened to look up at the roof of a cavern and discover the painted bison of Altamira Cave, in northern Spain, the magnificent art of the Paleolithic hunters has been a source of fascination. No other remains from our prehistoric past have been found in such a remarkable location, deep inside dark, damp, and narrow limestone caves.

To encounter the world of beliefs of Upper Paleolithic people is an experience marked by awe, anxiety, excitement, and wonder. Often it involves an expedition of a kilometer or more (about half a mile) into the depths of a mountain—walking, crawling on one's knees and elbows, and sometimes swimming across underground lakes and rivers. The remote location is characteristic of cave art. The experience itself, of isolation, darkness, and unnatural timelessness, must have been of vital importance to the people of that age when selecting a sanctuary. The explorer is overwhelmed by a sense that secret rites and ceremonies of great mystery must have taken place in these unreal surroundings.

←◑ The painted bison in the cave of Altamira, in northern Spain, are some of the most elaborate and well-known examples of Paleolithic art in the world. Painted some 12,000 years ago, they represent the highlight and also mark the end of a several-thousand-year-old artistic tradition in Europe.

↑ Hand stencils—a dramatic and personal message from the Ice Age.

RONALD SHERIDAN/ANCIENT ART AND ARCHITECTURE COLLECTION

GÖRAN BURENHULT

⚓ The famous rock shelter (or *abri*) of La Madeleine, which has given its name to the Magdalenian phase, is situated on the banks of the Vézère River, in the Dordogne, France. This site has yielded some of the finest pieces of portable art known, and appears to have been an important ceremonial gathering place.

⇨ A magnificent horse-shaped spear-thrower made of bone from Bruniquel, Tarn-et-Garonne, France. The spear-thrower (also known as a throwing stick or atlatl) is well known among many hunter-gatherers in more recent times, including the North American Indians and the Australian Aborigines. The technique is ingeniously simple. The spear-thrower has a hook on one end which engages with a hollow at the end of the spear, and the effect of this extension of the throwing arm is to improve both penetrating power and accuracy quite dramatically. A skilled hunter can bring down a deer from a distance of more than 30 meters (30 yards), and kill an animal with a direct hit from a distance of 15 meters (15 yards).
DAVID L. BRILL, ©1985/MUSEE DES ANTIQUITES NATIONALES, ST GERMAIN-EN-LAYE

De Sautuola was an amateur archaeologist, and at first no one believed that his finds were unique art treasures from Paleolithic times. The elegant, vividly painted animals were thought to be too perfect—too naturalistic and technically advanced—to have been created by a Stone Age man or woman. They were believed to be a hoax of recent origin. Don Marcelino died before the sensational age of the paintings was confirmed. It was only much later that new finds of cave art in or together with datable strata convinced the scientific world of their great age. These new finds consisted mainly of small, three-dimensional animals carved in antler and bone—examples of so-called portable art—and were crafted with the same remarkable skill to create astonishingly life-like images.

The time perspective alone is dizzying. The earliest images found are more than 30,000 years old. As far as we know at present, the Neanderthals never expressed themselves in art. The image as a means of expression belongs exclusively to modern humans, *Homo sapiens sapiens*, who appeared in Europe about 35,000 years ago in the form of the

people we know as the Cro-Magnon. There is nothing to indicate that Neanderthals were less able to express abstract thought in the form of imagery, but for some reason they never did.

What happened at the start of the Upper Paleolithic? Why did Ice Age humans suddenly need to express themselves in images? And why did they find their way, with the evident danger of being killed, through extremely difficult passages to the deepest parts of caves? Why are these caves to be found almost exclusively within an area in southern France and northern Spain? Were the cave paintings created by one person, or did entire communities find their way into the silent sanctuaries to perform their cult ceremonies? Who created the paintings? Were they men or women, or perhaps children?

No preliminary stages of paintings or carvings have been found, and this has been interpreted to mean that the cave art was created by a limited group of selected individuals—a sort of priesthood, in the form of medicine-men or shamans. Another possible explanation is that people trained on perishable materials, such as hides or wood, outside the caves.

A Time of Changes

To understand what led up to the beginnings of art, we have to look far beyond the art itself. The Upper Paleolithic period was a time of dramatic changes. The appearance of a new human species in Europe is sensational enough, but these newcomers were to introduce a number of social and technological innovations that radically changed conditions of life within a short period. The population grew markedly, and nomadic family groups began to gather in larger units and for longer periods than in earlier times. The archaeological record shows that goods were interchanged over greater distances, indicating a growing network of relationships between groups.

The most conspicuous change that occurred at this time was the development of a new and stylistically more complex tool technology. The stone tools of the Neanderthals consisted of a few similar types. Prepared, tortoise-shaped pieces of flint provided the raw material, from which flakes were struck off. These flakes were then retouched to make scrapers and points of different kinds. (This is known as Levalloisian technology.) *Homo sapiens sapiens* developed a more advanced blade technology, and were able to produce long, thin tools, such as blades in the shape of a laurel leaf. Many new types of tools were developed, including flint tools with double functions, such as retouched flakes where one end was shaped as a scraper, while the other served as a burin. The large variety of burins that have been found from this period clearly indicates that they served a range of specialized purposes.

The new tools were largely developed to enable people to work with bone and antler. Burins in particular were mainly used for this purpose. By the end of the Paleolithic period, during the Magdalenian phase, most artifacts—both those with a practical function and those that appear to have been ornaments or ritual objects—were made of these materials. Tens of thousands of portable works of art have been found in Europe, most of them in southern France. A large number of different kinds of harpoons and fish-spears, each with a specialized function, have also been found from this period, indicating that hunting small game and fishing were becoming more sophisticated and much more important as a means of subsistence.

Spear-throwers made of antler, often beautifully carved, were another addition to hunting weapons at this time.

But tools and works of art are not the only evidence of profound social change in the Upper Paleolithic period. New needs and traditions are reflected even more clearly in a series of spectacular finds which indicate that the people of this time had developed a rich ceremonial life based on complex concepts and rituals.

For the first time, evidence of regular burials appears, the bodies dotted with red ocher, many dressed in magnificent clothing and adornments, and accompanied by sets of tools. At Sungir, some 200 kilometers (125 miles) northeast of Moscow, four well-preserved burials dated to between 25,000 and 20,000 years ago have been found—a man, a woman, and two adolescent children. The man had been buried together with blades of ivory, and was dressed in a headband and a number of necklaces carrying some 3,000 beads of mammoth ivory. The cranium of a female had been placed on the grave in the course of his burial ritual. In a double grave in which a girl and boy were buried head to head, more than 10,000 ivory beads were found, together with rings, ornaments, the teeth of arctic fox, and 16 weapons in the form of spears, spear-throwers, and daggers. Similar burials from this period have been found at a number of other European sites, including Grimaldi, in Italy, and La Madeleine, in France.

◄ Carving of an animal head from Le Mas d'Azil, one of the most important Paleolithic sites in the French Pyrenees. The enormously rich finds of portable art as well as cave art at this site suggest that it was one of the main ceremonial gathering places in the Franco-Cantabrian region. The site has also yielded small pebbles with painted red dots.

JEAN VERTUT/COLLECTION DE SAINT-PERIER

◄ Ibex carved in a piece of bone from the cave of Isturitz, Basses-Pyrenées, France.
JEAN VERTUT/COLLECTION DE SAINT-PERIER

Together with the different kinds of art, both portable art objects and cave art, these burials clearly indicate that the people of this time felt the need to communicate abstract information by means of symbols. In the whole history of human evolution, this is the first evidence we have of the need to show group affiliation and social status—while the child burials are the first indication that status may have been hereditary. For this reason, it has been suggested that the Upper Paleolithic period may mark the beginning of the end of the totally egalitarian society.

As the population grew and these new and more complex patterns of social organization emerged, people clearly had a greater need to communicate both within their own group and with outside groups. The development of images and symbols can be directly linked to this growing need for communication, and it has been suggested that language may have undergone a parallel development at this time.

➤ Deer head carved in a piece of antler from the cave of Isturitz, Basses-Pyrenées, France.
JEAN VERTUT/COLLECTION DE SAINT-PERIER

◄ Bison carved in a piece of bone found in Magdalenian layers in the cave of Isturitz, Basses-Pyrenées, France.
JEAN VERTUT/COLLECTION DE SAINT-PERIER

⚥ Carving depicting a vulva at La Ferrassie, in the Dordogne.

DAVID L. BRILL, ©1985/MUSEE NATIONAL DE PREHISTOIRE, LES EYZIES DE TAYAC

☞ *Opposite:* Head of a Venus figurine from Brassempouy. This exquisite piece of craftsmanship, one of the earliest depictions of a human face, dates from the Gravettian phase, between 29,000 and 22,000 years ago. The checked pattern on the head has been interpreted as a hairnet.

☞ Elegantly stylized, headless female figures from Lalinde, at La Roche, in the Dordogne. Their buttocks are heavily marked. About 10 to 15 centimeters (4 to 6 inches) high, these carved figures date back to the Magdalenian phase.

The Artistic Revolution

Cave art, with its naturalistic images of animals, arose during a later stage of the Upper Paleolithic period. The first expressions of art in Europe consist of symbols of female sexuality. As early as 35,000 years ago, Cro-Magnon people carved images of vulvas on rock and other surfaces. Some millennia later, about 29,000 years ago, the first portable art appeared in the form of the famous Venus figurines, small female figures with a characteristically stylized form. They were to dominate artistic expression for nearly 10,000 years.

Most of these female figures have exaggeratedly swelling breasts and buttocks, while the head and legs taper off into a less defined shape, clearly being seen as of minor importance. They have been found over extensive areas, indicating widespread contacts and a common system of rituals throughout widely scattered communities during this period. Similar-looking Venus figurines have been found in great numbers from southern Russia in the east to the Atlantic coast in the west, a distance of more than 2,000 kilometers (1,200 miles). The most important sites include Dolní Věstonice, in the Czech Republic, Kostenki, in Russia, Willendorf, in Austria, and Brassempouy and Lespugue, in France.

Two possible explanations have been put forward to explain this emphasis on female genitals in the artistic and ritual life of the Cro-Magnon people and the distinctive characteristics of the Venus figurines. First, we know from the skeletons of this period that Cro-Magnon women were generally less robust than their predecessors, the Neanderthals, and had a considerably narrower pelvic opening. This may have resulted in more difficult childbirth and, as a result, a high death rate among mothers and babies. Second, it is not unlikely that the rapidly growing population led to increasing conflict, and conflict within traditional societies usually involves competition for women. In any case, women's vital role in ensuring the continued existence of a society whose survival was coming under increasing pressure may very well have given rise to a cult centered on women.

We can trace the growth in population by the number of sites that have been discovered from different periods. At present, we know of only six sites from the Neanderthal era in the Russian region—the area between the Black Sea and the ice edge in the north—while the same area has more than 500 settlements from the Cro-Magnon period. As people have more frequent contact with outside groups, they have a greater need to show who they are and what position in society they hold. In all traditional societies, this is done by wearing adornments and other objects indicating personal status, and also by different kinds of body decoration, in the form of tattoos or body painting. The beautifully carved ivory spear-points and spear-throwers, as well as many of the other portable art objects made of bone and antler, could have marked out individuals of high status in Upper Paleolithic society, while other artifacts might have been protective amulets.

It was not until about 23,000 years ago that cave art appeared. When it did, it was concentrated in one main area—the Franco-Cantabrian region of southern France and northern Spain.

JEAN VERTUT

THE VENUS FIGURINES

GÖRAN BURENHULT

Thirty-thousand-year-old fertility symbols, the Venus figurines are among the most fascinating and enigmatic works of art of the Upper Paleolithic period. They bear witness to beliefs in magical power and to advanced ritual ceremonies, to long-term planning and to a clear knowledge of the importance of fertility for survival. These magnificent works present the first glimpse into the world of beliefs of Ice Age hunters and mark the prelude to the use of images as a means of establishing contacts between people and the supernatural.

The appearance of the first human expressions of art is one of the most evident signs of the fact that *Homo sapiens sapiens* possessed mental capacities superior to those of their predecessors—the ability to communicate through symbols. But this abstract world of symbols also reveals the modern human's need of religious and ritual systems, emanating from a changed subsistence and thus a changed social organization.

DR LÍDIO CIPRIANO, 1932/NATIONAL MUSEUM OF ETHNOGRAPHY, STOCKHOLM

Venus figurine made of mammoth ivory from Des Rideaux, at Lespugue, in Haute Garonne, France, dating back to about 23,000 years ago. According to some, this figurine may indicate that steatopygia occurred among Ice Age women. Marija Gimbutas, on the other hand, has suggested that the exaggerated buttocks are a metaphor for the double egg or pregnant belly—a symbol of intensified fertility.

MUSEE DE L'HOMME, PARIS/J. OSTER

It has been suggested that the swelling buttocks of some of the Venus figurines indicate that steatopygia occurred among Ice Age women—that is, an extreme accumulation of fat at the hips which is used as a reserve during times of food shortage. Steatopygia still exists among the females of some traditional societies, including the Bushmen of the Kalahari, among whom it is also considered to have great aesthetic value.

⬤ This well-known Venus figurine of limestone was found in layers of Gravettian age at Willendorf, near Krems, in Austria.
NATURAL HISTORY MUSEUM, VIENNA

One might expect that the first symbols of the Upper Paleolithic big-game hunters would be linked to the most essential part of Ice Age survival—the game animals that constituted the main source of food across much of the European tundras. Instead, the world of images was centered on sexuality and fertility—another vital part of the struggle for survival: securing the continuity of the group.

The oldest known figures consist of carved vulva depictions, which may be linked to the Aurignacian tradition and which date back about 30,000 years. They have been found on rocks at, for example, Abri Blanchard, Abri Castanet, and La Ferrassie, in the Vézère Valley, in the Dordogne. But the famous Venus figurines, which have been found over a very large area, became the most characteristic kind of object in this world of beliefs. They were made out of a number of different kinds of materials, such as mammoth ivory, antler, bone, stone, and clay, and they all share the same standardized design: exaggeratedly swelling breasts and buttocks, and many of them appear to be pregnant. Most of them are naked and equipped with marked genitals. With a few exceptions, their heads are rudimentary and most often shaped only as little knobs, and, likewise, the swelling thighs taper off to poorly marked

feet. The fertility symbolism is evident—the important thing was reproduction, fertility, and pregnancy.

But not all of these little fertility goddesses—perhaps even depictions of the Mother Goddess herself—have been depicted pregnant. American archaeologist Marija Gimbutas has pointed out that probably not even the classic Venus figurines from Willendorf, in Austria, and Lespugue, in France, are pregnant. Breasts and buttocks are the focus of attention, and, moreover, their hands are placed over their breasts. Others, like those from Kostenki, in Russia, and the famous limestone bas-relief from Laussel, in France, have their hands placed over their abdomen and may be interpreted as being pregnant. Consequently, breasts and buttocks are not particularly marked in these figures.

The remarkable Venus tradition belonged primarily to the Gravettian phase, between 29,000 and 22,000 years ago, a period of increasing cold and advancing glaciers and ice sheets. The figurines had a standardized appearance over a distance of more than 2,000 kilometers (1,200 miles), from the Atlantic Ocean in the west to Russia in the east, and this bears witness to far-away contacts and intensive communication between the Upper Paleolithic big-game hunters along the Eurasian ice edge.

⬤ Found at the Upper Paleolithic site of Dolní Věstonice, in Moravia, in the Czech Republic, this Venus of burned clay is about 26,000 years old.
RONALD SHERIDAN/ANCIENT ART AND ARCHITECTURE COLLECTION

⬤ A 22,000-year-old Venus made of serpentine marble (steatite) from Savignano, in northern Italy. Her head has been interpreted as a phallus symbol.
MUSEO NAZIONALE PREHISTORICO EO ETNOGRAFICO "L. PIGORINI", ROME

⬤ This Venus, with both hands placed on her genitals, was found at the famous Upper Paleolithic burial site of Grimaldi, on the French-Italian border.
J. M. LABAT/AUSCAPE

⬤ This beautiful, amber-colored limestone Venus from Sireuil, in the Dordogne, France, dates back to about 23,000 years ago.
MUSEE DES ANTIQUITES NATIONALES, ST-GERMAIN-EN-LAYE/R.M.N.

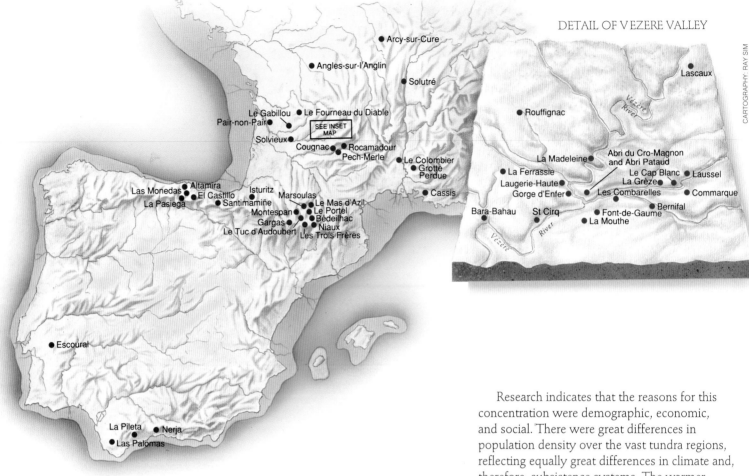

DETAIL OF VÉZÈRE VALLEY

CARTOGRAPHY: RAY SIM

UPPER PALEOLITHIC ART SITES

The major Upper Paleolithic art sites in France and on the Iberian Peninsula. The region along the Dordogne and Vézère rivers, in south central France, shown in the detail, is particularly rich in cave art. Coastlines as they were during the peak of the last glacial, some 18,000 years ago, are indicated.

The Franco-Cantabrian Heartland

At present, we know of more than 200 European caves with Paleolithic paintings and carvings. Of these, no fewer than about 180, or 85 percent, are located in southernmost France and northern Spain, in what is usually called the Franco-Cantabrian heartland. If we look at the spread of cave art outside this area, this concentration becomes even more striking. The remaining part of the Iberian Peninsula has another 20 or so caves with Paleolithic art, while about 10 have been found in Italy and only one in eastern Europe—Kapova Cave, in the Ural Mountains.

The fact that more than 90 percent of cave art is found in France and Spain cannot be explained by the lack of suitable caves in other regions. Very similar areas with cave systems are to be found in many other places in Europe, including the Carpathians, the Alps, and the Urals. Neither can we attribute it to insufficient research or accidental discoveries. During the present century, speleologists have penetrated and mapped most known cave systems in these regions. In the extensive area south of the ice edge, from France in the west all the way to the Urals in Russia in the east, a long series of Upper Paleolithic sites has been found, and almost all have yielded considerable quantities of portable art. This serves to make the concentration of cave art even more surprising.

Research indicates that the reasons for this concentration were demographic, economic, and social. There were great differences in population density over the vast tundra regions, reflecting equally great differences in climate and, therefore, subsistence systems. The warmer climate close to the Atlantic coast in southwestern Europe obviously led to an ecology significantly different from that of the permafrost steppes farther east. People in the southwest had less need to be nomadic, because fish and plant foods were abundant.

This is reflected in the archaeological record by a long series of settlements that can be interpreted as important meeting places and ceremonial centers. Some of these had complex stone structures, some of which may have served ritual purposes. At Solvieux, near Bergerac, in the Dordogne Valley, no fewer than 16 occupation levels dating from about 30,000 to 14,000 years ago have been unearthed. In the Dordogne, four sites dating from the Magdalenian period have yielded 1,400 portable works of art made of bone or antler— 80 percent of those so far known. This clearly indicates that people were concentrating in particular areas.

It has been estimated that about 20,000 years ago, between 2,000 and 3,000 people lived in what is now France, while the population of the rest of Europe, including Spain, cannot have exceeded 10,000. In the heart of the French area, at Les Eyzies, on the Vézère River, between 400 and 600 people lived side by side, at the same time, under the protection of four or five rock shelters known as *abri*. Similar gathering places located much farther apart are known further east—for example, at Dolní Věstonice, in the Czech Republic, and at Sungir and Kostenki, in Russia.

The evidence of increased mass killings of single species of animals also suggests that the population was growing substantially during this period—although it is usually difficult to determine whether the bone deposits in these kill sites are the result of a single hunt or have accumulated over a longer period from regular killings. Some sites in eastern Europe have yielded the remains of close to 1,000 mammoths. At Solutré, in eastern France, a kill site has been found with the bones of perhaps as many as 100,000 horses, which were either driven to their death over the cliffs or herded into the natural trap formed by the narrow pass below to be slaughtered.

A food resource often overlooked previously, salmon fishing, may have drawn people to the Franco-Cantabrian heartland during the Upper Paleolithic period. Images of salmon have long been known in several caves, particularly in the Pyrenees. The known temperature range between 20,000 and 10,000 years ago suggests that the rivers of the Franco-Cantabrian heartland would have provided ideal conditions for salmon. Even as late as the nineteenth century, the rivers in this area were among the best salmon-fishing areas in Europe. People may have settled in one place for longer periods to exploit the regular seasonal migrations and spawning time of salmon, and as the numbers of horses, mammoths, bison, and reindeer declined as a result of mass killings, fishing and food gathering would have become even more important. And, like the meat from mass killings, fish could be dried and stored.

While portable art is clearly associated with the nomadic big-game hunters of the extensive tundra area south of the ice edge, cave art is concentrated in an area that offered much more varied ways of subsistence and therefore encouraged a more settled way of life. It is in the context of these major social changes that we must understand the developing ceremonial world reflected by the remarkable works of art created in the dark of the caves.

⚘ The valley of the Vézère River, an area of unmatched natural beauty and charm, boasts the highest concentration of Paleolithic art in the world. The rich environment provided ideal conditions for human habitation during the last Ice Age, and the area seems to have been an important center for social and ceremonial activities.

A. BORDES/EXPLORER-AUSCAPE

↪ One of the main characteristics of Paleolithic art was the artists' habit of using pre-existing natural formations on walls as an integral part of their images. Most parts of this magnificent horse's head at Commarque, in the Dordogne, including the eye, the ear, and the forehead, are natural irregularities in the rock surface. Only the nostril, the muzzle, and the mouth have been carved by human hands.

↪ *Opposite page*: Paleolithic art in Europe developed over a period of 25,000 years. The earliest works of art consisted primarily of carved vulva images. Cave art appeared about 24,000 years ago, but the true flowering of mural art did not begin until the end of the Upper Paleolithic period, between 20,000 and 12,000 years ago.

AFTER ANDRE LEROI-GOURHAN'S DATINGS OF FRANCO-CANTABRIAN CAVE ART

♀ Depictions of salmon, such as this one from Gorge d'Enfer, in the Dordogne, indicate that fishing may have been an important part of the Magdalenian hunters' subsistence. Interestingly, depictions of purely salt-water species, such as different kinds of flatfish, have been found far within the central areas of the Dordogne and the Pyrenees. This may indicate that people spent parts of the year by the sea.

Encountering the Supernatural

As we have seen, the cave art tradition developed over a very long time and can be linked to social and demographic conditions as well as economic conditions and climate. Most works of cave art, more than 80 percent, were created between 17,000 and 12,000 years ago, and it is easy to forget that we ourselves are closer in time to the heyday of the Magdalenian artists than they were to their ancestors who created the first cave art and the first sculptures more than 30,000 years ago.

To encounter the works of art created by the big-game hunters is to encounter the supernatural. The meeting is in itself a fascinating experience. The almost inaccessible location of cave art is one of its most characteristic features. The images never or very seldom appear at the cave entrances, where people lived. Instead, we have to walk and crawl on our knees and elbows, or even swim

across swift, underground rivers or lakes, to reach the innermost parts of the sanctuaries, sometimes with obvious danger to life. Just imagine the thought of not being able to find your way back! Or of getting stuck in one of the many almost impassable passages! Often the explorer in search of cave art has to crawl backwards for hundreds of meters in galleries that turn out to be dead ends and are too narrow to turn around in. The danger and excitement must have been an essential part of Paleolithic ritual. Lamps fueled by animal fat, with wicks of dry fibers, could have been kept alight for up to five or six hours. In many caves, lamps of stone have been found, some of them elegantly carved, others consisting of simple limestone flags with hollows for the fuel. Never has a skeleton been found of a person who failed to return to the world of the living outside the cave.

Deep inside the least accessible galleries, these Paleolithic artists created their works of art. But even here, not on the obvious surfaces. Instead, they often chose an out-of-the-way location in a narrow passage, not immediately visible from the obvious vantage points.

Clearly, these artists, with their flickering lamps, sought a very special vision of the wall surfaces, one that brought life to the image from the real world they had in their mind's eye—a running horse or a charging bison. Among the irregularities of the rock surface, they searched for natural formations they could use as an integral part of the image. This is a distinctive feature of much cave art, including the magnificent mammoths of Rouffignac and the suggestive lioness of Les Combarelles, whose eyes consist of natural cores of flint embedded in the limestone.

It is often difficult to determine the angle from which the artist intended a particular image to be seen—or rather from which he or she would have seen it. Often it seems that the artist wanted to build in an element of surprise for the observer, who must crouch in an awkward position to see the image come to life. We find it hard to conceive how these artists were able to produce life-size images in correct proportion without being able to stand back and view the work as a whole.

Paleolithic art has sometimes been called "animal art", and it is true that the vast majority of paintings, carvings, and reliefs depict game animals, such as reindeer, horses, mammoths, bison, woolly rhinoceroses, deer, ibex, and aurochs (wild cattle). Occasionally, cave lions, bears, fish, and birds appear. But there are also some images of humans, often dressed in animal hides and equipped with hooves, horns, or other animal attributes. These probably depict shamans during cult ceremonies. There are many images of genitals, mainly vulvas, with or without the female body. In some caves, there are numerous

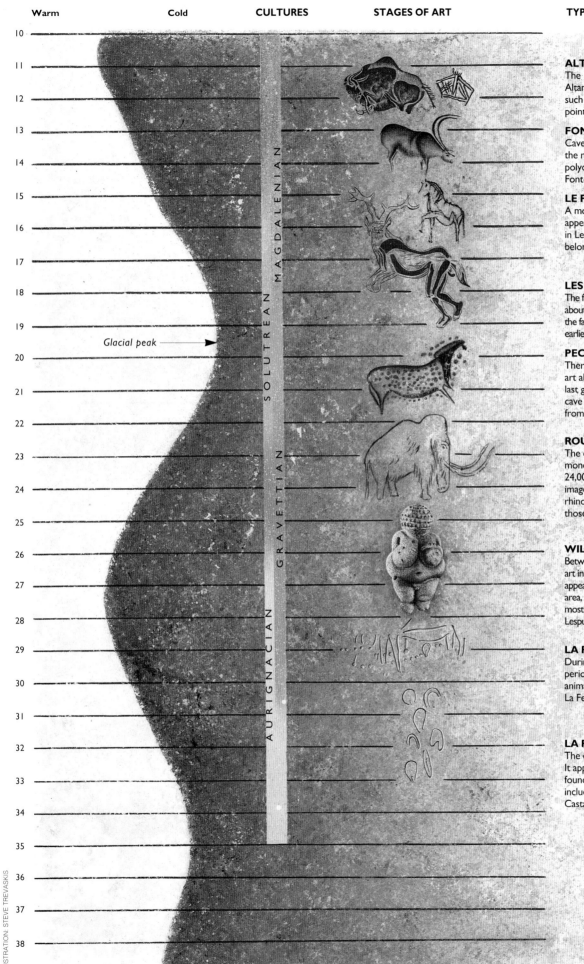

| Warm | Cold | CULTURES | STAGES OF ART | TYPICAL SITES |

10
11
12
13
14
15
16
17
18
19
20
21
22
23
24
25
26
27
28
29
30
31
32
33
34
35
36
37
38
39

Glacial peak ➤

THOUSANDS OF YEARS AGO

CULTURES: MAGDALENIAN · SOLUTREAN · GRAVETTIAN · AURIGNACIAN

ALTAMIRA AND FONT-DE-GAUME
The 12,000-year-old bison paintings in Spain's Altamira cave and the hut-like signs from caves such as Font-de-Gaume mark both the high point and the end of Ice Age art in Europe.

FONT-DE-GAUME
Cave art peaked about 13,000 years ago with the naturalistic carvings and monochrome and polychrome paintings found in such caves as Font-de-Gaume, Niaux, and Les Combarelles.

LE PORTEL
A more mature style of cave art started to appear some 15,000 years ago. The paintings in Le Portel and some of those in Lascaux belong to this period.

LES TROIS FRERES
The first polychrome cave paintings appeared about 18,000 years ago. These early images include the famous sorcerer from Les Trois Frères and the earliest depictions of animals in Lascaux.

PECH-MERLE
There was a marked proliferation of Ice Age art about 20,000 years ago, at the peak of the last glacial. The first evidence of ceremonies in cave sanctuaries, notably in Pech-Merle, dates from this time.

ROUFFIGNAC
The earliest cave art consists of carvings and monochrome paintings created between 24,000 and 22,000 years ago. Many of the images are of mammoths and woolly rhinoceroses, perhaps the most famous being those in the spectacular cave of Rouffignac.

WILLENDORF
Between 28,000 and 24,000 years ago, portable art in the form of carved Venus figurines appeared. These figurines are found over a vast area, from western Europe to Siberia. Among the most famous are the Venuses found at Willendorf, Lespugue, Brassempouy, and Kostenki.

LA FERRASSIE
During the early phases of the Gravettian period, schematic signs and images of archaic animals and vulvas appeared in such caves as La Ferrassie and Arcy-sur-Cure.

LA FERRASSIE
The earliest art consists mainly of vulva signs. It appeared about 33,000 years ago, and is found at a number of sites in the Dordogne, including La Ferrassie, Abri Cellier, and Castanet.

⚤ The main gallery of the famous cave of Lascaux—often called the Hall of Bulls. The cave with the remarkable paintings remained dark and unknown for several millennia, until a day in 1940, when four teenagers happened to discover it.

JEROME CHATIN/GAMMA/PICTURE MEDIA

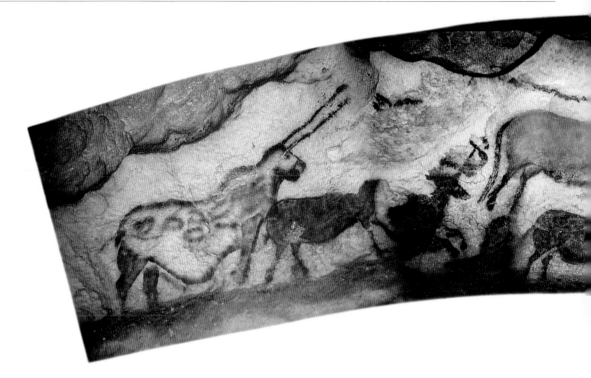

➡ Images of vulvas in the cave of El Castillo, Santander Province, northern Spain. Their exact age is unknown, but they were probably created during the middle of the Magdalenian phase.

JEAN VERTUT

➡ This carving of a human figure dressed as a bison, in Le Gabillou, in the Dordogne, may depict a shaman during a cult ceremony. Others have suggested that these figures with combined human and animal features represent spiritual beings in the form of "protectors" of animals and forests.

JEAN VERTUT

schematic symbols or signs, often in the form of standardized, geometrical figures. Different types of figures predominate in different regions. Schematic symbols, for instance, are much more common in the southern region—the Pyrenees and the caves of southern Spain, such as La Pileta, near Malaga.

Among the most dramatic cave art images are negative hand stencils, created by spraying color through a blowpipe over a hand placed on the rock surface. Many of these hands have mutilated fingers, a feature that has been interpreted differently in different caves. It may be that Paleolithic people deliberately amputated fingers, a practice known among many traditional cultures of recent times. This has a magical or religious purpose, being performed during times of severe

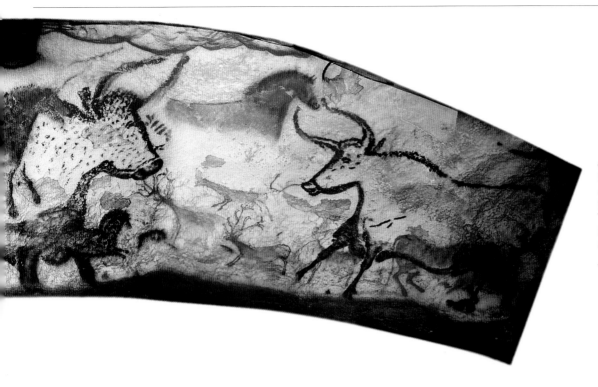

JEAN VERTUT

◄► Panorama of one of the two friezes in the main gallery of Lascaux, considered by many to be the finest Paleolithic paintings found to date. The small herd of galloping black horses is one of the few examples of composition in Paleolithic art.

JEAN VERTUT

◄► A remarkably realistic depiction of a Przewalski horse in Gallerie Noir (the Black Gallery) of the cave of Niaux, southern France. Parts of the image are now covered by white deposits of calcite.

♀ A bison painting in Gallerie Noir, the main gallery of Niaux. This huge sanctuary, situated more than 1,000 meters (3,000 feet) inside the mountain, mainly contains monochrome paintings of horses and bison.

adversity to appease the spirits. But many of the mutilated hands, such as those in the "cave of a hundred mutilated hands" at Gargas, in the Pyrenees, have been interpreted as depicting unintentional injuries such as frostbite, and it has also been suggested that the fingers may have been bent in a sort of sign language.

The range of images in cave art differs from region to region. Many caves have a unique character, and this must clearly be taken into account in any attempt to interpret the different groups of images. In certain caves, such as Rouffignac, images of mammoths and woolly rhinoceroses predominate. In others, such as Niaux and Lascaux, most images are of horses, aurochs, and bison.

The paint used by Paleolithic artists was made of pulverized rock—mainly iron oxide, which gives the red color, and manganese oxide, which gives the black—mixed with animal fat. Paintbrushes of different kinds and blowpipes have been found in numerous caves. In many cases, such as in Lascaux, holes have been found in the cave floor from scaffolding erected to enable the artists to reach suitable surfaces further up on the walls or on the roof of the cave. This, too, strongly suggests a systematically performed cult.

One of the great areas of debate in the interpretation of cave art has been whether the different images should be seen as parts of compositions, or whether each constitutes an individual, self-contained ritual. A problem is posed by the fact that there are many instances of images painted or carved over an earlier image. These superimposed images can be interpreted in a number of different ways. The new image may

MUSEUM FÜR VOR- UND FRÜHGESCHICHTE/BILDARCHIV PREUSSISCHER KULTURBESITZ

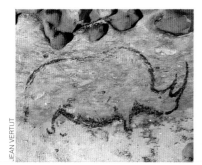

JEAN VERTUT

☝ Depictions of the mysterious woolly rhinoceros are rare and limited to the very earliest phases of Paleolithic art. This one is from the cave of Rouffignac, in the Dordogne.

♀ The spectacular cave of Rouffignac is dominated by very early monochrome paintings of mammoths and woolly rhinoceroses. The strange formations in the rock surface are natural cores of flint embedded in the limestone.

have been placed over the old one to make use of the existing supernatural power or, equally likely, to destroy it. Alternatively, the earlier image may have been regarded as unimportant and only happened to be at the site of a later ceremony. The same difficulties apply when trying to interpret the many puzzling signs and symbols which most often appear on or alongside the animals.

The animals are depicted in greatly varying sizes, even on the same section of rock surface, and are placed among each other in a seemingly formless muddle, with no perspective or horizon line. With the notable exception of the famous galloping black horses of Lascaux, it would seem that the concept of composition, in a traditional artistic sense, cannot be applied to Paleolithic art. However, modern research has revealed that cave art reflects a much more sophisticated understanding and use of symbolism than previously thought to be possible among the hunters of the Upper Paleolithic.

Interpretations and Reinterpretations

As is always the case with archaeological research, interpretations of cave art have changed as new findings have emerged. For a long time, Paleolithic art was thought to reflect the big-game hunters' need for decoration and beauty in their everyday surroundings—art for art's sake. No one was inclined to believe that "the primitive savage" would have had a religious or ceremonial life. Little attention was paid to the fact that almost none of the works of art were found in settlements and almost all were located in remote parts of caves.

It was not until the beginning of the twentieth century, when ethnographic studies made the world aware of the remarkable complexity and variety of beliefs that exist within traditional cultures, that researchers began to realize that the cave images probably had a more profound significance. The Australian Aborigines in particular excited much interest. Their rock paintings were shown to be ceremonial expressions of a complex

JEAN VERTUT

CENTRE NATIONAL DE PREHISTOIRE, PERIGUEUX, FRANCE

mythology. For the first time, the concept of totemism was discussed. This refers to a system of social organization based on tribes or clans in which each tribe or clan is distinguished by a totem—an object from the natural world, most often an animal—with which it considers itself to have a special, usually a blood, relationship.

The researcher who dominated the discussion of Paleolithic cave art from the 1930s to the 1950s was Abbé Breuil. He strongly supported the then current view that cave art was an expression of sympathetic hunting magic: by depicting the game animal and then injuring it symbolically by placing a feather-like symbol over it, supernatural powers were released and successful hunting was assured. This interpretation, however, left many aspects of the art unexplained.

First, why did the artists often depict hunting weapons as feather-like signs, particularly since most of these signs were placed outside the images of the game animals? Second, why do the most common game animals very seldom appear in cave art? This applies particularly to reindeer, which, judging by the enormous numbers of bones found in the settlement layers throughout this region, must have been one of the main sources of food during the Magdalenian period. Nor does it fully explain the dominating element of sexual symbolism in cave art, even if the many images of seemingly pregnant animals can be linked to the concept of fertility—perhaps within both the clan and the species.

Modern research began with André Leroi-Gourhan, whose important studies in the 1960s focused on the placing of the different images and their relationships to each other. By means of comprehensive statistical analysis, he revealed previously unsuspected patterns.

⊙ This historic photograph records the first investigation of Lascaux, in 1940. Standing third from right is the legendary cave art researcher Abbé Breuil. The boys sitting on the floor are two of those who discovered the cave.

PECH-MERLE:
A 20,000-YEAR-OLD SANCTUARY

GÖRAN BURENHULT

🌣 Thanks to its many stalagmites and stalactites, the huge cave of Pech-Merle, near Cahors, in Lot, France, is one of the most beautiful caves with cave art. Its famous dotted horses, painted on a fallen rock, occupy a prominent position. There is evidence that ceremonies took place in these unreal surroundings.

DEEP INSIDE THE CAVES of the Franco-Cantabrian region, Stone Age hunters left behind a remarkable testimony to their cult ceremonies, and to the magical beliefs and complex social systems that gave rise to them. What took place when these images were created is one of the most fascinating issues in the study of the Paleolithic period.

Among the many such caves known, a small number are exceptional, partly because of their size, and partly because of the way in which the artists used the natural features of the cave walls to enhance their images. They include such classic caves as Lascaux, Font-de-Gaume, and Rouffignac, in the Dordogne region; Niaux, in the Pyrenees; and Pech-Merle, near Cahors, in Lot, in southwestern France. The evidence from a number of caves strongly suggests that these magnificent underground halls were the site of recurring ceremonies—probably rites of passage—and that the images were created successively, never on just one occasion. Clearly, such ritual gathering places were an important part of Stone Age people's encounters with the supernatural.

Pech-Merle is one of the oldest known caves containing Paleolithic art. In contrast to most of the other caves, it is a dripstone cave, its forests of stalagmites and stalactites making it one of the most beautiful underground galleries. The startling paintings of dotted horses for which it is famous are prominently displayed in a huge hall, painted on a fallen rock surrounded by a large flat area that might have been used for dances and ceremonies.

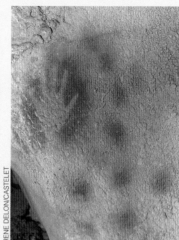

◄❂ I was here! The personal stamp of those who participated in the ceremonies, the hand stencils in Pech-Merle are eloquent evidence that rites of passage once took place here.

⚲ The footprints left behind in Pech-Merle, as in many other Paleolithic caves, are our closest and most immediate point of contact with the people who performed their cult ceremonies in the depth of the caves more than 20,000 years ago.

With the help of infrared light, we now know how these paintings were created. The red and black dots consist of different mixtures of paint and were placed on the horses on different occasions. The first figure represented a red fish and was placed slightly to the right of center on the rock surface. The outline of the first horse was then painted. Its head is inspired by the contour of the rock but is small and rudimentary—painted, with the neck, in black. The red and black dots were then sprayed onto the body through a blowpipe. When the body outline had been created, additional dots were placed outside the animal. The second horse was then created in the same way. Finally, hand stencils were placed on the rock, their obvious message being: I was here.

⚡ The two dotted horses for which Pech-Merle is famous are monochrome, and represent a rather early stage of Paleolithic art. Analyses of the dots have revealed important information about the cult ceremonies that lie behind the paintings—each dot was formed from a different mixture of paint, indicating that they were created on different occasions.

➥ Several monochrome paintings of the now extinct woolly mammoth have been found in secluded parts of the cave of Pech-Merle. These belong to the very earliest stages of cave art, and add to the mysteriousness of this remarkable underground gallery.

↪ The famous sorcerer from Les Trois Frères, Ariège, southern France. About 75 centimeters (30 inches) high, the image is partly painted and partly carved and has combined human, horse, deer, bird, and bear features. It probably depicts a shaman. The sketch was made by Abbé Breuil.

⚲ Two remarkably well-preserved bison sculptures of clay from Le Tuc d'Audoubert, southern France. A number of footprints of children, forming circular dance patterns around a group of sculptured clay phalluses, have been found in an adjoining chamber.

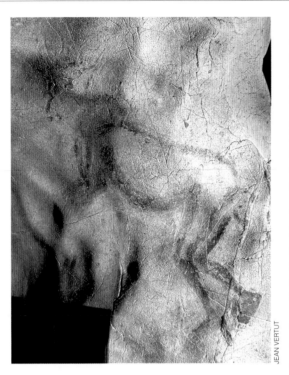

JEAN VERTUT

It was established that the figures in all Paleolithic caves appear in a dualistic relationship, with some species always appearing together, while others are never depicted on the same wall. More than half of the animal images depict horses and bison, two of the species that are always shown together.

The location of the images in the caves also shows a remarkable pattern. About 90 percent of all images of bison, aurochs, and horses appear in the central sanctuaries or main galleries, while all other animals are relegated to other, less prominent, locations in the caves.

CHARLES ALENARS/EXPLORER-AUSCAPE

Leroi-Gourhan interpreted the pairing of the animals as representing the relationship between masculine and feminine. In doing so, he also took into account the placing of the images in relation to the genital and schematic figures. He considered that horses were male symbols, while bison, aurochs, and mammoths were female symbols. Interestingly, another researcher, Annette Laming, came to the same conclusion independently at about the same time, except that she reversed the sexual symbolism, seeing the horses as female.

Details of Leroi-Gourhan's interpretations have been strongly criticized, but there is no doubt that his work raised a new set of questions and changed forever our perception of Paleolithic cave art. It is now accepted that this art was part of a deliberate and complex ritual system that was itself an integral part of the Paleolithic world of belief.

Ceremonies for Survival

Our new knowledge of the social and economic background to the rise of Paleolithic art does not, however, satisfactorily explain the individual peculiarities of the various groups of images, with their elements of sexual symbolism, fertility cult, hunting magic, shamanism, and totemism. The total picture is far too complex for a single explanation, and much of the substance of the rituals no doubt changed during the many thousands of years the cave art tradition persisted. However, recent research has revealed that many caves were used as ceremonial gathering places. A number of pieces of evidence clearly point to this.

Images of humans are comparatively rare in cave art, but a striking number of them combine human and animal features, and often the features of several animals. The most famous example is the "sorcerer" from Les Trois Frères, in the Pyrenees, a male figure with the antlers of a stag, a nose like the beak of a bird of prey, and staring, owl-like eyes. The figure also has a horse's tail and unnaturally short forelimbs ending in bear-like paws, with claws. His genitals are abnormally placed, under the tail. This strangely hunched, or crouched, figure seems to be engaged in a ceremonial dance.

Shamanism is the dominant element in the religion of most known arctic and subarctic hunter-gatherers, including the present-day Inuit (or Eskimos) and the reindeer hunters of north-eastern Asia. Shamans are men or women who have a special relationship with the spiritual world and are called upon in times of sickness and other troubles to mediate with the spirits on the community's behalf. For example, when a shortage of game animals threatens the community's survival, the shaman enters a trance and sends out his or her soul to find out why the spirit who controls the animals is withholding them, and to persuade the spirit to send more animals. Shamans are also called upon to cure sickness (which in many such societies is believed to result from the breaking of a taboo rather than from natural causes). It seems likely that similar beliefs were important to the big-game hunters of the Ice Age, and that shamans—or some equivalent—may have conducted ceremonies in the caves. What might these ceremonies have been?

Discussions of cave art have long been centered on the content and meaning of the images themselves, and in the process some important evidence indicating that ceremonial dance and other cult ceremonies took place inside the caves has been largely overlooked. For understandable reasons, this evidence has survived at only a few sites. In their eagerness to study paintings or carvings in a newly discovered cave, early researchers walked around on the moist and often soft floor surface, unwittingly destroying for all time the unique information that had remained untouched for tens of thousands of years: the footprints of the people who performed their ceremonies in the sanctuaries. A few sites where such evidence has been preserved have been known for a long time. The classic example is the cave of Le Tuc d'Audoubert, known for its well-preserved bison modeled from clay, where the footprints of six people have been found in an adjacent chamber. They are all those of children, and six rows of footprints reveal a distinct dance pattern.

In recent years, a number of cave chambers with well-preserved Paleolithic footprints have been discovered. The most spectacular example is in a previously unknown section of the big cave of Niaux, in the Pyrenees. More than 1,000 meters (3,000 feet) farther into the mountain than the famous sanctuary known as Gallerie Noir, with its black outline drawings of horses and bison, there are more than 500 footprints, the largest number so far discovered in any cave. The way in is extremely difficult, as three large underground lakes must first be negotiated.

The footprints have proved to be those of children between 13 and 15 years old. But, as in all known caves where footprints have survived, they are mingled with the tracks of adults. Flutes and the remains of what may have been other musical instruments have been found in many caves, indicating that the ceremonial dancing was accompanied by music.

Abbé Breuil, André Leroi-Gourhan, and others had earlier suggested that at least some Paleolithic cave art could be related to initiation rites of different kinds, but this was overshadowed by attempts to unlock the meaning of the images themselves. Within all traditional cultures, rites of passage are a crucial part of ritual and ceremonial life. They are related to birth, puberty, marriage,

JEAN VERTUT

☝ Deep inside the cave of Niaux, more than 500 footprints of 13 to 15-year-old children, as well as those of adults, have been found, indicating that ceremonies once took place here.

♀ The numerous rock shelters (or *abri*) in the Dordogne area were ideal dwelling places for people during the Paleolithic period, providing excellent protection from the elements.

GORAN BURENHULT

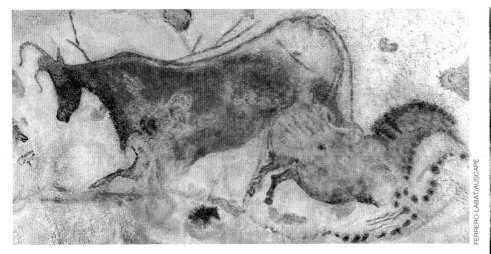

FERRERO-LABAT/AUSCAPE

♦ Polychrome paintings of a cow and a horse in one of the main friezes of the famous cave of Lascaux, in the Dordogne.

and death. Male initiation rites—when young boys, under the direction of a master, are initiated into the mysteries of the adult world—are often associated with isolation, darkness, and frightening experiences. Painful tests of manhood, such as tattooing and, sometimes, circumcision, are often an important element of these prolonged ceremonies. Dancing often accompanies such rituals, and among many traditional peoples today, including Australian Aborigines and the Bushmen of southern Africa, rock art is directly related to puberty rites of this kind. Nearly always, the rites are also used to impart knowledge of the mythological world. Animals play an important part in the mythology of most traditional peoples, particularly within totemistic societies, and often serve as sexual and fertility symbols.

As is the case with many archaeological findings, we may never understand the precise significance of cave art, with its many different images. Mythological symbols cannot simply be read like a book. Nevertheless, we are closer than ever before to understanding its function within Paleolithic society. The images in the caves are unique social documents, a kind of prehistoric encyclopedia, in which the different entries together reflect the need for communication, identification, and cohesion within a rapidly expanding and changing society. Contemporary evidence of ceremonial gathering places in the open as well as in caves suggests that some communities in this period had developed more accessible forms of ritual. Perhaps the most famous is the ceremonial center at Mezhirich, southeast of Kiev, in the Ukraine, built of 70 tonnes (almost 70 tons) of mammoth bones from 200 animals.

Art and ritual as forms of human expression would seem to represent one of the key ways in which people came to terms with a new, more demanding, and socially more complex way of life. The world of beliefs, and the ceremonies and rituals this engendered, were a means of binding the society together, protecting it, and preserving its values—ultimately, a strategy for survival.

Challenged only by Altamira, Lascaux cave contains some of the finest examples of polychrome painting yet discovered. These paintings represent the peak of the 20,000-year-old tradition of Ice Age art in Europe, a tradition that died out about 12,000 years ago.

COSQUER CAVE:
AN ANCIENT SUNKEN GALLERY

JEAN CLOTTES AND JEAN COURTIN

E ARLY IN SEPTEMBER 1991, professional undersea diver Henri Cosquer informed the French Ministry of Culture that he had discovered prehistoric paintings and engravings in a cave deep under the sea off Cape Morgiou, near Marseilles. At about the same time, three amateur divers, who had probably heard about the discovery, swam into the cave, became lost in its murky galleries, and drowned when their air supply ran out.

☝ Henri Cosquer, who discovered the cave, beside a large bison painted black, its head shown in three-quarter view while the horns are represented frontally and the body in profile.

☞ The entrance to Cosquer Cave lies at the base of a limestone cliff, 37 meters (120 feet) below sea level, at Cape Morgiou, between Marseilles and Cassis, in the south of France.

Four black horses were painted over numerous finger tracings dating from an earlier period. An ibex, its horns depicted from the front while its body is in profile, and many other lines were then engraved over the horses (middle of the photograph).

The Ministry of Culture responded swiftly to these events. With the help of Henri Cosquer, whose name was given to the cave, it organized a series of dives from 16 to 25 September. The other members of the expedition were combat divers from the French navy and Jean Courtin. We examined the cave closely, took many photographs, collected samples for analysis, and made a preliminary survey of the galleries. The entrance was later blocked with rock and railings to secure the cave and its contents and to deter would-be explorers.

Hidden Chambers under the Sea

The tiny cave entrance is at the bottom of a cliff, 37 meters (120 feet) under the surface of the Mediterranean Sea. A narrow passage slopes upwards for 160 meters (525 feet), opening into several huge chambers. Only the upper half of the chambers is above sea level, and it is here that a number of wall paintings and engravings were found.

The cave opening was flooded at the end of the last Ice Age, when the sea level rose 120 meters (400 feet)—probably about 10,500 years ago. The lower part of the main chamber must have remained above water for a long time, because it contains a number of large stalagmites, which could not otherwise have formed. Cosquer Cave is only one of a number of caves in the area—some of them

These large stalagmites in the lower part of the main chamber are now entirely underwater. As calcite cannot deposit under such conditions, this proves that the chamber was free of water for millennia before it was flooded.

⬆ One of the many stenciled hands discovered on the walls of the cave. This one and several others are exceptional in showing part of the forearm. Like the finger tracings, these stenciled hands are several thousands of years older than the animal paintings and engravings.

known for a long time—that could have sheltered groups of people who were living by the sea in Paleolithic times.

There were no traces of art in the long gallery leading up to the chamber. Any images on its walls would long since have been destroyed by the salt water, which has deeply corroded the limestone walls. The same applies to the flooded part of the main chamber.

Where the cave is above water, it expands into a chamber 50 meters by 60 meters (165 feet by 200 feet). The ground is covered with stalagmites and huge fallen rocks. There are numerous charcoal fragments scattered about, many of them covered with calcite (the mineral from which stalagmites are formed).

Two small hearths, about 30 centimeters (12 inches) in diameter, may have been used to light the cave, as no bones, flints, or other artifacts were discovered. This is a place where people came but did not stay long.

A Unique Gallery

The cave has not yet been fully surveyed, and many images undoubtedly remain to be discovered. So far, the following have been recorded. On the walls and parts of the roof, there are paintings of at least 23 animals. Two are indeterminate (not unusual in cave art), but all the others are recognizable. They include 10 horses, 5 bison, an ibex, a red deer, and the head of a cave lion. There are also three paintings

of the extinct great auk (*Alca impennis*), a flightless relative of the razorbill, which was hunted to extinction during the nineteenth century—the only images of these birds known in Paleolithic art.

Among the many engravings, there are 21 animals: 4 horses, 2 bison, 6 ibexes, 5 chamois, 2 seals, and two that can't be determined. Long, spear-like lines with a barbed top have been engraved over the top of a number of them. In addition, thousands of lines crisscross the walls, many of them obviously traced or scraped by human fingers.

There are also 26 negative hand stencils on the walls and calcite draperies (wide, thin sheets of stalactites), 19 black and 7 red. (These were created by placing

➥ This stag was painted on the roof of a very low passage, where there are only 40 centimeters (16 inches) between the roof and the floor, so the artist must have lain on his back. An ibex and two horses were also painted on the same ceiling. Bright white patches of calcite and a few stalactites have developed in this area and have covered parts of the animals.

One of the three black great auks—the only images of these birds known in an Upper Paleolithic cave. Like all the other animal paintings and engravings in this cave, they can be dated to between 18,000 and 19,000 years ago. The images of marine creatures—seals, fish, and possibly jellyfish or squid, as well as the auks—are one of the unique features of Cosquer Cave.

a hand on the wall and outlining the shape with paint blown through a blowpipe.) Most have incomplete fingers, as in the cave of Gargas, in the Pyrenees. The most likely explanation for this is that the fingers were bent in a sort of sign language.

As is to be expected, the images are very weathered. The lines of the paintings are eroded on the sides, and many are partly covered with calcite, which deposits slowly over decades. A random sample of charcoal taken from the ground was radiocarbon-dated at 16,490 BC plus or minus 440 years—that is, about

18,500 years old. This makes Cosquer Cave some 15 centuries older than Lascaux. Many other charcoal fragments were identified as belonging to two species of pine known to have grown in the area during the last Ice Age (*Pinus silvestris* and *Pinus nigra*), providing further confirmation of the date.

The conventions the artists followed in depicting the animals— showing the horns and antlers front on, when the bodies are drawn in profile; always omitting the hoofs; the stiff postures, with shortened, stick-like legs—are fully consistent with the radiocarbon date. The

Provence painters who came to this cave used the same artistic conventions as those who painted the cave of Ebbou, in the Ardèche Valley, about 150 kilometers (90 miles) to the northwest.

Cosquer Cave is the first cave containing mural art to be found in Provence. It is a find of great significance, adding much to our knowledge of Paleolithic art. The images are abundant and varied, and the seals and great auks are unique. Our only regret is that the sea, which has preserved the cave over millennia, has also destroyed so much of what it once contained.

SPREADING THROUGHOUT THE GLOBE

50,000 YEARS AGO – 10,000 YEARS AGO

Towards New Continents

GÖRAN BURENHULT

WE KNOW THAT MODERN humans first appeared in Africa between 200,000 and 150,000 years ago. From there they spread outward to the rest of the continent, to Europe, and to parts of Asia. Southwest Asia seems to have provided a natural passage for these pioneers.

Human remains have been found in the Levantine area dating to about 100,000 years ago, whereas Europe was first populated by *Homo sapiens sapiens* only about 40,000 years ago. These modern humans spread into unknown territory slowly but steadily. It was never a question of deliberate migration. Scattered groups extended their hunting grounds by only a few kilometers (2 or 3 miles) per generation, but this was enough for them to populate the world in some tens of thousands of years.

◄● Between 50,000 and 10,000 years ago, anatomically modern humans spread across the world. In pursuit of game, people gradually settled the vast and previously uninhabited tundras of Siberia and North America. Reindeer and, in North America, caribou were the favored game animals of these early pioneers.

◊ An Upper Paleolithic Venus figurine from southern Siberia.
MUSEE DE L'HOMME, PARIS/J. OSTER

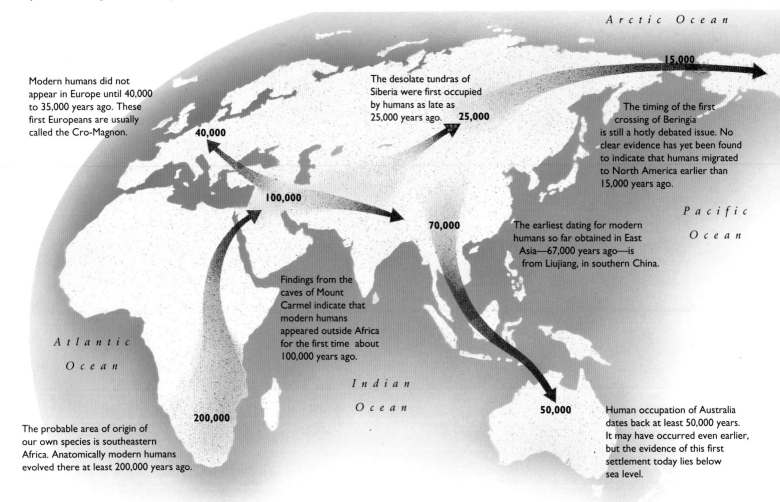

Arctic Ocean

15,000

Modern humans did not appear in Europe until 40,000 to 35,000 years ago. These first Europeans are usually called the Cro-Magnon.

The desolate tundras of Siberia were first occupied by humans as late as 25,000 years ago. **25,000**

The timing of the first crossing of Beringia is still a hotly debated issue. No clear evidence has yet been found to indicate that humans migrated to North America earlier than 15,000 years ago.

40,000

100,000

70,000

Pacific Ocean

The earliest dating for modern humans so far obtained in East Asia—67,000 years ago—is from Liujiang, in southern China.

Atlantic Ocean

Findings from the caves of Mount Carmel indicate that modern humans appeared outside Africa for the first time about 100,000 years ago.

Indian Ocean

200,000

The probable area of origin of our own species is southeastern Africa. Anatomically modern humans evolved there at least 200,000 years ago.

50,000

Human occupation of Australia dates back at least 50,000 years. It may have occurred even earlier, but the evidence of this first settlement today lies below sea level.

CARTOGRAPHY: RAY SIM

THE SPREADING OF MODERN HUMANS

About 100,000 years ago, anatomically modern humans began to spread outside Africa. The arrows indicate their assumed routes of expansion, and approximate dates of arrival are given.

The characteristics these modern humans acquired were to influence cultural evolution throughout the world. They were remarkably adaptable, which meant that they could inhabit areas that had been inaccessible to earlier hominids. For the first time, people settled in the arctic regions of Eurasia, adapting to the most difficult ecology on Earth. Ten to fifteen thousand years before Cro-Magnon humans entered Europe, their cousins in Southeast Asia had crossed 90 kilometers (56 miles) of open water by some form of sea-craft and reached present-day Australia and New Guinea. Some millennia later, groups of people took advantage of the low sea level during the last glacial to walk or paddle across present-day Bering Strait, entering the continent of North America. In the space of a few tens of thousands of years, modern humans opened up new worlds—in the north, the northeast, and the southeast.

Asian Anomalies

While cultural evolution in western Asia generally corresponded with that in Europe, East Asia developed characteristics of its own. Human fossils found there, dated to between 200,000 and 100,000 years ago—the period during which the

Neanderthals were evolving—look very different from those found in the west. As American anthropologist Richard Klein says, "At a time before 50,000–40,000 years ago when western Asia was variably occupied by Neanderthals perhaps derived from Europe or by very early moderns arguably derived from Africa, eastern Asia seems to have been occupied by a distinctive human type(s) that was neither Neanderthal nor modern".

The lack of modern excavations makes this period in East Asia difficult to evaluate. We have known for a long time that the blade tools that appeared in Europe with *Homo sapiens sapiens* were apparently not introduced or developed in East Asia. Instead, the flake and chopper tools used by *Homo erectus* survived there for more than 300,000 years, to as late as about 10,000 BC. Correspondingly, there seemed to be no evidence in eastern Eurasia of the cultural developments that took place in Europe during the Upper Paleolithic period—a wider and more sophisticated use of antler and bone, the rise of art, and evidence of a rich ritual life, with complex burial practices.

A number of important new finds indicate, however, that modern humans who had developed advanced stone and bone tools and a complex ritual and artistic life settled the southern, eastern, and southeastern parts of Asia during the very early phases of the Upper Paleolithic period. The remarkable fact that *Homo sapiens sapiens* populated Australia and New Guinea at least 50,000 years ago certainly points to this, but this is not the only evidence. Fossils of modern humans found at Liujiang, in China, have been dated to 67,000 years ago. At Batadomba lena, a cave in the southwestern part of Sri Lanka, settlement layers dating back to about 29,000 years ago have yielded the remains of modern humans, together with small, technically sophisticated stone tools (so-called geometric microliths) and bone tools. Apparently, sophisticated stone tools existed in Southeast Asia, but they were not widespread and not as standardized as those found further west. Because they existed side by side with more traditional tools, it would appear that they were developed locally. Consequently, the big, as yet unanswered, question is why *Homo sapiens sapiens* took new technology with them to the west but not to the east.

Between 35,000 and 20,000 years ago, Upper Paleolithic big-game hunters spread over the vast tundras of northeastern Siberia for the first time and soon became the first humans to set foot in America. Siberian stone tools differed from their contemporary European equivalents, being made from different raw materials and influenced by the blade cultures of the west and the flake cultures of the southeast. As time went on, this Siberian cultural tradition spread south and east to Mongolia, China, Korea, and Japan.

During the last glacial, northeastern Siberia had such low levels of rain and snow that ice sheets and glaciers like those in northern Europe never formed. The hunters who inhabited these immense, frozen, and treeless expanses had to cover vast territories in pursuit of game and other food. There were few caves and rock shelters for protection, so they had to build huts that could withstand the severe cold. They also needed effective fireplaces that would allow them to maintain fires almost continuously, and close-fitting clothes of fur and hide. Antler and bone implements were crucial aids to these enterprises. The mammoth became a sought-after game animal, because it provided food, hides, and large quantities of bones that could be used as fuel, building material, and tools.

Towards New Horizons

Some time between 50,000 and 40,000 years ago, groups of people in today's Indonesia became the first seafarers, paddling some 90 kilometers (56 miles) in canoes or on rafts across the Sunda Strait to present-day Australia and New Guinea. The lack of reliably dated material in Southeast Asia still makes it difficult to chart the appearance of modern humans in this region in any detail. The best-documented material has been found in

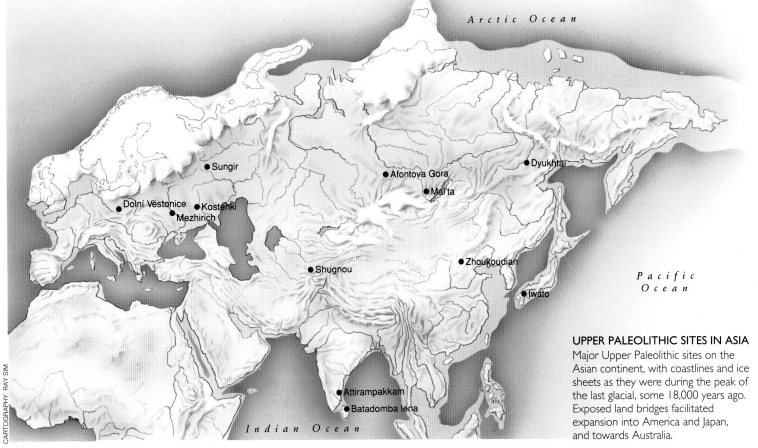

UPPER PALEOLITHIC SITES IN ASIA
Major Upper Paleolithic sites on the Asian continent, with coastlines and ice sheets as they were during the peak of the last glacial, some 18,000 years ago. Exposed land bridges facilitated expansion into America and Japan, and towards Australia.

CARTOGRAPHY: RAY SIM

125

Australia, and we now know that *Homo sapiens sapiens* had reached Tasmania, the southernmost part of the continent, before 30,000 years ago.

In tracing the stone tool cultures of Southeast Asia during the Upper Paleolithic period, two sites in Vietnam have long been important: Son Vi and Hoa-Binh. Modern excavations and radiocarbon datings have confirmed that the Sonviian tradition is the older of the two, suggesting that it existed between 18,000 and 11,000 years ago. The Hoabinhian tradition, which appeared about 14,000 years ago, became much more widespread, extending south to Sumatra and east to the Philippines. It survived in many different forms well into the Neolithic period. Pottery from Spirit Cave, in Thailand, for example, has been dated to

View from inside one of the Niah Caves, situated in the Gunung Subis limestone massif, in Sarawak, East Malaysia. This famous and spectacular site was used both for habitation and burial, and has yielded a human skull believed to be about 40,000 years old.

HANS HOFER/APA PHOTO AGENCY SIIN

PETER BELLWOOD

Excavation at the rock shelter of Hagop Bilo, one of the Baturong sites, in Sabah, East Malaysia. The site was occupied between 17,000 and 12,000 years ago.

this period, and in Vietnam, the bearers of this tradition were making pottery as early as 8000 BC.

The finds at Son Vi and Hoa-Binh are clearly much too recent to shed any light on the first Australians. However, newly found sites in Southeast Asia dated to earlier than 25,000 years ago may in time tell us much more about cultural development in this part of the world during the Upper Paleolithic period. Lang Rong Rien, in southern Thailand, is a particularly important site, the tools in its oldest layers dating back to about 40,000 years ago. Other important sites are Leang Burung and Wallanae River, in South Sulawesi, Indonesia; Tabon Cave, on the island of Palawan, and Cagayan Valley, in Luzon, both in the Philippines; Tingkayu, in Sabah; and Niah Cave, in Sarawak, East Malaysia. (See the feature *Tools and Cultures in Late Paleolithic Southeast Asia*.)

The closest fossils that could possibly be the ancestors of the Australian Aborigines and the Papuans of New Guinea are the classic skulls found at Ngandong and Wajak, in Java, Indonesia. These are almost certainly more than 60,000 years old, although they cannot yet be accurately dated. On this evidence, it seems likely that further finds of modern human fossils, considerably older than

those so far discovered, will soon be made in southern Asia.

At certain times during the last Ice Age (the Upper Pleistocene period, which extended from about 115,000 years ago to about 10,000 years ago), the sea level dropped as much as 120 meters (400 feet) as large amounts of water were frozen in the immense land glaciers in the north. During such periods, the area that today comprises Australia, New Guinea, and the Sahul Shelf was exposed as one landmass, known as Sahul or Greater Australia. Water-craft would still have been needed to cross the narrow straits separating the Sunda Shelf (of which Java, Sumatra, and Southeast Asia formed part) from Sahul.

⚭ Modern humans reached the steaming jungles of Southeast Asia at least 60,000 to 50,000 years ago. Fossil finds of early settlers in this region are, however, still very few.

TOOLS AND CULTURES IN LATE PALEOLITHIC SOUTHEAST ASIA

IAN C. GLOVER

IN THE 1940s, the American prehistorian Hallam Movius characterized the Paleolithic cultures of Southeast Asia as being a part of the "East Asian Chopper and Chopping Tool Complex", a tradition dominated by large flint-core tools showing little refinement and few specialized types. This tradition was thought to have survived throughout the Middle and Upper Pleistocene periods and to have persisted, with little change, into the early Holocene period as the Hoabhinian culture, which was largely replaced from 4000 BC by Neolithic cultures brought by intrusive southern Mongoloid populations expanding into the region from South China.

Recent excavations in several parts of Southeast Asia have shown that there was much greater variability, change, and specialization in the stone tool assemblages of the late Upper Pleistocene than was previously appreciated, and this period now promises to overthrow many previously held assumptions about cultural adaptations and processes in Southeast Asia. However, very little is yet known about the late Upper Pleistocene cultures of this part of the world.

IAN C. GLOVER

⊛ Excavating in Leang Burung 2.

⊛ The Tingkayu Plain, in Sabah, was covered by a lake from 28,000 to 18,000 years ago, and hunters left many bifacially flaked chert points by its shores.

⊛ In South Sulawesi also, excavations in 1975 revealed a Levalloisian point and blade industry at the rock shelter site of Leang Burung 2 (Bird Cave 2) which can be dated to between 30,000 and 19,000 years ago. The abundant animal remains from the cave show that the environment was little different from that of today. The rich flake assemblage includes some fine points with prepared platforms, and blades, scrapers, and flakes with edge gloss. The few cores confirm a knowledge of Levalloisian technology.
IAN C. GLOVER

☞ Hagop Bilo, a rock shelter in the Baturong limestone massif in Sabah, in the Malaysian part of the island of Borneo, was occupied by humans some 17,000 to 12,000 years ago and shows a typical island South East Asian Late Stone Age flake and blade industry. Flakes with a silica gloss are known, together with remains of modern animals including pigs, deer, monkeys, rats, snakes, lizards, tortoises, porcupines, and some birds, as well as three species of freshwater gastropods.

♀ Tabon Cave, on the island of Palawan, in the Philippines, has long been known for its long sequence through the Late Pleistocene period. Here, too, the assemblage is dominated by a flake tradition, although the coarse nature of the quartzite used limited the range of specialized tool types in comparison with other sites further south in the islands of Southeast Asia.

PETER BELLWOOD

PETER BELLWOOD

PETER BELLWOOD

⚓ Vietnam's Stone Age prehistory has been more extensively researched than that of any other Southeast Asian country, and yet a previously totally unknown Levalloisian flake industry dated to before 23,000 years ago has recently been found at Nguom Cave, in the limestone mountains of North Vietnam's Bac Thai Province, below a Hoabhinian assemblage, from which it was separated by layers of rock fall and breccia.

IAN C. GLOVER

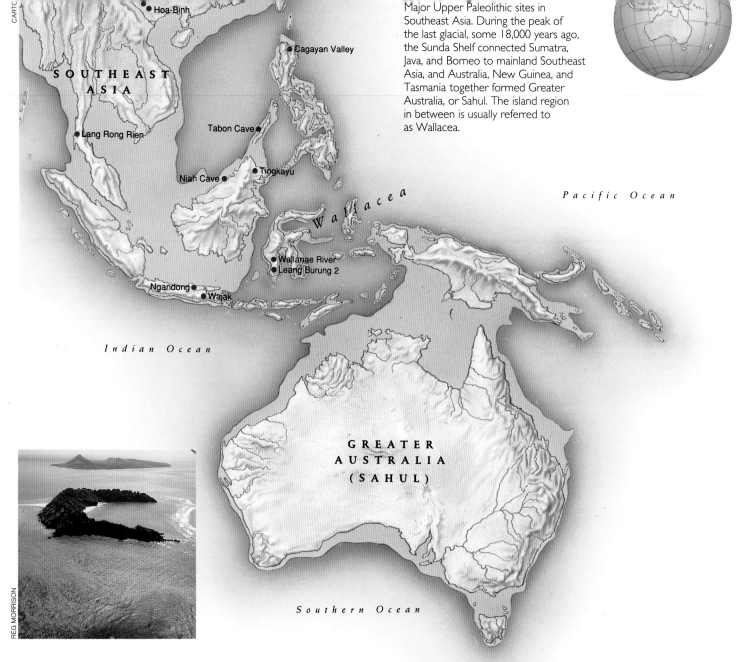

Hoa-Binh

SOUTHEAST
ASIA

Cagayan Valley

Lang Rong Rien

Tabon Cave

Niah Cave • • Tingkayu

Wallacea

Pacific Ocean

Wallanae River
Leang Burung 2

Ngandong • • Wajak

Indian Ocean

GREATER
AUSTRALIA
(SAHUL)

Southern Ocean

Major Upper Paleolithic sites in
Southeast Asia. During the peak of
the last glacial, some 18,000 years ago,
the Sunda Shelf connected Sumatra,
Java, and Borneo to mainland Southeast
Asia, and Australia, New Guinea, and
Tasmania together formed Greater
Australia, or Sahul. The island region
in between is usually referred to
as Wallacea.

🔊 The Mer Islands in Torres Strait—
isolated remains of the land area that
once connected Australia to New
Guinea. Some 8,000 years ago, the
land bridge was drowned, thereby
separating the populations of Australia
and New Guinea.

↦ Eastern Java, Madura, Bali, and
Lombok, in Indonesia, as seen from
space. It was in these waters that
people conquered the sea for the
first time, making possible human
occupation of the Australian continent.

The fact that sea journeys were necessary to
cross between the islands in Wallacea—the island
region between the Asian mainland and Sahul—
suggests that the early peoples who lived along the
coasts would have developed some sort of sea-craft.

About 53,000 years ago, and again about 35,000
years ago, the sea level dropped considerably,
making Sahul more accessible. Reaching Sahul
through Timor 53,000 years ago, however, still
involved a sea voyage of about 90 kilometers
(56 miles). In view of this, it seems likely that
Sahul was originally settled by accident. The first
occupants were probably small groups of people
landing in different places. Significant physical
differences between the New Guineans and the
Australian Aborigines suggest that separate groups
landed in different parts of Sahul and established
viable populations. The physical differences have
become more and more marked as these peoples
have adapted to vastly different environments
over a very long period.

Most of the settlements dating from the first
occupation of Sahul will never be found, as they
are now at least 100 meters (300 feet) below sea
level. The fact that no early materials have yet
been found may indicate that these earliest settlers
lived mainly on the coast. They gradually spread
throughout the continent, reaching the southernmost parts of Australia before 30,000 years ago.
By 20,000 years ago, they inhabited all environmental zones, including the central desert.

⤷ Mammoth ivory carvings depicting flying waterbirds have been found at the Upper Paleolithic site of Mal'ta, near Lake Baikal, in Siberia. Some of these bird figurines have female features, and it has been suggested that they represent a Bird Goddess.
SISSE BRIMBERG

The Arctic Challenge

In Europe, Neanderthals had occasionally ventured into the extensive tundra steppes of the north during the summer months, but they did not settle there permanently. To survive in a region where it was winter for nine months of the year required a quite different technology, and it was *Homo sapiens sapiens* who developed this technology. Many of the tools that made it possible for them to adapt to this harsh environment were made of antler and bone. The many perforated bone needles that have been found suggest that sewn leather clothing was common, and their sophisticated, often richly decorated spear-throwers made of antler made it possible for them to bring down animals from greater distances than previously—a necessity for hunters in this open, treeless landscape.

A series of more or less spectacular settlements stretching from the Czech Republic in the west to Siberia's Chukchi Peninsula, on Bering Strait, in the east indicates that the northern tundra steppes were settled between 30,000 and 15,000 years ago. The oldest of these settlements so far excavated is at Dolní Věstonice, in the Czech Republic, dating back to about 28,000 years ago, where a couple of large houses with central fireplaces were found.

On Russia's River Don, about 470 kilometers (290 miles) south of Moscow, lies the settlement of Kostenki, which has given its name to the Kostenki–Bershevo culture. Most sites from this tradition have been dated to between 27,000 and 13,000 years ago. The houses at Kostenki are known as pit dwellings, because the floors were dug about a meter (3 feet) into the ground to make the house as draftproof as possible. The rib-like frame of the arched roof was made out of mammoth tusks, and this was then covered with hides. The size of these houses, as well as the large number of fireplaces inside them, suggests that a number of families lived there at the one time.

Many of these magnificent settlements appear to have been places where large groups of people gathered for ceremonies and other social activities. The ritual function of these places is most obvious in the most remarkable of them all: Mezhirich, situated on the banks of the Dnepr, southeast of Kiev, in Ukraine. Dating back to 15,000 years ago, the five houses that have been excavated here were made entirely of ingeniously interlocked

⤊ More than 30 mammoth ivory figurines have been found in the remains of a dwelling at the Upper Paleolithic site of Mal'ta, in Siberia. Many of them, like this one, depict stiff-looking female figures.
MUSEE DE L'HOMME, PARIS/J. OSTER

mammoth bones and tusks, and the settlement covered more than 10,000 square meters (17,000 square yards). The houses were very large, each enclosing an area of 80 square meters (100 square yards). At least 50 people probably lived here at the one time. Finds of amber and shells, which must have been carried over distances ranging from 160 to 800 kilometers (100 to 500 miles), also strongly suggest that Mezhirich was a rendezvous for ceremonial activities and the interchange of commodities. (See the feature *Mammoth Bone Huts*.)

The famous and well-preserved graves discovered at Sungir, outside Moscow, allow us an even more telling glimpse of the ritual life and social organization of the Paleolithic big-game hunters. Here, both children and adults were buried with remarkably rich grave goods, dressed in magnificent clothes and headdresses, with decorations of thousands of pierced animal teeth. These burials have been interpreted as indicating the beginnings of social stratification among arctic hunter-gatherer societies of the Ice Age. (See the feature *Sungir: A Stone Age Burial Site*.)

GEORGE W. CALEF/MASTERFILE

The first immigrants in Alaska discovered a land of breathtaking vistas. The previously uninhabited continent was abundant in big game and must have been a land of milk and honey for the early Americans.

Siberian figurines, like some of those found at sites near Lake Baikal, represent the easternmost examples of the widespread and long-lived Venus tradition. Very similar carvings were created all the way to the Atlantic coast, nearly 8,000 kilometers (5,000 miles) away, indicating intensive contacts between the big-game hunters of Ice Age Eurasia.
SISSE BRIMBERG

Southeast of Samarkand, in central Asia, lies Shugnou, another riverside site and one of the world's highest Paleolithic sites. Bone deposits reveal that the most common game in this region were horses, aurochs, wild sheep, and goats. The oldest layers at Shugnou date back to about 20,000 years ago, and the location of the site indicates that the growing population was forcing people to settle further north and higher in the mountains.

During the Upper Paleolithic period, Siberia and northeastern Asia were inhabited by two entirely different cultural groups. The Mal'ta Afontova, which is probably the older, is named after two sites in the valley of the Yenisey, near Lake Baikal. People had settled in this arctic environment by about 22,000 years ago, living in longhouses and hunting big game, including mammoths and horses, locally and on the plains further south. Apart from retouched stone tools such as spear-points, scrapers, and burins, they made tools of bone, antler, and ivory, and female and bird figurines. Clearly, this group had close ties with contemporary cultural groups in the west, particularly those of eastern Europe.

The second group who had settled in this arctic region of northeastern Asia were the Dyukhtai, who lived largely around the rivers of Lena and Aldan, east of the Yenisey. They existed between 18,000 and 12,000 years ago, although there is some unconfirmed evidence of older occupation. Their tools were very different from those of the Mal'ta–Afontova tradition. Among other things, they made very effective tools from small chips of stone, known as microblades. We do not know where this practice originated, but similar tools have been found in northern China, dating from about 22,000 years ago, and also in Japan, although the latter finds have not as yet been reliably dated.

Unlike the Mal'ta people, the Dyukhtai were clearly orientated towards the east, and this is crucially important in tracing the first migration across Bering Strait into America. As time went on, the Dyukhtai proved adept at adjusting to climatic and environmental conditions very different from those traditional tundra hunters were accustomed to.

MAMMOTH BONE HUTS

ROLAND FLETCHER

AFTER THE END of the period of extreme cold between 20,000 and 18,000 years ago, people began to move back into the central Russian plain. In the winter and spring, they lived in huts made of mammoth bone. One such settlement, discovered at Mezhirich, in Ukraine, was occupied some time between 15,000 and 14,000 years ago. It lay a short distance from the junction of two rivers, on the higher, western bank of the main river. The hills were covered with grass. Pine trees, birch, and alder grew on the floodplains below. The community hunted mammoths (quite how we do not know), bison, horses, and reindeer. They also caught birds and a few fish, such as pike, and hunted arctic foxes and hares for their pelts. Between 30 and 60 people may have lived here. Each hut had a hearth, fueled by bone. Around the dwellings were fireplaces, storage pits for meat and bone, and areas where flint and bone tools were made.

♙ This engraved piece of mammoth ivory found at Mezhirich may be a picture of the huts—perhaps the oldest known map. Images of landscapes are very rare in Upper Paleolithic art.

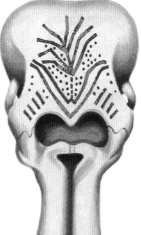

⬅ A mammoth skull elaborately painted with red ocher was found in one of the huts. Similarly decorated mammoth bones have been found at Mezin, 200 kilometers (120 miles) to the north. Small ivory figurines and beads made of amber from the Kiev area were also found.

♀ Mezhirich was excavated by I. Pidoplichko, N.L. Kornietz, and M.I. Gladin in several stages between 1966 and 1983. Olga Soffer, on whose work much of this description is based, analyzed the animal remains.

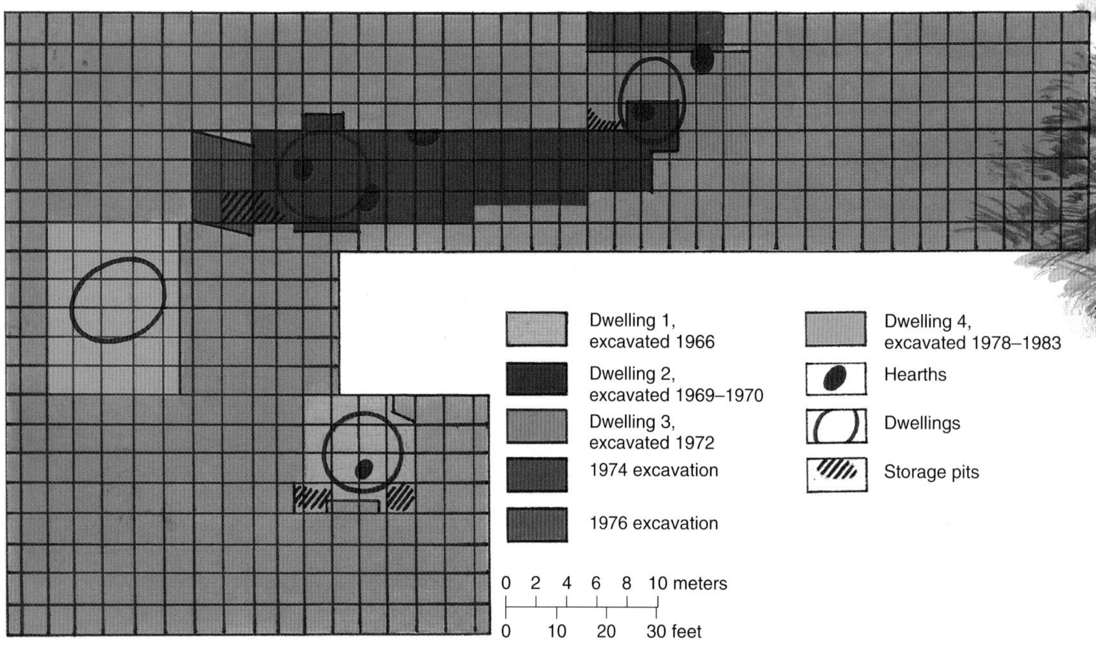

Dwelling 1, excavated 1966

Dwelling 2, excavated 1969–1970

Dwelling 3, excavated 1972

1974 excavation

1976 excavation

Dwelling 4, excavated 1978–1983

Hearths

Dwellings

Storage pits

0 2 4 6 8 10 meters

0   10   20   30 feet

ILLUSTRATION: JOHN RICHARDS

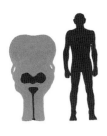

☞ Each hut had a solid base of large mammoth bones and a lighter superstructure. The bones were carefully interlocked, often in symmetrical patterns. Different bones predominate in each hut.. The base of one was built of mandibles; that of another, mainly of long bones. Some of the large bones have holes cut in them, probably to support a timber frame. Large tusks were fitted together to form the roof arch. The frame was presumably covered by skins and turf.

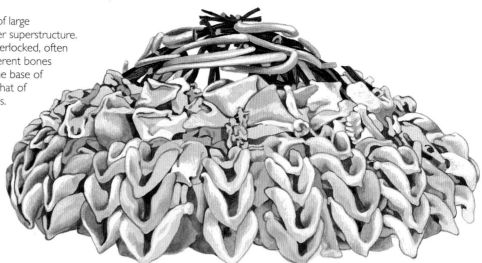

⚲ It would have taken 10 people about 15 days to build the settlement. The storage pits, which are about a meter (3 feet) deep, could only have been dug in warmer weather, when the ground was not frozen, so building would have started in the autumn. Between 150 and 650 bones were used for each hut—a total of 97 crania, 109 mandibles, 92 tusks, and several hundred other large bones. The biggest of the huts was made of 20 tonnes (just under 20 tons) of bone, including 46 crania, 95 mandibles, and 40 tusks. A single cranium weighs 100 kilograms (220 pounds), and a tusk can be as heavy as 200 kilograms (440 pounds). Most parts of the mammoth were used, and bones of the same animal are found in different huts. The bones probably came from a nearby natural "cemetery".

Arctic Ocean

Bluefish Caves

Akmak

Kurupka • Puturak
Ul'khum • • Dry Creek

• Dyukhtai

Pacific Ocean

One of the earliest examples of a people who adapted to a postglacial environment is provided by the Jomon culture of Japan, which developed about 12,500 years ago and was largely based on fishing and other marine resources. The rich resources along the coasts allowed the Jomon people to become sedentary, which, in turn, led to their becoming one of the first peoples in the world to make pottery. Dating back to 12,000 years ago, their pots were probably used for cooking mollusks and plants. In some areas, the Jomon culture survived unaltered right up to the beginning of the first century AD.

During two phases of the last Ice Age—from 50,000 to 40,000 years ago, and again from 25,000 to 14,000 years ago—the present Bering Strait was drained, as were large parts of the Arctic Ocean in the north and the Bering Sea in the south. This territory, often called Beringia, connected Alaska with Siberia's Chukchi Peninsula, making it possible for humans and animals to cross from one continent to the other. It is unlikely that humans migrated into North America during the first phase, as there is no evidence of human settlement in northeastern Asia from this period. It

is also very unlikely that people crossed the Arctic Ocean in the intermediate period, between 40,000 and 25,000 years ago. A boat trip across Bering Strait would have been a very difficult undertaking indeed at that time. The warm climate and waters of Southeast Asia were much more conducive to seafaring, as we know from the fact that people crossed the Sunda Strait to reach present-day Australia and New Guinea.

The most likely time for people to have crossed Bering Strait is clearly between 25,000 and 14,000 years ago. This corresponds with the known spread of modern humans into the arctic regions of Europe and with the earliest finds of big-game hunters' settlements within the Mal'ta and Dyukhtai traditions of northeastern Siberia, which date back to between 18,000 and 15,000 years ago. The oldest known tools on both sides of Bering Strait exhibit a similar microlithic blade technique: those within the Dyukhtai tradition, in Siberia, and those found in sites such as Bluefish Caves (c. 13,000 BC), Dry Creek (9000 BC), and Akmak (c. 8000 BC), in Alaska. In spite of intensive efforts to find older signs of human occupation in Alaska, there are at present no reliable finds older than those from Bluefish Caves, going back 15,000 years. Tools of a similar age have been excavated from several Upper Paleolithic sites in the Chukchi Peninsula, including Kurupka, Puturak, and Ul'khum, which undoubtedly housed the ancestors of the first Americans.

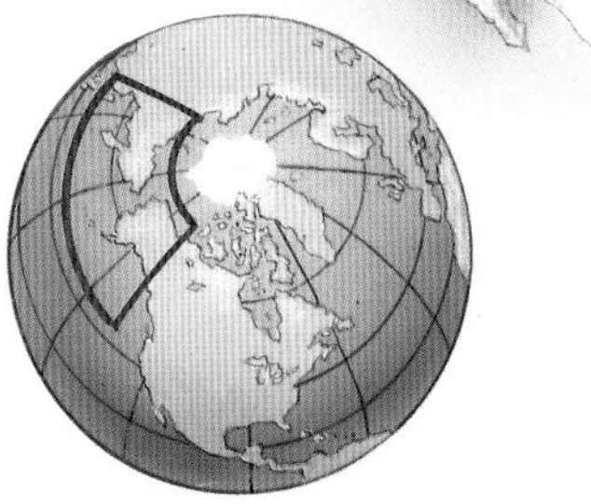

THE ICE AGE LAND BRIDGE OF BERINGIA

Between 25,000 and 14,000 years ago, eastern Siberia and Alaska were connected by a land bridge usually referred to as Beringia. The timing of the first crossing of people into North America is the subject of intense debate. Coastlines and ice sheets are shown as they were during the peak of the last glacial, some 18,000 years ago.
CARTOGRAPHY: RAY SIM

◄● Only some 80 kilometers (50 miles) of icy waters today separate Russia's Chukchi Peninsula from Alaska. During the last Ice Age, Bering Strait was drained, allowing humans to cross by land from Asia to the New World. Shown here are the Diomede Islands, situated in the middle of the strait.

SUNGIR: A STONE AGE BURIAL SITE

OLGA SOFFER

THE SITE OF SUNGIR, containing the richest Upper Paleolithic burials found in the world to date, is located on the outskirts of the city of Vladimir, some 200 kilometers (125 miles) east-northeast of Moscow, in Russia. The site was discovered in 1955 during brick quarrying and was excavated between 1956 and 1977.

The cultural layer of the site, 15 to 90 centimeters (6 to 35 inches) thick, was situated on a 50 meter (164 foot) promontory formed by the banks of the Klyazma River and those of its tributary, the Sungir. It was found some 3 meters (10 feet) below the present-day surface and lay on top of soil formed during a somewhat warmer period that occurred between about 29,000 and 25,000 years ago. Radiocarbon dates obtained on wood charcoal from the site put its age between some 25,500 and 22,000 years ago, with the former age probably being the more accurate one.

Although people occupied Sungir during a warmer spell of the last Ice Age, they were nonetheless living in a tundra environment when climatic conditions were severe enough to produce permafrost (permanently frozen ground). Climatic conditions worsened after the site was abandoned, and the cultural layer was significantly disturbed by repeated freezing and thawing of the deposits.

Sungir measured some 10,000 square meters (108,000 square feet) in area, of which 4,500 square meters (about 48,500 square feet) were excavated. The opened area contained five concentrations of cultural materials, consisting of the remains of surface dwellings; numerous hearths and pits of various sizes; work areas where stone and bone implements were manufactured; and remains of at least six burials, three of which were undisturbed. The nature of the animal remains (reindeer, horses, mammoths, arctic foxes, and a few wolves, bears, wolverines, arctic hares, and bison) and the transitory nature of the dwellings indicate that people occupied Sungir during the summer to early autumn, while the distribution of cultural remains suggests that the site was visited repeatedly over a number of years.

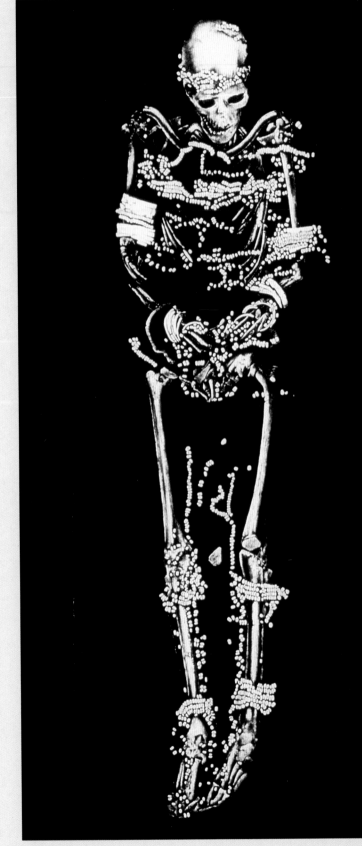

MUSEE DE L'HOMME, PARIS/O. BADER

More than 3,000 ivory beads were sewn onto the clothing of the older male buried at the Upper Paleolithic site of Sungir.

Tools and Ornaments

Sungir's stone tool inventory consisted of more than 50,000 pieces made from locally available cobbles. The stone tools (3.6 percent of the total inventory) include bifacially retouched triangular points, Aurignacian pieces, and archaic Mousterian forms, and point to the site's early Upper Paleolithic age. Scholars disagree on its cultural affinity. Some assign the inventory to an Aurignacian tradition with leaf points, while others see it as a younger stage in the development of the local Kostenki–Streletskaia culture.

Sungir also produced a very rich inventory of worked bone, ivory, and antler pieces shaped into a variety of implements; remains of jewelry made of stone, bone, ivory, shell, and belemnites; and perforated arctic fox canine teeth fashioned into beads, bracelets, pins, pendants, and rings. Carved decorative objects found included two animal figurines (a horse or saiga antelope and a mammoth) and perforated ivory and stone disks. Most of these objects were found in the graves described below.

Double burial of an adolescent boy and girl at the Upper Paleolithic site of Sungir with a rich inventory of ivory spears, lances, and jewelry. Close to 6,000 beads were sewn onto the clothing, but these were removed before the photograph was taken.
MUSEE DE L'HOMME,PARIS/ARLETTE LEROI-GOURHAN

The Human Evidence

Although remains of nine anatomically modern people (*Homo sapiens sapiens*) have been found at Sungir to date, two intact burials of three bodies found in the southwestern part of the site have made it world famous. These, consisting of a single grave of a 45 to 60-year-old male (burial 1) and a double grave where a 13-year-old boy was interred head to head with a 9 to 10-year-old girl (burial 2), were found some 3 meters (10 feet) apart. Both graves, measuring 2.05 by 0.7 meters (6 feet, 9 inches by 2 feet, 3 inches) and 3.05 by 0.7 meters (11 feet, 6 inches by 2 feet, 3 inches), respectively, were situated inside dwellings and had been dug into permafrost to a depth of 65 to 75 centimeters (26 to 30 inches). The bottom of the graves was covered with a layer of black charcoal, then white limestone, then red ocher.

The bodies were laid out extended on their back, with arms folded across their pelvis, and all three burials were liberally sprinkled with red ocher. The placement of thousands of beads sewn on their hide and fur clothing suggests that all three were clad in shirts, long pants with attached footwear, over-the-knee fur boots, and short outer cloaks. The males were wearing fur hats, and the girl wore a hood.

The man's clothing was decorated with some 3,000 ivory beads, his hat or cap was circled with perforated arctic fox teeth, and his forehead and biceps were bedecked with ivory bracelets. Just under 5,000 beads were sewn onto the boy's clothing, and he wore a belt made of more than 250 drilled arctic fox canines and a bracelet and pendant made of ivory. An ivory sculpture of a mammoth had been placed underneath him. A spear measuring 2.4 meters (nearly 8 feet) and weighing more than 20 kilograms (44 pounds) lay beside him, along with assorted ivory spears and lances and a perforated ivory disk with a latticework design. At his left side, near the edge of the grave, lay a human femur with broken epiphyses which was filled with red ocher.

The girl's burial was the most elaborate. The grave contained 5,274 beads and bead fragments; numerous ivory lances, including one 1.6 meters (5 feet, 3 inches) long; two perforated and decorated pieces of antler known as *bâtons de commandement* (sometimes called shaft straighteners); and four carved round ivory disks with a latticework design, one of which was inserted into an ivory shaft.

While both the single and the double burials were dug down from the same cultural layer into the underlying loess–loam stratum, microstratigraphic observations suggest that the two children were buried earlier than the adult male, who may have been interred a few seasons after them. The children's grave was superimposed by the burial of another adult, whose almost totally decomposed remains, minus the head, were interred in the upper part of the grave. The top part of the adult male's grave, on the other hand, was covered with a large ocher stain on which sat a sizable boulder and the poorly preserved cranium of an adult female. The headless adult must have been buried some time after the children, but the cranium of the female was placed over the interred adult male in the course of his burial ritual.

What Was the Social Structure?

The stylistic similarity in the burial features and associated inventories indicates that the man and the children belonged to the same social group. The wealth of the burial inventory, measured by the labor invested in the making of the grave goods found, suggests that these individuals may have had special status in their community. Since the children were too young to have achieved high status through their skills or talents, some scholars believe the abundance of goods buried with them to indicate that they may have been related to people of high status and thus inherited their important social position. If this were so, then the Sungir burials show us that some Upper Paleolithic groups lived in complex social units. But messages from the grave can be equivocal, and the wealth of these burials may simply reflect the high status these individuals achieved in death itself, the wealth buried with them bearing no relationship to high status in life.

↪ At Matanuska Glacier, in Alaska, one can get a feeling of what it was like to live along the ice edges of glacial Eurasia and North America.

🔥 Typical tools of the Hamburg culture include coarse points with tangs—so-called *kerbspitze* (**a**)—and a very specialized gimlet called a *zinken* (**b**), both made of flint. The latter was used for splitting bones (**c**). The *riemenschneider* (**d**), a crescent-shaped tool probably used for leatherwork, consists of a coarse flint point mounted in a piece of reindeer antler.
ILLUSTRATIONS: RAY SIM

The Settling of Northern Europe

At the end of the last Ice Age, between 15,000 and 8,000 years ago, the climate changed dramatically throughout the world. These changes decisively altered the patterns of human life and, in time, led to the birth of agriculture. As the climate in western Europe improved rapidly and the ice edge retreated, the herds of reindeer and horses, so important to the big-game hunters of the Magdalenian period, moved north. With the spreading forests came totally different forms of subsistence. Some groups of people followed the animals north, while others adjusted to the new conditions where they were. This meant a change from big-game hunting to fishing, beachcombing, hunting small game, and—an activity that was to become increasingly important—gathering plants. For the big-game hunters, the desolate tundras of Scandinavia provided a short-lived refuge for their several-thousand-year-old way of life.

Towards the end of the Ice Age, groups of reindeer hunters related to both the European Magdalenian tradition of the west and to more eastern cultural groups appeared in northern Germany, Holland, and Belgium.

Among the earliest was the so-called Hamburg culture, named after the Hamburg area, in which a number of sites dated to between 17,000 and 12,000 years ago have been found. These include Meiendorf, Stellmoor, Borneck, and Poggenwisch. The oldest sites, such as Meiendorf, appear to have been summer hunting grounds, whereas the more recent ones also show traces of winter settlement. These people were predominantly reindeer hunters, but they also hunted wild horses, hares, foxes, and wildfowl. Some settlements were very close to the ice edge, where the harsh tundra climate allowed only birch and willow to take root in the frozen ground.

The tools of the Hamburg culture are very distinctive. They include coarse spear-points with tangs for hafting (known as *kerbspitze*); knives with handles of reindeer antler (*riemenschneider*), probably used for leatherwork; and bent gimlets (*zinken*), used for splitting bones. Many more hunting sites dating from about 10,000 BC have been found in northern Europe—for example, Usselo and Tjonger, in Belgium and Holland, and Wehlen and Rissen, in northern Germany. These are all known as Federmesser cultures, after a feather-like spear-point characteristic of them all.

These big-game hunters gradually spread into the vast tundras of northern Europe, ranging of necessity over large areas. Population was sparse, and large areas in the west which today are covered by the North Sea were part of the reindeer hunters' territory. About 13,000 years ago, reindeer hunters from the Federmesser cultures were the first to move into the ice-free regions of southern Scandinavia. Reindeer skeletons and antlers have been found in Denmark and southern Sweden,

LATE GLACIAL SITES IN NORTHERN EUROPE

Important sites in northern Europe at the end of the last glacial, some 13,000 years ago. At this time, Scandinavia was the only part of Europe still under ice. By about 6000 BC, the ice sheet had melted away completely.
CARTOGRAPHY: RAY SIM

but the age of the bones indicates that these kill sites resulted from short visits, perhaps of only a few weeks. This is almost certainly why so few settlements from this time are known: Bromme, on the island of Zealand, in Denmark, and Segebro and Finja Lake, in the province of Scania, in Sweden. All have been dated to about 10,000 BC. Similar blade tools have been found at Bromme and Segebro, including scrapers, burins, borers, knives, and points with tangs. A bent gimlet, or *zinken*, of the Hamburg type has also been found at Finja Lake. No organic material has survived at these sites, but as well as reindeer, the people probably ate elk and wildfowl, and also some fish.

Since the vast majority of people in western and northern Europe hunted reindeer, a similar range of tools is found throughout these areas until about 10,000 BC, when, in response to climatic changes, the forests spread north. This led to an increase in both big and small game and also made plants a more important source of food, and new tools were gradually developed to suit local conditions and the new subsistence patterns. With a vastly richer ecosystem, smaller areas of land were able to support larger groups of people, leading to rapid population growth, and clear seasonal settlement patterns developed within different regions. Coastal

Atlantic Ocean

●Komsa

●Fosna

●Finja Lake
Bromme● ●Segebro

Meiendorf ●Ahrensburg
● ●Stellmoor
Poggenwisch

As early as 10,000 years ago, small groups of people from the east settled the barren but ice-free coasts of Europe's northern outposts. In Norway's Nordland, they established the so-called Komsa culture.

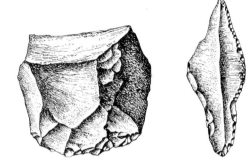

settlements became more common, although we know very little about these, as most coastlines that existed during the late Ice Age, like those of the early postglacial period known as the Holocene, have long since been submerged by the rising seas.

A northern German culture known as the Ahrensburg, after a village north of Hamburg, is an important example of a culture that changed in response to changing conditions. Existing between 9000 and 8300 BC, these people had most of the tools characteristic of the Paleolithic world, none of the clearly Mesolithic ones—notably axes and microliths (having no need of axes in the tundra landscape)—but a series of tools showing the transition from one subsistence pattern to another. As the climate improved and hunting small game, fishing, and plant gathering gradually became more important, they tended to make smaller tools for these new purposes—not yet microliths, but what might be called precursors of microlithic technology. These included small, bifacially trimmed points with tangs (known as *stielspitze*), indicating that bows and arrows were in use in the north. The Ahrensburg culture thus represented the end of the late glacial tundra economies in northern Europe.

Big-game hunting did not, of course, disappear entirely as a way of life. The hunters who spread to southern Scandinavia probably moved further north along the ice-free coastal areas of western Scandinavia, where they established various hunting-gathering economies that survived unaltered for thousands of years in the form of the Fosna culture. In the extreme north, scattered groups of reindeer hunters from the tundra steppes of eastern Europe reached the ice-free coasts of the Kola Peninsula and Nordland, establishing the so-called Komsa culture, which survived until about 2000 BC—well into the late Neolithic period.

In most of Europe, however, a new era was just around the corner. Mesolithic peoples were showing a remarkable ability to adapt to a diverse range of environments and ecosystems, and in time these successful hunter-gatherers would adopt herding and farming as an increasingly necessary part of their subsistence.

The tools of the first Scandinavians are very similar to those of other late glacial reindeer hunters in northern Europe, consisting mainly of scrapers, burins, and points with tangs. The examples illustrated here are from Segebro, in southern Sweden.
ILLUSTRATIONS: RAY SIM

Huge rock carvings depicting reindeer have been found at the water's edge at Sagelven, in Norway's Nordland, in northernmost Europe. These works of art are attributed to the Komsa people, who arrived in the area some 10,000 years ago.

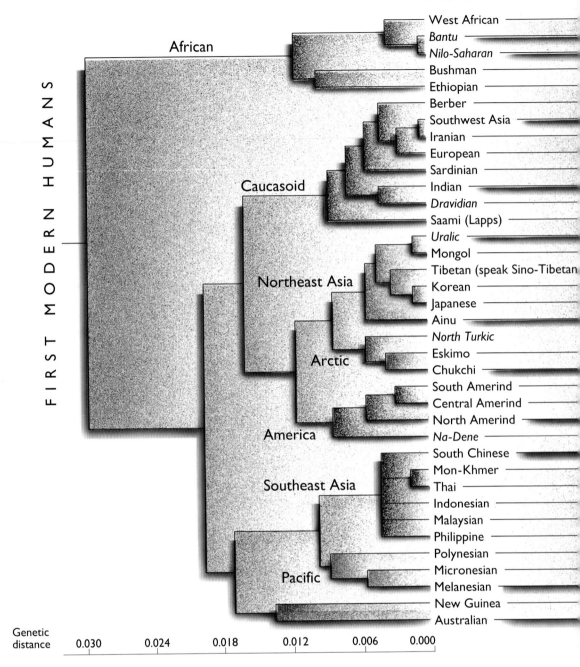

POPULATION

West African
Bantu
Nilo-Saharan
Bushman
Ethiopian
Berber
Southwest Asia
Iranian
European
Sardinian
Indian
Dravidian
Saami (Lapps)
Uralic
Mongol
Tibetan (speak Sino-Tibetan
Korean
Japanese
Ainu
North Turkic
Eskimo
Chukchi
South Amerind
Central Amerind
North Amerind
Na-Dene
South Chinese
Mon-Khmer
Thai
Indonesian
Malaysian
Philippine
Polynesian
Micronesian
Melanesian
New Guinea
Australian

African

Caucasoid

Northeast Asia

Arctic

America

Southeast Asia

Pacific

FIRST MODERN HUMANS

☞ Revolutionary new evidence suggests that language may be linked to our genetic origins. The "family tree" shown here is controversial, but reflects some of the latest research in this fascinating area.

Closeness of relationship is indicated by how far to the left one has to go to find a line connecting two populations. Thus, in the Caucasoid group, the two closest groups are the Iranian and Southwest Asian populations. Next closest are Europeans, and next after them come Berbers—and so on, until the Saami are included as the most distantly related population within the Caucasoid group.

Higher-order groups are connected still further to the left: the Caucasoid, Northeast Asian, Arctic, and American groups form one such higher-order group, which is still more distantly related to the Southeast Asia–Pacific–Australia–New Guinea higher-order group. African populations are more distantly related to the other groups, a factor supporting an African origin for all living humans. If modern humans evolved elsewhere, diverged, and later spread into Africa, then modern Africans and their closest non-African relatives should form a linked higher-order group, but no such group exists.

Italics indicate populations that are defined linguistically rather than ethnically.

Genetic distance is calculated from the average frequencies of 120 genes in the various populations studied.

Genetic distance

0.030   0.024   0.018   0.012   0.006   0.000

GENES, LANGUAGES, AND ARCHAEOLOGY

PETER ROWLEY-CONWY

RECENT GENETIC EVIDENCE indicating that all living humans trace their descent to a single hypothetical woman ("Eve") who lived in Africa less than 250,000 years ago is of immense importance. Even more recently, several new lines of work have come together to support this picture and are beginning to give us a revolutionary new insight into our origins.

Genetics have provided one "family tree". The various human populations are not characterized by the simple presence or absence of particular genes, but have different

frequencies of different genes. By analyzing a huge body of genetic data, L.L. Cavalli-Sforza has recently produced the family tree shown in the chart. The populations he studied are listed down the middle. Most are ethnically defined, but a few are linguistically defined, and these are shown in italics. The interrelationships are shown at left, calibrated against the scale of genetic distance (or difference) between the various populations (see the caption). African populations are distantly related to all the other groups, a factor that supports an African origin for all living humans.

LANGUAGE FAMILY

- Niger-Kordofanian
- Nilo-Saharan
- Khoisan
- Afro-Asiatic
- Indo-European
- Dravidian
- Uralic
- Altaic
- Korean
- Japanese
- Ainu
- Eskimo-Aleut
- Chukchi-Kamchatkan
- Amerind
- Na-Dene
- Sino-Tibetan
- Austro-Asiatic
- Daic
- Austronesian
- Indo-Pacific
- Australian

LANGUAGE MACROFAMILY

- CONGO-SAHARAN
- NOSTRATIC
- EURASIATIC
- DENE-CAUCASIAN
- AUSTRIC

"PROTOWORLD"

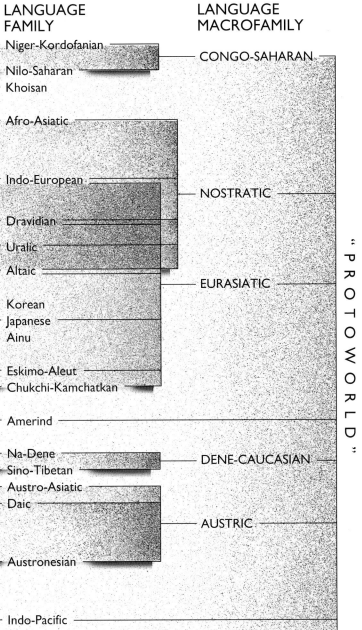

ILLUSTRATION: DAVID WOOD

Languages have only recently been brought into this debate, and their role is highly controversial. The right-hand side of the chart shows the language families corresponding to the genetic populations Cavalli-Sforza studied. Clearly, many populations that are genetically quite closely related also speak closely related languages.

The extent to which languages reflect ancestry is currently under debate. People cannot change their genetics, but they can obviously change their language. For example, black Americans are genetically like Africans but linguistically like Europeans. The chart shows more problems of this kind. Ethiopians are genetically Africans but speak an Afro-Asiatic language.

These problems aside, some scholars are beginning to believe that languages may reflect ancestry and population movements, such as when early farmers spread out, replacing hunter-gatherers in other regions. This is plausible but difficult to prove, because the various agricultural dispersals took place long before writing was developed. Very recently, a minority of linguists have gone even further,

proposing language groups bigger than those labeled "language family" in the chart. If these groups are valid, the implications are enormous. Vladislav Illich-Svitych has proposed a "Nostratic" macrofamily, while Joseph Greenberg has suggested a different but overlapping "Eurasiatic" macrofamily. This would imply that, at some time, perhaps 15,000 to 10,000 years ago, a "proto-Nostratic" or "proto-Eurasiatic" language was actually spoken somewhere. As people dispersed, this branched out into distinct regional languages, which themselves later split into the languages that are now spoken.

Other such higher-level groups are currently being suggested, and these, too, are indicated in the chart. But considerable difficulties remain. The proposed Dene–Caucasian macrofamily would link not only American and Southeast Asian populations, but also the Basques. These people live in the border region between France and Spain and speak a language usually thought to be unrelated to any other in the world, so this seems a most unlikely grouping. Merrit Ruhlen has suggested, however, that even these macrofamilies have links. In other words, they may all descend from a single language, for which the term "protoworld" has been coined. It has been suggested that this language may have been spoken in Africa.

Are distant echoes of a linguistic "big bang" still reverberating? Could it be that the speech of all of us reflects, however distantly, a single original "protoworld" language, spoken by the first modern humans in Africa? Most linguists believe that such a language existed, but do not accept that any trace of it persists to this day.

Archaeology is also coming up with evidence, in two main ways. First, it is obviously not possible to excavate a language, but it may be possible to detect in the archaeological record the type of symbolic thought processes without which a spoken language of modern complexity could not exist. Art and other evidence of

symbolic thought appear only about 35,000 years ago, and tool types start to become stylized at about the same time. There is also some (controversial) evidence, derived from studies of the lower parts of skulls, that Neanderthals would not have been able to make all the complex sounds we can make. William Noble and Iain Davidson have recently suggested that language as we know it is no more than about 50,000 years old—an unexpectedly short time span. If this is so, it seems just possible that linguistic traces of a "protoworld" language could have survived into the present.

Second, archaeology can provide fossil evidence of our origins. New finds, and new dating methods, currently support the hypothesis that modern humans originated in Africa. The earliest dated finds of modern humans are African, going back more than 100,000 years. These people were living at the same time that Neanderthals were living in Europe. Dates from finds in Israel show that modern humans were present there 90,000 to 100,000 years ago. The next dates we have for modern humans are 67,000 years ago, for human remains found at Liujiang, in China, and about 50,000 years ago, when Australasia was colonized. Europe was colonized about 35,000 years ago, the Americas about the same time or later. This pattern indicates that humans did indeed originate in Africa and spread from there to the rest of the world.

These three lines of evidence— genetics, linguistics, and archaeology—*can*, therefore, be brought together to tell a single, coherent story. All three are controversial and need much more detailed testing before the story can be accepted as fact. Only two things are certain. First, by the time you read this in print, significant new developments will have taken place. And second, if these three lines of evidence are not disproved by future work, we are on the threshold of a colossal breakthrough in our understanding of ourselves.

THE SETTLEMENT OF ANCIENT AUSTRALIA

50,000 YEARS AGO – 10,000 YEARS AGO

The First New World

J. Peter White

EVERY SOCIETY HAS its own ways of explaining how it came to be. Australian Aborigines trace their own and their country's origins to the great Spirit Ancestors of the Dreamtime. These beings, the Aborigines believe, created the world and determined the pattern of life as Aborigines know it. They remain a vital influence on Aboriginal life today, particularly through the medium of ceremonies during which stories and song-cycles telling of the events of the Dreamtime are recited and enacted. Parts of two creation accounts are given here, to introduce Aboriginal ways of looking at Australia's past—and present. For "Dreamtime" is an English translation of a term that doesn't refer to a past or a future, but to an eternal present. We translate these stories into a time frame, but for most Aboriginal people, creation is a continuing process.

Our own industrial society's version of Australia's history comes from recent scientific research. It is less personal than the Aboriginal accounts, and chronology, or when things happened, is given greater prominence.

The common element in both the Aboriginal and the scientific accounts is that they seek to explain the emergence of a new world. The humans who settled Australia were the first people to break the sea barriers that had previously kept humans in the Old World. Australia was *Homo sapiens'* first New World.

◄◌ On the shores of Lake Mungo, people camped, fished, and buried their dead more than 35,000 years ago. As the eastern margins of these lakes were built up by wind and water, the evidence of these activities was buried. Today, these sandy shores are eroding, exposing ancient relics.

⬆THE NATURAL HISTORY MUSEUM, LONDON

Sun Mother and the Creation

Once the earth was completely dark and silent; nothing moved on the barren surface. Inside a deep cave below the Nullarbor Plain slept a beautiful woman, the Sun. The Great Father Spirit gently woke her and told her to emerge from her cave and stir the universe into life. The Sun Mother opened her eyes and darkness disappeared as her rays spread over the land; she took a breath and the atmosphere changed, the air gently vibrated as a small breeze blew.

The Sun Mother then went on a long journey, from east to west and from north to south she crossed the barren land and wherever her gentle rays touched the earth, grasses, shrubs and trees grew until the land was covered in vegetation. In each of the deep caverns in the earth, the Sun found living creatures which like herself had been slumbering for untold ages. She stirred the insects into life in all their forms and told them to spread through the grasses and trees, then she woke the snakes, lizards and many other reptiles and they slithered out of their deep hole. Behind the snakes mighty rivers flowed, teeming with all kinds of fish and water life. Then she called for the animals, the marsupials and many other creatures to awake and make their homes on the earth. The Sun Mother then told all the creatures that the days would from time to time change from wet to dry and from cold to hot, and so she made the seasons. One day while all the animals, insects and other creatures were watching, the Sun travelled far in the sky to the west and as the sky shone red, she sank from view and darkness spread across the land once more. The creatures were alarmed and huddled together in fear. Some time later, the sky began to glow on the horizon to the east and the Sun rose smiling into the sky again. The Sun Mother thus provided a period of rest for all her creatures by making this journey each day.

Karraru Tribe

The Origin of Lake Eyre

An old woman was out hunting when she saw a huge kangaroo in the distance. From her belly a young boy, Wilkuda, jumped out and chased the kangaroo west, hoping to spear it. He chased it until his spear finally reached its mark and, thinking it was dead, he threw it over his fire to cook and went to sleep. When he awoke the kangaroo had jumped off and escaped him. Wilkuda followed that kangaroo from sunrise to sunset for many days, until finally he grew weary. An old man with a dog came across their path, and with the aid of his dog, killed the kangaroo. Wilkuda said the old man could have the meat from his kangaroo, but he needed the skin.

Then Wilkuda travelled back east and threw the skin down east of Anna Creek, where it changed into a huge lake, Lake Eyre. Wilkuda is today seen as a boulder by the shores of the lake.

Arabana Tribe

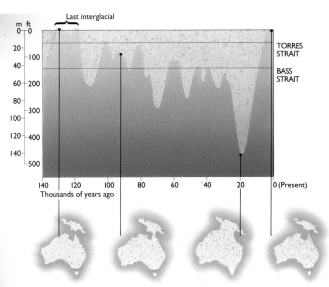

The balance between land and sea
Sea levels have been lower than they are at present
for most of the last million years. This has not only
increased the land area available for people to live
on but has also allowed easier movement between
what we now think of as different countries. The
drowning of previously inhabited areas by
8,000 years ago has destroyed much
of the archaeological record.

ILLUSTRATIONS: JON GITTOES

Wallacea

M odern maps give a poor idea of the
landmass described in this chapter.
Ancient or "Greater" Australia, also
sometimes referred to as Sahul, comprises
present-day Australia, Tasmania, and New
Guinea. These lands have been joined as
one continent for at least 80 percent of the
time during which they have been occupied
by human beings.

Greater Australia itself was separated from
the other great landmasses of the world tens
of millions of years ago, and for all of that time
there has been a continuous sea barrier between
it and Asia, its closest neighbor. Called Wallacea
(after the naturalist A.R. Wallace, who recognized
its importance 150 years ago), this area of island-
studded sea marks the division between the
world's two great faunas: oriental mammals,
birds, and insects, and their Australian counterparts. Thus, on one side, there are apes, elephants,
tigers, and pigs; and on the other, kangaroos,
koalas, and wombats.

Australia: a land apart
Australia's unique mammals are often described as
primitive, but its monotremes (the platypus and the
echidnas) and marsupials (for example, koalas and kangaroos)
are highly specialized animals that have adapted in sophisticated
ways to the continent's unusual vegetation and unpredictable
environment. They have evolved in different directions from
animals in other parts of the world for millions of years.

◂◦ This single-outrigger canoe was observed by Abel Tasman off New Ireland in 1643. It was being used for shark fishing, as the propeller-like floats between each man indicate. It would have been quite seaworthy, but have taken a great deal of effort to paddle between islands.

⬩ Outrigger canoes propeled by paddles are now found throughout the tropical Pacific and are both stable and seaworthy. John Forrest observed islanders near New Guinea hunting pigs from such a canoe in 1775.

⊙▸ A raft and paddles made of mangrove wood, hibiscus bark, and twine. Used by the Kaiadilt people of Mornington Island to cross rivers and as spearing platforms, this example was made in 1987. Craft like this would not be used to travel between distant islands.

⚲ Tasmanian Aborigines observed in 1802 made canoe-rafts consisting of three bundles of tied bark or dried reeds lashed together with grass string. Being very buoyant, these handled well in rough water, but they became waterlogged on voyages of more than 10 kilometers (6 miles).

AUSTRALIAN NATIONAL MARITIME MUSEUM

AUSTRALIAN NATIONAL MARITIME MUSEUM

Greater Australia looked very different from the Australia of today. Where now the roaring forties blow uninterrupted across Bass Strait, 10,000 years ago there was a broad, flat plain with several isolated hills. Between Australia and New Guinea stretched a similar but tropical plain, the sea covering the last spit of Torres Strait only about 8,000 years ago. And until the sea finally rose to its present level about 6,000 years ago, the coasts extended further than they do now, sometimes by only a little, sometimes by several hundred kilometers (about 200 miles), as we can judge from the offshore contours. This means that today's sea boundaries are not a good guide to cultural boundaries in the past. Obviously, some resources that would have been available in the Pleistocene period were not available more recently, while almost all evidence of life in shoreside areas more than 6,000 years old has long since been submerged by the rising seas.

The First Settlers

The people who settled in Greater Australia unquestionably came from Southeast Asia. Several different lines of evidence point to this. First, we may be certain that *Homo sapiens* did not evolve in Greater Australia. No primates (apes, monkeys), or even more distant human relatives, are found east of Java, Sumatra, and Borneo. The permanent water barrier of Wallacea kept early people out, as it did other recent mammals. All human remains found in Australia belong to *Homo sapiens sapiens,* our own modern species. No earlier forms have been found. This suggests that only modern people developed the cultural ability to cross water barriers by means of boats or rafts.

Second, Southeast Asia is the closest landmass from which people might have come. There were no sophisticated sailing craft 50,000 years ago, and people could not have paddled in bark canoes or on bamboo rafts from India, China, or Africa and survived. The most likely craft would therefore be outrigger canoes or single-log hulls with outriggers. The island chains of what is now Indonesia offered a pathway. Indeed, the tropical, generally calm, waters of these areas would have provided a kind of sheltered nursery, where, for the first time in human history, people could learn safely to exploit the sea and its resources.

Finally, humans have been in Southeast Asia for at least the last million years. Skeletal remains of earlier hominids, *Homo erectus,* have been found in Java, as well as the remains of more modern, but still ancestral, humans. We do not know the precise routes people followed when they came to Greater Australia. Every move from island to island was probably made by a few people traveling to the next piece of visible land, or land they inferred to exist from bushfire smoke, clouds, or bird movements. Almost certainly, there was no large-scale, deliberate migration. On the other hand, it seems likely that different parts of Greater Australia (New Guinea and Australia, for instance) were settled by different groups of people. Today, New Guineans and Australians are more closely related than either is to anyone else in the world, but they are still two identifiable groups, although similar enough to suggest a common origin. Although it is unlikely, each group may have descended from a single boatload of people, whose descendants inter-married relatively little and whose gene pool was little affected by later comers.

We cannot say exactly when people came to Greater Australia. Because people of the time could not make long sea voyages, they probably traveled when sea levels were lower, island areas were more extended, and sea crossings were shorter. One period when the sea level was lower was between about 55,000 and 50,000 years ago. At these ages, the reliable tool of radiocarbon dating is stretched to its limits. The fact that many human sites throughout Greater Australia have been dated to between 28,000 and 37,000 years ago, but that there are very few older sites, may mean only that we are at the limits of the technique. Or it could mean that by that time the population had grown large enough to leave traces in the archaeological record. Other radio-metric dating techniques (most of which involve measuring the ratios of certain radioactive isotopes in specimens) are being used, and if we accept current scientific claims, they show that humans came to Greater Australia at least 50,000 years ago. Two sites, both in the north of the continent, have been dated by the thermoluminescence technique as slightly younger than this date. (See the feature *Thermoluminescence Dating.*) We are never, of course, likely to find the very first site!

The Oldest Sites

Bobongara is a hillside that rises out of the sea on the north side of New Guinea's Huon Peninsula. Unusually for New Guinea, it is in a rainshadow area and covered with grass, so the series of horizontal terraces making up its surface can be seen clearly. Each terrace is formed by an old coral reef. At some time in the past, the flat top was a lagoon. The terraces have been gradually lifted out of the sea by the steadily rising rock base on which they are built. Scattered across the hillside are scores of large and heavy stone artifacts, up to 2 kilograms (between 4 and 5 pounds) in weight, made of big flakes knocked off river boulders. They look like axeheads and have a notch on either side in the middle, which seems to have been intended for some kind of handle.

Scores of waisted tools have been found in the raised reefs of Bobongara Hill. They are made of very large flakes struck from water-rolled boulders, and the side notching (or "waist") was clearly intended for hafting. These tools are usually thought of as axes, but they are not very sharp, and it seems likely that they were used as wedges or digging tools.
J. PETER WHITE

Raised coral reefs extend up Bobongara Hill like a series of steps from sea level to a height of more than 1,000 meters (3,300 feet). The youngest reef was lifted out of the sea some 6,000 years ago. Each reef once comprised a flat lagoon, with waves breaking against the steep front. Artifacts more than 40,000 years old have been found here.

ROBERT RAYMOND

THERMOLUMINESCENCE DATING

RICHARD G. ROBERTS

Archaeologists use a variety of dating techniques, each suited to different materials. Radiocarbon dating can be used on organic materials, such as charcoal and bone, while inorganic materials, such as quartz and feldspar crystals, can be dated by thermoluminescence (TL). These crystals occur in most soils (clay, silt, and sand), as well as in flint and volcanic ash. The TL method can date materials up to about 200,000 years old (or more in favorable circumstances), and dates are usually accurate to within about 10 percent.

The method relies on the fact that there is a low level of radioactivity within the crystals themselves and in the surrounding soil and rock. During the process of radioactive decay, small quantities of radiation (alpha particles, beta particles, and gamma rays) are regularly released, producing free electrons within the crystals. These electrons eventually become trapped at defects but can be released if the crystals are heated to 500 degrees Celsius (932 degrees Fahrenheit) or exposed to sunlight for several hours. The TL method exploits this fact.

Dating Pottery

TL was used originally to date pottery that has been fired in a kiln or open fire to make it hard. This firing causes all the trapped electrons to be released and thus sets that pot's TL "clock" at zero. Once the pot (or a fragment of it) is buried in the ground, electrons once again start to become trapped within its crystals. This continues until the pot (or fragment) is reheated. When this is done in a darkened laboratory, the release of electrons is visible as a quantity of light, which can be measured. The greater the quantity of light, the greater the number of electrons released, and so the older the pot. The method is widely used to authenticate pottery and ceramics for museums and art sales.

Dating Sediments

TL dating can also be used on flint artifacts that have been heated, and buried sediments that have been exposed to sunlight at some time in the past. For example, excavated soil containing stone tools can be dated. The method in this case relies on the fact that the TL clock was set at zero when the soil was last exposed to sunlight. Using TL in this way is trickier, since sunlight rarely releases all the electrons, and so the clock is not truly set at zero. Some allowance must be made for the number of trapped electrons remaining since the sediment was last exposed, and this is done by measuring the number of electrons retained by similar sediment in an exposed area. A closely related technique, known as optical dating, is currently being developed to avoid this problem of incomplete zeroing by sunlight.

Because electrons are trapped at different rates in different samples, the rate of electron trapping is determined for each sample. This is done in the laboratory by exposing separate portions of each sample to different amounts of radiation and then measuring the quantity of light released by each portion when heated. To calculate the amount of radiation that the pot has accumulated since it was buried (the paleodose), the quantity of light released by the "as collected" portion of the pot is compared with the light from the irradiated portions. The same procedure is used to date flints and sediments.

Establishing the Date

To finally obtain an age for a sample of pottery, flint, or sediment, it is necessary to know not only the paleodose but also the amount of radiation that the sample received, on average, each year that it was buried (the annual dose). The sample age is equal to the paleodose divided by the annual dose. In the case of pottery, the annual dose results mainly from the radioactive decay of uranium, thorium, and potassium, which are present in the clay from which the pot is made and in the soil surrounding the buried pot. In the case of sediment, the sample and the surrounding soil often have the same mineral composition and hence the same radioactivity. For pottery, it is important to measure the radioactivity of the soil as well as that of the pot itself to obtain an accurate date. Consideration must also be given to the water content of the sample, averaged over the period it was buried, because the annual dose is reduced by the presence of water in pottery and soil.

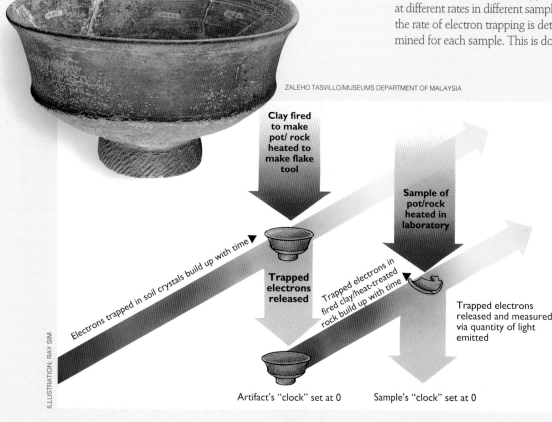

Clay fired to make pot/ rock heated to make flake tool

Sample of pot/rock heated in laboratory

Electrons trapped in soil crystals build up with time

Trapped electrons released

Trapped electrons in fired clay/heat-treated rock build up with time

Trapped electrons released and measured via quantity of light emitted

Artifact's "clock" set at 0

Sample's "clock" set at 0

The TL clock is reset when a pot is fired in a kiln or open fire. When the pot is later reheated in the laboratory, the quantity of light emitted is related to the number of electrons released, and hence the time elapsed since the pot was fired.

While most of these tools have been found on the surface, three have been found stratified between the weathered volcanic ash that blankets the surface of reef IIIA and the front of reef IV. Reef IIIA is dated to between 45,000 and 53,000 years ago. Reef IIIB, where there is no ash, is dated to 40,000 years ago. The ash surrounding the waisted axes has been dated by the thermoluminescence technique to more than 40,000 but less than 60,000 years ago. It seems probable, therefore, that the tools are about 45,000 years old, or possibly a little older.

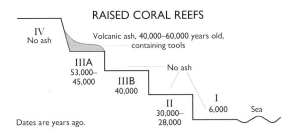

RAISED CORAL REEFS

IV
No ash

Volcanic ash, 40,000–60,000 years old, containing tools

IIIA
53,000–
45,000

IIIB
40,000

No ash

II
30,000–
28,000

I
6,000

Sea

Dates are years ago.

Of the three tools found embedded in the ash, two were waisted in the usual way but one has a groove over both faces, showing even more clearly that these tools were meant to be hafted. Scientists have speculated that they were axes used to clear small spaces in the forest that would have grown there at a time of higher rainfall. These clearings might have been made to allow edible fruit trees or other plants more room to grow, or to get wood for houses. Such explanations, however, are difficult to test.

Another site with evidence of human occupation going back 50,000 years is Malakunanja II, a large rock shelter near the Arnhem Land escarpment. It consists of more than 4 meters (13 feet) of sand deposit, the upper 2.6 meters (8 feet 6 inches) of which contain stone artifacts. These are less distinctive than the waisted blades, consisting only of flakes and chunks with sharp edges. But there are many more of them: more than 100 have been collected from the lowest 20 centimeters (8 inches) of the occupation deposits in a pit only a meter (just over 3 feet) square. It is significant that artifacts have not been found below 2.6 meters (8 feet, 6 inches), suggesting that the site was not occupied before this time.

Some researchers have claimed that humans came to Greater Australia much earlier than 50,000 years ago, but none of these claims has so far been generally accepted. The two main reasons for this are that the material alleged to prove early occupation, such as an increase in charcoal in a lake bed or an accumulation of shells on a seashore, cannot be proved to have resulted from human actions, and that the association between the dated material and artifacts made by humans could also result from more recent events. Despite considerable research in likely areas, such as old lake shores, no human remains or artifacts have been found that are older than about 50,000 years.

RICHARD G. ROBERTS

	Depth of sample below surface		TL date
	in cm (in)		given as most likely range
STONE ARTIFACTS PRESENT	149–155 (59–61)		12,000–18,000
	190–209 (75–82)		19,000–29,000
	230–236 (91–93)		36,000–54,000
	241–254 (95–100)		41,000–48,000
	254–259 (100–102)		48,000–74,000
NO STONE ARTIFACTS	295–315 (116–124)		51,000–79,000
	339–362 (133–143)		65,000–97,000
	452–458 (178–180)		86,000–128,000

⚑ The large rock shelter known as Malakunanja II sits at the base of the spectacular sandstone escarpment of northwest Arnhem Land. The site faces onto a flat, sandy plain and has been occupied for some 50,000 years.

◄ TL dates for Malakunanja II. The upper (younger) levels of this site have also been dated by the radiocarbon method, and the correlation between these two techniques, along with normal scientific caution, suggests that the younger end of each TL age range should be used at present. (That is, stone artifacts were present at least 12,000 to 48,000 years ago.)

Colonizing the Continent

From what is known of past climates, people who arrived in the north of the continent would have found climatic conditions very little different from those they had left. People coming from Asian tropical coastal environments would not have found their new home particularly strange, except for the animals. Most of the fish and shellfish would have been similar, and so would the plants, including the edible ones. It thus seems highly probable that settlers would most rapidly have occupied tropical areas: the coasts and lowlands of New Guinea and northern Australia; the land between; and the large, visible islands of New Britain and New Ireland.

A real contrast existed further south. Temperate Australia (see map) was not only climatically different, it was also the home of different plants and animals, whose habits, availability, and usefulness to humans needed to be learned before the country could be occupied permanently. Temperate Australia 50,000 years ago has been called a "land of lakes", indicating the effect of an increased rainfall on the country around the arid core, then much smaller than it is today. But these lakes did not last. Gradually the rainfall decreased, temperatures declined, and the arid core of the continent expanded. By about 25,000 years ago, temperate Australia was as dry as it is now; and by 20,000 years ago, much drier, colder, and windier.

The theory that the continent may have been colonized in two stages is supported by the types of stone artifacts that have been found: notably waisted, sometimes stemmed, blades and stone axe (or hatchet) heads, with working edges sharpened by grinding. The technique of grinding tough stone to create and sharpen artifacts is a relatively recent invention. In Europe and other parts of the Old World, it goes back about 10,000 years (thus falling within the Holocene period), and is usually found within farming communities. But there is now widespread, if not extensive, evidence that this technique was used in the north of Greater Australia at least 25,000 years ago.

Ground-edge tools like modern Australian hatchet heads have been found at the Nawamoyn and Malangangerr sites of Arnhem Land and dated to about 20,000 years ago, as have similar tools found in Cape York and the Kimberleys, while one found at Nombe in the New Guinea Highlands has been dated to 26,000 years ago. The waisted blades, which are generally flaked, not ground, are older still, being the main tools found at Bobongara. Other, younger, or surface (and therefore undatable), finds of waisted blades have been made throughout New Guinea and in Cape York.

The relationship between these two groups of tools is not clear. Most researchers are inclined to think of both as axes or hatchets, or something similar, but why there were two forms in the Pleistocene period when one served the full range

⚲ Many of Australia's temperate landscapes have a sandstone base, most often either flat or steeply scarped. As soils are commonly thin and acidic, the vegetation is highly specialized. People lived along the river valleys in areas such as Grose Gorge, in the Blue Mountains of New South Wales, using the ridge tops for their ceremonies and as a route to other areas.

of (presumably) similar functions in the Holocene in both areas is not known. The significant point is that both groups of tools are found only in the tropics and that there is no evidence of them in temperate Australia until less than 5,000 years ago (with the possible exception of a few examples on Kangaroo Island, off the coast of South Australia). This indicates cultural differences between the two areas during the Pleistocene period, a difference that continues—underlined by the physical separation of New Guinea and Australia—until the present. The rock engravings found in the tropical and temperate areas of Greater Australia (discussed below) similarly suggest such a cultural division.

Once people learned how to use the country of temperate Australia, perhaps more than 40,000 years ago, there is evidence that they expanded into it quite rapidly. Early dates from Tasmania, southwestern Australia, and inland regions—though not the central desert—are all around 35,000 to 40,000 years ago. After that time, the most extensive climatic change, which affected the whole continent except for some coastal regions, was at the peak of the cold, dry period that occurred about 18,000 years ago, when few or no people lived in large parts of the inland.

More local environmental effects occurred at other times, however. In Tasmania, people stopped using all the known southwestern sites about 12,000 years ago. The warmer climate

REG MORRISON

caused the forests to increase, apparently making the landscape unfit for certain animals and plants and therefore unfit for the humans who depended on them for food. As a result of such changes, people moved gradually to other parts of the country which generally did not support such large populations. As the sea level rose, local changes certainly occurred in some coastal

⚲ Today, at least two-thirds of Australia is arid or semi-arid, and even more of the continent was dry in the Pleistocene period. Despite appearances, these environments support a diverse range of plants and animals, but because rainfall is low and unpredictable, few people can live in them.

☦ A grindstone from the lower levels of Malakunanja II, excavated in 1989. At about 50,000 years old, it is currently one of the oldest grindstones in the world. It was probably used for preparing ochers for painting on bodies, artifacts, or walls.

D. MARKOVIC

locations, but we have no record of these changes before the sea reached its present level about 6,000 years ago.

We cannot accurately estimate the number of people who might have lived in the country at a particular time: our archaeological records are too sparse. We can say, however, that there are unlikely to have been more than a million in Australia or 1.5 million in New Guinea, which is a generous estimate of the numbers at the beginning of European colonization in AD 1788. But once the entire Greater Australian continent had been occupied, there are unlikely to have been fewer than 250,000 people, or we would not have the kinds of archaeological records we have. There must always have been enough people to sustain an organized social system, with appropriate marriage and other networks. Families cannot live in isolation for very long.

The population was not, of course, spread evenly over the country. Many people would have lived along the coast, as they did in more recent times, but the remains of their settlements have long since been drowned by the rising seas. Within Australia, they also settled around rivers and lakes. Traces of occupation during the last 35,000 years have been found at sites along the Darling River, and on the shores of the Willandra and other overflow lakes in western New South Wales. The population in different areas of Australia has always been closely related to rainfall and the availability of water, for obvious reasons.

The distribution of people in what is now New Guinea is harder to determine. Apart from the coasts, people certainly used the highlands from early on, although few areas were completely free from tropical disease. It is unlikely that many lived in the inland lowlands, with their high rainfall, malaria, yaws, and other tropical diseases.

The People of Australia

Many anthropologists have attempted to show not only that Australian Aborigines and New Guineans are genetically different but that modern Aborigines have developed from different races which came here at different times. Early anthropologists either classified mainland Australians and Tasmanians separately, or divided the people of these two islands into three groups—basically, northern, central and southern, and rainforest (Queensland and Tasmania). The data on which these judgments were based were either literally superficial, relying on such surface features as skin color and hair form, or consisted of a few skull measurements. It was assumed at the time that such factors were not subject to selection pressure or random change and that they reflected the original differences between groups, preserved for tens of thousands of years. We now know that this is a false assumption.

A more reliable source of information about

D. ELFORD/WESTERN AUSTRALIAN MUSEUM

ancient populations is provided by remains of human skeletons dating from prehistoric times. Some of the largest and best preserved accumulations of these in the world have been found in Australia, especially the southeast. These records of the Aboriginal past can tell us a great deal about the history of both individual peoples and human settlement in Australia.

The study of human bones has been controversial in Australia for the last 20 years. While some Aborigines are interested in learning what scientists can add to their knowledge of the past, many think the dead should not be disturbed. Until recently, most scientists—like most white Australians—were prepared totally to ignore the affront that digging up bones and putting them in museums gives to Aborigines. Many now understand, however, that once Aboriginal control of the Aboriginal past is accepted, cooperative research may be possible.

The oldest Australian skeletons so far identified come from three burials on the shores of Lake Mungo, in western New South Wales, dated to more than 20,000 years ago. Many more date from 15,000 to 10,000 years ago, when people along the Murray River Valley,

in particular, buried their dead in riverside sands at Kow Swamp, Coobol Creek, and other locations. Analysis of these skeletons has shown conclusively that all are of modern humans, *Homo sapiens sapiens*. Beyond that, there are two schools of thought.

Some physical anthropologists have contrasted the very thick skulls, large teeth, and heavy brow ridges of some skeletons with the much thinner, lighter, and more gracile build of others, and on this basis have divided the skeletons into two groups. The more robust group they compare with ancient Indonesian skeletons, and the more finely built group with some ancient Chinese skeletons, suggesting that there were two migrations to Australia, from different places and at different times. They believe the robust group to be the older but have not yet been able to demonstrate this.

Others have re-examined the finds and concluded that no sharp distinction can be drawn between "robust" and "gracile" skeletons and that there is no significant demonstrable difference in their age. Rather, they claim that most larger skeletons are male, while most smaller, lighter skeletons are female. The fact that the two oldest skeletons are relatively gracile they attribute to chance, given the small sample represented by these finds. On this view, the skeletons simply show that some Pleistocene Australians were bigger than those of the Holocene and that the population as a whole was physically more varied than in the later period, but that is true of many human populations in the world at that time.

↩ This necklace of sea shells was recently excavated from a rock shelter in the northwest of Australia. It is more than 30,000 years old—which roughly corresponds to the time humans all over the world began to decorate themselves.

⚲ Pits of this kind are found in tropical areas from 20,000 years ago. They seem to be the result of many years of cracking nuts and pounding ocher to use as pigment. This series of pits in Kakadu National Park, in Arnhem Land, is particularly extensive.

REG MORRISON

ART OF THE LAND

PAUL TACON

PAUL TACON

PAUL TACON

AUSTRALIAN ABORIGINAL PEOPLES have been marking their rocky landscapes with engravings and paintings for tens of thousands of years. Archaeologists using a variety of experimental dating techniques may not agree on the age of the oldest rock art, but they are convinced that many forms have survived for at least 15,000 years. These include some petroglyphs, such as macropod or bird tracks and circular designs, that are covered by a thick silica skin or rock varnish, and some pictographs from the escarpments of northern Australia. The painted images are of immense interest, as they show perishable objects and aspects of life of which there is no other record.

☗Boomerang stencils are among the oldest stencil forms of Arnhem Land, in the Northern Territory. Boomerangs have not been used as weapons in Arnhem Land for more than 6,000 years, but many of the older styles of painting include depictions of figures fighting and hunting with boomerangs.

☗A large, barbed spear protrudes from the breast of an emu painted in the Pleistocene "dynamic figure" style of Arnhem Land. The dashes near its open beak may be an early visual symbol of sound. Dynamic human figures are also shown with such dashes when they are chasing or in opposition to each other.

PAUL TACON

☗Macropod (kangaroo and wallaby) and bird (often emu) tracks are common in the oldest petroglyphs of Australia. These examples from Kakadu National Park have a thick silica skin covering them. Much current research is devoted to dating these skin formations more precisely.

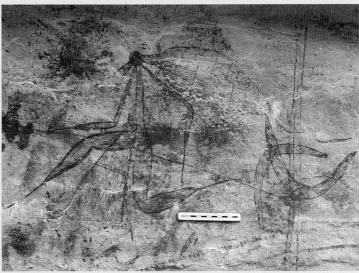

⚤ Male dynamic figures often carry large spears and boomerangs and are often shown in combat, hunting, or carrying out domestic activities. They depict a way of life that has not been seen in Arnhem Land for more than 10,000 years.

⚤ Female dynamic figures are rare, but they, too, are animated and painted along with their material artifacts, such as digging sticks and baskets. Sometimes, they are shown interacting with males, animals, or beings with animal heads.

⚤ So-called Bradshaw figures, similar to the dynamic figures of the Northern Territory, were painted in the Kimberley region in the far north of Western Australia. They, too, are shown with boomerangs, spears, grass skirts, and elaborate headdresses. Investigations currently focus on whether the two have a common age and origin.

GREATER AUSTRALIA

Eighteen thousand years ago, the sea level dropped about 150 meters (500 feet) as glaciers spread across the northern hemisphere, locking up sea water. In the Pleistocene period, this created the landmass of Greater Australia. People lived throughout the continent, but the only surviving records are from areas that are above the modern-day sea level. During the Pleistocene, all of modern-day Australia was in the temperate zone, and much of it was quite cold and arid.

It does not mean that there was more than one founding group.

There is less evidence from New Guinea. Only a few small fragments of Pleistocene skeletons have been found, but at present we believe that the first inhabitants were of the same stock as the original Australians. Australians and New Guineans look very different from each other now as a result of many factors, including climate, isolation, selection, and genetic drift. But the differences are mostly only skin deep: genetically, the two groups are quite close.

Caves and Shelters

Remains from Pleistocene times are found throughout Greater Australia. Where they are found depends on two factors: where people lived in the past and where their debris has survived until the present. Caves and rock shelters are good places to look for evidence: the rubbish people left behind in the course of repeated visits is protected from the weather, and from the layers that build up over the years we can construct an historical sequence. Malakunanja II (see map) is one such site. In many places, however, stone tools and charcoal are the only evidence to have survived, since local conditions, such as acid ground water, often destroy organic materials. Tasmania is a notable exception. (See the feature *Hunters on the Edge of the Tasmanian Ice*.)

Rock shelter and cave sites often yield evidence of long-term changes in human occupation. At Lawn Hill station, in northern Queensland, for instance, Peter Hiscock has shown that when the site was first occupied about 20,000 years ago, people made their tools from various kinds of stone, some found only on the plains to the north, others on the plateau to the south. Then, at the peak of the cold, dry period that occurred about 18,000 years ago, local rock shelters close to permanent water were used more intensively, and people made stone tools mainly from material close at hand. After about 13,500 years ago, when the climate improved, they reverted to the earlier pattern. What we can see here, then, is the long-term impact of environmental change on human behavior—changes that were probably not obvious to those living at the time.

But most Pleistocene sites are not found in protected locations. Consistent with the fact that most people lived in the open air, making only temporary shelters, the majority of sites consist of scatters of material resulting from short-term stays in one place.

Riverside Middens

Jane Balme and Jeanette Hope recently carried out research in western New South Wales showing both the impact of environmental change on human behavior and how changes in the local environment determine the nature of the archaeological record. They researched the 15,000 square kilometers (5,800 square miles) of the lower Darling River basin, an area of very flat country through which run the current river channel and a string of anabranches (Talyawalka, Tandou, and Redbank creeks) representing the course of the river before 9,000 to 7,000 years ago. There are also two sets of overflow lakes created by the flooding of present and past rivers.

Balme and Hope found middens of freshwater shellfish along the river and anabranch banks and the lake shores, usually consisting of small concentrations of shells and freshwater crayfish carapaces surrounding a small fireplace. The middens were preserved only if they had almost immediately been covered by slow-moving river or lake silt. Once the material had been uncovered by wind erosion, it soon deteriorated. Clearly, we cannot judge settlement patterns in prehistoric times simply from surviving sites. Most sites will long since have been destroyed by the elements.

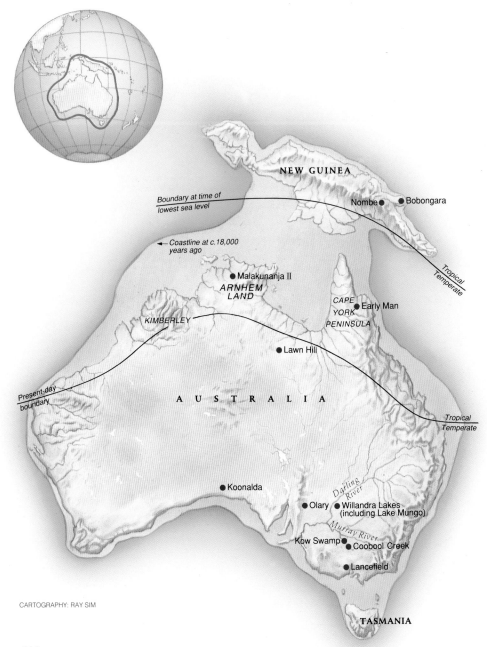

Boundary at time of lowest sea level

NEW GUINEA

Nombe ● ● Bobongara

← Coastline at c.18,000 years ago

● Malakunanja II

ARNHEM LAND

Tropical / Temperate

CAPE YORK PENINSULA

● Early Man

KIMBERLEY

● Lawn Hill

Present-day boundary

A U S T R A L I A

Tropical / Temperate

● Koonalda

Darling River

● Olary ● Willandra Lakes (including Lake Mungo)

Murray River

Kow Swamp ● ● Coobool Creek

● Lancefield

TASMANIA

REG MORRISON

◄● Freshwater shellfish, usually the bivalve *Velesunio* sp., inhabit many rivers and lakes throughout temperate Australia and have long been part of the Aboriginal diet. The discarded shells are often found in archaeological sites, such as here at Lake Mungo. As well as giving an insight into the environment of the time and people's eating habits, shells can be radiocarbon-dated and thus help to establish the age of sites.

As the map shows, however, carbon dates of shell middens in this area reveal a clear pattern of settlement. Pleistocene dates are found only along the anabranches and around the adjacent overflow lakes. Sites less than 7,000 years old are found along the modern river and its lakes, such as Lake Menindee. In the period between 9,000 and 6,000 years ago, very high river flows clearly filled Ratcatchers Lake and other lakes, and for a short time provided conditions favorable to both Aboriginal settlement and the preservation of midden sites.

Research on the shell middens of this area showed Balme and Hope that Aborigines were present in some part of the area almost continuously from about 27,000 years ago. Combined with data from another set of middens and hearths found around overflow lakes from the Lachlan River, about 100 kilometers (60 miles) south, the record shows that people have lived in this general area continuously for about 35,000 years. No single set of archaeological materials, however, provides a complete and reliable picture of how humans related to their environment over this period.

The Lake Mungo Burials

More dramatic but rarer finds give us an insight into the day-to-day lives of ancient people. The most famous of these are the burials at Lake Mungo. Mungo I is the burial of the remains of a cremated woman. The body was burned while

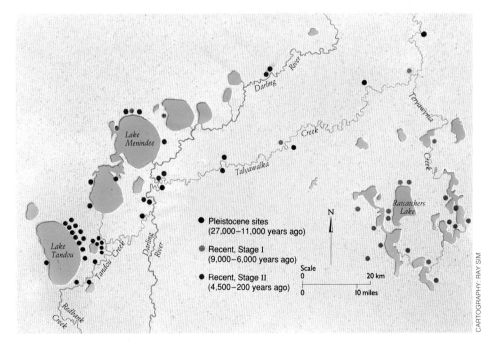

CARTOGRAPHY: RAY SIM

lying on its left side, after which the bones were gathered up, broken into small pieces, and placed in a pit near or perhaps under the pyre. Mungo III is the burial of an adult man, who is lying on his back. Pink ocher powder was sprinkled over the upper part of his body before he was buried. We do not know whether the differences between these burials stem from time, sex, totem, or some other cause. But these complex burial practices show that Pleistocene Australians, like people

MODERN AND FOSSIL LAKES

The lakes of western New South Wales are mostly dry today, but at various times in the past they have been filled. People in Australia have always settled around rivers and lakes, water often being a scarce resource.

⚊ This 26,000-year-old bone bears the tooth marks of the extinct carnivore *Thylacoleo*, a relative of modern possums.

⚊ Lower jaws (mandibles) of the extinct kangaroo *Sthenurus*, which lived in the more forested parts of eastern Australia.

⚲ Many of the prehistoric engravings in the rock walls of Early Man Shelter, in Cape York, appear to be symbolic.

elsewhere in the world at the same time, had some kind of relationship with a spiritual world. (These Mungo remains were recently returned to the local Aboriginal community.)

Humans and the Environment

One of the major puzzles in the archaeology of early Greater Australia concerns the relationship between humans and their environment. We know that in recent times much of temperate and arid Australia was regularly burned, a practice its Aboriginal owners described as "cleaning it up". The long-term effect of this method of land management is difficult to evaluate, as is the interaction between Aborigines and the animals that used to inhabit the country. One account of the animals involved, and one view of their relationship, is given in the feature *The Lost Animals of Australia*. Here is another.

Prehistoric people have certainly hunted animals to extinction elsewhere in the world. Where this has happened, many bones of extinct animals have been found at human sites. This is not the case in Greater Australia. The evidence to date does not show a great deal of interaction between humans and animals.

Excavations at Lancefield Swamp, in southern Australia, have revealed a large bone bed, some 2,000 square meters (2,600 square yards) in area, resting on green clay and sealed in by about 70 centimeters (27 inches) of black clay. Below the bone bed, which consists of thousands of bones of all sizes, a small channel has been eroded into the green clay. It contains bone fragments and charcoal. This charcoal has been dated to about 25,000 years ago, and the bone bed that seals it in must be younger than this, although not much. Most bones are of one species of extinct kangaroo,

but there are a few pieces of diprotodon and of extinct bird species. These bones are not cut or burned, so they did not accumulate as a result of the animals being hunted, butchered, or cooked. They are more likely to be the remains of *Thylacoleo* prey, because some bones bear tooth marks fitting the pattern of this animal's sharp carnassial teeth. (*Thylacoleo* was a large carnivore closely related to possums—a meat eater similar to a panther or a leopard, rather than a bone crusher such as a hyena or, the Australian equivalent, *Sarcophilus*. Both are now extinct.)

The Lancefield findings show that at least some animals that are now extinct lived long after people arrived. This is also shown at Nombe in the New Guinea Highlands, where diprotodon bones and the bones of three different macropods (animals from the kangaroo family), which were apparently killed by humans, were found with stone tools and material of human origin in levels dated to between 25,000 and 15,000 years ago. None of the animals is very big: the diprotodon is about the size of a pig.

If people were responsible for the extinction of these animals, the process was different from that in other parts of the world. Elsewhere, many species of birds and mammals disappeared rapidly after humans arrived. As with more modern examples from our industrialized world (the dodo, the passenger pigeon, and some whales, seals, and bears), large animal populations were wiped out in only a few centuries. This is not the case in Australia, and given that we have no good evidence of large-scale killing, climatic change has been suggested as the most likely cause of these extinctions.

But is this feasible? We know that there have been many climatic changes during the last two million years, and we have no reason to believe that the most recent changes were more extreme or wide-ranging in their impact than earlier ones. To claim that climatic change during the last 50,000 years caused so many extinctions would seem to require evidence of a large-scale catastrophe, such as an extreme drought and consequent dust storm—and even then, such an event is highly unlikely to have affected the whole of Greater Australia. What does seem likely is that both climate and humans have been involved in these extinctions, each contributing differently in different areas. Humans probably played a bigger part in the tropics, and climate in the arid zone, but with local variations.

Art in Early Australia

Recent developments in dating techniques show that during the Pleistocene there was a wide range of decoration on rock surfaces. The best-documented of these is at Early Man Shelter, in Cape York, where Andrée Rosenfeld found engravings on a rock wall against which were

banked 13,000-year-old archaeological deposits. The figures included spirals, "bird tracks" and other three-pronged shapes, and meandering lines—none directly representational and some appearing to be symbolic.

Very similar figures have been found engraved on rocks throughout nontropical Australia. Known as the Panaramitee style, after a site in central Australia, their distribution has been cited as evidence for a kind of "community of culture" throughout Pleistocene Australia and Tasmania. Certainly, it is interesting to note that this engraving style has not been found in New Guinea or in Arnhem Land. It may, in fact, help to demarcate the temperate province of Greater Australia.

Direct dating of some engravings by the new cation-ratio method, however, puts the age of many in dispute. This technique, which involves correlating mineral ratios with radiocarbon dates, is not yet totally accepted, but seems to give consistent results when used in various parts of the world. According to this, the lowest levels of desert varnish (a deposit made by microorganisms that oxidize manganese and iron) covering rock engravings in the semidesert of South Australia's Olary region range between 1,500 and perhaps 30,000 years old, but the older dates are less reliable with this technique. If confirmed, these dates would suggest that such engravings were being made from the time humans first came to Australia, as well as at the same time as a whole range of rock paintings, nearly all of which are thought to date from the last few thousand years. Too little is known of the reasons behind engraving and painting to say that such a range of ages is impossible, but an artistic tradition that continued unchanged for 30,000 years would be surprising. Other radiocarbon-based dating techniques suggest that the more recent dates are more probably correct.

There are other examples of Pleistocene art. Deep inside South Australia's Koonalda Cave, many hands have traced multiple lines on the soft

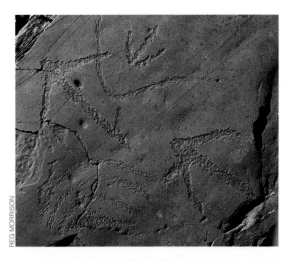

◄ Engravings such as these have been found in several areas of Australia. Known as the Panaramitee style, they look like kangaroo and emu footprints and sometimes occur in a line. Although they are usually called engravings, they are actually pecked into the rock surface. When paintings are found at the same site, the engravings always appear below them and are presumably older.

↧ Elaborate "rayed" circles of this kind have been found together with Panaramitee-style art at some sites. This particular symbol has not yet been dated.

◄ Peckings found in the Olary region include a wide range of Panaramitee-style motifs. They were probably done in the course of ceremonies and used to transmit traditional knowledge and law. In time, they became covered with desert varnish, a layer of predominantly organic material which can be dated.

REG MORRISON

❂➤ This rock painting in Arnhem Land depicts the thylacine (commonly known as the Tasmanian wolf), which has been extinct on the Australian mainland for more than 3,000 years.

PAUL TACON

❂❂ Naturally occurring red and yellow ochers, usually oxides of iron, were mined for use as pigments to decorate bodies, tools, weapons, and rock walls.

REG MORRISON

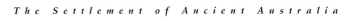

cave walls when the cave was used at least 15,000 years ago. Hands stenciled in red paint have been found in Tasmanian caves last occupied 12,000 years ago, while lumps of ocher found near the Mungo burials suggest that the practice of painting bodies or artifacts is very old indeed. There have even been serious attempts to show that a few paintings of some extinct large animals survive, but the evidence for this is much more disputed. The only good examples are of the Tasmanian "wolf", *Thylacinus*, which became extinct on the Australian mainland between about 3,000 and 4,000 years ago. Our present knowledge of Pleistocene art suggests that it was much more restricted in range of motif, use of color, and elaboration of design than more recent art, but whether this is because it was used for different purposes, or whether it only appears to be so because so little has survived, has yet to be determined. (See the feature *Art of the Land*.)

How Much Do We Know?

By 30,000 years ago, the entire continent of Greater Australia had been settled by descendants of Asian tropical foragers, who crossed sea barriers and discovered and settled environments ranging from the familiar to the subtemperate, from rainforest to near-desert. Even the desert core was probably occupied, although sparsely. These people were the direct ancestors of most of today's Aborigines.

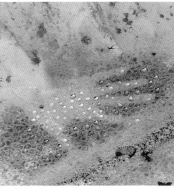

⚤ Aboriginal paintings have been found in several Tasmanian caves. Most are hand stencils, made by blowing red paint through a pipe around a hand held against a rock wall. The organic material—perhaps saliva or blood—mixed with the paint to make it stick has been dated to about 10,000 years ago.
JOHN VOSS FOR TASMANIAN DEPARTMENT OF PARKS, WILDLIFE AND HERITAGE

⚥ Koonalda is one of many sinkholes that dot the Nullarbor Plain. Today, many people visit the site, as the tracks indicate, but few are allowed to descend into this ancient mine.

⚤ From deep underground in Koonalda Cave, Aborigines mined flint to make tools. The charcoal deposits from the fires they lit to work by have been dated to between 15,000 and 20,000 years old. The soft limestone walls near the mining areas are covered with engravings made with sharp stones or sticks, and with fingers.

REG MORRISON

HUNTERS ON THE EDGE OF THE TASMANIAN ICE

RICHARD COSGROVE

The colonizing of Tasmania in late Pleistocene times represents a surprising and important chapter in the story of the spread of anatomically modern humans throughout the globe. Archaeological evidence now being won from limestone caves in southwest Tasmania shows that humans had traversed the vast continent of Greater Australia, from the tropical north and the islands of Melanesia to the glacial south, at least 35,000 years ago, demonstrating a remarkable ability to exploit the entire range of ecological habitats.

☗ A small artifact made of Darwin glass, recovered from Nunamira Cave.

R. COSGROVE/SOUTHERN FORESTS ARCHAEOLOGICAL PROJECT

Over the past five years, the Southern Forests Archaeological Project at La Trobe University, Melbourne, has recorded more than 100 radiocarbon dates for material excavated from seven widely dispersed cave and open sites in southwest Tasmania (see map). These cover a period from 35,000 years ago to 11,000 years ago. The oldest of these dates has significantly changed our thinking about the people of the Late Stone Age. We now know that hunter-gatherers did not survive and thrive solely on coastal, lake, and river resources, but were able to exploit subantarctic inland and upland environments previously thought to have been too harsh for settlement. The finds are of particular interest, because they mark the southernmost appearance of humans on the planet at this time.

An Ancient Land Bridge

Until recently, it was thought that humans arrived in Tasmania only about 23,000 years ago, when the world was entering a period sometimes referred to as the Big Chill. At this time, so much water froze that the sea level was 60 meters (200 feet) lower than at present. About 20,000 years ago, it dropped to a maximum of 120 meters (400 feet), exposing the land under what is now Bass Strait. We now know, however, that people arrived some 12,000 years earlier, in a milder part of the last Ice Age, when the sea was at its previous lowest level.

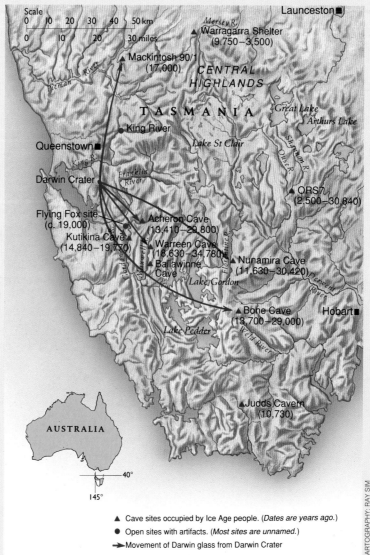

LATE PLEISTOCENE SITES IN SOUTHWEST TASMANIA

Scale
0   10   20   30   40   50 km
0   10   20   30 miles

Launceston ■

▲ Warragarra Shelter (9,750–3,500)

▲ Mackintosh 90/1 (17,000)

CENTRAL HIGHLANDS

TASMANIA

● King River

Great Lake
Arthurs Lake

Lake St Clair

Queenstown ■

Darwin Crater

■ ORS7 (2,500–30,840)

Flying Fox site (c. 19,000)

Acheron Cave (13,410–29,800)

Kutikina Cave (14,840–19,770)

Warreen Cave (18,630–34,780)

Ballawinne Cave

▲ Nunamira Cave (11,630–30,420)

Lake Gordon

▲ Bone Cave (13,700–29,000)

Hobart ■

Lake Pedder

▲ Judds Cavern (10,730)

AUSTRALIA

40°

145°

▲ Cave sites occupied by Ice Age people. (*Dates are years ago.*)
● Open sites with artifacts. (*Most sites are unnamed.*)
➤ Movement of Darwin glass from Darwin Crater

CARTOGRAPHY: RAY SIM

herb fields developed in their place, attracting such animals as wallabies and emus. Because of the rain-shadow effect of the western mountains, the drier eastern part of the island had a much lower rainfall. Destabilized soils and cold northwesterly winds inhibited plant growth. Summers were probably short and cool. Although rainfall was reduced by about half, south-west Tasmania probably did not suffer the fluctuating drought conditions of the east, so its resources were more predictable than those in the southeast of the island.

Subantarctic Hunter-gatherers

Despite the bleak conditions, most of the cave sites in southwest Tasmania have yielded exceptional quantities of human food remains. At Nunamira Cave, in the Florentine Valley, more than 200,000 pieces of bone, amounting to 30 kilograms (66 pounds), have been excavated from less than a cubic meter (about 35 cubic feet) of deposits. Of this, 90 percent are remains of the red-necked wallaby. Large quantities of emu shell found at some sites indicate that these sites were occupied in late winter and early spring. This is important, because it is the most difficult time of the year for hunter-gatherers and their prey, especially in a subantarctic environment.

The human occupants of these caves were able to exploit a range of animals according to their needs.

At this time, temperatures were declining, reaching their lowest level in Tasmania 18,000 years ago, when the annual average temperature was between about 2 and 4 degrees Celsius (35 and 40 degrees Fahrenheit). During this cold period, glaciers developed above many of the western valleys occupied by humans. Trees could not flourish at heights above 250 meters (820 feet), and patches of grassland and

These thumbnail scrapers, from Nunamira Cave, are 23,000 years old.
R. COSGROVE/SOUTHERN FORESTS ARCHAEOLOGICAL PROJECT

Numerous stout bone-points made from the lower leg of the wallaby have been found, indicating that these people were making clothes at least 26,000 years ago. Many have polished ends, suggesting that they were used to work hides, and some have been shaped into fine needle-like forms. Others were probably used as spear-points.

At all these sites, a range of small tools, or thumbnail scrapers, has been found. These have been dated to between 23,000 years old (in Nunamira and Bone Caves) and 18,500 years old (in Warreen Cave), while some found outside the southwest zone at Cave Bay Cave, in northwest Tasmania, are about 19,000 years old. They are made from a variety of raw materials, including fine-grained chert, silcrete, hornfels, quartz, and, most important, glass from Darwin Crater, which was formed by the impact of a meteorite some 700,000 years ago. This glass material has been found at all sites, and was used over a long period, between 27,000 and 13,000 years ago. It has been found up to 100 kilometers (60 miles) from its source, indicating that these hunter-gatherers traveled long distances throughout the region, almost certainly seasonally.

A recent find of cave art has given us a new insight into the life of these Stone Age people, suggesting that it had an intellectual and spiritual dimension beyond the realm of mere day-to-day survival. More than 30 human hand stencils have been discovered in two of the caves, Ballawinne Cave, 60 meters (196 feet) underground, and Judds Cavern, 60 meters (196 feet) underground.

Significantly, at the same latitude (43 degrees North) and throughout this glacial period, on the other side of the world—in France, Spain, and Russia—people were also creating art deep inside caves and hunting a range of animals including bison, reindeer, horses, and ibex under similar glacial conditions. This suggests that modern humans had similar ways of adapting to their environment and exploiting physically inhospitable landscapes.

What Drove Them Out?

The combined archaeological evidence shows that these Tasmanian Ice Age people had developed a technology and a social system that allowed them to exploit the southwest region for more than 25,000 years. Clearly, they were no mere puppets of environmental change. But about 12,000 years ago, almost all the caves were abandoned. Why this happened we don't know, but it has been suggested that with the rapid change in climate at the end of the Pleistocene period the zone was covered in unproductive temperate rainforest, which drove out the game animals—and the humans who had hunted them for more than a thousand generations.

Bone and stone tools excavated from Bone Cave.
R. FRANK/SOUTHERN FORESTS ARCHAEOLOGICAL PROJECT

A selection of points, made of wallaby leg bones, excavated from Warreen Cave.
B. DOUGLAS/SOUTHERN FORESTS ARCHAEOLOGICAL PROJECT

Nunamira Cave, Florentine River valley.

R. FRANK/SOUTHERN FORESTS ARCHAEOLOGICAL PROJECT

THE LOST ANIMALS OF AUSTRALIA

TIMOTHY FLANNERY

THE HISTORY OF AUSTRALIA'S ANIMALS over the past 50,000 years has been largely one of extinction. The time has been far too short for new species of large animals, such as mammals and birds, to evolve. Yet over this period nearly one-third of Australia's mammal species have become extinct, along with nearly all the large reptiles and many of the flightless birds. The cause of these extinctions is still hotly debated. One school of thought suggests that humans caused the extinctions, and the other that they were due to changes in climate.

ILLUSTRATIONS FROM KADIMAKARA, EXTINCT VERTEBRATES OF AUSTRALIA, 1991, PRINCETON UNIVERSITY PRESS. BY P. V. RICH AND G.F. VAN TETS. DRAWINGS BY FRANK KNIGHT. © MUSEUM OF VICTORIA

🜨 The size of a large rhinoceros, diprotodons were the largest land mammals ever to have existed in Australia. The trunk shown here is conjectural.

The greatest problem in evaluating these theories is that we do not know precisely when these animals became extinct. Fossils from a number of well-dated cave and lakeside sites suggest that all the now-extinct species had vanished by 35,000 years ago—but a few other sites suggest that giant marsupials might have survived until 25,000 years ago, or even as late as 6,000 years ago. We know that Australia's climate has changed greatly over the past 40,000 years. Between 25,000 and 15,000 years ago, the sea level dropped by more than 100 meters (320 feet), and the continent experienced an extremely arid phase. Clearly, the timing of the extinctions is of critical importance. If they can be shown to coincide with the arrival of humans, about 50,000 years ago, then circumstantial evidence would point to humans as the cause. If, however, the giant marsupials survived until 25,000 years ago, then the increased aridity would seem to be the more likely cause.

Australia's Ancient Giants

Before these great extinctions, Australia was a very different place. Fires were probably less frequent than they are now, because large, now-extinct marsupial herbivores (of which there were about 40 species) reduced the standing crop of vegetation. Rainforest plants were more widespread in the drier parts of Australia. (Today, their distribution is limited not by lack of water but by bushfires, which kill them.)

The largest marsupial species was the diprotodon, which, like other Australian marsupial giants, was about one-third the weight of its ecological equivalent elsewhere. It probably weighed between 1,000 and 2,000 kilograms (2,200 and 4,400 pounds), while the elephant of Afro-Eurasia weighed about 5,000 kilograms (11,000 pounds). The relatively small size of the Australian marsupial giants has been attributed to Australia's extraordinarily poor soils and erratic climate, both factors that inhibit plant growth.

Judging by the teeth of extinct species, there were many specialist grazers and browsers, paralleling the great mammal communities of Africa today. But the Australian carnivores were very different. For example, there was no equivalent of a lion (the Australian marsupial lion, *Thylacoleo carnifex*, was only about the size of a leopard), and no equivalent of the vast number of cat-like and dog-like carnivores of Africa. Among the larger carnivorous mammals, Australia had only one cat-like species (the marsupial lion), one dog-like species (the thylacine, *Thylacinus cynocephalus*), and one scavenger (the Tasmanian devil, *Sarcophilus harrisii*). The larger Australian carnivores were all reptiles. The gigantic snakes of the genus *Wonambi* were more than 6 meters (20 feet) long and were the major predators throughout Australia, while over the warmer three-quarters of the continent, the 7 meter (23 foot) long goanna

↩ The marsupial lion was Australia's largest warm-blooded carnivore. Closer to a leopard than a lion in size, it evolved from herbivorous ancestors.

Magalania prisca, and the 3 meter (10 foot) long land crocodile *Quinkana fortirostrum*, were the main predators.

There were never vast numbers of most species. Large, warm-blooded creatures were at a disadvantage, their prey being limited by the continent's poor soil and erratic climate. The cold-blooded reptilian carnivores, which required less energy, were therefore able to dominate.

The Impact of Humans

Humans had evolved in their Afro-Eurasian homeland as a medium-sized member of a very large community of mammalian carnivores and omnivores. By 40,000 years ago, they were taking an extraordinarily broad range of prey, including mammals much larger than themselves. They had thus become highly successful and generalized predators. Studies have shown that when humans or other predators arrive in areas where there have previously been no ecologically equivalent species, they invariably have a profound impact. For example, over the last thousand years, Polynesians in Hawaii have destroyed more than 70 percent of the island's bird species; during the nineteenth century, sealers on Macquarie Island severely depleted many seal species; and after rats (*Rattus rattus*) were introduced on Lord Howe Island in 1918, nine species of birds became extinct.

Australian animals were particularly vulnerable to the impact of humans. Marsupial herbivores were adapted only to avoiding predation by large but relatively unintelligent reptiles. Although there were many species of large animals, their numbers were probably quite small. Humans, then, are the most efficient and largest warm-blooded predators that have ever existed in Australia.

From the upper mountain rainforests of Irian Jaya to Australia's desert center, extinctions emptied landscape after landscape, until finally the largest remaining mammals were humans them-

selves. The medium-sized species, weighing between 10 and 100 kilograms (22 and 220 pounds), either became extinct or shrunk in size over thousands of years. Gray kangaroos are now half the weight they were, while koalas, Tasmanian devils, and the larger wallabies weigh on average one-third less than formerly. In general, the larger the species, the more it has reduced in size—with the exception of humans, and possibly wombats (which might have been protected

because of their burrowing habits). This, too, may be attributable to human hunting practices. If hunters claimed the largest individuals of these species, fast-maturing dwarfs would have been more likely to survive to maturity. Increasingly, they would then have produced smaller offspring.

Only the smallest mammals, those weighing less than 10 kilograms (22 pounds), survived largely unaltered, although some may have been restricted to fewer

areas. This changed with the arrival of Europeans towards the end of the eighteenth century. Over the course of the following century, 21 medium-sized species of mammals and one large species—the sole remaining native carnivore, the thylacine—became extinct.

⚲ The thylacine, Australia's only dog-like carnivore, had vanished from mainland Australia by 3,000 years ago but survived in island Tasmania until the 1930s.

THE FIRST PACIFIC ISLANDERS

30,000 YEARS AGO – 10,000 YEARS AGO

Pioneers of the Oceans

J. PETER WHITE

EAST OF AUSTRALIA and New Guinea in the Pacific Ocean lie a number of islands that gradually decrease in size. The largest are New Britain and New Ireland, close to New Guinea and each other. Manus and the other Admiralty Islands to the north, as well as Bougainville and the other Solomon Islands to the southeast, are much smaller, and cannot be seen from the larger islands. Some of the Solomon Islands are no more than the hills remaining from a larger Pleistocene landmass. All these islands can be called Near Oceania, and this chapter is about the people who lived there. They developed skills and technologies that allowed them, ultimately, to visit almost all the islands in the Pacific and to settle on many of them.

The settlement of Near Oceania involved sea crossings of more than 100 kilometers (60 miles), some out of sight of land. Nowhere else in the world has sea travel of this kind been known until the last few thousand years, when islands such as Cyprus and Crete were first visited. Seafaring developed much earlier in the Pacific region, because the sea and climate are warm and there are many intervisible islands stretching east from Southeast Asia. So the people who entered Near Oceania were already accustomed to traveling by sea.

◄◉ The Solomon Islands were the first large islands to be reached by people who had to voyage out of sight of land to find them. Thirty thousand years ago, when people first arrived here, many of the present islands were the mountainous interior of a much larger island.

⌘ RAY SIM

THE FIRST PACIFIC SITES

All the Pleistocene sites of Near Oceania, shown here, have been discovered within the last decade. Their antiquity, which matches that of Australia and New Guinea, is a surprise, since early people would have to have made a long sea voyage to reach some of these islands. Even now, only a handful of sites is known—enough to establish their great age, but too few to do more than hint at the area's history. It seems likely that most sites have not survived, since they were in the open air. Logging, plantation development, and resettlement during this century have also destroyed many sites.

↬ Rainforests are the most diverse ecosystems in the world, housing an enormous variety of vegetation. They are also very fragile, since all available nutrients are constantly in use by plants and animals, rather than some being stored in the soil, as occurs in temperate climates. Much rainforest life is found in the upper canopy, and only along streams, where sunlight penetrates to the forest floor, is there a profusion of ground-level plants.

☗ At the long-occupied cave site of Balof 2, excavated animal bones—each pile from a different excavation square and level—are set out to dry after being washed. All are remnants of human meals eaten thousands of years ago.

We do not know what kinds of craft were used on such voyages, since none have survived. They must have been more than simple rafts or small canoes, but whether they were paddled or had sails as well, we cannot tell. Both kinds have been used in the last few centuries of Pacific travel, although paddling canoes were used for shorter voyages and in more protected waters. Sailing vessels seem more likely for longer journeys, as do boats big enough to carry several adults and some supplies. Single-hulled outrigger canoes with a riding platform, the all-purpose craft of recent Pacific peoples, had probably already been developed. Moreover, a boatload of people would have had a much better chance of establishing themselves than would any castaway couple.

Given the location of these islands and our knowledge of climate change, it is likely that these islands were as covered with rainforest throughout the Pleistocene period as they are today.

In the last decade, traces of occupation during the Pleistocene period have been discovered on four of the main island groups. Two sites from New Ireland and one from the northern Solomons have been radiocarbon-dated to about 30,000 years ago. (No sites of this age have been discovered in New Britain, but because it is the closest island to New Guinea, they probably exist.) All the oldest sites are in the rock shelters or limestone caves of old reefs now raised above the sea. (See the feature *Relics of the First New Ireland Settlers*.) Because of their alkaline properties, these have preserved bone, shell, and some other organic materials, as well as providing protected locations for the accumulation of debris. They have, therefore, played an important part in preserving evidence of human occupation.

Food Sources: Animals and Plants

Being seafarers, the people were accustomed to using the ocean as a source of food, especially its shellfish and fish. It is surprising to find, however, that early sites show no evidence of trolling or other techniques used to catch large, open-sea fish. The surviving fish bones have proved to be of reef-dwelling species that can be caught by trapping or spearing.

Our best information about the animals of the area comes from New Ireland, where all five known Pleistocene sites have yielded the remains of animals that were cooked and eaten. At Balof 2, for example, 5 cubic meters (180 cubic feet) of deposits have produced the bones of between 250 and 300 possums, along with those of rats, bats, lizards, snakes, and, in more recent layers, wallabies. Other sites have produced similar quantities of bones.

often carried around today for later use as food and decorative fur, and also as pets. Because these animals were introduced so long after human settlement, I believe that they were most likely introduced by accident. (See the feature *Moving Animals from Place to Place* for a different view.)

The situation in New Britain—which covers an area of about 37,000 square kilometers (14,300 square miles)—and the Admiralty Islands is less clear, as there are fewer sites, with fewer animal remains, and no prehuman deposits known so far. But both islands have a very small range of marsupials today. New Britain has two phalanger species, one wallaby, and one bandicoot, while the Admiralties have one phalanger and one bandicoot. This contrasts strongly with the main island of New Guinea—820,000 square kilometers (317,000 square miles) in area—where there are 53 species of larger marsupials, including at least 9 bandicoots, 8 phalangers, and 14 wallabies and kangaroos. The differences can be explained to some extent by the fact that the islands are smaller than New Guinea, with less diverse environments. But if animals migrated there naturally, we would expect them to have done so over many millennia. We would then see both greater evolutionary differences between animals on different islands and considerably more species on large than on small islands. Since we find the same few species on each island, it seems likely that they are all recent arrivals, brought deliberately or accidentally by humans.

🦇 *Pteropus temincki ennisae* is a newly discovered subspecies of bat so far known only from the northern part of New Ireland. Its close relatives live in New Britain and some small islands nearby. It is one of only two New Ireland mammals (the other being a rat) to have evolved sufficiently to be different from animals elsewhere in the Bismarck archipelago.

ILLUSTRATION: PETER SCHOUTEN/AUSTRALIAN MUSEUM

Particularly interesting is the vertical distribution of these bones within the deposits, indicating when they were thrown away. In the lowest levels of each site, both in the natural soil and in the early human deposits, there are no marsupials at all: the only animal remains belong to two species of rats, many species of bats, and several species of reptiles. Then, between 14,000 and 10,000 years ago, possum bones first appear, and in considerable numbers. Wallaby bones occur later, from about 7,000 years ago at the earliest. As it is highly unlikely that people would not have hunted them if they had been present, we must assume that these animals, so common elsewhere, were introduced. We cannot tell whether this happened deliberately or accidentally, but we know that "wild" animals of this kind, especially phalangers (a family of tree-dwelling marsupials which includes cuscuses and brush-tailed possums), are

➔ The dusky pademelon (*Thylogale brunii*) is widely found throughout the eastern two-thirds of New Guinea, in forest and upper alpine grasslands. It does not inhabit lowland savanna. It probably breeds throughout the year and is thus able to adapt fairly easily to new habitats.

JEAN-PAUL FERRERO/AUSCAPE

MOVING ANIMALS FROM PLACE TO PLACE

TIMOTHY FLANNERY

Human beings are the only vertebrate predators that relocate some of their prey species in order to establish new populations. This is very unusual behavior, and we have to look to certain ant species, which are known to relocate sap-sucking insects such as aphids, to find anything similar in the animal world. Like music and mathematics, this is one of the things that set us apart from other vertebrates. It is of particular interest, because it may represent the first step towards domesticating animals.

The history of moving, or translocating, animals in this way is difficult to trace, because there is rarely any clear evidence in the fossil record. For example, if early humans moved a herd of deer from one valley to another where they were not naturally found, there would be no way of judging this from fossils alone. The evidence would be the same if the deer had migrated there of their own accord. For this reason, the clearest evidence for animal translocation comes from islands, especially in areas where animals differ markedly from island to island and island animals are different again from those of nearby continents. Obviously, if an animal is clearly out of place on an island, it must have been brought there.

The Earliest Evidence

The islands of Melanesia are ideal for studying animal translocation. Not surprisingly, they have yielded the earliest evidence of this practice. New Guinea, the largest island in the region, has more than 200 indigenous species of mammals, including 2 species of monotremes, 63 species of marsupials, 59 species of rat-like and mouse-like rodents (including some very large ones), and 79 species of bats. Before humans arrived, there were also some giant marsupials, weighing up to 300 kilograms (660 pounds). This extraordinary diversity of species is in marked contrast to the

JEAN-PAUL FERRERO/AUSCAPE

☝ An inhabitant of the lowland rainforests of northern Melanesia, the northern common cuscus (*Phalanger orientalis*) spends the day hidden in epiphytes in the treetops and becomes active at dusk, when its loud snarls and dog-like, yapping calls are often heard in the rainforest.

situation on nearby islands, such as Halmahera, which has only 27 indigenous mammal species, all but two of which are bats, and New Ireland, which has 29 indigenous species, again all bats except two.

We know more of New Ireland's prehistory that we do of that of any other island in Near Oceania, and it is here that the earliest evidence of animal translocation has been found. The species in question is the northern common cuscus (*Phalanger orientalis*), brought to New Ireland between 19,000 and 10,000 years ago.

The Adaptable Cuscus

Over the last 20,000 years, the northern common cuscus has been translocated repeatedly, making it one of the most widespread marsu-

pials. The reason for this is found in its biology. There is good reason to believe that the translocated animals were "back young"—that is, young that have developed fur and no longer depend on the mother's milk, but, for a brief period, are carried around on her back. Younger animals are susceptible to hypothermia and starvation, and older, less tractable animals are liable to be injured on capture and often suffer from "capture myopathy", a debilitating form of shock that is sometimes fatal.

Moreover, the northern common cuscus is unique among northern New Guinea's larger marsupials in that it usually bears twins. Because of this, a single female with back young could quite easily found a new population.

This would be much less likely in the case of any of the other marsupials, which bear only one young at a time. Most New Guinean mammals do not breed seasonally, so, assuming that the young are carried on the mother's back for only one month out of the 12 in the breeding cycle, the chance of obtaining back young is 1 in 24. (On average, half the animals captured will be males.) The likelihood of capturing two females, one with a male and one with a female back young, at the right time (shortly before a trading voyage), is very remote indeed.

If the northern common cuscuses in New Ireland do indeed descend from a brother and sister, there should be considerable evidence of inbreeding. Preliminary studies suggest that this may be the case, particularly among those found on the Solomon Islands (which most likely derived from New Ireland).

If a species is to be translocated successfully, two vital conditions must be met. It must be able to exist on whatever food its human captors offer it, and it must be able to survive at its release site, which may not have been very carefully chosen. Obviously, adaptable animals will do better than those with very precise food and habitat needs. The little that is known of the northern common cuscus's diet and habitat requirements suggests that it is such a generalist.

Animal translocation is similar to animal husbandry in important ways. In both cases, only a few species are suitable, and in both, animals and humans must live in close contact. It seems remarkable that prehistoric people did not take that small step further and domesticate the northern common cuscus. Perhaps it does not reproduce readily in captivity, or there may be other biological reasons why it was not domesticated. It may also be that the early Melanesians' way of life was simply not conducive to keeping domesticated animals.

1 Selecting the stone
Stone for tools is taken either from seams of good rock or, as here, from river gravels. Pebbles and cobbles are smashed by throwing them down so that the newly broken surfaces can be inspected and their quality assessed.

HEAT TREATMENT: A 50,000-YEAR-OLD TECHNOLOGY

J. PETER WHITE

2 Building an oven
As direct contact with fire will cause the stone to shatter and split, the rocks are buried in sand to a depth of 4 or 5 centimeters (1 or 2 inches) and a fire lit over the top. Modern researchers use a sand bath in an oven.

FOR THE LAST TWO MILLION YEARS, people have flaked stone to make tools and other artifacts. The stone used has usually been brittle and fine-grained, without large crystals, rather than tough or very crystalline. This is because brittle rocks such as flint, chert, and obsidian flake cleanly, giving a sharp edge. More crystalline rocks, such as quartzite and silcrete, are more difficult to flake, because the force of the flaking hammer must travel around all the tiny crystals, resulting in an edge that is less sharp.

Heat treatment makes stone flake more readily by driving water out of the interstices between the crystals and increasing the number of internal microfractures. The flaking force can thus travel through the crystal lattice rather than around it. This makes the rock more brittle, reducing its tensile strength by about half. Heat treatment, therefore, allows a wider range of rocks to be flaked more precisely, and also produces sharper, though more brittle, edges. The procedure is shown in the illustrations.

Heat-treated rocks usually have a glossy appearance when flaked, since the flaked surfaces are flatter. They may also change color, either on the surface or all through, becoming redder as a result of the oxidation of microscopic quantities of iron.

Heat treatment appears to have been invented within the last 50,000 years. Flakes struck from heat-treated stone have been recovered from Late Pleistocene sites in Siberia, the Americas, and Australia.

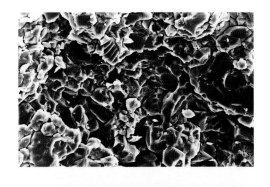

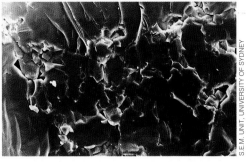

S.E.M. UNIT, UNIVERSITY OF SYDNEY

⬆ Scanning electron microscope photographs of the surface of a flake from the same piece of stone (magnified 2,500 times) made before (top) and after (below) heat treatment. The force of a blow can travel through most rock grains after heat treatment.

3 Slow heating, slow cooling

The fire needs to be small but maintained continuously. The temperature of the rock is raised over several hours to around 275 degrees Celsius (527 degrees Fahrenheit) and held for about 8 hours. The rock is then allowed to cool gradually, to avoid thermal shock.

4 Flaking

Flakes can be struck by placing the stone to be flaked (the core) on an anvil and hitting it with another stone, as shown here, or the core can be held in one hand and the hammer in the other.

⚱ A man from the Eastern Highlands of Papua New Guinea uses a sharp flake to cut long barbs in an arrow. Throughout Near Oceania, flaked stone tools were commonly used for woodworking tasks such as this. Heat treatment produced sharper flakes, but they were more brittle.

6 Wrapping the core

Small cores are sometimes wrapped in fiber or cane to avoid hitting the fingers when the flake is struck. This also keeps the flakes together and helps produce longer, thinner flakes.

5 Splitting the core

Once the core is split, sharp edges are created. These pieces may be used as they are, or further flakes may be struck.

ILLUSTRATION: JOHN RICHARDS

7 The final flake

Flakes of any size can be used for cutting and scraping. Their edges are often as sharp as a steel knife, but not as durable.

FROM STONE TO TOOLS: RESIDUE ANALYSIS

TOM LOY

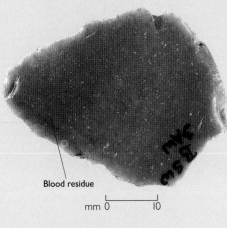

Blood residue

mm 0   10

☉ The dark discoloration from the blood residue can be seen on the cutting edge, at left.
TOM LOY

A hundred thousand years ago, an artisan who lived at Barda Balka, along a river in northwestern Iraq, picked up a small grey nodule of flint, with a few blows created a tool, used it, and threw it away. With hundreds of others, this tool was excavated and analyzed by a research team from the Oriental Institute in Chicago. They found nothing unusual about the artifact, and on the evidence of shape and flaking patterns decided that it had been a scraper or a knife. But some years ago, traces of blood were discovered on its surface. Microscopic and biochemical analysis of the organic residues has since been able to tell us a surprising amount about how the tool was used.

Traces of woody tissue with characteristic pits in the cell walls

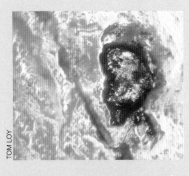

☉ Photomicrograph showing the blood residue from the Barda Balka tool at 600 times' magnification. The reddish brown and brown areas are where the blood residue is very thick, the yellowish areas where it is much thinner. The flint itself is light grey.

were found along the working edge of the Barda Balka tool, indicating that it was used, probably only once, to scrape a coniferous softwood. While scraping, the artisan was cut, but continued to work. Analysis of serum albumin, hemoglobin, and immunoglobin G molecules removed from the reside has shown that the blood is human. Wood fragments were preserved in the blood film as it dried. No human skeletons were excavated from the Barda Balka site, but the date suggests that the person who used the tool was probably a Neanderthal. The DNA contained in the white blood cells found in the blood residue may eventually be used to study the genetic relationship between the tool user and ourselves, and ultimately indicate the user's sex.

Evidence through the Ages

Such residues are often found. They have been discovered on artifacts from open-air and cave sites, arctic regions, the desert, tropical jungle swamps, and most environments lying between these extremes. Biochemical analysis of preserved residues indicates that blood molecules may survive throughout the millions of years that human beings have been using and making tools.

This analysis does not only tell us about human beings. Far removed from Barda Balka, 11 chert knives were found at a site known as Toad River Canyon, near the northern end of the Rocky Mountains in western Canada. (They were eventually deposited in the Royal British Columbia Museum in Victoria, Canada.) The acidic, subarctic soils in this region do not preserve animal bones, but analysis of the tool residues has revealed that mountain sheep and caribou were among the animals butchered by the prehistoric hunters. More significantly, many traces of blood tissue and hair from North American bison

were found on the tool surfaces. Bison are no longer found in the region, and were not thought to have been among the animals slaughtered for food at that time.

Because the site was destroyed after the tools were collected, conventional methods could not be used to date the collection. However, advances in the radiocabon dating of minute amounts of carbon have allowed 50 micrograms (or 1/500,000 of a gram) purified from blood proteins on one of the tools to be dated at about 3,000 years ago. This collection of tools has given us the first animal DNA from blood residues. With our current methods, which can detect DNA from a single cell, the way has now been opened to directly analyzing a variety of animal species in terms of their taxonomy and evolutionary relationships.

New Insights into Ancient Lives

Blood and tissue are not the only materials that have survived. Starch grains and plant tissue preserved on 27,000-year-old tools from the Kilu Cave site in the north Solomon Islands, in the Southwest Pacific, document the oldest known use of root vegetables. The starch grains have been identified as taro, *Colocasia esculenta*, a staple food throughout Southeast Asia and the Pacific. Preserved seeds or plant tissue are rarely found at archaeological sites, but the direct analysis of plant remains on stone tools will fill in many gaps in our knowledge of the long history of gathering and cultivating wild and semiwild plants that culminated in the development of Neolithic farming methods.

The scientific methods developed to study these microscopic and molecular remains are able to provide much greater detail than traditional methods of classification. They represent a major advance in archaeological research, allowing us a vastly greater insight into the lives of ancient peoples.

Sample for DNA analysis

Sample for radiocarbon dating

Hairs

mm 0   10

☉ Abundant hairs can be seen slightly to one side of the tip of this tool excavated from the Toad River Canyon site in northern British Columbia, Canada. For the purposes of radiocarbon dating and DNA analysis, blood residues were taken from the areas indicated.
TOM LOY

☉ Low-power photomicrograph showing the hair and blood residue found on the Toad River Canyon tool. The hairs have been identified as belonging to the North American bison (*Bison bison*), and analysis of DNA extracted from the blood residue has confirmed this.

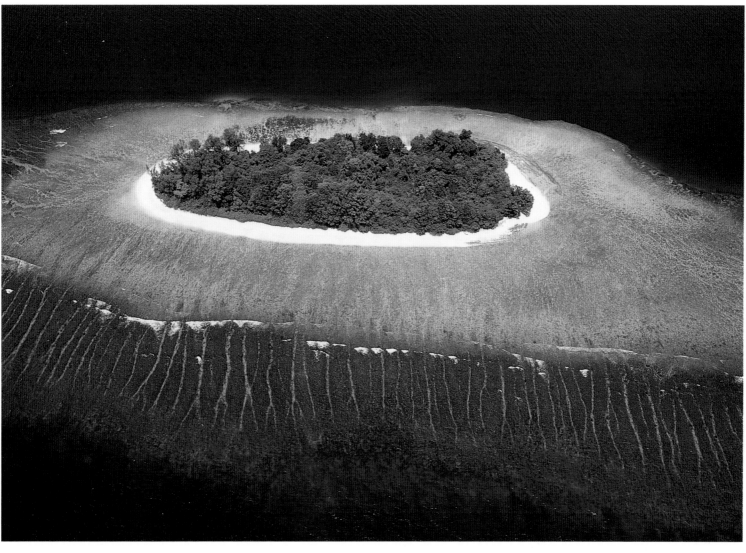

On the Solomon Islands—39,000 square kilometers (15,000 square miles) in area—the picture is different. The earliest levels excavated at the Kilu site (see map) contain the remains of five species of rats, as well as of bats and two lizard-like reptiles. The rats are all highly distinctive, ranging up to 2 kilograms (between 4 and 5 pounds) in weight. They are clearly not recent introductions. Two of these species disappeared in the course of human settlement, presumably because they were hunted to extinction or because their habitat changed. Remains of nonnative animals do not appear after 3,000 years ago, with the exception of one piece of phalanger jaw found in a 10,000-year-old level, which may be a relic of trade in smoked meat or an introduced animal that did not escape into the wild.

These studies of human–animal relationships have broad implications, showing not only that hunters and gatherers can cause animals to become extinct, but also the extent to which they alter the natural environment to their own advantage. In the light of the archaeological evidence, theories of island biogeography that suggest a direct and simple relationship between numbers of animal species and island size, environmental diversity, and distance from a potential population source, such as a continental landmass, need to be reconsidered. The present "wild" fauna of the Pacific islands is in large part the result of human action.

🜄 A classic Pacific island, with dense vegetation, golden sands, an extensive reef, and the sea—an island one might visit to catch fish, shellfish, and perhaps birds, but one not likely to have fresh water or soil good enough for gardens.

◄◯ The king rat, *Uromys rex*, is one of the large, mosaic-tailed rats of the Solomon Islands—so called because the tail scales do not overlap but fit together, like a mosaic. It is about 60 centimeters (2 feet) long, half its length being the tail. A tree dweller, it is still found on some islands, but is now rare.

⬥ *Canarium indicum* trees are native to the New Guinea area and have been transplanted to other Pacific islands, being valued for their plentiful crop of edible nuts and also their bark, which can be used to treat burns. The trees are sometimes grown near villages, as shown here, but more commonly, trees growing naturally in the forest are owned and looked after by villagers, who harvest the nuts.

⬥ Canarium nuts have a high protein content. They can be eaten raw, either alone or used as flavoring for sago or taro, and can also be dried over a fire, after which they can be stored for many months.

As well as useful animals, useful plants were being transported across the sea. At the Pamwak site on Manus Island—about 2,100 square kilometers (800 square miles) in area—the nuts of *Canarium indicum* ("galip" nuts), which are native to mainland New Guinea, have been found. These shiny black nuts are about the size of a golf ball and grow on a large, easily propagated tree. The nut kernels are high in protein and are good to eat, as well as being easily stored, particularly when smoked. Canarium nuts have also been found in levels 10,000 years old at the Kilu site in the Solomons, while taro starch residues have been found on stone tools from the earliest levels. (See the feature *From Stone to Tools: Residue Analysis.*) Whether these taro were simply wild plants that were collected and scraped before they were cooked, or whether they were cultivated, has not been determined.

This plant evidence suggests that islanders were looking after wild plants in the Pleistocene period. These people would not have had large fenced gardens, but rather a formal system whereby people owned, cared for, and harvested food plants growing naturally in the tropical jungle.

Artifacts

All the cave and shelter sites contain a range of artifacts, either discarded tools or manufacturing waste from tools. Surviving materials are stone and bone, although some organic residues, mainly plant tissues and blood, cling to the used edges.

In New Ireland, the stone artifacts consist solely of sharp flakes and the cores from which they were struck, both of which were used as tools. Many were made from local stone, including partially marbled limestone and coarse-grained volcanic rocks collected as cobbles from stream beds. In their lower levels, all sites contain tools made from hard, fine-grained rocks such as variously colored cherts. But the sources of these rocks are problematic. At Balof, neutron activation analysis of 102 specimens showed that they belonged to two groups. A few, found in the lowest levels and about 14,000 years old, were calcium–aluminium silicates of volcanic origin, while the rest were cherts and quartzites, which form in marine environments. The volcanic group must have originated at least 30 kilometers (18 miles) from where they were found, as there are no closer volcanic sources, but no precise source has been determined. They might even have come from another island. (Sources of this kind are often very small, and are unlikely to be found unless local people remember them.) Cherts and quartzites have not been found in the local limestone, which was, of course, formed under water or as pebbles in local stream beds. In this case, an offshore source seems likely, in the form of a layer of limestone long since drowned by the rising seas during the Holocene period. None of

these fine-grained rocks were used more recently than 8,000 to 10,000 years ago.

The other major rock type used for tools is obsidian, a type of volcanic glass. This is found in only three small areas of New Guinea and Near Oceania: Fergusson Island, several outcrops around Talasea in New Britain, and one small island in the Admiralties (see map). All the obsidian more than 3,000 years old found in New Ireland derives from a source known as Mopir, near Talasea. The oldest obsidian has been found at Matembek, which is about 400 kilometers (250 miles) from Mopir, in levels dated to about 19,000 years ago, suggesting that people over a wide area have valued this material for thousands of years.

In the Holocene period (the last 10,000 years), obsidian was carried much further out into the Pacific. What it was exchanged for we do not know, but a whole range of local goods, such as feathers, food, and wood carvings, may have been involved. We might surmise that this extensive distribution network was organized by specialized traders, but this seems unlikely among earlier hunters and gatherers. More loosely organized group-to-group trading, as takes place today, is more probable.

The presence of obsidian on New Ireland has puzzled archaeologists. It appeared at Matembek about 19,000 years ago, but was first found at Balof and Panakiwuk less than 10,000 years ago.

These sites are on the same island, and not far apart, so such a difference is unlikely to have resulted from lack of contact between them. It is possible, of course, that the dating is inaccurate, but this too seems unlikely, because each site has yielded a set of internally consistent radiocarbon dates taken from different materials. Perhaps the activities carried out at Balof and Panakiwuk more than 10,000 years ago did not require the use of obsidian, but nothing else points to this—indeed, there seems to have been very little difference in the ways these cave sites were used. There might have been some kind of cultural barrier, or a prohibition on the use of obsidian in the northern part of the island, but research to date has yielded

⊕ The volcanic landscape of Willaumez Peninsula, New Britain. Obsidian from some of its volcanoes was distributed widely throughout the western Pacific, but living in this volcanically active area was risky.

no evidence of this either, and such propositions are in any case difficult to test.

How were stone artifacts used? Again, this is often hard to judge, as their form is not always a reliable guide. However, recent research in two areas—the microscopic analysis of the wear patterns on artifacts, which are then compared with those resulting from various known uses, and organic residue analysis—has given us new insights into the lives of ancient peoples. At Balof, for example, Huw Barton has found that all artifacts made from fine-grained rocks, including obsidian, were used on wood or other parts of plants, including the starchy parts (possibly tubers used as food). He also found a few fragments of bird feathers but little blood, indicating that very few tested tools were used on animals. The bones of many complete animals were found at the site,

including burned and chewed bones, which clearly indicate that the animals were cooked on a fire and eaten there. Perhaps wooden tools were used to skin and butcher them.

The Pamwak site on Manus Island contains stone tools made from local chert that has been heat-treated to make flaking easier. (See the feature *Heat Treatment: A 50,000-year-old Technology*.) Obsidian, presumably from outcrops on nearby Lou Island, first appears at the site about 12,000 years ago. And in New Britain, where only one clearly Pleistocene site has been discovered, levels dated to 11,000 years ago contain five small flakes of obsidian and some charcoal. This island is an important link in the settlement of Near Oceania, although given the high level of volcanic activity in the last 20,000 years, it remains to be seen how many of its Pleistocene sites will be accessible.

⚲ Kavachi volcano erupting in the Solomon Islands. Once the eruption ceases, this lava cone will be slowly colonized by plants and insects. If the final eruption consists of ash, which makes good soil, it will be colonized more rapidly.

MICHAEL McCOY

RELICS OF THE FIRST NEW IRELAND SETTLERS

CHRISTOPHER GOSDEN

The site known as Matenkupkum, on the southeast coast of New Ireland, close to Papua New Guinea, is a dry limestone cave 18 meters (59 feet) long by 10 meters (33 feet) wide. It sits just above present-day sea level on an uplifted limestone terrace, and its mouth faces southeast, looking out over the Pacific Ocean.

This cave was first excavated in 1985, a year after archaeologists discovered it. The excavation team consisted of myself, Pru Gaffey (another archaeologist from the Australian National University), and five people from the local village of Hilalon, where we stayed. We had two aims: to find out when the cave was first occupied, and to gain an understanding of the lives of the people who used it. We thought it likely that the light would have influenced the nature of the activities carried out in the cave, and so we decided to excavate a trench 10 meters by 1 meter (33 feet by 3 feet) from the mouth of the cave back to the center.

Our decision turned out well. We stripped the soil off one layer at a time along the whole trench, and in the middle found a series of hearths, which we later dated to between 14,000 and 12,000 years ago. These hearths consisted of pits, sometimes lined with limestone blocks, which had been redug and reused over 2,000 years. The hearths and their associated piles of rubbish provide a remarkably consecutive record of how people have used the cave over 80 or so generations.

Laboratory analysis showed that much of the soil we excavated was, in fact, ash from the hearths. Behind the hearths, in the darker part of the cave, we found a pile made up of shell taken from the nearby reef, the bones of rainforest animals (the northern common cuscus, *Phalanger orientalis*, rats, bats, birds, lizards, and snakes—all potential food sources), and large pieces of flaked stone from a local

⚑ The cave of Matenkupkum had its first human visitors some 33,000 years ago. Obsidian found here in 12,000-year-old deposits had been brought by sea a distance of 350 kilometers (220 miles).
CHRISTOPHER GOSDEN

river. There were also pieces of obsidian, a type of volcanic glass which has a sharp cutting edge. This came from volcanoes on the island of New Britain, about 350 kilometers (220 miles) away. It must have been transported by sea, showing that people who used the cave were in contact with people on other islands.

From Distant to Recent Past

Evidence unearthed at the front of the cave dated from quite a different period. During the Second World War, Japanese soldiers had occupied the cave to prevent the sabotage of a telephone line running along the coast. They dug a trench across the front to protect themselves from attack, and when they left they filled it with rubbish. The trench destroyed most of the prehistoric deposits at the front of the cave, and contained a range of everyday objects—saucepans, beer bottles, shoes, and so on—which provided an interesting insight into an ordinary soldier's life and the nature of jungle war.

Beneath the levels where the hearths were found, there was evidence that the cave was used between 21,000 and 18,000 years ago. Here we found fine layers of sand and ash, hard to distinguish

in excavation, which probably resulted from sporadic occupation of the cave over a long period. The fact that there was no obsidian or cuscus bones in these levels may indicate that the people of this time were not in contact with groups from outside. The base of the deposit was sand from an old beach, formed before the cave was uplifted to its present position. In this, we found evidence of the first use of the cave some 33,000 years ago: tools made from local stone and large shells picked from previously untouched reefs, as well as some bones of bats, rats, snakes, lizards, and birds.

These lowest deposits contained no trace of hearths, and rubbish appeared to have been scattered at random. If only small numbers of people had visited the cave infrequently, they would not have needed to clean up. The fact that rubbish was piled up in a more orderly way in later years, from about 12,000 years ago, indicates that more people lived on New Ireland at that time and visited the cave more frequently.

Although it is only one point in a landscape over which people may have ranged widely, the cave of Matenkupkum can tell us a great deal, both about the initial colonization of a large Pacific island and the changes that took place on it over 20,000 years.

mm 0   10

⚑ These limestone blocks may have been used as a hearth base 12,000 years ago.
CHRISTOPHER GOSDEN

CHRISTOPHER GOSDEN

⚑ For 20,000 years, people used stone tools like these, made from local river cobbles.

◄ Shells harvested from the local reef 33,000 years ago.

MODERN PEOPLE IN THE NEW WORLD

12,000 YEARS AGO – 10,200 YEARS AGO

The Clovis Mammoth Hunters and the Goshen and Folsom Bison Hunters

GEORGE C. FRISON

FOR MORE THAN HALF A CENTURY, archaeologists have been probing the geological deposits of the late Pleistocene period in their quest to identify the first humans to set foot in North America. These efforts have been both frustrating and rewarding. Although much information has come to light, the identity of the first migrants and their Old World ancestors, the entry route they used, and the conditions under which they arrived are still vigorously debated. (See the feature *Who Were the First Americans?*)

To date, the earliest cultural complex in North America that all archaeologists recognize is known as Clovis. (A cultural complex refers to a group of distinctive cultural artifacts found in association with each other and presumably used by a single population, perhaps over several generations.) It appeared somewhere between 12,000 and 11,000 years ago, just before the last of the large mammals (or megafauna) of the Late Pleistocene period became extinct. Two other cultural complexes, Folsom and Goshen, appeared not long after Clovis, and the surviving evidence of these three cultures constitutes our knowledge of the early North American Paleoindian hunters.

◄◙ Present-day herd of bison (*Bison bison*). Although bison are naturally gregarious, herd size changes as small groups split away and other groups join. Mature males may be solitary or form small separate groups, except during the breeding season. Late Pleistocene bison were larger and were the mainstay of the Plains Paleoindian economy.

⬦ A Clovis point from the Colby site, in northern Wyoming.
GEORGE C. FRISON

At the time of the last glacial maximum, about 18,000 years ago, huge ice sheets covered nearly all of Canada and extended south of the present-day Great Lakes in the eastern United States. So much water from the oceans was frozen in glaciers around the world that sea levels dropped, exposing a continental shelf that included a large, unglaciated landmass known as Beringia connecting northeast Asia and present-day Alaska. Beringia was a flat, well-vegetated landmass capable of supporting not only the giant animals of the late Pleistocene era but also human predators crossing into the area from the west.

As the glaciers melted, sea levels began to rise, gradually submerging the exposed continental shelf. By 12,000 years ago, the Laurentide ice sheet had retreated to the east and the Cordilleran ice sheet to the west, resulting in an open corridor between them that stretched south from present-day Yukon across Canada to Montana. Usually referred to as the "ice-free corridor", this is believed by many prehistorians to have been the route the earliest big-game hunters took to reach the Great Plains of North America. Others think they entered from Alaska, south along the northwest coast.

A New Environment

Significant climatic and environmental changes took place between 12,000 and 10,000 years ago. When the Clovis Cultural Complex first appeared, between 12,000 and 11,000 years ago, winters were warmer and summers were cooler, so

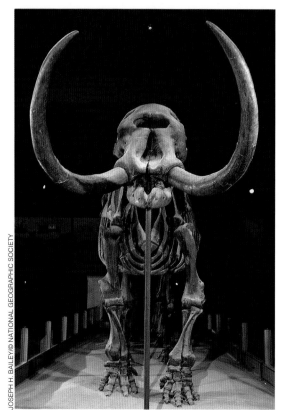

➻ The mammoth stood no taller than a modern Asian elephant but was unique for its massive tusks. It was a grazing animal adapted to the open grasslands, while the mastodon was more of a browser adapted to forested areas.

seasonal extremes of temperature were less marked than at present. Vegetation was different: tall grasses, for example, covered the short-grass plains of today. The giant animals of late Pleistocene times were on the edge of extinction. They included mammoths, mastodon, horses, camels, and giant sloths. Large bison would survive for another 3,000 years. Perhaps even more impressive were the carnivores, such as the short-faced bear—twice the size of a present-day grizzly bear—and the American lion and American cheetah—again, both bigger than their present-day African counterparts. There were many small animals as well. The collared lemming, for example, a tiny creature that can survive only in cold environments, lived around the margins of the glaciers. It can still be found today in arctic glacial environments.

Some time after about 11,000 years ago, another environmental shift occurred. Seasons became more marked, with long periods of sunlight and warmer temperatures, while snowfall and annual rainfall declined. These changes culminated about 10,000 years ago, at the beginning of the Holocene period, when climatic conditions were similar to those we know today.

Although many archaeologists are convinced that humans were present in North America during pre-Clovis times, all agree that Clovis tools and weapons are the earliest found to date that would have enabled people to hunt the large animals present at that time. This strongly suggests that the Clovis hunters were related to the Upper Paleolithic hunters of the Old World, who had pursued and killed mammoths, bison, reindeer, and other large animals for many thousands of years previously.

The First Paleoindian Finds

Early this century, it was generally believed that humans had arrived in North America relatively recently in prehistoric terms. Then, in the 1920s, a black cowboy, George McJunkin, made an historic discovery when he noticed some large bones exposed in the earthen bank of an arroyo (a steep-sided channel) while herding cattle near the small town of Folsom, in northeast New Mexico. The find was brought to the attention of the Colorado Museum of Natural History, and in 1926 paleontologists from the museum found stone weapons of a type later to become known as the Folsom projectile point, along with butchering tools, among the bones, which proved to be those of an extinct species of bison. But archaeologists were not convinced that the tools and weapons were associated with the bones, and several eminent scientists of the time, including Barnum Brown, a paleontologist from the American Museum of Natural History, and Frank H.H. Roberts Jr, of the Smithsonian Institution, were called in to view a projectile point in place

MAJOR PALEOINDIAN SITES IN NORTH AMERICA

The Bluefish Caves and Meadowcroft sites have strong claims for pre-Clovis occupations. Dry Creek has unfluted points about the same age as Clovis. Charlie Cave has yielded a fluted point with a date of 10,500 years ago.

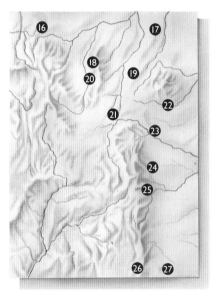

1   Bluefish Caves

2   Dry Creek

3   Charlie Cave

4   Richey-Roberts Clovis cache, Washington State

5   Simon Clovis cache, Idaho

6   Lange-Ferguson, South Dakota
    Clovis mammoth kill

7   Lehner and Murray Springs, Arizona
    Mammoth kill and camp site (respectively)

8   Blackwater Draw, New Mexico
    Clovis mammoth kill and camp site
    Folsom kill and camp site

9   Domebo, Oklahoma
    Mammoth kill

10 Kimswick, Missouri
    Clovis points and mastodon remains

11 Vail, Maine
    Camp site with Clovis points

12 Debert, Novia Scotia
    Camp site with Debert-style points

13 Meadowcroft Rockshelter,
    Pennsylvania (?19,000)

14 Thunderbird, Virginia
    Clovis camp site

15 Aucilla River, Florida
    Underwater site with Clovis-age
    ivory artifacts

16 Anzick Clovis cache, Montana

17 Mill Iron, Montana
    Goshen bison kill

18 Hanson, Wyoming
    Folsom camp site

19 Carter/Kerr-McGee, Wyoming
    Goshen; Folsom bison kill

20 Colby, Wyoming
    Clovis mammoth kill

21 Casper, Wyoming
    Hell Gap-age bison kill

22 Agate Basin, Wyoming
    Folsom bison kill

23 Hell Gap, Wyoming
    Goshen and Folsom bison kill
    and camp site

24 Lindenmeier, Colorado
    Folsom camp site

25 Dent, Colorado
    Clovis mammoth kill

26 Cattle Guard, Colorado
    Folsom bison kill and camp site

27 Folsom, New Mexico
    Folsom bison kill

28 Taima-taima (?13,000)

29 El Inga (9,000)

30 Pachamachay (10,500)

31 Pikimachay (?25,000–?15,000)

32 Pedra Furada (?35,000)

33 Tagua-Tagua (11,500)

34 Monte Verde (?33,000)

35 Fell's Cave (11,000)

All dates are years ago.

MAJOR PALEOINDIAN SITES IN SOUTH AMERICA

The Taima-taima, Pedra Furada, and Monte Verde sites have strong claims for pre-Clovis occupations. Some Fishtail-type points, such as those from Fell's Cave, are examples of a true fluting technique.

CARTOGRAPHY: RAY SIM

Excavations at the Dent site, in Colorado, during the summer of 1933. In 1932, large bones discovered near Dent, along the South Platte River, proved to be the remains of several mammoths. Father Conrad Bilgery, of Regis College, Denver, directed excavations at the site, and on 5 November a Clovis projectile point was recovered close to the bones. In 1933, the Colorado Museum of Natural History continued the excavations, and a second Clovis point was found.

PHOTO ARCHIVES, DENVER MUSEUM OF NATURAL HISTORY

Removing a cast block of bison bones from the arroyo at the Folsom site, in northeast New Mexico.

PHOTO ARCHIVES, DENVER MUSEUM OF NATURAL HISTORY

among the bones. It was only after a third year of excavation that all archaeologists and paleontologists agreed that the evidence was overwhelming: humans had indeed inhabited North America much earlier in prehistory than was previously believed to be possible and had successfully hunted long-extinct animals.

In 1932, a flood along the North Platte River, in northern Colorado, exposed the remains of several mammoths. When the site was excavated, two projectile points were found among the mammoth bones and later confirmed to be Clovis fluted projectile points. But it was a concentration of finds from a site known as Blackwater Draw Locality No. 1, near the town of Clovis, in eastern New Mexico, that gave the Clovis Cultural Complex its name. As the town of Clovis is on the western edge of the Llano Estacado, the complex is also sometimes known as Llano.

Blackwater Draw is a drainage channel that, during a much earlier geological period, was a stream flowing southeast across the Llano Estacado. By Clovis times, because of climatic changes, all that remained was a series of shallow seasonal ponds that collected sediment during runoff periods. These ponds were natural gathering places for large animals such as mammoths and bison. Hunters either killed the

animals at the waterholes or followed prey wounded elsewhere back to the water, where the animals sought to alleviate their suffering. Tools and weapons preserved in stratigraphic sequence in the continually accumulating sediments attest to several thousand years of Paleoindian hunting and butchering activities around Blackwater Draw. There can be no doubt that Clovis hunters were killing mammoths and bison some 11,000 years ago. Immediately above the Clovis level is evidence of the Folsom hunters, who, a short time later, were killing bison, but not mammoths.

The Blackwater finds came about because the culture-bearing sediments were buried under gravel, a scarce commodity on the Llano Estacado. As the gravel was being excavated for road building, mammoth and bison bones were exposed, along with human tools and weapons. However, the site was turned into a gravel pit, and archaeologists had to salvage what they could (although the operator of the gravel pit deserves credit for cooperating with them). In 1956, an attempt was made to have an area of 2 hectares (5 acres) set aside for future research, but this was unsuccessful. As a result, what was possibly the major part of the most significant Paleoindian site in North America was lost to posterity.

With the discovery of Clovis and Folsom

remains, most archaeologists believed that Clovis was the oldest culture, followed closely by Folsom. This view was challenged in the 1960s by excavations at Hell Gap, in southeast Wyoming, one of the earliest and largest Paleoindian sites in North America. Being a deeply stratified site, Hell Gap helped to establish a reliable chronology for the Paleoindians of the Northern Plains. A small number of chipped stone artifacts discovered beneath a Folsom level at Hell Gap were at first believed to be Clovis. More detailed analysis soon showed that they were neither Clovis nor Folsom but included projectile points closely resembling a type recovered from the Southern Plains and known as Plainview. However, because the Plainview culture was believed to be more recent than Folsom, and the Hell Gap finds were clearly older than Folsom, the new finds were given the new name of the Goshen Cultural Complex, after the county in which they were found. Although further Goshen artifacts have since been discovered, Goshen's relationship to both Clovis and Folsom remains unresolved.

The Clovis Cultural Complex

When the people we now know as the Clovis Cultural Complex began to spread south of the continental ice sheets, they emerged into an area populated by large animals that had not previously been exploited by human predators. Clovis people developed superior types of tools and weapons and became efficient hunters. There was no competition for food resources, so they had little, if any, need to defend their hunting territories. They lived in small bands, and when

resources diminished, they could simply move on to a new area. This could explain why the Clovis culture spread so rapidly and widely over the ice-free areas of North America, and why similar tools and weapons are found over vast distances. In contrast to later Paleoindian groups, the Clovis hunters were not forced to adopt specialized subsistence strategies that would have restricted their mobility and required them to modify their tools and weapons to suit local and regional conditions.

Evidence of Clovis occupation—in the form of their distinctive fluted projectile points and variations of these weapons—has been found in mammoth kill sites across the whole of North America. In the 1950s, the search shifted to the San Pedro Valley area of southern Arizona.

⬆ Location of the deeply stratified Hell Gap site, in southeast Wyoming, which has provided a reliable chronological sequence of Paleoindian cultural complexes in western North America.

◄ Clovis projectile points from the Murray Springs mammoth and bison kill site, in Arizona. Clovis weaponry was well designed, demonstrates superior technology, and was made from the best of raw materials.

WHO WERE THE FIRST AMERICANS?

DAVID HURST THOMAS

T<small>HE MOST SIGNIFICANT</small>, if least dramatic, event in the history of the Americas occurred when the first human footprint appeared in the New World. No one knows exactly when this happened, or where. We do not know what these Paleoindians wore, looked like, spoke, or thought. We do not know when they left their Asian homeland, or what conditions they experienced along the way.

And yet there remains no reasonable doubt that the first Americans did indeed travel from Asia during the late Pleistocene. Biology, language, and archaeology all point to an Asian homeland. It is the timing and conditions surrounding their arrival that remain unknown.

In this chapter, George Frison has argued that Clovis is the earliest cultural complex in the New World, established some time between 12,000 and 11,000 years ago. This relatively conservative estimate remains reasonable, because despite decades of concerted research, no undisputed evidence of pre-Clovis occupation has been uncovered anywhere in the Western Hemisphere.

Considerable nonarchaeological evidence also supports this position. Joseph Greenberg's recent reanalysis of American Indian languages suggests that there were three waves of migrants into the New World and that the earliest took place about 12,000 years ago: these were the people of the Clovis Complex. Other investigators, independently analyzing human tooth morphology and blood genetics, have come to the same conclusion.

But considerable controversy surrounds Greenberg's broad-brush linguistic reconstructions, and numerous skeptics question the relevance of the dental and genetic evidence in this prehistoric context. Moreover, although it is still controversial, archaeological evidence emerging from a number of sites suggests that people arrived considerably earlier. Many archaeologists have begun to acknowledge, if sometimes only privately, that people might well have arrived in the New World as early as 40,000 years ago.

TOM D. DILLEHAY

➡ This pressure flaker made of antler, a flintknapping implement used to remove channel flakes, was found in the Woodland occupation level at Meadowcroft Rockshelter.
MERCYHURST ARCHAEOLOGICAL INSTITUTE, ERIE, PENNSYLVANIA

🔥 Finds at the Monte Verde site include wooden pegs tied to an adjacent floor timber, remnants of junco-reed knots, and flattened pegheads.

MERCYHURST ARCHAEOLOGICAL INSTITUTE, ERIE, PENNSYLVANIA

➡ The Meadowcroft Rockshelter before excavation in 1973, looking to the west. This remarkably well-stratified site in southwestern Pennsylvania has yielded radiocarbon dates as old as 19,000 years ago, and the oldest stone artifacts appear to date from between 15,000 and 14,000 years ago.

Hints of Pre-Clovis Occupation

Numerous sites throughout North and South America have provided tantalizing suggestions of pre-Clovis occupation, but none has yielded ironclad proof acceptable to all archaeologists. Some of the best evidence comes from excavations at Meadowcroft Rockshelter, a remarkably well-stratified site in southwestern Pennsylvania. Here, James Adovasio and his colleagues have documented a sequence of more than 40 radiocarbon dates in near-perfect stratigraphic order. The oldest cultural date is a little more than 19,000 years ago, and the oldest stone artifacts appear to date from between 15,000 and 14,000 years ago. Evidence of early human habitation found in the various occupation levels consists of fire-pits, stone tools and by-products of tool-making, a wooden foreshaft, a piece of plaited basketry, and two human bone fragments.

Although many archaeologists consider the evidence from Meadowcroft to be conclusive, others remain unconvinced. The stone implements are scarce and small, and don't tell us much. They are also disturbingly similar to much later artifacts. Surprisingly, there are no remains of the giant animals known to have existed in the Pleistocene era, and the plant remnants recovered are clearly of types that grow in temperate zones, whereas, for part of this time, the ice front should have been less than 75 kilometers (47 miles) to the north.

Another leading pre-Clovis candidate is Monte Verde, an open-air residential site in southern Chile. Excavator Tom Dillehay and his colleagues have unearthed four distinct zones of buried cultural remains. The foundations and fallen pole-frames of close to 12 residential huts have been excavated, with fragments of skin (perhaps mastodon) still clinging to the poles. Abundant plant remains have been found in the deposits, as well as numerous shaped stone tools, including several grooved *bola* stones.

Dillehay argues that the upper layers at Monte Verde contain "well-preserved and clear, conclusive evidence" of human habitation about 13,000 years ago. Even more controversial are the deep layers, where remains associated with possible cultural features and several fractured stones have been radiocarbon-dated to 33,000 years ago.

TOM D. DILLEHAY

A worked bone awl from the Late Archaic occupation level at Meadowcroft Rockshelter.

MERCYHURST ARCHAEOLOGICAL INSTITUTE, ERIE, PENNSYLVANIA

Architectural foundations discovered at the Monte Verde site, in southern Chile, indicate that about 12 semirectangular huts once stood here. Fallen pole-frames were also excavated, with fragments of skin (perhaps mastodon) still clinging to them.

Tortoiseshell bowl fragment from the Woodland occupation level at Meadowcroft Rockshelter.

MERCYHURST ARCHAEOLOGICAL INSTITUTE, ERIE, PENNSYLVANIA

TOM D. DILLEHAY

A Paleoindian projectile point (Miller Lanceolate type) from Meadowcroft Rockshelter.

MERCYHURST ARCHAEOLOGICAL INSTITUTE, ERIE, PENNSYLVANIA

Modified mastodon tusk and burned rib fragments from Monte Verde.

Big-game Hunters or Foragers?

These controversial findings suggest not only that humans arrived in the New World much earlier than previously thought, but also that the earliest Americans were not the glamorous big-game hunters associated with the sophisticated Clovis Complex and its elegant stone tools. Rather, the plant and animal remains from Monte Verde suggest that they were hunter-gatherers who lived mainly on wild plant foods and shellfish. They may also have scavenged, and hunted slow-moving mammals such as seals, but these would have been secondary activities.

Yet, despite the findings from Meadowcroft, Monte Verde, and numerous other sites, we have no unequivocal, indisputable archaeological evidence that the New World was inhabited before Clovis times. The debate rages on, and until more substantial evidence comes to light, claims as to the identity of the first Americans are likely to be based, as one skeptic has put it, as much on psychological as on archaeological grounds.

A site close to the Mexican border discovered in 1951, Naco, contained a single mammoth and 8 Clovis projectile points. Further down in the valley, the Lehner site has yielded the remains of several mammoths and 13 Clovis points, 3 of which are fairly small and made of quartz crystal. In the same valley, at Murray Springs, evidence was found in the 1960s of both a mammoth and a bison kill of Clovis age lying immediately under a geological feature known as the "black mat"—a dark layer several centimeters (about an inch) thick believed to have been derived from organic materials. The Clovis occupation surface was so well preserved that it has even been suggested that depressions in part of the site area are mammoth tracks. An artifact of carved mammoth bone found here, thought to have been a device used to straighten shafts, is almost identical to at least one recorded from northeast Asia.

In the 1970s, another mammoth kill site was found at Colby, in northern Wyoming. In this case, the animals had been driven into the cul-de-sac formed by the steep walls of a dry arroyo to be killed. Two piles of mammoth bones found here provide clear evidence of human activity. One pile was made up of the left front quarter of a mammoth, with the long bones of several other mammoths stacked around it, and was capped by the skull of a juvenile male mammoth. A fluted projectile point was found at the bottom of the left part of the ribcage. Because of the northerly location of the Colby site, it has been suggested that this pile of bones is the remains of a frozen meat cache that was never used. Nearby is a dispersed pile of mammoth bones, also containing the partial remains of several animals. This second pile is thought to be a similar meat store that had been opened up and used.

The piles are similar to caches of caribou meat that arctic people of more modern times are known to have kept. Long bones were stacked around the meat that had been stripped from the carcasses and stored for future use. The skull was placed on top of the pile, which was then packed with slush to freeze the contents and protect them from scavengers and carnivores. These were short-term winter caches, and meat that was not used would have spoiled with the coming of spring. For the Clovis people, such stores of frozen food were necessary to provide for the long, intensely cold winters on the Northwest Plains. If not needed, the meat was simply allowed to spoil.

Other mammoth kill sites containing only one or two animals have been found, including the Domebo site, in Oklahoma, and the Lange-Ferguson site, in western South Dakota. At the Kimswick site, in Missouri, Clovis weapons were found together with mastodon remains. Sites without mammoth remains but containing characteristically fluted Clovis projectile points include the Debert site, in central Nova Scotia, the Lamb site, in New York, the Vail site, in Maine, the Bull Brook site, in Massachusetts, and the Thunderbird and Williamson sites, in Virginia. Together they show that Clovis hunters ranged widely throughout the northeast of the United States and southeast Canada.

Fluted projectile points and cylindrical-shaped, carved ivory objects found in rivers in northern Florida are almost identical to a specimen from a Clovis site in the extreme east of Wyoming. At least two stone flaking sites in western Kentucky cover more than 40 hectares (100 acres) each and are located alongside sources of high-quality chert. Clovis fluted projectile points are common finds in plowed fields in Ohio and Illinois, and further south, in the lower Mississippi Valley, fluted points are regularly found where Clovis-age landforms are exposed. They are also found in the southwest, in California, and in the Great Basin. Sites where the stratigraphy can be radiocarbon-dated are rare, however, and are largely confined to the Plains and the southwest, where conditions of erosion and deposition are most likely to have left the cultural materials in good stratigraphic sequence with other Paleoindian cultural complexes.

In Texas, at the Pavo Real site, near San Antonio, Clovis stone artifacts were found in an undisturbed context buried underneath younger cultural layers and separated from them by nearly a meter (3 feet) of noncultural deposits. Cores, blades, and blade tools are very similar to those found in Upper Paleolithic sites in Europe and Asia. Similar evidence has been recovered from the large surface sites mentioned in western Kentucky, and at least two Clovis blade caches have been found in the southwest of the United States. Together, these finds suggest that the Clovis tradition was closely linked to the Upper Paleolithic tradition of the Old World.

Clovis Tool and Weapon Caches

In 1961, rancher William Simon was operating a large earthmover on the Big Camas Prairie near the small town of Fairfield, in Idaho, when something caused him to stop and look back at the area shaved by the machine's blade. Exposed but undamaged were five unusually fine examples of Clovis projectile points. Further examination revealed other stone artifacts, several of which had been damaged by the earthmover. This became known as the Simon Clovis cache and was the first of several such finds.

In 1968, workers operating an end loader near the small town of Wilsall, in Montana, exposed a cache containing more than a hundred items,

♦ A device made of mammoth bone found at the Murray Springs site, in Arizona, thought to be a shaft-straightening tool, was probably used like this. The shaft, also of mammoth bone, was found at the Anzick site, in Montana.

including Clovis points, bifaces (chopping and cutting implements with a sharp edge formed by percussion flaking from each side), tools, carved bone, and a small amount of skeletal material from two juvenile humans. There were also several carved cylindrical artifacts made of heavy long bone, probably mammoth, which may have been foreshafts for holding Clovis projectile points. Some of these have a single-beveled, cross-hatched end, with the other end tapered to a cone shape, while others have both ends single-beveled and cross-hatched. Everything was heavily coated with red ocher. Known as the Anzick site, this is the only known example of a Clovis burial.

A cache unearthed in 1988 during trenching operations in an orchard by the Columbia River, near the town of Wenatchee, in Washington, contained cylindrical bone artifacts similar to those found at Anzick, as well as exceptionally large Clovis projectile points, bifaces, and tools. A further cache found at about the same time in northeast Colorado contained 13 Clovis points, most of which were made from Alibates dolomite, a distinctive material found only in the Texas Panhandle, north of Amarillo, while others were made of a local material known as Flat Top chert. There were also some ivory fragments.

The publicity that surrounded the Wenatchee finds brought to light a cache of 56 Clovis artifacts discovered many years earlier, now known as the Fenn cache. We will never know exactly where it was discovered, as the person who made the discovery died many years ago, but it was somewhere in the area where Utah, Idaho, and Wyoming join. It included complete and reworked Clovis points, bifaces, a single blade tool, and a crescent. Three quartz crystal points were made of material similar to that of several bifaces from the Simon site. Several items were made of obsidian (a type of volcanic glass) that has been traced to a source in southeast Idaho. One of these is a projectile point with longitudinal scratch marks on the flute (the smooth area on each side of the point where the channel flakes were removed) that are identical to those found on obsidian Clovis points from California and Oregon. The crescent-shaped object is identical to crescents found on the surface in the Great Basin and long thought to be of Clovis age. All items were heavily coated with red ocher, reminiscent of the Anzick cache, but unfortunately we will never know if human skeletal remains or ivory or bone artifacts were also present.

Many of the bifaces and projectile points are made of a type of stone found only in a narrow strip of land stretching from northwest Utah, across the southeast corner of Wyoming, and into western Colorado. Other items are made of an extremely high-quality chert that comes from the Bighorn Mountains of northern Wyoming. One specimen from each of the Simon and Anzick

caches and two from the Fenn cache were made of the Bighorn Mountain material.

We can learn a lot about the Clovis tradition from these caches. Now that several have been found, they can be seen as an integral part of the Clovis cultural system rather than as anomalies. The Anzick cache gives us an insight into Clovis burial practices. If platform burials—where the dead are exposed for some time before burial—were the norm, this would help to explain the scarcity of Paleoindian burials. The use of red ocher in three of the caches strongly suggests ritual activities and a possible relationship with those associated with human burials among

⚲ Remains of what was possibly an unused frozen meat cache at the Colby site, in Wyoming. A protective cover of mammoth long bones was stacked around the left front quarter of a mammoth, and the skull of a five-year-old male mammoth placed on top.

CLOVIS WEAPONS: A MODERN EXPERIMENT

GEORGE C. FRISON

The archaeological record leaves no doubt that the North American High Plains Paleoindians hunted several species of large animals very successfully, including mammoths. Although archaeologists will never be able to reproduce the hunting conditions of this period, nor acquire the expertise of these Paleolithic hunters, experiments with African elephants can give us an insight into both the weapons they used and the animal behavior they would have encountered. The main limitation of such experiments is that there are bound to be some differences between elephants and mammoths and also differences in the natural environment between then and now.

Clovis projectile points from mammoth kills have survived, however, and we can compare the physiology of elephants with that of frozen mammoths recovered from Siberia. We know that mammoths and African elephants have hides of similar thickness, although elephant hides have a more armor-like surface, probably because elephants inhabit regions characterized by thorny vegetation. Mammoth hide is covered with long hair and short, thick fur that would have offered little resistance to an expertly propeled Clovis projectile point.

⟨⊙ This replica of a Clovis projectile point, mounted on a foreshaft inserted into the end of the mainshaft, was used in the elephant experiments.
GEORGE C. FRISON

In the national parks of Zimbabwe, elephant herds have multiplied beyond the carrying capacity of the ecosystem, and a program of controlled killing, or culling, has been instituted. The Zimbabwe Division of Wildlife agreed to allow experiments with Clovis weapons to be carried out, provided that only dead or dying animals were targeted.

The strategy used to cull African elephants is to kill an entire family— the oldest female, all of her offspring, and her family's offspring, except for males beyond puberty. Because elephants have a matriarchal social structure, random killing is ill advised. Animals from one family are not accepted by other families, and those lacking a matriarch leader become outcasts, which are a danger to national park visitors.

An internationally known flint-knapper, Dr Bruce Bradley, has made replicas of Clovis projectile points from several different kinds of raw-stone flaking materials. The points were mounted on short wooden shafts (foreshafts) which could be used with either a thrusting or throwing spear, or an atlatl—a type of throwing stick—and long shaft. The thrusting or throwing spear is either held in both hands at the time of impact or thrown with one arm from a distance. The purpose of the atlatl is to add length to the throwing arm. It has a hook on one end which engages with a shallow cup on the end of the long shaft, allowing the shaft to be propeled.

The best part of the animal to aim at is probably the lung cavity, halfway between the bottom of the ribcage and the top of the back. On the average young adult elephant, the hide here is 8 to 10 millimeters (a quarter to half an inch) thick, and the ribs are rounded, which usually allows the projectile point that hits a rib to

slide around it and penetrate the ribcage. Lower down, the ribs are wider and flatter, making it difficult to penetrate the heart, which lies close to the bottom of the ribcage. Higher up, the hide is thicker. If the spear penetrates the flesh at the top of the back, this produces a painful wound that will eventually prove fatal only if the spear has penetrated the interior of the ribcage.

It requires considerable strength to penetrate an elephant's hide with a thrusting spear. A spear thrown from a distance is effective, but a great deal of practice is needed to throw it accurately. An atlatl and dart were found to be the most effective method, the dart having a combined weight—shaft, foreshaft, and projectile point— of 478 grams (16 ounces) and a combined length of 220 centimeters (7 feet 2 inches). But each hunter needs to experiment to find the length and weight that suit him personally.

During the culling operations, a mature female elephant that was mortally wounded and left for dead managed to climb to her feet, thus allowing a throw at a standing elephant using an atlatl

and darts. From a distance of 20 meters (22 yards), an elephant's body is much higher off the ground than, for example, a bison's, and the first shaft passed just under the animal's belly. But the second shot, into the lung cavity, was lethal, although it was difficult to get a sharp enough angle of elevation on the spear shaft to allow for the height of the animal.

Several things rapidly became apparent in these experiments that would not have been evident simply from the archaeological record. Hunters must spend a considerable amount of time in making and maintaining their weapons. For example, the shaft must be straight, or the force will not be properly applied to the base of the projectile point. Similarly, hidden flaws in a piece of stone flaking material can cause a projectile point to break at the critical moment, allowing the animal to escape or even causing serious injury to the hunter. Weapons become an extension of the hunter, and careful maintenance and continual practice are required if hunting is to be a successful strategy for survival.

☚ A dart launched by an atlatl from a distance of nearly 20 meters (22 yards) penetrated the hind quarter of this juvenile African elephant to the end of the foreshaft.

GEORGE C. FRISON

Upper Paleolithic hunters and gatherers in the Old World.

Some of the stone items in these caches represent the finest efforts of Clovis flintknappers and are made of the finest available materials, while others are broken and somewhat carelessly reworked. If these collections were, in fact, burial offerings, then the term cache is probably inappropriate, since there would have been no intention of recovering the materials for use at a later date. In this case, some of the best flaked stone artifacts would have been lost for future use. Some of the raw materials found in the caches had obviously been brought from far-off sources, indicating trade or other contacts between widely dispersed groups.

Clovis flintknappers were masters of percussion flaking—that is, shaping stone materials with stone and antler hammers. Unless new discoveries prove otherwise, the Clovis hunters were the first to exploit North America's stone resources, and it can be assumed that there were adequate surface supplies of all materials for their purposes. Clearly, Clovis flintknappers recognized and sought out stone with exceptional flaking qualities, and when they acquired it, crafted it into objects of exceptional quality, such as their projectile points. There are many highly accomplished flintknappers today, and they find that it requires considerable effort to acquire the kind and

quantity of flaking materials, and to develop the technology, necessary to duplicate the artifacts found in the Clovis caches. Quarrying of stone has been documented at the Knife River flint sources, in central North Dakota, between 11,000 and 10,000 years ago, suggesting that the best surface materials had been depleted by the end of Clovis times.

Mammoth Hunting in Clovis Times

Mammoth hunting has captured the imagination of students of human hunting strategies more than the hunting of any other large animal. Unfortunately, most modern illustrations of mammoth hunting—as, indeed, of most forms of big-game hunting in prehistoric times—are highly misleading. A more pragmatic approach to this question is needed, based on a knowledge of animal behavior and human hunting ability.

We know from studies of frozen mammoths recovered from Siberia that the hide covering a mammoth's ribcage was as much as 12 millimeters (half an inch) thick. Clearly, well-designed weapons were needed to penetrate it. Either by design or accident, Clovis weapons were aesthetically pleasing as well as functional. The Clovis projectile point is an example of good structural design that minimizes breakage under stress. Flutes extending distally from the base allow the point to be easily inserted and bound into a notched foreshaft, and rough edges of the point were ground smooth for some distance distal to the base to prevent the blade edges from cutting the shaft bindings upon heavy impact.

Moreover, if the point snaps off, it can be repaired with simple tools in a matter of minutes. The point was attached to either a thrusting spear or an atlatl (a spear-thrower) consisting of a long, heavy mainshaft and a foreshaft. Since a flaw in the stone can render the point useless and put the hunter in danger, all points would have to have been carefully tested before use, particularly before hunters set off on a large-scale kill.

⬆ This fluted projectile point from the Fenn Clovis cache is an example of highly controlled diagonal percussion flaking. The point is made of a red, opaque chert found in Wyoming.
GEORGE C. FRISON

➤ A fluted Clovis point of high-quality chert from the Anzick cache, in southwest Montana.
GEORGE C. FRISON

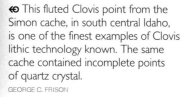

◄ This fluted Clovis point from the Simon cache, in south central Idaho, is one of the finest examples of Clovis lithic technology known. The same cache contained incomplete points of quartz crystal.
GEORGE C. FRISON

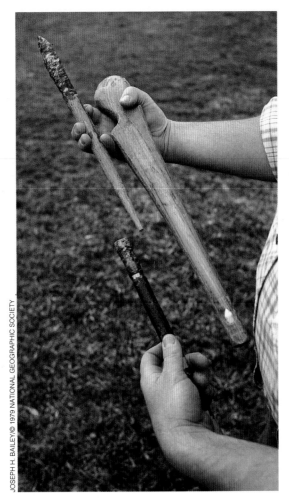

JOSEPH H. BAILEY/© 1979 NATIONAL GEOGRAPHIC SOCIETY

➼ Paleoindian weaponry components, including a throwing stick (atlatl), a wooden foreshaft with a stone projectile point attached with sinew, and the forward end of a long mainshaft wrapped with sinew. The tapered end of the foreshaft is inserted into a hole in the mainshaft carefully designed for an exact fit.

🔥 One of four fluted Clovis points from the Colby mammoth kill site, in Wyoming. They were found in association with the partial remains of eight mammoths scattered along the bottom of an arroyo for nearly 100 meters (about 110 yards).
GEORGE C. FRISON

Morphologically, mammoths are similar to modern elephants, although mammoth hide is not quite as tough as that of African elephants in the wild. Experiments on African elephants have shown that Clovis weapons are effective, and we can assume that Clovis hunters would have been skilled hunters. (See the feature *Clovis Weapons: A Modern Experiment.*) The family structure of African elephants, based on a strong matriarch to protect the family, places certain limits on their procurement, since any attempt to harm a family member brings instant retaliation by the matriarch. It would seem likely that mammoths had a similar family structure, but this is something we will never know.

The evidence is too limited to allow us to say whether the Clovis people hunted mammoths opportunistically or in seasonal campaigns, or both. Finds of the remains of one or two animals around a water source suggest opportunistic hunting, while the Lehner and Colby sites seem to represent the remains of kills made over a period of time, possibly as the result of a more systematic and predictable hunting strategy. It has been suggested that the mammoths found in the Lehner site may represent a whole family killed on one occasion, but this seems unlikely in view of the fact that this would have created a surplus of meat

far beyond the means of a small hunting group to process and store.

Most modern artists' depictions of mammoth hunting show an animal incapacitated in a bog or pit, surrounded by hunters, some with spears and darts, others throwing rocks. Dogs are barking, a dead or maimed hunter is being dragged from the scene, women and children are in the background, and the whole operation appears to be one of noise and confusion. This goes against the rules of intelligent hunting. If a healthy mammoth were submerged in a bog to the extent that it could not extricate itself, a hunting band would not have been able to extract it either. Butchering the animal would have been an even bigger problem. A far better strategy would be to kill the animals on solid ground, and Clovis hunters had both the weapons and the hunting expertise to do this.

The Folsom Cultural Complex

The hunting groups known as the Folsom Cultural Complex appeared about 10,900 years ago, close on the heels of Clovis, and survived for about 600 years. Folsom remains are not found over such wide areas as Clovis, being confined to the Great Plains, the southwest, the central and southern Rocky Mountains, and several intermontane basins partly or entirely within the Rocky Mountains. These people did not hunt mammoths but mainly targeted a now-extinct species of bison, along with occasional pronghorn and mountain sheep. A few camel bones, usually in the form of tools, have been found in some Folsom sites, but there is little evidence to suggest that camels were hunted.

In 1934, amateur archaeologists discovered fluted projectile points identical to those found earlier at the Folsom site, in New Mexico, at a site in northern Colorado now known as the Lindenmeier site. To this day, Lindenmeier remains the largest and most complex Folsom site known. The large number and variety of tools, weapons, and other artifacts found here shows that the Folsom groups were very skilled at making and using stone tools. A small but significant number of bone tools and decorative items show that they were equally adept at working bone. Their flake tools, made from carefully selected materials, exhibit a wide variety of skillfully prepared edges, points, and corners that equal or surpass those of any other Paleoindian cultural complex in the archaeological record of the New World. Microscopic analysis of wear patterns on tool edges suggests that these tools were used to work bone, wood, hide, and possibly other materials as well.

Folsom projectile points are crafted extremely skillfully, and reflect a knowledge of flake technology equal to that known anywhere else in the world. The fluting is a refinement of that found on Clovis points, although many of today's most skillful flintknappers find it difficult to accept that Clovis stone technology was a direct precursor of Folsom technology. Whether Folsom fluting should be considered an aesthetic rather than a functional feature is open to question. The fluting process required high-quality flaking stone and also carried a high risk of failure, which inevitably would have meant that much of this prized raw material was wasted. On the other hand, experiments on modern bison show that fluting is of little, if any, benefit in the hafting process. Therefore it has no effect on the point's ability to produce a lethal wound.

Much has been written about the fluting process because of the difficulty of replicating it. However, many present-day flintknappers have been able to produce very close approximations, using a variety of methods. The key factors are to understand the principles of flaking, to be able to recognize and acquire stone of adequate quality, and, finally, to be able to control the amount and direction of the pressure needed to remove the channel flake that forms the flute. Numerous devices, some simple and some more complex, can be used to remove the channel flakes. Two

⚓ An outstanding example of a Folsom projectile point. The flutes on each side were removed as a single flake.
GEORGE C. FRISON

PHOTO ARCHIVES, DENVER MUSEUM OF NATURAL HISTORY

↞ Two ribs of an extinct subspecies of bison and a Folsom point in their original position in a block of matrix from the Folsom site, in northeast New Mexico. This confirmed the association of human weaponry and extinct bison in North America.

⊕ A Folsom bison kill site in eastern Wyoming's Agate Basin. The partial remains of at least eight bison were found here, along with those of at least four pronghorn (*Antilocapra americana*). The animals were probably killed in the arroyo adjacent to the bone bed, and the Paleoindian group would have camped alongside the meat supply during the winter months.

GEORGE C. FRISON

⚲ Topography of the Agate Basin bison kill site. The animals were driven up arroyos (from right to left of the photograph), where natural and/or artificial barriers formed traps.

GEORGE C. FRISON

punches, one made of elk antler and the other from the rear leg bone of a bison, were excavated from a Folsom level at the Agate Basin site in the midst of a scatter of channel flakes and projectile points broken at various stages of manufacture. These are believed to have been used, in conjunction with some sort of simple leverage device, to remove channel flakes.

The Evidence of Paleoecology

The Folsom level at the Lindenmeier site was buried in sediments up to several meters (10 feet) thick, and was exposed in the banks of an eroding, or downcutting, arroyo. Radiocarbon dating had not been invented at that time, and

since the site is located on a dry tributary of the Cache La Poudre River, which originates in the Colorado Front Range of the Rocky Mountains, a geological project was set up to try to date the Folsom deposits in relation to river terraces that could be correlated with glacial events in the mountains during the late Wisconsin Period. These efforts met with some success, and this encouraged an interdisciplinary approach to investigating archaeological sites. As with the Lindenmeier site, many important Paleoindian sites, particularly those on the Plains and in the southwest, are found in stratified geological deposits. If we are to reconstruct the ecological conditions of the late Pleistocene and early Holocene periods as accurately as possible, and to understand how humans and animals would have fitted into this environment, we need to draw upon the expertise of many different specialists, including geologists trained in quaternary studies, soils specialists, palynologists (who study fossil pollen), paleobotanists, paleoclimatologists, and others. Interdisciplinary studies are continually being refined in ways that help archaeologists to interpret their finds in cultural terms.

Killing Fields and Bone Beds

Bone beds resulting from the killing, butchering, and processing of bison in prehistoric times are the most visible of Paleoindian archaeological sites. The location of these kill sites is largely determined by topography. Arroyos are common landscape features throughout the Great Plains. They changed continually through time as a result of geological processes, and from time to time a combination of landforms occurred that formed a natural bison trap. Sometimes the prehistoric hunters may have added a fence or drive line— stone lines believed to have been used to strengthen wooden fences often remain.

Continuing geological activity has destroyed most archaeological evidence of arroyos used for large-scale bison kills, but sometimes these same processes act to preserve such sites. Arroyos continually undergo cycles of erosion and deposition. The bone bed at the bottom of an arroyo that is aggrading (or filling up) may be temporarily protected and preserved by a layer of sediments. Later on, during the degrading (or downcutting) cycle, the bone bed is usually destroyed. But in rare cases, the arroyo may take a different course during the downcutting cycle, and the bone bed, or parts of it, may be preserved intact.

A bone bed results from the activities of human hunters and is therefore a valuable source of cultural information. The investigation of bone beds falls under a branch of science known as taphonomy, which deals with the study of animal remains between the time the animals were killed and the time the bones are exhumed. Archaeologists use many kinds of taphonomic data. For example, changes to bones that result from human activity can usually be distinguished from those caused by carnivores and scavengers, and bones stacked and piled by humans can be distinguished from piles of bones washed together by floods. Stages of bone weathering can often tell us for how long and under what conditions a bone bed was exposed in the past. Where large numbers of animals were involved, we can often determine whether the bones resulted from a single mass kill or accumulated gradually over a longer period from a number of hunting episodes.

Paleontologists alerted archaeologists to the fact that the teeth of animals such as bison erupt at particular stages, allowing the age of young animals to be determined to within a few weeks. Not only are teeth more likely to be preserved than other animal parts, but especially during Paleoindian times, mandibles were usually discarded intact when carcasses were butchered and processed, because they were of little use as food. If a bison kill included young animals, we can work out fairly accurately at what time of year it took place by adding the animal's age to the time of its birth— which we know from the fact that the young are born within a short period during spring. By contrast, if bison or other animals were taken throughout the winter, rather than in a single kill, we can establish this, too, by examining the teeth to see which had erupted and/or the stages of development of fetal remains. Bone beds can also give us information about butchering methods and the amount of meat Paleoindian hunters acquired. When drawn together, all this information helps us to reconstruct the Paleoindian way of life.

Bison Hunting in Folsom Times

Many other Folsom sites have been located throughout the Great Plains and intermontane basins in the Rocky Mountains since the Lindenmeier site, and most show evidence of bison hunting. The Lipscomb Bison Quarry, in the northeast Texas Panhandle, contained the carcasses of at least 14 (and probably more) extinct bison, along with Folsom fluted projectile points and stone tools. At the Folsom site itself, in northeast New Mexico, are the remains of about 30 extinct bison, which may or may not represent a single kill. One area of the Lindenmeier site, known as the "bison pit", contains the bones of 9 or more extinct bison. (See the feature *The Paleoindian Bison Hunters*.)

The Hell Gap site is topographically similar to the Lindenmeier site, having a permanent water source and opening onto a plain that would have been ideal for the grazing megafauna of the late Pleistocene and early Holocene periods. Bison bone and carcass remains found here indicate that Paleoindian hunters killed small groups of bison over a period of nearly 3,000 years, using a natural barrier or an artificial trap made of logs (or a combination of both) located in the arroyo.

For at least a thousand years since Folsom times, Paleoindians have trapped bison in arroyos around the Agate Basin site in east central Wyoming, to the north of the Hell Gap site. One winter kill made during Folsom times contains the partial remains of eight bison. The hunting group

apparently camped alongside the butchered animals, using the meat, which was probably frozen, as needed. The arrangement of activity areas, artifacts, and other features suggests that they lived in small, above-ground structures very similar to Plains Indian tipis. The site is located on the arroyo floodplain, a good place to live in winter but one that would have flooded and become uninhabitable with the approach of warm weather and spring runoff.

⬆ Looking up Wild Horse Arroyo at the location of the Folsom site before excavation in 1926. The bison bone bed is exposed near the arroyo bottom. The arroyo becomes much narrower and the gradient increases sharply immediately beyond the bone bed, creating ideal conditions for a natural trap.

THE PALEOINDIAN BISON HUNTERS

GEORGE C. FRISON

PALEOINDIAN BISON HUNTERS on the plains of North America were familiar with their hunting territory and the day-to-day habits of the animals, and they had developed the best weapons known anywhere in the world during that period. The communal hunt was an important social event as well as a means of acquiring food. The entire band, or even several bands, gathered at a designated location not only to provision the group with meat but also to perform numerous social obligations and related activities that served to reinforce the solidarity of the group and helped to ensure its continued existence.

Communal bison hunts were events in which the chances of failure were always present, so the supernatural was called upon to reinforce the chances of success. The religious leader, or shaman, performed the necessary rituals involved in calling in the animals and ensuring that the spirits of the dead animals were properly treated. In this way, future hunting success would not be imperiled, since the general belief among hunting societies such as these was that the animals made themselves available for the benefit of humans, but only as long as they were accorded the proper respect through the performance of established rituals. Repeated failures could be blamed on the shaman, but he could protect himself by claiming that the failure was due to someone in the group neglecting to observe the proper rituals.

Many Paleoindian sites on the plains bear witness to as much as 2,000 to 3,000 years of repeated use, owing to topographic features that in their natural form or with slight modification formed traps for animals. Since the teeth of bison are known to erupt at certain ages, especially in young animals, and the calving season is restricted to a short time in early spring, we know from the fossil evidence that many Paleoindian bison kills were carried out in late autumn and winter. Evidence from some kill sites on the Northern Plains indicates that surplus meat was temporarily frozen and placed in protected caches for use as needed.

GEORGE C. FRISON

⊕ Skull and other bones of butchered bison at the Casper site, in Wyoming.

↩ A modern model of the parabola-shaped dune used to trap bison at the Casper site.

GEORGE C. FRISON

↪ The spectacular Olsen-Chubbuck site, in eastern Colorado, has revealed the carcasses of more than 200 large Pleistocene bison, killed when they were stampeded into a deep, narrow arroyo about 10,000 years ago. Stone projectile points among the bones indicate that some animals were dispatched by the hunters. The herd included males and females of all ages. Many animals at the bottom were so deeply buried under other animals that they could not be retrieved. This was an unusual situation, since in other known Paleoindian bison kills there was little waste.

♣ Bones of bison butchered 10,000 years ago lie in the trench of a parabolic sand dune at the Casper site, in Wyoming. At the time of the kill, the trench was several meters deep and at least 150 meters (160 yards) long. Animals driven into the trap would have had to reverse direction in order to escape, during which time they would have been extremely vulnerable.

Further north, in the Powder River Basin in northeast Wyoming, the burning of coal beds more than 30 meters (100 feet) thick, estimated to have occurred several million years ago, caused an area of land more than a kilometer (half a mile) wide and several kilometers (almost 2 miles) long to subside. This eventually collected water to form a shallow lake. Tall grasses growing along the lake margins would have attracted grazing megafauna, and, with time, arroyos formed as runoff water drained into the lake. One of these became a major bison trap and is now known as the Carter/Kerr-McGee site. It very nearly duplicates the Paleoindian cultural record of the Hell Gap site. The location and configuration of the arroyo would have made it an ideal trap for large animals during Paleoindian times.

One of the larger of the known Folsom sites is the Hanson site in the Bighorn Basin, in north central Wyoming. Once again, it is near the head of an arroyo that opens up into a large area where bison would have grazed in Folsom times and so would have been an ideal bison trap. Bison would have moved naturally or been driven along the arroyo to a point where there was a natural or artificial trap. The number of bison bones found in the Folsom level of the site strongly indicates that there was a kill area nearby.

The Sand Dunes National Monument, in the San Luis Valley of southern Colorado, was formed when sand moving across the eastern part of the valley was stopped by steep mountain slopes. Several Folsom bison kill sites were found on the margins of the dunes. One of these, known as the Cattle Guard site, is very close to the surface but nonetheless contains a collection of artifacts in an undisturbed context. This was undoubtedly a favorable area for killing bison in Folsom times, although we cannot be sure which hunting strategy was used. A U-shaped sand dune was

used as a bison trap 10,000 years ago in central Wyoming, and similar features may have been present and used during Folsom times in the San Luis Valley.

The Goshen Cultural Complex

For nearly two decades after the Hell Gap site was investigated, nothing appeared in Paleoindian sites to kindle any interest in the Goshen Complex. This changed in the early 1980s with the discovery of the Mill Iron site, in southeast Montana. Projectile points and tools eroding out of a steep rocky slope near the crest of a flat-topped butte were strikingly similar to those recovered from the lowest level at the Hell Gap site and given the name of Goshen. As the Mill Iron site had evidence of only one Paleoindian culture, there was no possibility of stratigraphic comparisons with Clovis and Folsom layers, but radiocarbon dating indicates that the artifacts are about 11,000 years old. Although two mammoth rib fragments—one used as a tool or the haft of a weapon—were recovered from the Mill Iron site, there is no evidence to indicate that mammoths were killed there. Mammoth bones would undoubtedly have been present and used for some time after the animals became extinct.

A bison bone bed at the Mill Iron site contained the partial remains of at least 31 animals that were killed in mid or late winter. Extreme erosion in the area has removed so much of the landforms that would have been present when the site was occupied that no clue remains as to the hunting strategy used at the time. Nor is it possible to determine if the bone bed represents more than a single kill.

♀ These remains of bison carcasses have been preserved in the same position as they were after butchering in the sand dune trap at the Casper site.

Many Folsom sites have been found in the San Luis Valley, in southern Colorado. Deep sand deposits have collected at the eastern side of the valley, and Folsom bison kills have been found at the edge of the dunes. The floor of the valley lies at an elevation of about 2,400 meters (8,000 feet), and the mountain peaks in the background rise above 4,250 meters (14,000 feet).

A Goshen projectile point from the Mill Iron bison kill site, in southeast Montana.
GEORGE C. FRISON

Excavations in the poorly preserved bison bone bed at the Mill Iron site revealed the partial remains of at least 31 animals, killed in late winter or early spring. They were probably killed close by, but erosion has removed all evidence of nearby landforms suitable for a trap.

At the Carter/Kerr-McGee site mentioned earlier, in the central Powder River Basin in northern Wyoming, a small remnant of a cultural level with Goshen-style projectile points was found underneath a Folsom level. This is another case where the stratigraphic evidence suggests that Goshen is older than Folsom. Judging by its location, the Carter/Kerr-McGee site must have been used as an animal trap, but in the Goshen level, only a metatarsal bone of a late Pleistocene camel was found, along with several unidentified fragments of heavy long bone. As was the case at Hell Gap, this was first thought to be a Clovis level, but a closer look at the projectile points revealed that they are more likely Goshen.

The technology represented by Goshen projectile points is very similar to that of Folsom except that Goshen points are not fluted. Instead, several pressure flakes extend distally from the base—presumably to make the base thinner as an aid to hafting—but there is nothing that can be called a flute. The tools found are similar to both Clovis and Folsom tools. Taking all this evidence into account—types of tools and projectile points, stratigraphy, and hunting strategies—it seems reasonable to conclude that Goshen may have been the immediate precursor of Folsom.

Current archaeological investigation of a small basin within the Rocky Mountains near the headwaters of the Colorado River, known as Middle Park, has yielded both Folsom and Goshen sites. Goshen projectile points have been found at a kill site containing at least 13 bison, located at an elevation of about 2,620 meters (8,600 feet). In a nearby camp site, Goshen and Folsom artifacts are found together. It is clear from this evidence

that bison frequented higher elevations during the late Pleistocene and early Holocene periods. Since the bison remains are located where a major game trail reaches the crest of a steep hill, it seems likely that hunters forced the animals up the trail, to be killed when they were winded after the steep climb and less alert to danger by other hunters waiting at the crest of the slope.

Although sites such as these are still being discovered, we do not yet have enough information to be sure of the relationship between the Clovis, Goshen, and Folsom cultures. The evidence to date, however, based on both radiocarbon dates and stratigraphy, indicates that the Clovis hunters arrived in North America about 11,000 years ago, and that both the Goshen and Folsom cultures followed very soon afterward.

The Great Animal Extinctions

What happened to the giant animals of the late Pleistocene period that were present, but apparently on the verge of extinction, when the Clovis hunters arrived? This is a fascinating question. Unless evidence is uncovered showing that highly efficient hunters were present in North America in pre-Clovis times, we cannot attribute their demise to human predation alone. Although the Clovis culture was widespread in North America, there is very little to suggest that these people could have hunted these animals to extinction—although they may well have delivered the *coup de grâce* in some cases, in particular to mammoths. Nor does it seem likely that either horses or camels were seriously hunted by humans in North America, while bison survived as the main prey of Paleoindian hunters on the Plains for at least 3,000 years after the Clovis hunters disappeared. The large-scale animal extinctions at the end of the Pleistocene period have yet to be satisfactorily explained and probably resulted from several contributing factors. (See the feature *The Fate of North America's Early Animals*.)

Beyond Bones and Stones

Paleoindian studies involve many and varied disciplines, but in the final analysis, the surviving evidence must be interpreted within a framework of human behavior. The archaeological record shows that Paleoindians developed the ability to make different types of stone tools and weapons. However, weapons (especially projectile points) changed in form over time, and it is on the basis of these changes that archaeologists are able to identify different cultural complexes. Tools do not show as much change, and are therefore a less reliable guide to time. Because of this, the enduring stone projectile point has become the "guide fossil" for North American archaeologists. This, along with stratigraphy and radiocarbon dating, has allowed us to establish a chronology for the various Paleoindian groups that inhabited North America.

We cannot project ourselves back in time and observe Paleoindian groups at first hand, but we can use our knowledge of recent hunter-gatherer societies at a similar cultural stage in different parts of the world to shed light on the past. For example, Inuit (or Eskimo) groups who hunt caribou and sea mammals and the historic record of the bison hunters of the North American Plains provide good bases for comparison and allow us to look at the Paleoindians as human societies rather than archaeological sites. We must remember, however, that we can compare such groups only in general terms.

On this basis, we can conjecture that Paleoindian communities consisted of small groups of nomadic *Homo sapiens sapiens* concerned with problems of day-to-day survival. They lived in close harmony with a harsh and unforgiving environment, where a single mistake in the everyday quest for food could mean death or disablement and even result in the family starving to death. They had to compete directly with large predators and scavengers for food, and they had to protect stored surpluses from these and other dangers. For example, rodents burrowing into a food cache from below could have the same end result as a grizzly bear tearing the cache apart from the outside.

The mainstay of the Paleoindian economy was hunting, which was a male-centered activity. Women butchered the meat from the kill, prepared it for consumption, and gathered plant foods. While the latter was a less prestigious activity than hunting, plants were an important part of the everyday food supply. Paleoindians lived in small bands, the only political leadership being provided by the male who claimed the greatest charisma by virtue of being the most accomplished hunter and provider. Bands ranged in size from 20 to 50 individuals made up of 4 to 10 nuclear families. For most of the year, the band fragmented into smaller single or multiple family groups to exploit the available food resources more efficiently. Communal hunting or a windfall in the form of surplus food would have brought the entire band or even several bands together. The wide-ranging sources of the stone used to make the flake tools found at the Lindenmeier site, in northern Colorado, suggest that more than one band may have gathered there to take part in communal bison hunting.

♀ Mule deer (*Odocoileus hemionus*) grazing the lush grass away from the edge of the sand dunes in the San Luis Valley. Trees at the base of the sand dunes indicate that conditions would have been ideal for bison in the past, with running water.

JIM BRANDENBURG/MINDEN PICTURES

Bands were territorial, and resources within the territory were exploited systematically, although boundaries were less distinct than those defining modern-day states or countries. Bands were exogamous—that is, members took partners from outside the band—and this involved crossing territorial boundaries. In hunting societies such as these, it was the women who moved to the husband's residence, since it was vitally important to survival that the intimate knowledge of the hunting territory be passed on from father to son.

Hunting groups such as these had a special relationship to the animal world. Hunting magic and ritual dominated most animal hunting activities, especially where the chances of failure were high, as in the case of a communal bison kill. These people believed that animals made themselves available to humans, but that a well-defined measure of respect was expected in return. The animal spirits had to be treated appropriately at every stage of the hunting process, and if this was not done, the animals would no longer make themselves available. The shaman, or medicine-man, was present at communal hunts to ensure that the proper rituals were observed. Shamans also had a role in curing sickness, which was generally believed to result from breaking taboos, rather than from natural causes.

These Paleoindian hunting societies survived for thousands of years, and one of the secrets of their enduring success was cooperation. No matter who killed the animal or gathered the food, all members of the group shared, since not every hunter or gatherer could be successful at every attempt. When food was in short supply, sharing was even more important. It was considered reprehensible to hoard food, and in these kinds of societies it was next to impossible to do this without being found out. The people most admired were those who were the best providers and who shared the most. Storing food in caches was quite different from hoarding and was strictly a short-term measure to provide for periods of extreme cold or other times when it was not possible to go out and search for food. Caching may also have been more common in the Arctic, and was not as necessary for groups living in warmer areas.

It is difficult to imagine humans, however acclimatized they may have been, surviving the winter in the colder regions without adequate clothing and shelter. The archaeological record tells us very little about this aspect of Paleoindian life, and very few sites offer clues to the nature of winter living quarters. What evidence there is suggests that they lived in simple structures, perhaps similar to the tipis of the North American Plains Indians, consisting of hides of large animals stretched over a conical framework of poles. Such shelters are, in fact, remarkably warm in winter when well insulated with snow and heated with

WARREN MORGAN

small fires. Even so, it is difficult to imagine them surviving subzero temperatures without adequate clothing, especially footwear, and we know that they possessed the tools to make such clothing. For example, eyed bone needles not unlike the metal ones of today have been recovered from Folsom sites.

Ideally, the archaeologist hopes to find sites with undisturbed cultural levels, containing characteristic projectile points along with organic material that can be radiocarbon-dated. Unfortunately, this rarely happens. But we should never lose sight of the fact that Paleoindian archaeology deals with people, much like ourselves, who managed to survive under very difficult environmental conditions, to raise families, and to maintain the continuity of human populations from one generation to the next. It is much more than the mere study of artifacts of stone and bone.

☝ Two Clovis points from the Richey-Roberts cache at Wenatchee, Washington, along the Columbia River—the first Clovis cache to be excavated by professional archae-ologists. Other items included blades, blade tools, unfinished projectile points, and carved cylindrical items of mammoth bone similar to those from the Anzick site.

THE FATE OF NORTH AMERICA'S EARLY ANIMALS

Donald K. Grayson

Towards the end of the Pleistocene era, some 35 genera of mammals became extinct in North America—in the sense either that they no longer existed anywhere on Earth (29 genera), or that they disappeared from North America while continuing to exist elsewhere (6 genera). Large herbivores were prominent among the losses, including mastodon, mammoths, musk oxen, horses, camels, huge ground sloths, and giant beavers. Many others were carnivores that probably preyed upon the herbivores, such as the sabertooth cat, the American cheetah, the American lion, and the dire wolf.

The archaeological and paleontological records leave little doubt that virtually all of these mammals were extinct by the end of the Pleistocene era, 10,000 years ago. What is far from clear is when the extinctions began—and what caused them.

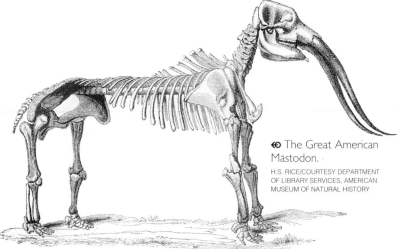

The Great American Mastodon.

H.S. RICE/COURTESY DEPARTMENT OF LIBRARY SERVICES, AMERICAN MUSEUM OF NATURAL HISTORY

Lion-sized predators, sabertooth cats were widespread in North America during the Pleistocene era.

Nearly all of the extinct mammals appear to have survived the glacial maximum that occurred between about 22,000 and 18,000 years ago. Indeed, since the mid-1960s, it has been generally assumed that virtually all the extinctions occurred between about 12,000 and 10,000 years ago, but this is not borne out by recent detailed investigations of the available radiocarbon dates. Of the 35 extinct genera, only 9, including horses, camels, mammoths, and mastodon, can be reliably shown to have existed later than 12,000 years ago. The remaining 26 may have become extinct during this period, but we cannot be sure: they may have started to die out thousands of years before the end of the Pleistocene era.

Until we know a lot more about the timing of the extinctions, we can only conjecture as to what may have caused them. Two main explanations have been put forward. The best-known theory is that developed by paleoecologist Paul S. Martin, who points out that the extinctions seem to have coincided with the appearance of Clovis hunters in North America. He argues that these Paleoindian hunters emerged south of the glacial ice about 11,500 years ago, where they came upon a great variety of what they saw as large game mammals. Because these herbivores had never before encountered human predators, they had not developed any form of defensive behavior. Taking advantage of this massive, naive, and accessible food supply, the human hunters multiplied and spread southward very rapidly. Behind them, they left a trail of extinct populations—and, ultimately, extinct genera—of mammals. As their prey disappeared, so, too, did such carnivores as the sabertooth cat, the American cheetah, and the American lion.

Although intuitively appealing, the "overkill hypothesis" has fallen

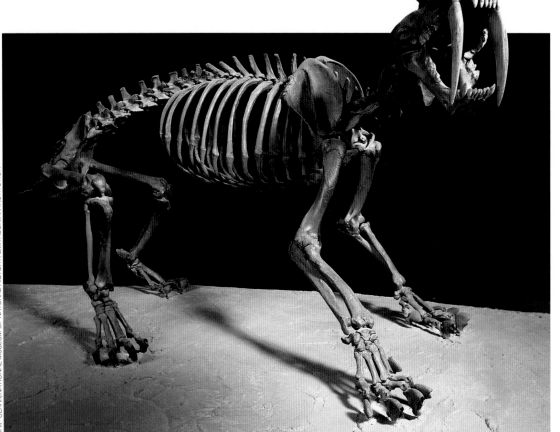

out of favor in recent years. To begin with, there is evidence to suggest that Paleoindians ate a far more varied diet than this hypothesis assumes. Moreover, only mammoth and mastodon remains have ever been found in a context indicating that the animals were killed by humans.

Although our knowledge of how Paleoindians subsisted is very limited, the fact that no kill sites have been found for mammals other than mammoths and mastodon appears to be compelling. In the continental United States, the most frequently found fossils are those of horses (followed by mammoths), but there are no kill sites for horses. Similarly, the third most commonly found fossils are camels (followed by mastodon), and, again, none of the camel sites appears to be a kill site.

As the overkill explanation has lost support, climatic explanations have become more widely accepted. These have been developed in detail by paleontologists Russell W. Graham, R. Dale Guthrie, and Ernest L. Lundelius. While they are complex, they are all based on the fact that massive environmental changes took place in the period during which the extinctions occurred, including, in many areas, changes in the seasonal distribution of temperatures and dramatic alterations in the nature of the vegetation. As a result, the distribution of small mammals changed tremendously, and the larger mammals, which were not as numerous and made greater demands on their environment, could not survive. While the proponents of the climatic explanations do not exclude the possibility that humans may have had a role in making some of the mammals extinct— perhaps delivering the *coup de grâce* to some species—they maintain that the ultimate cause is to be found in the dramatic environmental changes that marked the end of the Pleistocene era in North America.

CHIP CLARK/NATIONAL MUSEUM OF NATURAL HISTORY, SMITHSONIAN INSTITUTION

⬆ Reaching a height of some 5.5 meters (18 feet) and with an estimated body weight of just over 3 tonnes (3 tons), Harlan's ground sloth was the largest of the four genera of ground sloths that existed in North America towards the end of the Pleistocene era.

PIONEERS OF THE ARCTIC

2 5 0 0 B C — A D 1 5 0 0

The Last of the Habitable Lands

MOREAU MAXWELL

THE ARCTIC, the last of the habitable lands, was occupied quite late in human history, about 4,500 years ago. Survival in this most harsh and bitter of environments depended ultimately on people's ability to kill animals for food, clothing, and fuel. This was an almost unbelievably awesome task. It could require, on occasion, a solitary hunter, armed with only a flimsy spear, to face and defeat a polar bear standing twice his height, knowing that with one blow of its great paws it could break him in two.

Drinking water, that most basic of human requirements, was extremely difficult to obtain. In the frozen Arctic, fresh water is locked away in rock-hard ice and must be melted for use. In many parts of the region, the only firewood is driftwood. As this is too scarce to rely on for fuel, early Arctic people burned the fat of sea mammals instead.

◄ Towards spring, the ice packs of the eastern Arctic break into drifting fields, with open-water leads between. Hunters on the ice may drift away from shore, to be lost forever. Rough hummocky ice is formed when drifting ice fields collide. These hummock ridges may rise 5 meters (15 feet) or more above the flat surface of the ice.

◊ Wooden mask with carved bone eyes from an Old Bering Sea culture burial. The mask probably covered the face of the skull.

NORTH POLE

● Independence Fiord

GREENLAND

● Bache Peninsula
● Port Refuge
● Sarqaq sites

Lancaster Sound

● Cape Denbigh

ALASKA

Baffin Bay

● Pond Inlet

● Naknek

● Ekulluk sites

● Kapuivik
● Igloolik

Davis Strait

● Great Bear Lake

Pacific Ocean

● Lake Harbour sites

Hudson Strait

Atlantic Ocean

● Great Slave Lake

● Arnapik

● Saglek

C A N A D A

Hudson Bay

Labrador

Quebec

CARTOGRAPHY: RAY SIM

⚓ ARCTIC SMALL TOOL TRADITION SITES

Some early prehistoric sites occupied between 2000 BC and AD 500.

⚓ THULE CULTURE SITES

The ultimate distribution of the Classic Thule culture from AD 1200 to AD 1500.

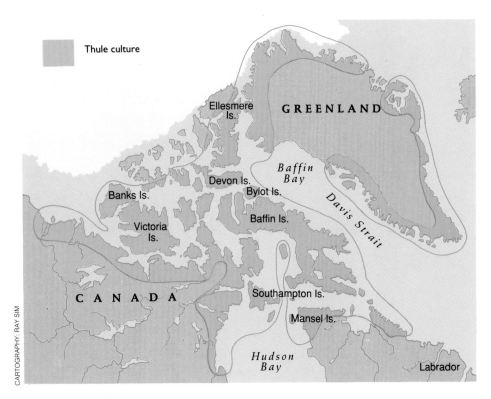

Thule culture

Ellesmere Is.

GREENLAND

Baffin Bay

Devon Is.

Banks Is.

Bylot Is.

Victoria Is.

Baffin Is.

Davis Strait

C A N A D A

Southampton Is.

Mansel Is.

Hudson Bay

Labrador

CARTOGRAPHY: RAY SIM

As well as providing fat for fuel, seals were the main source of food and clothing. Hunting was a difficult and dangerous task, especially in winter. At that time of the year, seals are best hunted in the strip of open water between the sea-ice and the wide expanse of ice frozen fast to the shore. Here, the hunter had to wait patiently for a seal's head—smaller than a volleyball—to surface, presenting a fleeting target for his harpoon. Throughout the often long wait, he had to remain constantly alert for a low roar from the ice he was standing on, signaling that it was breaking away from the shore, carrying him out to sea with it. Even today, hunters at the ice edge sometimes drift away, never to return.

Days of labor were required to make a single harpoon. The hunter would first collect scarce and precious bits of driftwood, which he would join skillfully to make the shaft. He would then spend many hours carving the head out of hard ivory and flaking a flint point for its tip. Finally, he faced the perilous task of finding and killing seals and other prey. A successful hunter, returning with a small seal carcass, would have barely enough to feed his family for a week. Then the task would have to be repeated.

What Is the Arctic?

The Arctic is the northernmost region on Earth, extending right up to the North Pole. It can be defined in terms of degrees of latitude or distance from the equator. The southern boundary of the Arctic—the Arctic Circle—girdles the Earth at about 66 degrees 30 minutes North, running through the far north of Alaska, Canada, and Scandinavia and crossing Siberia. Here, on one day of the year, about 21 June, the sun does not set, and about 21 December, it does not rise. At the northern limit of land, there is no sunlight from about the middle of February to the middle of March, and few daily hours of darkness until early October. This dramatic fluctuation between sunlight and darkness has marked effects on both biological growth and human behavior.

As our interest here is in how early humans adapted to life in the Arctic, it is useful to consider the region in terms of its low annual "heat budget", or lack of heat energy. This does not mean that the Arctic has the lowest maximum temperatures: in many inland regions of Siberia and the Yukon, winter temperatures sometimes drop to levels never reached in the Arctic. Rather, it is the relative absence of heat energy throughout the year that distinguishes the Arctic and creates a unique environment. Scientists sometimes define the limits of the Arctic environment in terms of the average July temperature. An isothermic line connecting all regions of the north where the average July temperature does not exceed 10 degrees Celsius (50 degrees Fahrenheit) provides a useful boundary.

Two other lines that can be plotted on the Earth's surface, the permafrost line and the tree line, are also used to define the Arctic region, corresponding roughly to the isothermic line. The permafrost line marks regions where, except for a thin active surface, the ground remains permanently frozen. The more visible tree line, to the north of which forests cannot grow, is related to the permafrost region, because the frozen ground prevents tree roots from penetrating deeply and inhibits the subsurface drainage of meltwater. The tree line marks the border between boreal taiga to the south—the coniferous forests that extend across much of the subarctic—and treeless tundra to the north.

Adapting to Life in the Arctic

Although many species of mammals and birds wander back and forth across the tree line, certain animals have adapted specifically to this environment and are considered to be Arctic species. The polar bear is the best known of these. It sometimes spends the summer below the tree line, waiting for the sea-ice to freeze so that it can resume its hunting activities. (See the feature *Arctic Animals*.) Other Arctic animals include white arctic wolves, foxes, and hares; seals and walruses; arctic char

WAYNE LANKINEN/BRUCE COLEMAN LTD

⬆ An erect polar bear standing some 3.5 meters (11 feet) or more tall would be a fearsome beast to a hunter armed with only a spear.

➛ Razor-sharp microblades of chert and quartz crystal barely 10 millimeters (three-eighths of an inch) wide were pressed from carefully prepared cores. These artifacts, frequently found in Arctic Small Tool Tradition sites, were utility knives. Their sharp edges were especially useful for cutting seal and caribou skin patterns for clothing.

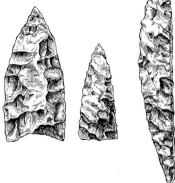

🔥 Stone tools from the Denbigh Flint Complex. The top two are burins. The second row, left to right, are two harpoon endblades and a sideblade for hafting in the side of an arrow.
ILLUSTRATIONS: KEN RINKEL (AFTER MOREAU MAXWELL)

(a type of sea trout that travels from the sea up a river or into coastal waters to spawn); caribou; and migratory ducks and geese. These were all prey for early people of the Arctic.

Humans adapted to Arctic conditions in a number of ways. They developed specialized techniques—in particular, various types of harpoons—for hunting animals on land, sea, and sea-ice. As well as food, animals provided skins and feathers for clothing and fat for fuel. People also learned to build shelters that offered them protection from the extreme cold. The evidence of these activities that has been preserved in the archaeological record is sufficiently clear to allow us to distinguish between Arctic people and the people of the boreal taiga, to the south. In more recent times, we know these two groups as Inuit (or Eskimos) and Indians.

The First Paleoeskimos

The first inhabitants of North America are thought to have crossed the broad land bridge of Beringia, between eastern Siberia and Alaska, as early as 20,000 years ago. At this time, the sea level was much lower, and this region was exposed as a broad plain of tundra and artemisia bush. In pursuit of the giant animals that roamed the American continent during the Pleistocene period, including mammoths, mastodon, and bison, these early hunters penetrated first southwards, into the northern American plains, and then beyond, on into South America. These ancestors of present-day Indians continued to live in the unglaciated interior of Alaska until about 6000 BC.

This Paleoarctic tradition, its distinctive stone tools grouped by experts into such cultural entities as Akmak, Anangula, Chindadn, and Denali, may have had its origin deep in the Aldan River region of Siberia as early as 30,000 years ago. These early people fished in the rivers and hunted land animals, particularly caribou, but did not develop the techniques of sea-ice hunting that were characteristic of later Arctic peoples.

The culture generally considered to be the forerunner of the first North American people to adapt to the Arctic was named the Denbigh Flint Complex, after Cape Denbigh, in Alaska, where the oldest flint tools belonging to the western Paleoeskimo tradition were found. It appears in the archaeological record several thousand years after the Akmak and Anangula cultures. Radiocarbon dating is less reliable in the Arctic than elsewhere, because the different types of organic materials available for analysis, such as bone, antler, and ivory tusks, seem to take up the carbon isotope at varying rates that are not yet well understood. It suggests, however, that Denbigh emerged not much earlier than 2000 BC. Denbigh's origins are unclear. It may have evolved from Akmak, or it may be related to some later Siberian tradition brought by hunters across Bering Strait.

The Arctic Small Tool Tradition

All that has survived of the Denbigh culture in Alaska is a distinctive set of stone tools found in a number of sites north and east along the Alaskan coast, from the base of the Alaska Peninsula to the Canadian border. The tools include burins (or gravers) only 2.5 centimeters (1 inch) long, used for carving bone, antler, and ivory; delicately flaked, bipointed endblades used to tip bone and antler arrowheads; sideblades of flint and quartz crystal for inserting into bone arrowheads and spearheads (to increase the loss of blood in land prey such as caribou and musk oxen and thus bring them to ground faster); triangular endblades, probably used to tip harpoon heads; and tiny blades of flint or quartz crystal known as microblades, no more than 10 millimeters (three-eighths of an inch) wide, used for such purposes as cutting skins and carving wooden handles. Other, less distinctive, tools include endscrapers and sidescrapers for working hard materials and dressing skins, and a few examples of polished adzes.

Except for the adzes, these tools and weapon tips are so small that they have become known as the Arctic Small Tool Tradition, which can be traced through several cultural complexes along the Arctic coast eastwards to Greenland. It is because the tools and weapons of these various complexes are so similar that the Denbigh Flint Complex is seen as the ancestral North American Arctic culture.

The earliest Denbigh sites are inland on the Kobuk and Brooks rivers, at the base of the Alaska Peninsula. Both sites have yielded evidence of caribou hunting and riverine fishing. Settlements consisted of clusters of two or three shallow pit houses 60 centimeters (2 feet) deep, each with a sloping entryway and a central fireplace. Early Denbigh hunters appear to have used coastal sites only during the short summer. Later sites seem to have been used throughout the year, perhaps because by then hunters had developed the skills necessary to kill sea mammals along the frozen coast.

The Denbigh Complex appears to be the only logical ancestor of the Arctic Small Tool Tradition, which spread eastwards from Alaska to Greenland. However, there is a problem with the dating of Denbigh that has yet to be resolved. Radiocarbon dates from the initial site on Cape Denbigh and several Brooks River sites suggest that the complex goes back to about 2000 BC. Equally reliable dates from the easternmost sites where the Arctic Small Tool Tradition is found, in Greenland, also go back to about 2000 BC, or even a few centuries earlier.

It is highly unlikely that early hunting bands would have migrated the 4,800 kilometers (3,000 miles) from western Alaska to northern Greenland in less than a century. Even four or five centuries would be rapid for such a migration. In addition, there is no obvious impetus for it.

JOHNNY JOHNSON/BRUCE COLEMAN LTD

FRANCOIS GOHIER/AUSCAPE

↩ Some small herds of caribou remained in arctic valleys throughout the winter, but most migrated from southern forests in huge herds in the spring, retreating to the south in late autumn.

🜨 The killer whale was too dangerous to be hunted frequently from kayaks. Bones from sites as early as Sarqaq, however, indicate that these whales were occasionally killed or the bones scavenged from dead animals washed ashore.

ARCTIC ANIMALS

People who live in the Arctic are far more dependent on animals for food and clothing than other hunter-gatherers. Today, supplies—even watermelons—can be flown in to isolated settlements, but before the advent of European explorers meat constituted 90 percent of the diet.

Seals of many species—ringed, bearded, harp, gray, and bladder-nosed—were the main source of food, and their layers of fat blubber provided fuel for cooking lamps. The skins of caribou killed in the autumn had hollow, air-filled hair, providing good insulation for winter clothing, and the meat was a welcome change from seal. Bear meat, loaded in spring and summer with trichinosis, was dangerous to eat then, and to eat the liver, with its concentration of vitamin A, was lethal. In winter, bear steaks were good, and the skin useful for trousers and mittens.

NORBERT ROSING/BRUCE COLEMAN LTD

🜨 Even today, large numbers of polar bears congregate at Churchill, on Hudson Bay, to wait for the sea-ice to freeze, so that they can hunt seals again. Here, two young males spar with each other in establishing dominance. They are more a marine than a terrestrial animal, living most of the year on sea-ice and capable of swimming long distances in the open-water leads between ice fields.

⚓ In spring, when sea-ice and open-water hunting was difficult and caribou meat thin, the appearance of migrating geese and ducks was a welcome sight.
VARIN-VISAGE/JACANA-AUSCAPE

⚲ A baby harp seal, a white coat, lies on the sea-ice off Newfoundland. Later in the spring, the harp seal will migrate northwards along the Labrador coast, following the melting pack-ice to Greenland. Skins of white coats were particularly used for babies' clothing. Large adult skins were useful for parkas, trousers, and waterproof boots, and the thick layer of blubber was used as fuel for fires.

DR ECKART POTT/BRUCE COLEMAN LTD

JEFF FOOTT/AUSCAPE

ERWIN AND PEGGY BAUER/BRUCE COLEMAN LTD

🐂 Musk-ox meat tastes like good beef, but the thick, woolly hides of these animals were more useful for sleeping skins than for clothing. Horns could be carved, steamed, and bent for use as spoons.

⚓ Walrus meat and blubber were used, but the ivory tusks were especially valued for making weapons and tools. The 2.5 centimeter (1 inch) thick hide was split and used as covering for umiaks.

Indians moving north into Alaska during the period of global warming that occurred between about 2500 BC and 1600 BC may have put pressure on Arctic people. Moreover, 4,000 years ago, to the east, Hudson Bay and Hudson Strait were free of glacial ice. Their unoccupied shorelines, with few animal predators, may have been so rich in prey that they lured people onward.

The most likely explanation of this seemingly conflicting evidence is that some of the dates from both Denbigh and Greenland are inaccurate, but the fact that very few sites have been found between Alaska and Greenland suggests that these early people did indeed migrate eastwards within fewer than 500 years.

Greenland, the Earliest Eastern Settlement

The earliest evidence of the eastward spread of the Arctic Small Tool Tradition comes from a complex named Independence I, after a fiord in northeast Greenland. According to radiocarbon dates derived from local willow remains, the people of this complex moved into the unglaciated Arctic desert of Peary Land between 2050 BC and 1700 BC. The complex extended west and south through Ellesmere Island to Devon Island and south along Greenland's east coast to at least as far as Dove Bay.

Independence I was uniquely a High Arctic culture (north of 75 degrees North latitude), adapted to one of the Arctic's most inhospitable regions. Food resources were scarce, since the fiords were free of ice for only a few months during the summer, and hunting was curtailed by nearly three months of total darkness. Unlike most Arctic people, the people of Independence I did most of their hunting inland, except during the short summer, when they harvested a few ringed seal and arctic char from the coast and coastal rivers. Their main prey was musk oxen, along with hare, ptarmigan, and geese. Fuel, in this icy inland desert, was limited to occasional pieces of driftwood, tiny stems of willow, and the greasy bones of the musk ox.

Their stone tools were those of the Arctic Small Tool Tradition: burins, microblades, and a variety of endscrapers and sidescrapers for dressing skins and working hard materials. Their weapons included bipointed endblades for arrow tips, and sideblades for arrows or lances. Larger, bifacially flaked blades that are tapered and notched at the blunt end have also been found, and may have been lance tips or knives. Bone needles with tiny, drilled eyes are among the few artifacts recovered from Peary Land made of materials other than stone, and indicate that skins were sewn to make clothing.

An Independence I site at Port Refuge, on Devon Island, has yielded harpoon heads made of ivory and antler that differ significantly from most harpoon heads found in the eastern Arctic. One

By June, the sea-ice has broken into a few drifting pans, and kayak hunting by weaving around the ice chunks is again possible. Polar bears, whose natural domain is the solid sea-ice, are forced onto land, where their only source of food is the tiny lemming. They are particularly dangerous at this time.

MARK NEWMAN/AUSCAPE

The ptarmigan, here in winter plumage, remains in the Arctic throughout the winter. It is a useful survival food in these lean times.

Y. LANCEAU/JACANA-AUSCAPE

Meat of the arctic fox is strong in ammonia and barely edible. Fox fur was used for babies' clothing and to trim parkas.

⚱ A round, soapstone oil lamp from a Sarqaq site. A small core of soapstone would be placed in the middle to hold a moss cotton wick.

⚱ A typical Sarqaq non-toggling harpoon head. The pointed base would fit into a round socket, and the slotted tip would hold a stone blade.

end is tapered to fit into a hollow socket, and the position of the line holes does not allow the head to act as a toggle—that is, to open outwards after penetrating the prey. Instead, it held the prey with only two side barbs, making it less efficient for hunting sea mammals than the harpoon heads found from later cultures, such as Canada's Pre-Dorset culture. The latter fitted into a blade-like foreshaft and toggled beneath the skin, providing a secure hold for retrieving the prey.

Independence I summer sites are often marked only by stone fireboxes, indicating that shelters were little more than simple tents. The most distinctive shelters were probably the winter dwellings. As evidenced by the rocks still in place that were used to anchor tent edges, tents were elliptical and occupied an area of 3 meters by 4 meters (10 feet by 13 feet). A structure of parallel, vertical stone slabs was set in the center, divided into storage sections for food and a central firebox for heating—to be fueled by such scanty materials as were available. A family would spend the dark winter wrapped in musk-ox skins in the shelter of their smoky skin tent, sleeping as much as possible and limiting food and water to the bare minimum needed for survival in order to reduce the need to go outside the tent—much as Arctic travellers trapped in a storm still do.

The Sarqaq to the South

A period of increasing cold may have brought an end to northeast Greenland's Independence I culture about 1700 BC. To the south, along the relatively ice-free west coast from Upernavik to Julianehaab, archaeologists have found sites with artifacts similar to, yet significantly different from, the Arctic Small Tool Tradition. The stone tools and weapons of these people, known as the Sarqaq (or, in Greenland, the Saqqaq), are similar to those of both Denbigh and Independence I—

burins and burin spall tools (the latter made of chips of stone); arrow, lance, and harpoon tips; microblades and scrapers—but are smaller and more delicately flaked than those found in Independence I sites. Unlike Independence I artifacts, many of the burins and endblades are polished. The few Sarqaq harpoon heads that have been found are of the non-toggling type found in Independence I sites rather than the open-socketed type found in later Paleoeskimo sites. Small, round, soapstone oil lamps, not found in Independence I sites, are also common in Sarqaq sites.

Both the coastal seal-hunting sites and inland caribou camps of the Sarqaq appear to have been more densely populated than the Independence I sites, probably because of a readier supply of food and improved hunting technology. Nonetheless, summer hunting in the open waters was fraught with danger. Evidence from Sarqaq sites indicates that narrow, kayak-like boats were in use from early times. Throwing a harpoon from these inherently unstable craft was highly dangerous, and represented a feat of remarkable skill. Even up to recent times, drowning was the most common cause of death among men in the Arctic. An additional hazard faced by hunters waiting for seals on still water is a form of vertigo that commonly occurs when the sea and sky merge to form an expanse of light and no horizon is visible. In these conditions, the kayaker often senses, incorrectly, that the craft is tipping, and in trying to right it, overturns it.

The first Sarqaq sites discovered were dated at no later than 1900 BC, which led to the theory that Sarqaq people were descendants of an Independence I community driven south by increasing cold. More recent radiocarbon dating of local willow remains indicates that these sites go back to at least 2200 BC. This suggests that, while Independence I people were entering Greenland via a northern route over Ellesmere Island and Smith Sound, other people, whose artifacts more closely resembled those of the Canadian Pre-Dorset culture, might have entered from the south. This would have meant crossing the wide expanse of Baffin Bay, which consists of open water or drifting ice for much of the year, or the ice fields of Davis Strait.

Few organic materials remain from most Sarqaq sites. A notable exception is Qeqertasussuk, on Disco Bay, the earliest site known to date, where a surprising collection of organic artifacts was found. Near a fireplace formed of small stones lay a carved spoon of whalebone, the side-prong of a fish spear, and fragments of wooden bowls. Close by were the shoulder blade of a killer whale, fragments of a wooden bow, wooden arrows, fragments of a slender boat, and the bones of the earliest domestic dog yet found in the Arctic. More than 60,000 bones of birds and animals used for food were recovered, indicating that these early people had adapted to their harsh environment more successfully than might have been expected.

The Pre-Dorset People of Northern Canada

The third of the earliest Paleoeskimo cultures in the eastern Arctic region, called the Pre-Dorset, was restricted to northern Canada, extending from Ellesmere Island, along the coasts of several intervening islands, to the middle of Labrador, and west to Banks and Victoria Islands. Radiocarbon dates suggest that the Pre-Dorset culture goes back to at least 1800 BC and possibly even to 2000 BC. In a late stage of the culture, about 1000 BC—perhaps because of increasingly colder climates—it extended south into the Keewatin Barren Grounds and onto the edge of the boreal taiga. Pre-Dorset stone tools are similar to those of the Arctic Small Tool Tradition, with a variety of burins (some polished at the tip), drill bits, many microblades, several types of endscrapers and sidescrapers, and sideblades for inserting into antler lanceheads. A few polished slate knives and small soapstone lamps have been found in later sites dating to about 900 BC.

Artifacts made of organic materials—bone, antler, and ivory—seldom survive from the more southerly sites. In the colder, drier conditions north of the Arctic Circle, harpoon heads of antler and ivory, antler lances with sideblades, bow parts of antler and wood, bone arrowheads, fish spears, and needles with tiny, round, drilled eyes have been found. A few bones of domestic dogs have also been found, suggesting that dogs may have been used for hunting.

This stone Sarqaq knife inserted in a wooden handle wrapped with whale baleen was found in a Qeqertasussuk dwelling radiocarbon-dated to 2200 BC to 2300 BC.
NATIONAL MUSEUM OF DENMARK, DEPARTMENT OF ETHNOGRAPHY

A Pre-Dorset chert burin. The left-hand corner has a chisel-like edge for carving ivory and caribou antler.
MOREAU MAXWELL

By mid-June, most of the snow cover has melted from the land—a view of Baffin Island from near the coast.

NORMAN TOMALIN/BRUCE COLEMAN LTD

EARLY ARCTIC CULTURES

Moreau Maxwell

FROM THE EARLIEST periods to modern times, carved antler and ivory artifacts have been characteristic of Arctic cultures. Harpoon heads, foreshafts, needlecases, and combs carved at first with flint burins and later with burins of meteoric or European iron all had distinctive regional shapes and designs. Changes to individual features of harpoon heads through time provide us with the most reliable method of dating them relative to each other. Much Arctic carving was in the form of weapon decoration, but Dorset people in particular often carved three-dimensional human and animal figures that had magical and artistic significance.

IPIUTAK

Ipiutak ivory carvings, including elaborate open spirals, single-piece linked chains, and swivels, were probably made possible by tools of imported Siberian iron.

BIRNIRK

This prehistoric western pottery decorated by impressing the soft clay with curvilinear designs only rarely spread to eastern Thule sites.

IPIUTAK

Masks of ivory segments covered the faces of some Ipiutak dead.

PUNUK

Possibly representing a bowhead whale, this ivory carving may have been a fetish to sew on a whaler's clothing for luck.

OLD BERING SEA

With walrus in ready supply, most Old Bering Sea carvings were of ivory and elaborately engraved. This bear is one of the few naturalistic carvings.

DENBIGH

Denbigh flint weapons were more precisely flaked than most other blades of the Arctic Small Tool Tradition. With their careful rows of parallel flakes, they are almost art forms.

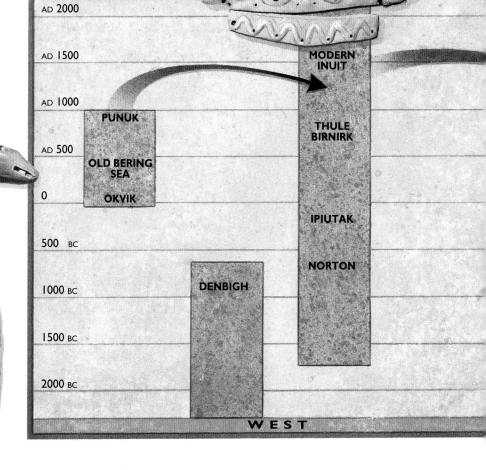

AD 2000

AD 1500

AD 1000

AD 500

0

500 BC

1000 BC

1500 BC

2000 BC

PUNUK

OLD BERING SEA

OKVIK

MODERN INUIT

THULE BIRNIRK

IPIUTAK

NORTON

DENBIGH

WEST

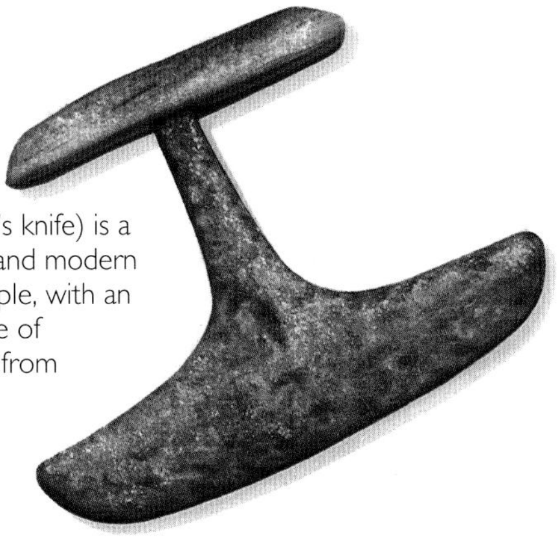

INUIT

This tanged ulu (woman's knife) is a shape typical of ancient and modern Inuit cultures. This example, with an antler handle, has a blade of hammered local copper from the Coppermine River.

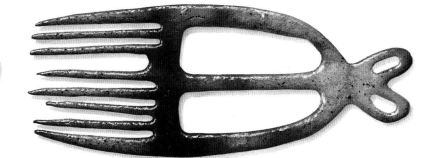

THULE

In spite of their apparent technical ability, Thule carvers made few artistic pieces. Elaborate openwork and engraved bone or ivory combs were among the few examples.

PRE-DORSET

Most of the recovered Pre-Dorset harpoon heads have open sockets into which a foreshaft fitted. They did not toggle within the prey's body.

THULE

Narrow-slitted snow goggles of bone, antler, or ivory, essential for sea-ice hunting in the bright glare of springtime, were used before sunglasses were introduced. Even gray, overcast days can produce the crippling pain of snowblindness.

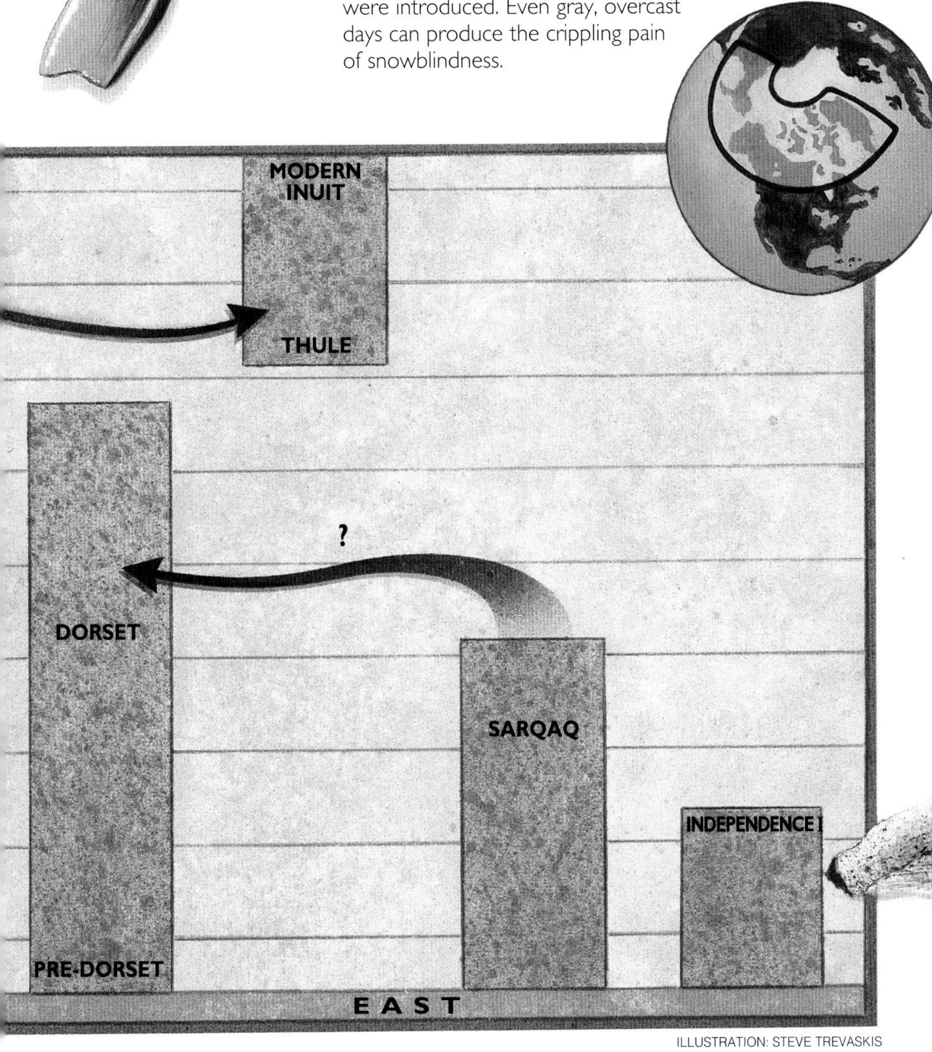

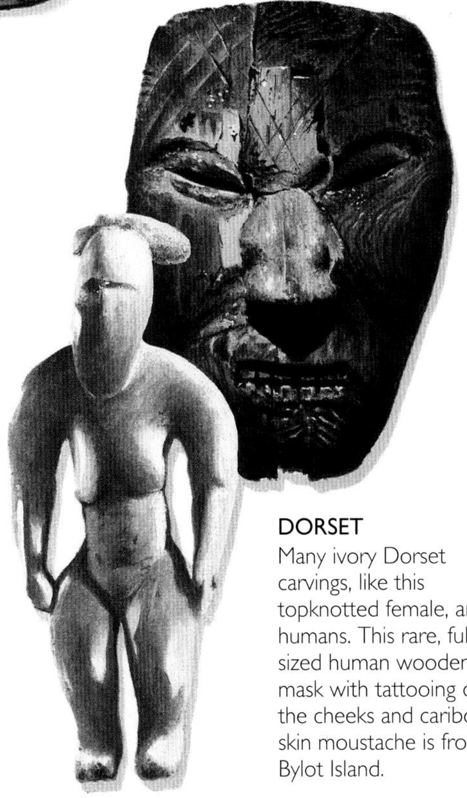

DORSET

Many ivory Dorset carvings, like this topknotted female, are of humans. This rare, full-sized human wooden mask with tattooing on the cheeks and caribou-skin moustache is from Bylot Island.

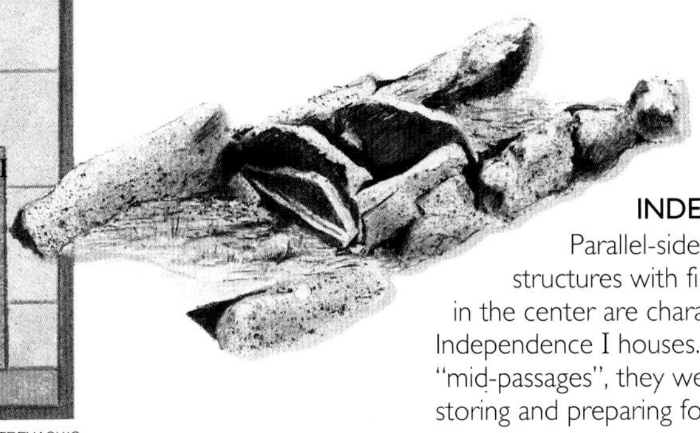

MODERN INUIT

THULE

DORSET

SARQAQ

INDEPENDENCE I

PRE-DORSET

EAST

INDEPENDENCE I

Parallel-sided stone structures with fireboxes in the center are characteristic of Independence I houses. Originally called "mid-passages", they were probably for storing and preparing food.

ILLUSTRATION: STEVE TREVASKIS

⚓ A typical Early Dorset ivory toggling harpoon head with a chert endblade. An internally carved basal socket (not visible) would have fitted over a blade-like foreshaft of caribou antler.
MOREAU MAXWELL

↪ An ivory fish spear from a Dorset site on northern Baffin Island. Such spears were used for arctic char, which swim upstream from the sea to spawn in the late spring.
MOREAU MAXWELL

⚲ Typical Middle Dorset harpoon heads of ivory and antler. The small ivory hunting fetish would probably have been hung on a hunter's clothing.
MOREAU MAXWELL

Remains of animals used for food indicate that these Pre-Dorset people hunted all of the available prey, with the probable exception of beluga and narwhal whales, which would have been too large for their hunting equipment. Faint traces of tent rings, often surrounding a flat rock on which seal fat was burned for heat, are generally the only remaining indications of shelter. On the Labrador coast, however, several sites have remains of houses with central structures built of parallel stone slabs resembling those found at Independence I sites.

Radiocarbon dating of Pre-Dorset sites is difficult. Dates of about 2000 BC, much the same as those from Independence I and Sarqaq sites, have been derived from the remains of sea mammals, but these do not give accurate ages, because the fossil sea water they appear to have ingested can result in dates several centuries older than they should be. More reliable dates derived from wood are no earlier than 1800 BC. Whether this means that the Canadian Pre-Dorset culture represents a later immigration from the west, or simply that we have not recovered adequate earlier materials for dating, is a problem yet to be solved.

From Sarqaq/Pre-Dorset to Dorset

The cultural transition from the Pre-Dorset to the Dorset periods—and, in Greenland, from Sarqaq to Dorset—presents an equally knotty dating problem. While some scholars see a smooth continuation of artifact types from one culture to the next, occurring somewhere between 900 BC and 500 BC, others see Dorset artifacts as being sufficiently different as to indicate a major cultural change. A group of sites discovered in the more southern areas of Labrador and Newfoundland complicates the problem. The stone artifacts found here are distinctly different from, yet still within, the Arctic Small Tool Tradition. Known as Groswater Dorset, this complex appears from radiocarbon dates to overlap both the late Pre-Dorset and early Dorset cultures.

Early Dorset sites are found on Baffin Island and in northern Labrador from the onset of permafrost, about 600 or 700 BC. Artifacts useful for hunting on sea-ice appear here at the same time. These include small sleds, sled shoes made of ivory, snow knives (for cutting blocks of snow to make igloos), and so-called ice creepers, consisting of pieces of antler fastened to boot soles for walking on sea-ice. The fact that these antler and ivory artifacts, as well as bone and wooden objects, have been found at these sites may, however, tell us nothing more than that organic materials are preserved in permafrost, whereas before the onset of permafrost they would have disintegrated. Because permafrost preserves even skin and feathers, we know much more about Dorset than about preceding cultures.

The Dorset culture—named after Cape Dorset, on Baffin Island—presents an interesting contrast to the Pre-Dorset. Dorset people occupied the same coasts as did those of Pre-Dorset times, but from Dorset times, the same style of harpoon head is found throughout this vast region. Whenever it changed, the new style appears simultaneously in sites throughout the region, providing us with our most reliable means of distinguishing between Early, Middle, and Late Dorset phases. Although the line holes in Dorset harpoon heads often appear to be round, they were not drilled, as in Pre-Dorset times, but scratched in with fine flint tips.

Dorset stone tools are generally typical of the Arctic Small Tool Tradition, with numerous microblades and scrapers. In several regions, however, early Dorset culture is marked by the appearance of various types of slate knives notched on the sides near the base, allowing them to be bound to wooden handles, and burin-like tools made of polished flint, chalcedony (a type of translucent quartz), and nephrite (a type of jade), which replaced the earlier spall burins. We do not know why, but bows and arrows, drills, and hunting dogs, all so widespread in Pre-Dorset times, completely disappeared in the Dorset period.

Dorset artifacts made of organic materials include a variety of ivory and antler harpoon heads for hunting seals and walruses, antler lanceheads for hunting caribou and polar bears, and handles made of bone, antler, wood, and ivory for knives, burin-like tools, and microblades.

Caribou skin was essential for winter clothing, but hunting caribou was both difficult and dangerous. These wary animals have excellent hearing, and to stalk them over the treeless landscape and get close enough to kill one with nothing but a handheld lance, as Dorset people did, required exceptional hunting skill. Women in the camp then had the long and arduous task of scraping and tanning the skins, cutting patterns with razor-sharp microblades, and sewing the material with stitches tiny enough to ensure water-tight seams.

NATIONAL MUSEUM OF DENMARK, DEPARTMENT OF ETHNOGRAPHY

On the coasts of Labrador and Newfoundland, Dorset houses were well-defined structures, often with the central passage of stone slabs found in Independence I and some Pre-Dorset houses. North of Hudson Strait, a few small, shallow pit houses have been found, some of them with a roof framework of driftwood, but most shelters were simply skin tents, of which the only surviving evidence is the boulders used to hold down the flaps. In Late Dorset times, "longhouses" were built of rectangular rows of boulders. These structures, which could be as much as 45 meters (148 feet) long, enclosed a number of individual family tents when local communities gathered in the spring. (See the feature *A Dorset Camp*.)

Dorset Art

The most fascinating aspect of Dorset culture is its art. Hundreds of miniature ivory, antler, and wood carvings have been recovered, particularly from later Dorset sites. These range from naturalistic to impressionistic and schematic images of local animals and birds. Humans and bears are the most common subjects, and are usually depicted with skeletal engravings—like X-ray paintings—on the surface. Often the belly or throat of both the human and bear carvings is slit and filled with red ocher, suggesting a form of sorcery against enemies. Occasionally, humans are represented by small wooden dolls with removable arms and legs. The only life-size carvings known are one complete and two fragmentary wooden masks from the Button Point site on Bylot Island.

Cultural Developments in the West

While the sequence from Independence I, through Sarqaq and Pre-Dorset, to Dorset was occurring in the eastern Arctic, similar cultural changes were taking place in Alaska and on islands to the west, in the Bering Sea. The Denbigh Complex changed little throughout most of its region until about 700 BC, except that stone artifacts from Late Denbigh times tend to be less delicately flaked than those of the "classic" Denbigh period. Coastal sites were used only during the summer, inland hunting and fishing still being the main means of subsistence.

To the north of Bering Strait, from Kotzebue to the Firth River, a new complex, known as Choris, appeared about 1600 BC. Its artifacts of chipped stone are generally continuations of Denbigh types, but larger. New types of projectile points, designed for the tips or sides of antler arrows and lances, have been found here, and a few types of stone tools are noticeably absent. Clay pottery, decorated with linear stamping, and stone labrets—ornaments worn in a slit in the lower lip—appear for the first time. Choris seems to represent a more flexible approach to life in the interior and on the coast, with a number of regional variants. Slate knives for separating seal blubber from meat are common finds in coastal sites, whereas large flint knives for butchering caribou are more common in the interior. In the settled communities on the coast, houses were large, measuring 12.5 meters by 7 meters (42 feet by 24 feet), whereas tents were used in the hunting camps in the interior.

⚱ Female figurines like this group of carved wooden Thule figures from a site at Angmagssalik, East Greenland, are typically found in Thule sites.

SISSE BRIMBERG

⚱ This crudely carved Dorset human figurine is from the Knud Peninsula, Ellesmere Island. The pierced chest was filled with red ocher.

⬆ Intricately carved segments of bone and ivory covered the skeletal faces of some Ipiutak burials. Eyes would have been ivory disks, with pupils of black jet.
A. ANIK AND J. BECKETT/COURTESY DEPARTMENT OF LIBRARY SERVICES, AMERICAN MUSEUM OF NATURAL HISTORY

↪ This Ipiutak ivory swivel would have been screwed into a socket of wood or antler. The elaborate Ipiutak ivory carvings were probably made possible by tools of imported Siberian iron.
RAINEY, 1940/COURTESY DEPARTMENT OF LIBRARY SERVICES, AMERICAN MUSEUM OF NATURAL HISTORY

Choris, as a cultural complex, disappeared about 700 BC. There then appears to have been a cultural hiatus. Both Choris to the north and Late Denbigh to the south were separated from Norton, the succeeding complex, by some 200 years.

Extending from the Alaska Peninsula to the Firth River, Norton existed at the same time that the shift from the Pre-Dorset to the Dorset culture was taking place in the east, but there is no evidence of contact between the Dorset and Norton peoples. Rather, Norton was an amalgam of characteristics from the south and west, with oil lamps and check-stamped pottery from Siberia (created by patting wet clay with wooden paddles carved with checkered or curvilinear designs) and stone vessels and ground slate tools from other cultures south of the Alaska Peninsula. Compared with the preceding cultures, Norton settlements were larger and more stable, and the people exploited the sea to a greater extent. Coastal pit houses were large, and 1 to 2 meters (3 to 6 feet) deep, with a central hearth and a tunnel entry extending 2 to 3.5 meters (6 to 11 feet). Many types of stone tools are continuations of Denbigh types, although they are larger and more often ground and polished. Drills, not found in Dorset, are common. Specially designed spears for birds and fish suggest that these were becoming more important sources of food.

Caribou Hunters of the North

In the late stages of the Norton culture, at about the beginning of the Christian era, a distinct and fascinating culture appeared to the north of Bering Strait. This was the Ipiutak, best known from a site at Point Hope. It owed some of its stone tool ancestry to Norton but, unlike Norton, lacked pottery, ground slate tools, oil lamps, and houses with tunnel entries. Surprisingly, in view of its location on the migratory route of the baleen whale, the Ipiutak site at Point Hope shows no evidence of whale hunting. Some seals and walruses were taken, but the evidence suggests that these people had not really adapted to a coastal way of life. Rather, the abundance of animal bones and caribou-hunting weapons found here indicates that they survived mainly on caribou. If a substantial number of the more than 600 small, square house pits at Point Hope were ever occupied simultaneously, the site would have been the largest prehistoric settlement in the Arctic.

One hundred and thirty-eight Ipiutak graves have been excavated, and they provide strong indications of status distinctions and the power of shamans in the culture. Many weapons, carvings, and tools were buried with the dead, more than 100 arrows sometimes being found in single graves. Some skulls were covered with elaborate bone masks, with ivory eyeballs, pupils of jet, ivory nose plugs in the shape of birds' heads, and ivory lip covers representing the sewing together of lips. Other graves contained collections of ivory chain-links, swivels, and pretzel-shaped objects, all apparently made for the purpose of demonstrating carving skill. Ivory carvings of animals and humans are elaborately engraved in what has been called a Scytho-Siberian style. Iron tools imported from Siberia—which gave Ipiutak artists much greater scope than stone carving tools—are found here for the first time in the Arctic. After AD 800, Ipiutak people deserted the coast and moved to smaller hunting camps around lakes in the interior.

In contrast, during the same period, the people who inhabited St Lawrence and Punuk Islands, in the Bering Sea, were successfully hunting large marine mammals—walruses and baleen whales—among the drifting ice floes. Two distinct styles of artifacts, known as Old Bering Sea and Okvik, also appeared towards the beginning of the Christian era in St Lawrence Island sites. Although Old Bering Sea and Okvik artifacts were first described by scholars in 1937, there is still dispute as to whether they represent new cultural complexes or are simply stylistic variants of a single culture.

The artifacts found, mainly harpoons, are richly engraved with complex designs. Harpoon heads, wings for harpoon shafts, harpoon sockets, and a number of other objects whose use has not been identified are decorated with geometric, curvilinear, and circular designs, which may have had some ideological significance. The Old Bering Sea style is more Asiatic in its orientation than Okvik. Graves excavated on the Chukchi Peninsula of Siberia contain materials identical to those found on St Lawrence Island. In a later cultural complex, known as Punuk—after the island in the Bering Strait where it was found—sea mammals were hunted even more intensively. As a result, settlements were bigger and more densely populated, some having as many as several hundred people.

Ancestors of the Present-Day Inuit

Between AD 500 and AD 800, a culture known as the Birnirk emerged. Best known from excavations near Point Barrow, it is clearly at least one of the ancestors of the modern Inuit (Eskimo) culture— if, indeed, we cannot trace their ancestry back to the Denbigh culture. Birnirk appears to represent a combination of Ipiutak traditions and hunting techniques derived from people of the Bering Sea, and it spread along the Alaskan coast and as far west as the Kolyma River. By AD 1000, the Birnirk and Punuk cultures had merged and developed into the fully Arctic-adapted Thule culture. Thule carried into the eastern Arctic the skin kayaks and umiaks, the dog sleds, and the techniques of hunting on sea-ice that today we associate with traditional Eskimos. One of the most important of these techniques was that of hunting ringed seal through the breathing holes they maintain in the sea-ice. This technique, probably developed about AD 1200, made it possible to take more game during the long winter months. The hunter had to keep a long, patient watch at the hole until the fluttering of a wisp of duck down he had placed over it indicated that a seal was breathing in the water below, whereupon he would make a swift thrust with his harpoon.

As the Thule whale hunters moved into the eastern Arctic between about AD 1000 and AD 1200, the preceding Dorset culture disappeared. Thule technology, with its more efficient hunting weapons, may have displaced the Dorset culture, but it has also been suggested that Dorset people may have died out a century or two before the Thule culture appeared.

Although there is still much to be learned about how early humans adapted to the Arctic, one conclusion is clear: surviving the dangers and difficulties of this extraordinarily harsh environment was undoubtedly one of humankind's most remarkable achievements.

An ivory hat ornament from the Old Bering Sea period, with jet eye inlays and lateral holes for hair and wooden plugs. Such ornaments, signs of superior hunting skill, were fastened to wooden peaked hats used to shield the eyes when kayak hunting.
SMITHSONIAN INSTITUTION/ COURTESY MUSEUM OF ANTHROPOLOGY AND ETHNOGRAPHY, ST PETERSBURG

These Punuk artifacts include an ivory rectangular wrist guard and an unidentified ivory object possibly related to hunting with a bow and arrow. The wrist guard would protect the bow hunter's wrist from the slap of the bowstring. Bows and arrows and other implements of war proliferated as growing Punuk populations led to social tensions.
SMITHSONIAN INSTITUTION /COURTESY MUSEUM OF ANTHROPOLOGY AND ETHNOGRAPHY, ST PETERSBURG

A rectangular wall
5 meters (16 feet) wide and
45 meters (148 feet) long enclosed
approximately 18 individual family
tents used for sleeping and eating.
Across a narrow bay, a row of hearths
and food-storage platforms provided
cooking areas for each family.

A DORSET CAMP

Moreau Maxwell

Tʜɪs 1,200-ʏᴇᴀʀ-ᴏʟᴅ Dᴏʀsᴇᴛ ᴄᴀᴍᴘ on the Knud Peninsula, just south of the Bache Peninsula, on Ellesmere Island's east coast, is unique, although others like it may exist in the Dorset realm. Here, Dr Peter Schledermann and assistants excavated a late spring gathering site for Dorset people coming together after a winter spent isolated in hunting camps on the sea-ice. The location was ideal. It is near a polynya, an open-water pond in the sea-ice, which acted as a magnet in the spring for air-breathing sea mammals. On one occasion, the excavators counted 300 walrus congregated in the open-water polynya.

The surplus of food animals available at this time enabled the whole band of some 100 people to assemble for social and religious purposes. Here, mates could be chosen, marriages performed, and kinship obligations strengthened. Many of the beautiful Dorset ivory carvings appear to have magical–religious significance, and this gathering was undoubtedly a time for some religious ceremony—possibly in celebration of the coming short, warm period of summer.

Here, on a flat beach, the people have built a rectangular enclosure of waist-high rocks. Inside this enclosure, 5 meters (16 feet) wide and 45 meters (148 feet) long, the distribution of recovered artifacts and animal bones suggests that each family had its own skin tent for sleeping and eating. All of the cooking was done across a narrow bay on a row of individual hearths 32 meters (105 feet) long. Adjacent to each low hearth was a rock platform for storing food (such as seal carcasses). On shore, several men are shown struggling to drag ashore a walrus, which may have weighed a tonne or more (about a ton).

At this time of the year, the arrival of migratory birds—ducks and geese—would have increased the food supply. Some caribou might have been taken in the hills inland, but in spring the animals are thin and their hides of little use for clothing. The band might have stayed together, if food were available, through the summer until the collective caribou drives in the autumn. At that time, the hides would be thick and ideal for clothing. There is some evidence that Dorset people—as did the later Thule people and the still later modern Inuit—drove the caribou through V-shaped fences of rock piles shaped like men. Standing behind each rock pile, a man armed with a lance would have killed the animals as each ran through.

☞ Radiocarbon dating of wood excavated from cooking hearths by Dr Karen McCullogh suggests a date of ᴀᴅ 800 to ᴀᴅ 900.

⚲ Dr Peter Schledermann and assistants excavate the area within the enclosure. Recovered artifacts and animal bones suggest that the site was occupied by people of the Late Dorset culture in the late spring and early summer.

ILLUSTRATION: JOHN RICHARDS

MARTHA COOPER/NATIONAL GEOGRAPHIC SOCIETY

MARTHA COOPER/NATIONAL GEOGRAPHIC SOCIETY

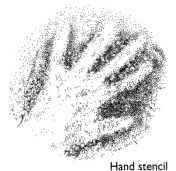
Hand stencil

GLOSSARY

abri
French word meaning "shelter", used to refer to the Paleolithic natural rock shelter sites characteristic of the limestone region of southern France.

absolute dating
Dating that can be expressed in calendar year ages on the basis of measurable physical and chemical constants or historical associations such as coins and written records. See also *relative dating*.

Acheulean
An industry of the Lower Paleolithic period, linked to the erectines, the first to use regular bifacial flaking, producing hand axes along with flakes and other cores. The culture is named after the site of St Acheul, in northern France.

adze
A heavy, wide-bladed cutting tool which is attached at right angles to a wooden handle. It was used for trimming and smoothing timber and for such tasks as hollowing out a dug-out canoe.

Arctic Small Tool Tradition
A distinctive set of stone tools and weapon tips from the early Arctic Denbigh culture, recovered from sites along the Alaskan coast and eastwards to Greenland. All but the adzes are of small size—hence the name.

arroyo
A steep-sided dry gully. Such geomorphic features were used by Paleoindians as natural traps to capture mammoths and bison.

atlatl
A New World version of a spear-thrower or throwing stick. A hook at the distal end fits into a depression at the proximal end of the spear, in effect extending the throwing arm.

Aurignacian
The earliest Upper Paleolithic technological phase in western Europe. It occurred between 38,000 and 22,000 years ago, and is characterized by the use of bone tools and a blade flint technology, with scrapers and burins. Aurignacian peoples produced the earliest art. Industries of Aurignacian type are found across Europe and western Asia, and sites are often in deep, sheltered valleys. The culture is named after the site of Aurignac, in southern France.

australopithecine
An evolutionary stage of extinct hominid (including *Australopithecus* itself) with a small cranial capacity, huge, protruding jaws, and upright gait that existed in Africa between four and one million years ago. The word *Australopithecus* means "southern ape", and these hominids were so named because their fossils were found first in southern Africa.

Azilian
The final Upper Paleolithic culture in southwestern France and northern Spain, from about 9000 BC to 8000 BC, characterized by flat harpoons, carved spear-throwers made from deer antlers, and stone pebbles painted with red dots. The culture takes its name from the massive cave of Le Mas d'Azil, in the French Pyrenees.

Beringia
The part of the continental shelf that connects Northeast Asia with present-day Alaska. When exposed at the time of the last glacial maximum, 18,000 years ago, it was a large, flat, vegetated landmass.

bifacial
A term used to describe a stone tool shaped on both faces. The technique is typical of the hand-axe tradition of the Lower Paleolithic period.

bipedal
Walking upright on two legs. For early humans, it had the advantage of leaving the hands free.

blade
A long, narrow flake struck from a stone core (often flint) selected for its flaking properties. The blade was either used as a tool in itself or became the blank from which other tools were manufactured. In Europe, blades and blade tools appear at the start of the Upper Paleolithic period, and are first associated with the Aurignacian culture and the arrival of modern humans.

BP
An abbreviation of "Before Present", BP is used in radiocarbon dating to mean "before AD 1950", the standard radiocarbon-dating reference year.

burin
A short, pointed blade tool with a chisel end, used to carve and engrave wood and bone (particularly antlers, which were made into spearheads and harpoon tips). The most common form has a sharp tip, formed by the intersection of two flake scars. The burin is associated with Upper Paleolithic cultures, especially the Magdalenian.

burin spall tool
Small cutting tools made from chips or splinters of stone driven or pressed from the edges of burins.

C14
The radioisotope carbon-14. Its known rate of decay is the basis of radiocarbon dating.

candelabra model
One of the theories of human development, also known as the regional continuity theory. Modern humans are seen as descending from *Homo erectus* in Africa, Europe, and Asia. The opposing theory, known as the Noah's Ark model, holds that modern humans originated in one single area of Africa.

channel flake
A long, thin blade of stone removed by percussion or pressure from the center line of either face of a projectile point. The smooth depression it leaves behind is known as a flute or channel.

Chatelperronian
A cultural phase of the Upper Paleolithic period, between 36,000 and 32,000 years ago, characterized by bone tools and weapons (made of ivory or reindeer antler) and flint knives. The culture is named after the site of Châtelperron, in France.

Cordilleran ice sheet
The ice mass that covered the coastal mountains along the Pacific Ocean coast of North America from northern Washington state into southern Alaska. At its maximum extent, about 20,000 years ago, it connected with the Laurentide ice sheet to the east and with the Pacific Ocean to the west, and reached a thickness of some 3 kilometers (1 mile).

core
A lump of rock used in the manufacture of stone tools. Blades and flakes are struck from the core by hitting it accurately with a pebble or bone. The core may also be fashioned into an implement, such as a chopper or scraper.

Cro-Magnon
The earliest known modern humans in Europe, who were characterized by a long head, a tall, erect stature, and the use of blade technology and bone tools. They were associated with the Aurignacian culture, which produced the earliest European art. The name comes from a rock shelter in southwestern France where, in 1868, *Homo sapiens* remains were first found in association with Upper Paleolithic tools.

cultural complex
An assemblage of artifacts and other physical evidence that regularly occur together within a restricted area, and are thought to represent the material remains of a particular group of people, perhaps over several generations.

cultural layer
Deposition of materials from settlements or other prehistoric areas of activity that accumulate over a relatively continuous time. Several such layers create a stratigraphic and chronological sequence.

dendrochronology
The construction of chronologies from tree-ring sequences. The annual tree-rings on timber recovered from a site are compared with an established sequence of ring patterns that extends back to about 9000 BP.

diprotodon
A large Australian herbivorous marsupial, now extinct, of the group that includes kangaroos, koalas, and wombats. It was characterized by two prominent incisors on the lower jaw.

DNA
The basic material of chromosomes, which includes the genes. Analysis of the DNA of different primate groups has been used to determine the evolutionary line of modern humans, and DNA techniques have also been used to show for how long the various regional human populations have been separated from each other. DNA analysis of blood residue, both human and animal, on prehistoric tools and weapons may one day provide fresh information on the evolutionary relationships between a range of animal species, and between prehistoric and modern humans.

endocast
An internal cast, as of the inside of the human skull.

endblade
A small blade tool. Bipointed endblades were used to tip bone and antler arrowheads; triangular endblades were probably used to tip harpoon heads.

endscraper
A blade tool with a steeply angled working edge on the end of the blade, used to work hard materials and to dress skins. It appeared in Europe during the Upper Paleolithic period.

Eocene
The geological epoch from 55 million to 38 million years ago. It occurred

within the Tertiary period, following the Paleocene and preceding the Oligocene. During this epoch, mammals consolidated their status as the dominant land vertebrates.

erectine
A now-extinct member of the genus *Homo*, including *Homo erectus*, who lived in Africa, Asia, and Europe during the Lower and Middle Pleistocene. Erectines walked upright, may have used fire, and are often associated with the Acheulean industries, especially with hand axes.

estrus cycle
The regular reproductive cycle of female mammals, marked by a series of physiological changes in the sexual and other organs that signal a period of availability for mating.

ethnography
The collecting and study of basic research material, such as artifacts, for analysis of social and cultural structures and processes.

"Eve" theory
The hypothesis that all modern humans are descended from a common first mother who lived in southern Africa about 200,000 years ago. The "Eve" theory is similar to the Noah's Ark model, and is based on genetic research showing that as modern humans spread throughout the world, they rarely, if at all, interbred with existing, but more archaic, humans, such as the Neanderthals. The "Eve" theory does not imply a creationist view, only that there has been a chance survival of a single line of mitochondrial DNA.

flake tool
A tool made from a thin, sharp-edged fragment of stone struck off a larger stone (the core).

flintknapping
The technique of striking flakes or blades from a larger stone (the core) and the shaping of cores and flakes into stone implements. The most commonly used stone was flint (also called chert), a hard, brittle stone, commonly found as pebbles in limestone areas, that breaks with a conchoidal fracture rather than along predetermined cleavage planes. Obsidian, basalt, and quartz were also fashioned into tools. Flintknapping began with the simple striking of one stone against another. Later methods include the use of antler and wooden strikers for both direct and indirect percussion, and bone and antler pressure-flaking tools.

flute
The smooth longitudinal groove left on a projectile point after the removal of a channel flake.

fluted projectile point
A stone projectile point associated with the Clovis and Folsom cultures of North America. Flutes were formed by removing flakes from the base towards the point by percussion or pressure. The sharp ridges of the flutes were ground smooth near the base of the point, to prevent them from cutting the bindings when the point was inserted into a notched foreshaft.

foramen magnum
The hole at the base of the skull where the spinal cord enters. Its position is an indication of posture. If the foramen magnum is far forward on the skull base, it indicates an upright posture, like that of humans, with the head balanced on top of the spine.

genome
The complete set of genetic material—the chromosomes and the genes they contain—that makes up any cell and determines hereditary features.

glacial maximum
The peak of an Ice Age, when the ice sheets are at their greatest extent and temperatures at their lowest. The last glacial maximum occurred between 22,000 and 18,000 years ago.

graver
A stone tool used for engraving stone, bone, and wood, also referred to as a burin.

Gravettian
A cultural tradition of the Upper Paleolithic period, between 29,000 and 22,000 years ago, which follows the Aurignacian and is characterized by the appearance of Venus figurines, small pointed blades, burins, and bone spearpoints. Gravettian-type industries are found from France and Spain, across central Europe, to southern Russia. The culture is named after the site of La Gravette, in southern France.

grinding stone
A stone used to grind to powder foodstuffs (such as grains), medicines, and pigments for decorating rock walls and bodies.

habiline
An early member of the genus *Homo*, including *Homo habilis*, known from fossils in Africa dating from 2.4 million to about 1.5 million years ago. Habilines made simple stone tools and are the precursors of *Homo erectus* and the erectines.

hand axe
A type of stone tool that is typical of the Acheulian tradition and linked mainly to the erectines of Africa, Europe, India, and Southwest Asia. Hand axes consist of a nodule that has been bifacially worked. They vary in size and shape, but usually one end is pointed. The hand axe probably had a wide range of uses, such as cutting, digging, and scraping.

hand stencil
The impression of a hand produced by spraying thick paint (made from white clay or red or yellow ocher) through a blowpipe around the edges of a hand placed against a rock surface.

haft
The handle part of an implement such as an axe, knife, or adze.

harpoon
A spear-like missile with backward-pointing barbs, loosely hafted, and attached to a line. When hurled at marine mammals, such as seals, the point, if it finds its mark, is separated from the shaft, and the barbs prevent it from being dislodged. The line is used to retrieve the catch. The appearance of the harpoon is associated in particular with the Magdalenian culture, which is known for finely carved single-barbed and double-barbed harpoon heads made of antler or bone.

Holocene
The present geological epoch, which began some 10,000 years ago. It falls within the Quaternary period and followed the Pleistocene. The Holocene is marked by rising temperatures through-out the world and the retreat of the ice sheets. During this epoch, agriculture became the common human subsistence practice.

hominid
A member of the Hominidae, the family that includes both extinct and modern forms of humans and, in most modern classifications, the Great Apes.

hominoid
A member of the primate family that includes both humans and the apes, and their extinct evolutionary precursors.

ibex
A wild goat with large, recurved horns, common in European and central and West Asian mountain systems. They were often depicted by Upper Paleolithic artists.

interglacial
A period of warmer temperatures and diminished ice sheets occurring between periods of glaciation. The last 10,000 years (the Holocene) is probably an interglacial, since its temperatures and the distribution of vegetation are similar to those of earlier interglacials.

isothermic line
A line on a map linking places of equal temperature at a given time or period.

labret
A decorative plug of shell, bone, ivory, metal, or pottery inserted through a hole in the lip.

lancehead
A large, flat missile point of stone, bone, or ivory. The lancehead was mounted on a long shaft to form a lightweight lance or javelin-like weapon for war or hunting. A lancehead is larger than an arrowhead, but smaller than a spearhead.

Laurentide ice sheet
The ice mass that covered most of Canada and parts of the United States, including the Great Lakes area and northern New England. At its maximum extent, about 20,000 years ago, it was connected with the Cordilleran ice sheet to the west.

Levalloisian flake technique
A technique that produced flakes of a predetermined form by means of trimming the core to a certain shape before the flakes were struck off. The core was then discarded. A Levalloisian flake shows scars of the preparatory work on one side and is flat on the other. The technique is associated with the Middle Paleolithic period in Europe.

Lower Paleolithic
The first part of the Paleolithic, beginning about two million years ago. The era of the earliest forms of humans and of tool-making.

macropod
A grazing Australian marsupial with short forelimbs, long hind limbs adapted for hopping, and a long, muscular tail, such as the kangaroo, the wallaby, and the tree kangaroo.

Magdalenian
The last major culture of the Upper Paleolithic period in Europe. It was adapted to the cold conditions of the last Ice Age and based on the specialized hunting of deer. Characteristic artifacts are barbed harpoons and carved spear-throwers of reindeer bone and antler decorated with naturalistic carvings of game animals. It is also the period when cave art reached its peak. The culture lasted from 18,000 to 12,000 years ago and is named after the rock shelter of La Madeleine, in southwestern France.

Harpoon

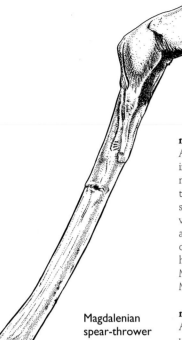

Magdalenian
spear-thrower

mastodon
Any of various now-extinct species of large, elephant-like mammals. The American mastodon (*Mammut americanum*), an extinct form of the family Mammutidae, is classified as a browser from its low-crowned teeth, as opposed to the woolly mammoth (*Mammuthus primigenius*), of the family Elephantidae, which, because of its high-crowned teeth, is classified as a grazer.

megafauna
The large, now-extinct animals of the Late Pleistocene period—including mammoths; mastodon; giant bison, sloths, and camels; and diprotodons. The term also covers extinct larger species of quite small animals.

Mesolithic
Literally, the "Middle Stone Age". A transitional period between the Paleolithic and the Neolithic, marked by the retreat of the Pleistocene glaciers and the appearance of modern forms of plants and animals. Its peoples were hunter-gatherers whose flint industries were characterized by microliths. The term Mesolithic is limited to Europe.

microblade
A very small, narrow bladelet, less than 10 millimeters (half an inch) wide, shaped by pressure-flaking a prepared core. Microblades were often retouched into various forms of microliths.

microlith
A very small arrowhead, barb, or other implement, most commonly of flint, made by removing a triangular, trapezoidal, or parallelogram-shaped section from a microblade. Microliths were mounted in wooden or bone shafts as arrow tips, or along one or both sides of a shaft to form a barbed spear or harpoon, or set in rows on sickles. Microliths were characteristic of the Mesolithic period in the Old World.

midden
An extensive deposit of settlement refuse, which may include the remains of shells, bones, ashes, and discarded implements. Middens are commonly built up over many years and mark the site of previous human habitation.

Middle Paleolithic
The middle part of the Paleolithic, starting some 150,000 years ago and ending with the extinction of the Neanderthals, about 33,000 years ago. It was the era of the Neanderthal peoples and flake tools. The Middle Paleolithic is equivalent to the Middle Stone Age in sub-Saharan Africa.

Miocene
The geological epoch between 7 million and 2.6 million years ago. It occurred within the Tertiary period, following the Oligocene and preceding the Pliocene. During this epoch, many mammals of modern form, such as dogs, horses, and human-like apes, evolved.

molecular clock
A method of tracing evolutionary lines based on the changes in the protein structure and DNA of living organisms that take place over long periods of time. By establishing the degree of difference between the proteins of two species, it is possible to calculate how long ago they shared a common ancestor.

Mousterian
A culture of the Middle Paleolithic period that appeared throughout Europe from the last interglacial through to about 33,000 years ago. It is characterized by the appearance of flint scrapers and points and is associated with the Neanderthals. Mousterian peoples lived in cave mouths and rock shelters. The culture is named after Le Moustier, a rock shelter in southwestern France.

Neanderthals
An extinct form of humans that appeared during the Upper Pleistocene era, some 100,000 years ago, and is known to have existed throughout unglaciated Europe and as far east as Uzbekistan. Neanderthals had prominent brow ridges, a receding forehead, and a brain of similar size to that of modern humans. They made flake tools in the form of scrapers and points. In Europe, they are associated with the Mousterian culture. The Neanderthals persisted into the Upper Paleolithic period, some 33,000 years ago. The name comes from the Neander Valley, near Düsseldorf, Germany, where skeletal remains of this type of human were first found in 1856.

neutron activation analysis
A method of determining the origin of flint artifacts by matching the trace element concentrations with those of flint from various known sources.

Noah's Ark model
The theory that modern humans originated in one single area of Africa and spread throughout the world, replacing other, more archaic, human types. It is also known as the replacement hypothesis. This view is supported by the so-called "Eve" theory, which postulates that all modern humans are descended from a common mother. The opposing hypothesis is often called the candelabra model.

obsidian
A black, glassy volcanic rock often used to make sharp-edged tools.

Oldowan
A term used to refer to the oldest known Paleolithic artifacts of South and East Africa, consisting of simple chipped pebble tools. The word comes from Olduvai Gorge, an important Paleolithic site in Tanzania, where fossil remains of early humans were found in association with such artifacts.

Oligocene
The geological epoch between 38 million and 28 million years ago. It occurred within the Tertiary period, following the Eocene and preceding the Miocene. During this epoch, many of the older types of mammals became extinct and the first apes appeared.

paleoanthropology
The study of prehistoric humans as revealed by fossil remains.

paleobotany
The study of ancient plants from fossil remains and other evidence, such as vegetable materials, preserved by charring, desiccation, or in water-logged deposits. Paleobotany provides information about the climate and environment and about materials available for food, fuel, tools, and shelter.

Paleocene
The geological epoch from some 65 million to 55 million years ago. It occurred within the Tertiary period and preceded the Eocene. During this epoch, there was great development of primitive mammals. The earliest known primates date from the Paleocene.

paleoclimatology
The study of past climates, using information such as vegetation and sedimentary records, geomorphology, and animal distribution.

Paleoeskimo
The earliest prehistoric Eskimo people, before the beginning of whale hunting. Later whale-hunting people are called Neoeskimo.

Paleoindians
The big-game hunters of the Americas from the earliest known, about 12,000 years ago, to about 8,000 years ago. Some investigators regard the term as referring to all hunting groups involved with now-extinct mammals, in which case the peoples who hunted the species of bison that became extinct about 6,500 years ago would also be classified as Paleoindians.

Paleolithic
Literally, the "Old Stone Age". It began some two million to three million years ago with the emergence of humans and the earliest forms of chipped stone tools, and continued through the Pleistocene Ice Age until the retreat of the glaciers some 12,000 years ago. The Paleolithic is equivalent to the Stone Age in sub-Saharan Africa.

paleontology
The study of life forms present in previous geological periods as represented by plant and animal fossils.

palynology
The analysis of ancient pollen grains and the spores of mosses and lichens to reveal evidence of past environments.

Panaramitee style
Rock engravings featuring circles and tridents (possibly kangaroo and emu tracks) found in many parts of Australia. Many probably date to Pleistocene times.

percussion flaking
The reduction of a stone core by hitting it with a hammer of stone or bone.

permafrost line
A line demarcating regions where the subsoil is permanently frozen. It is related to the tree line, because the frozen ground prevents tree roots from penetrating deeply and inhibits the subsurface drainage of meltwater.

petroglyph
A picture or symbol engraved, pecked, or incised into a rock.

pit house
A dwelling with the floor dug down below ground level to make it easier to weatherproof against wind. Often all that remains on an archaeological site is a large, shallow pit.

platform burial
The practice of placing a corpse on an artifical, above-ground structure; the body was sometimes retrieved at a later date for interment.

Pleistocene
The first epoch of the geological period known as the Quaternary, preceding the Holocene (or present) epoch and beginning some two million years ago. It was marked by the advance of ice sheets across northern Europe and North America. During this epoch, giant mammals existed, and in the Late Pleistocene, modern humans appeared.

Pliocene
The geological epoch from some seven million to two million years ago. It occurred within the Tertiary period, following the Miocene and preceding the Pleistocene. During this epoch, modern mammals became dominant and ape-like humans appeared in Africa.

pressure flaking
The technique of removing flakes by means of pressure applied to a specific spot with the point of a tool made of stone or bone.

projectile point
A weapon tip made of flint, antler, or bone.

polygyny
The mating of a male with more than one female.

protein sequencing
Analysis of the sequence of the amino acids that make up a protein. Comparison of the sequences in different species is one way of working out their degrees of interrelationship.

protoworld language
A single, original language, hypothesized to have been spoken by the first modern humans in Africa, from which all modern languages may descend. It has been suggested that linguistic traces of this language have survived into the present.

Quaternary
The most recent geological period, subdivided into the Pleistocene and the Holocene, beginning some two million years ago.

relative dating
A dating sequence that establishes which sample is older or younger than the other by means of its position in a stratified section of an excavation, or by placing it in an age sequence relative to other samples, none (or only some) of which have been dated by absolute dating methods. Relative dating does not give exact dates in calendar years.

sagittal crest
The crest along the top of the skull where the chewing muscles are attached, found only in very large-jawed species, such as male gorillas and orang-utans, and the australopithecine genus *Paranthropus*.

scraper
A core, flake, or blade with a steeply retouched edge either at the side (side-scraper) or end (endscraper). Scrapers were used to dress hides and to shape wood, bone, and ivory artifacts.

sexual dimorphism
The differences in shape, size, or color between males and females that occur generally in any population. Males are usually larger than females, but the reverse is sometimes the case.

shaman
A person believed to have supernatural powers. In times of sickness, shortage of game, or any other threat to a community's survival, the shaman is called upon to mediate with the spirit world on the community's behalf. The shaman presides over rituals, and may also be responsible for the keeping of laws and the continuity of traditions. Shamanism is the dominant element in the religion of most known arctic and subarctic hunter-gatherers. Most shamans are male.

sideblade
A narrow flake with a sharp edge on one side, often inserted into bone arrowheads and spearheads to increase loss of blood and thus bring prey to ground faster.

sidescraper
A flake tool having a steep, retouched edge on one side of the flake, used for working hard materials and dressing skins.

Solutrean
A culture of the Upper Paleolithic period which precedes the Magdalenian in western Europe and flourished from some 22,000 to 18,000 years ago. It is characterized by the use of pressure flaking to make large, thin, leaf-shaped bifacial points, in particular the laurel leaf point, for use as lanceheads. Some, however, are so finely tapered and delicate that it seems likely that they were made for ornamental purposes rather than for use in hunting or warfare. Bone needles with eyes appeared in this period. The culture is named after the site of Solutré, in southeastern France.

spear-thrower
A stick with a notch at one end into which the butt of a spear is fitted, thus giving increased leverage in throwing and making it possible to bring down animals from a distance. Spear-throwers made of reindeer antler are characteristic of the Magdalenian period in Europe. Similar weapons were used in the New World, where they are known as atlatls; in the Arctic; and in Australia, where they are often called woomeras.

Stone Age
The earliest period of technology in human culture, when tools and weapons were made of stone, bone, and wood. The Stone Age comprises the Paleolithic, the Mesolithic, and the Neolithic (literally, the Old, Middle, and New Stone Age). In sub-Saharan Africa, the Stone Age is equivalent to the Paleolithic.

stratigraphy
A term borrowed from geology to describe the layers of human artifacts and other remains in successive levels of occupation as revealed in a vertical section of an archaeological excavation. By following the principle that a deposit overlying another must have accumulated at a later time, it is possible to establish a relative chronological sequence of levels, providing there has been no subsequent disturbance.

tang
A long, slender projecting strip or prong of a tool, often fitted into a handle or shaft.

taphonomy
The study of the natural processes that act on the remains of a plant, animal, or human between its death and the incorporation of its remains into an archaeological or paleontological deposit.

Tertiary
The geological period preceding the Quaternary and comprising the Paleocene, Eocene, Oligocene, Miocene, and Pliocene epochs. It began about 65 million years ago and ended about 2 million years ago.

totem
An object from the natural world, usually an animal, with which a particular clan or tribe considers itself to have a special, often a blood, relationship.

tree line
A line marking the point in the Arctic north of which no trees grow, because the subsoil is permanently frozen. See also *permafrost line*.

umiak
A large, open boat used by Arctic peoples, made of skins stretched on a wooden frame.

Upper Paleolithic
The last part of the Paleolithic, starting some 40,000 years ago, during which modern humans replaced the Neanderthals. It is characterized by blade technology, human burials, and art.

Venus figurines
Small carved or sculptured figurines of naked women, usually with exaggerated features, such as a large abdomen, swelling breasts and buttocks, and marked genitals. These figurines appeared in the Gravettian phase about 29,000 years ago, and were made from a variety of materials, including antler, bone, stone, and clay. Figurines with a standardized appearance have been found across a distance of more than 2,000 kilometers (1,200 miles), from the Atlantic coast in the west to Russia in the east.

Wallacea
The area of island-studded sea that has separated Australia from Southeast Asia for all of the last 70 million years. It marks the division between two major faunal groups: oriental animals (such as elephants, tigers, and apes) and the animals of Australia (such as kangaroos, wombats, and the monotremes). It is named after the British naturalist A.R. Wallace, who first recognized its significance.

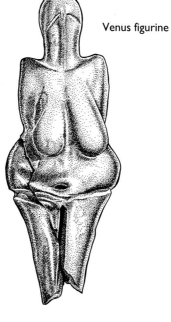
Venus figurine

Björn E. Berglund

Björn E. Berglund has been Professor of Quaternary Geology at Lund University, Sweden, since 1971. His main research area is Late Pleistocene and Holocene paleoecology, particularly the impact of humans on the environment. He has been a member of the Swedish Academy of Sciences since 1989. From 1976 to 1987, he led a UNESCO geological correlation project on past environmental changes, and from 1982 to 1990, he led a Swedish project on long-term changes in the human landscape. His books include *Handbook of Holocene Paleoecology and Paleohydrology* and *The Cultural Landscape during 6000 Years in Southern Sweden*.

Svante Björck

Svante Björck is Associate Professor of Quaternary Geology at Lund University, Sweden, working mainly in the area of environmental and sea level changes during the Late Cenozoic. As Visiting Scientist at the University of Minnesota, he worked on the deglaciation, paleoclimate, and revegetation of the midwest of North America from 13,000 to 8,000 years ago, and most recently, he has conducted paleoclimatic research in the polar regions.

Göran Burenhult

Göran Burenhult has been Associate Professor of Archaeology at the University of Stockholm, Sweden, since 1981 and is acknowledged internationally as a leading expert on prehistoric rock art and megalithic traditions. Between 1976 and 1981, he was director of the Swedish archaeological excavations at Carrowmore, County Sligo, Ireland, excavating one of the earliest known megalithic cemeteries, and he has undertaken field work on prehistoric rock art throughout the world, including the rock painting areas of the central Sahara Desert. Most recently, he has conducted ethnoarchaeological expeditions to the islands of Sulawesi and Sumba, in Indonesia, to the Trobriand Islands of Papua New Guinea, and to the island of Malekula, in Vanuatu, to study megalithic traditions, social organization, and primitive exchange. He is the author of numerous scholarly and popular books on archaeology and ethnoarchaeology, and has contributed to journals, magazines, and encyclopedic works. Between 1987 and 1991, he produced a series of international television programs about aspects of archaeology.

Jean Clottes

Jean Clottes is Conservateur Général du Patrimoine at the French Ministry of Culture and Chairman of the International Committee for Rock Art. For 21 years he was Director of Prehistoric Antiquities for the Midi-Pyrénées region, and he has excavated several Upper Paleolithic caves in France. He currently chairs the Société Préhistorique Ariège-Pyrénées and the Association pour le Rayonnement de l'Art Pariétal Européen.

Richard Cosgrove

Richard Cosgrove is a research archaeologist and Lecturer in the Department of Archaeology at La Trobe University, Melbourne, Australia. His main area of interest is Pleistocene human settlement and subsistence behavior in southern Tasmania. He has worked in this field for more than ten years, six of them as a research and consultant archaeologist for the Tasmanian Department of Parks, Wildlife and Heritage. He was involved in the surveying and excavation of Late Pleistocene sites in the Franklin, Maxwell, and Gordon river systems, now within a World Heritage Area.

Jean Courtin

Jean Courtin is Directeur de Recherches at the Centre National de la Recherche Scientifique, France. For a number of years, he was Director of the Département des Recherches Archéologiques Sous-Marines and Director of Prehistoric Antiquities for the Provence region. His scientific work is mostly concerned with the Neolithic period. He was the first archaeologist to enter Cosquer Cave.

Iain Davidson

Iain Davidson is Associate Professor in the Department of Archaeology and Paleoanthropology at the University of New England, Armidale, Australia. He is currently working in the area of language origins, with William Noble, and on the archaeology of northwestern Queensland. He has undertaken research in Australia into the colonization of the arid zone, and into trade, rock paintings, and engravings. He has also worked on the fauna and economy of Upper Paleolithic sites in Spain.

Irenäus Eibl-Eibesfeldt

Irenäus Eibl-Eibesfeldt is Professor of Zoology at the University of Munich; Director of the Research Institute for Human Ethology at the Max Planck Society, Andechs, Germany; and President of the International Society for Human Ethology. He has undertaken field studies in many remote parts of the world, including the Upper Orinoco, in South America; Namibia and Botswana, in Africa; and Papua New Guinea, Bali, and the Trobriand Islands. He is the author of 15 books, including *Ethology, the Biology of Behavior* and *Human Ethology*, and of more than 450 articles.

Timothy Flannery

Timothy Flannery is Head of Mammals at the Australian Museum, Sydney, Australia. His research interests include fossil and modern mammals of Australia and the Pacific.

Roland Fletcher

Roland Fletcher is Senior Lecturer in the School of Archaeology, Classics and Ancient History at the University of Sydney, Australia. His major fields of interest are a worldwide comparative study of the way humans use space, and the logic of archaeological theory. His theoretical concerns are with the development of long-term, large-scale models of human behavior.

George C. Frison

George C. Frison is Professor of Anthropology at the University of Wyoming, USA. His main area of interest is the study of the North American Paleoindians, and in particular animal procurement strategies on the High Plains, where he has applied his specialist knowledge of wild and domesticated animals to better interpret ancient hunting societies. He has published seven books and numerous journal articles, and is a past president of the Society for American Archaeology.

Ian C. Glover

Ian C. Glover is Senior Lecturer in the Department of Prehistoric Archaeology at the Institute of Archaeology, University College London, UK. He has located and excavated archaeological sites in Timor and Sulawesi, in Indonesia, and his field work has also taken him to western Thailand, where he surveyed and excavated prehistoric, protohistoric, and historic sites.

Christopher Gosden

Christopher Gosden is Lecturer in the Department of Archaeology at La Trobe University, Melbourne, Australia. He is currently researching the prehistory of Papua New Guinea and has undertaken field work on Pleistocene and Holocene sites there.

Donald K. Grayson

Donald K. Grayson is Professor of Anthropology at the University of Washington, USA. His research has focused on the history of mammals in North America, on the analysis of vertebrate faunal remains from archaeological sites, and on the history of archaeology. His most recent work was on the Middle and Upper Paleolithic faunal assemblages from archaeological sites in southwestern France. He is the author of *The Establishment of Human Antiquity* and *Quantitative Zooarchaeology*.

Colin Groves

Colin Groves is Reader in Biological Anthropology in the Department of Archaeology and Anthropology at the Australian National University, Canberra, Australia. His research interests are human evolution, primatology, mammalian evolution and taxonomy, and animal domestication. He has conducted field work connected with wildlife conservation on primates and other mammals in Kenya, Tanzania, Rwanda, Indonesia, and India, and has also worked as a consultant on wildlife conservation in the Middle East. He is the author of four books, including *A Theory of Human and Primate Evolution*.

Michelle Lampl

Michelle Lampl is a physician and physical anthropologist in the Department of Anthropology at the University of Pennsylvania, USA. She is interested in both living humans and our extinct ancestors. Her primary concerns are the biological basis of human behavior, in particular how humans develop into adults, and the reconstruction of extinct patterns of human behavior.

Walter Leutenegger

Walter Leutenegger is Professor of Anthropology at the University of Wisconsin-Madison, USA. His main areas of interest are primate evolutionary biology and biological anthropology.

Ronnie Liljegren

Ronnie Liljegren is Head of the Laboratory of Faunal History at Lund University, Sweden, and since 1986 has led the Swedish Late Quaternary vertebrate faunal history project. Before that, he spent ten years studying the paleoecological effects of water level changes in the Baltic Sea.

Tom Loy

Tom Loy is Research Fellow in the Department of Prehistory, Australian National University, Canberra, Australia. His main area of interest is the analysis of organic residues on prehistoric tools, using microscopy, protein biochemistry, and DNA analysis. He has developed methods to screen for blood residues and to identify the species of their origin.

Moreau Maxwell

Moreau Maxwell is Emeritus Professor of Anthropology at Michigan State University, USA. His area of specialization is Arctic archaeology. He has undertaken field work on several prehistoric and historic sites in the midwest of North America, and for more than 30 years has conducted Arctic archaeological research on Ellesmere and Baffin islands. His books include *Eastern Arctic Prehistory*.

William Noble

William Noble is Associate Professor of Psychology at the University of New England, Armidale, Australia. He is currently engaged, with Iain Davidson, in a project investigating hominid and human behavioral evolution, especially language. He has published numerous articles, and is the author of a book on hearing impairment.

Richard G. Roberts

Richard G. Roberts is Postdoctoral Fellow in the Department of Prehistory, Research School of Pacific Studies, at the Australian National University, Canberra, Australia. He is a specialist in thermoluminescence dating and is applying this technique to the dating of early human colonization sites in Australia, most recently to sites on the Nullarbor Plain, in southern Australia. During excavations in Kakadu National Park, in northern Australia, he established the oldest secure dates for human occupation in Australia—50,000 to 60,000 years ago.

Peter Rowley-Conwy

Peter Rowley-Conwy is Lecturer in the Department of Archaeology at the University of Durham, UK. He obtained his PhD with research on the Late Mesolithic and Early Neolithic history of Denmark, and has subsequently researched the European Paleolithic, Mesolithic, and Neolithic periods and the origins of agriculture in Southwest Asia. He has also worked on the economic archaeology of the Nile Valley in the Late and post-Pharaonic periods.

Wulf Schiefenhövel

Wulf Schiefenhövel is Research Associate at the Research Institute for Human Ethology at the Max Planck Society, Andechs, Germany, and Professor of Medical Psychology and Ethnomedicine at the University of Munich. He has conducted field work in Papua New Guinea, Irian Jaya, Bali, East Java, and the Trobriand Islands. His main areas of interest are the evolutionary biology of human behavior, ethnomedicine, and anthropology, especially reproductive strategies, birth behavior, early socialization, nonverbal communication, aggression and aggression control, and cultural diversity and the evolution of culture. He serves on the boards of many publications.

Olga Soffer

Olga Soffer is Professor of Anthropology at the University of Illinois at Champaign-Urbana, USA. Her special area of interest is Late Pleistocene hunter-gatherers in the Old World, and she is currently investigating the Eastern Gravettian groups who occupied central and eastern Europe some 30,000 to 10,000 years ago. With Moravian, Ukrainian, and Russian colleagues, she has excavated sites at Dolní Věstonice and Mezhirich.

Paul Tacon

Paul Tacon is Scientific Officer in the Division of Anthropology at the Australian Museum, Sydney, Australia. His special area of interest is Aboriginal material culture and Aboriginal art forms. He has conducted archaeological and field research in northern Australia at Kakadu National Park, Arnhem Land, and Cape York Peninsula, in central and eastern Australia, and in Canada, the USA, and the UK. Much of his work has focused on rock art and contemporary indigenous art forms.

David Hurst Thomas

David Hurst Thomas is Curator of Anthropology at the American Museum of Natural History, New York, USA. He is a specialist in the archaeology of the American Indians. He discovered and excavated the Gatecliff Shelter, in Nevada, the deepest rock shelter known in the Americas, with tightly stratified deposits spanning the past 8,000 years. He is the author or editor of many distinguished publications, has written more than 60 monographs and scientific articles, is on the editorial board of several journals, and is a founding trustee of the National Museum of the American Indian. In 1989, in recognition of his services to American archaeology, he was elected to the National Academy of Science.

J. Peter White

J. Peter White is Reader in Prehistoric Archaeology in the School of Archaeology, Classics and Ancient History at the University of Sydney, Australia. He has a special interest in the prehistory of Australia and the Pacific, especially Melanesia. He began research work in New Guinea in 1963, excavating for prehistory and studying the technology of highlanders who grew up in the Stone Age. More recently, he has worked in New Ireland and undertaken taphonomic studies in the Flinders Ranges, Australia. He is co-author, with Professor J. O'Connell, of *A Prehistory of Australia, New Guinea and Sahul* and has edited the journal *Archaeology in Oceania* since 1981.

◄● This carving of a bison found at the Upper Paleolithic rock shelter site of La Madeleine, in the Dordogne, France, once decorated a spear-thrower.
R.M.N.

Aborigines, Australian 93
  Dreamtime stories 147-8
  interaction between animals and 162
  origins of 156-60, 165
  puberty rites 116
  rock paintings 110
  Tasmanian 156-60
abri see rock shelters
Abri Blanchard, Dordogne, France
  28, 103
Abri Castanet, Dordogne, France 103, 107
Abri Cellier, Dordogne, France 107
Abri Pataud, Dordogne, France 92
accelerator mass spectrometric (AMS)
  technique 94
Acheulean tradition *endpapers, 20,*
  55, 64, 64, 66
Admiralty Islands 171, 180
  animal species on 174
Adovasio, James 190
Africa
  Acheulean tradition in *20,* 64
  Australopithecine sites 60
  climate zones in *83*
  dating of sites 75
  early *Homo* in East 60-1
  erectine sites 63
  Homo erectus 49
  Homo sapiens in 50, 77, *77-81, 78*
  Neanderthals in 67, 71
  spreading of modern humans from
    123, *124*
  vegetation zones in 83, *83*
Afropithecus 34, 43
  turkanensis 34
Agate Basin site, Wyoming, North
  America *187,* 198, *198,* 199
aggression 17, 23, *23*
  averting 26, *27*
  conflict within groups 93
  external and internal triggers 26
  as a positive force 27
  ritualized 26
  and war 26-7
agriculture 46, 140
Ahrensburg culture 143
Akmak, Alaska 137
Akmak culture 212
Alca impennis 120, *121*
Altamira Cave, Spain 91, 97, *97, 107*
Ambrona, Spain 46
Americas
  colonization of 46
  Homo sapiens in 50
  Paleoindian sites in *187*
  see also North America
amino acid racemization 75
Amud Cave, Israel *48,* 67
Anangula culture 212
Andamanese 93
animal translocation 175
antelope, saiga *87*
Antilocapra americana 196, *198*
Anzick site, Montana, North America
  187, 192, 193, *195*
apes
  evolution of 33-6
  sexual dimorphism 41
  similarities with humans 50
  see also chimpanzees; gorillas
Arago, France *48,* 66
Arago skull *50, 66,* 67, 84
Arctic
  animals 214-15
  ice packs *208-9, 217*
  settlement of 132-7, 209-27
Arctic Small Tool Tradition 212,
  213, 217
  sites *210*

Arcy-sur-Cure cave, France *107*
Arnhem Land, Australia 2-3, 153, *153,*
  158, 164
art 17, 18, *29*
  "Bubalus period" *81*
  cave *89,* 91, 97-121, 100, *107*
    bison *97*
    boomerang stencils *158*
    Franco-Cantabrian *104,* 104-5
    hand stencils *97,* 108, *113,* 120,
      120, 167, 165, *165*
    horse's head *106*
    inaccessible location of 106
    interpretations of 110-16
    polychrome paintings *89, 107,*
      116, 117
    salmon 105
    saltwater species 93
    superimposed images 109
    Upper Paleolithic sites *104*
    vulva images *107, 108*
  Dorset 223
  early Australia 158-9, 162-5
  evolution of *21*
  fertility symbols 102-3
  Komsa people *143*
  and language 46
  Magdalenian 91
  and memory 28
  origins in Southeast Asia 124-5
  portable *98,* 99, *99,* 104, *107*
  sexual symbolism 88, 100, *100,* 106,
    107, 108
  as status symbols 95
  Thule *223*
  Venus figurines 88
artifacts 28, 100
  analysis of wear patterns on 182
  Arctic 217
  Birnirk *220*
  bone and antler 98-9
  bone plaque from Abri Blanchard *28*
  carved bison *99,* 234
  Clovis 192-5
  Cro-Magnon 85
  deer head *99*
  Denbigh 223
  depicted in rock paintings *159*
  Dorset *221,* 222
  eyed bone needles 205
  Folsom 196-8
  ibex 99
  Ipiutak *220, 224*
  from Le Mas d'Azil *99*
  Magdalenian 91, *99, 99*
  mammoth ivory carvings *132*
  mammoth ivory figurines *132*
  from Meadowcroft Rockshelter *191*
  from Mezhirich *134*
  from Near Oceania 180-2
  oil lamps *218,* 224
  Okvik 224
  Old Bering Sea *220,* 224, *225*
  personal ornaments 30-1
  pottery 126
  Pre-Dorset 219
  Punuk *220, 225*
  sea shell necklace *157*
  sculptured clay phalluses *114*
  shells and amber 88
  statuettes *22*
  from Sungir 139
  Thule *221*
Asfaw, Berhane *38-9*
Asia *see* Southeast Asia
Atapuerca, Spain *48*
Aterian culture 80-1
Aucilla River, Florida, North
  America *187*

Auel, Jean 70
auk, great 120, *121*
Aurignac, France 85
Aurignacian tradition 77, 85, 88,
  89, 107
  split-base spear-point *77*
  vulva images 103
aurochs, North African *81,* 106,
  109, 114
Australia
  colonization of 46
  distribution of people in ancient 156
  Greater *160*
  modern humans in 22, 50, 124,
    124, 125
  settlement of ancient 147-69
Australopithecus 30, 37, *37,* 55, 57, *58*
  aethiopicus 50, 51
  afarensis 37, 37, 39, *50, 51*
    sexual dimorphism 41
  africanus 33, 40, *40, 50, 51,* 52, 60
    sexual dimorphism 41
  boisei 21, 41, 50, 51
  robustus 50, 51
Azilian tradition 91

Baffin Island *218-19, 222, 222*
Bahn, Paul 92
Ballawinne Cave, Tasmania, Australia 167
Balme, Jane 160
Balof, New Ireland 172, *172,* 180,
  181, 182
Ban Mae Tha, Thailand 63
bandicoots 174
Barda Balka, Iraq 178
Baringo, Africa *48*
Barton, Huw 182
Batadomba Iena Cave, Sri Lanka 125
bats 172, *211,* 174, 175, 179, 183
  New Ireland subspecies *174*
bear cult 43, 70, 73
bears
  cave 43, 70, 73, *86*
  depicted in cave art 106
  polar 211, *211,* 214, *214*
  short-faced 186
beavers, giant 206
Belohdelie, Africa *48*
Beringia *124,* 137, *137,* 186, 212
Biache, France *48*
Bighorn Mountains, Wyoming, North
  America 193
Bilgery, Father Conrad *188*
Bilzingsleben, Germany *48,* 49, 66
Binford, Lewis 61, 64
Bir el Ater, Tunisia, Africa 80
birds 183
  Arctic 212, 227
  extinct species 162
Birhor, northern India 93
Birnirk culture *220,* 225
bison *184-5,* 186, 188, *188,* 196, *197,*
  212, 234
  depicted in cave art 106, 109,
    109, 120
  hunting 199-202
  kill sites *198, 201, 202, 203*
  steppe *87*
Bison bison 184-5
  "bison pit" 199
Bison priscus 87
Black, Davidson *63*
Black Skull *45, 50*
Blackwater Draw, New Mexico,
  North America *187,* 188
Bluefish Caves, Alaska 137, *187*
Blumenbach, Johann Friedrich 33
Bobongara, Huon Peninsula, New
  Guinea 151, *151,* 154

Bodo, Africa *48, 50,* 67
bone beds *198,* 198-202, *202, 203*
Bone Caves, Tasmania, Australia 167, *167*
Border Cave, Africa 49, *76-7,* 78
Borneck, Germany 140
Bougainville 171
Boule, Marcellin 67
Bradshaw figures *159*
Brain, C.K. 60
brain size 52, *52*
  Australopithecus africanus 40
  and childbirth 62
  evolution of *Homo sapiens* 55
  Homo 45
  Homo erectus 48, 62
  increased 66
  and language 46
  Olduvai species 44
  Turkana Newcomer 47
Brassempouy, France *31,* 100, *101, 107*
Breuil, Abbé 92, 111, *111, 114,* 115
Bromme, Denmark 142
Brooks River, Alaska 212
Broom, Robert 37
Brown, Barnum 186
Brubus, Indonesia *48*
Bruniquel, Tarn-et-Garonne, France *98*
Bubalus antiquus 81
"Bubalus period" *81*
Bull Brook site, Massachusetts,
  North America 192
burials *80,* 88
  Clovis 193
  in Europe *84*
  first evidence 99
  hereditary status 95, 99
  indications of status distinctions
    132, 224
  ivory disks *224*
  Lake Mungo, Australia 161
  Neanderthal 46, 70, *70,* 72-3
  Old Bering Sea *209*
  oldest Australian skeletons 156-60
  social status 95, 99
  Sungir 138-9, *138-9*
Bushmen of the Kalahari 93
  aggressive behavior 26, *26*
  steatopygia *102*
  puberty rites 116

Cagayan Valley, Philippines 126
camels 186
  extinction of 206
camp sites *see* settlements
Canada 219-22
Canarium indicum 180, *180*
Canarium nuts 180, *180*
"candelabra" model 49, 80
  "pre-*sapiens*" finds 84
Canis lupus 86
Cann, Rebecca 80
cannibalism 65, 70, 72
canoes *150,* 151, 172
  in the Arctic 218, 225
Cape Denbigh, Alaska 212
Cape Dorset, Baffin Island 222
Cape York, Australia 154
caribou *122-3,* 212, *214,* 224, 227
  skins for winter clothing 214, 222
Carneiro, Robert 93
Carter/Kerr-McGee site, Wyoming,
  North America *187, 202, 203*
Casablanca, Morocco, Africa *48*
Casper site, Wyoming, North America
  187, 201, 202
Castanet, Dordogne, France *107*
cation-ratio method 163
Cattle Guard site, Colorado, North
  America *187,* 202

Cave, A.J.E. 67
Cave Bay Cave, Tasmania, Australia 167
cave bear cult 46
caves *see* rock shelters; settlements; shelters
ceremonial life 93
  depicted in cave art 97-121
  Franco-Cantabrian cave art 105-16
  Paleolithic period 91, 95
  rites of passage 112, 115-16
  shamanism 114-15
  see also ritual behavior; shamans
chamois, depicted in cave art 120
char, Arctic 211, 217
Charlie Cave, North America 187
Chatelperronian tradition 85, 85-8, 89
cheetah, American 186, 206
Chemeron, near Lake Baringo, Africa 44
chemical methods of dating 75
Chesowanja, Kenya 46, 55
  erectine sites 63
chimpanzees 23, 35, 53
  aggression 23, 26, 27
  brain 52
  evolution of 33-6, 43
  learning language 51, 51-2
  skull shape 49
  threat display 26, 26
  using tools 51, 53, 56-7
China 48
  Homo sapiens in 50
Chindadn culture 212
Choris Cultural Complex 223-4
Chukchi Peninsula, Siberia 132, 136, 137, 225
circumcision 116
Citellus citellus 87
Clactonian technology 66
The Clan of the Cave Bear 70
climate 186
  in ancient Australia 154, 155
  Arctic environment 211
  causing extinctions 162, 168, 207
  changes in skin color 62-3
  curves, global 82
  evolution of *Homo sapiens* 57
  fluctuations in global 72
  in ice-age Tasmania 166
  zones in Europe and Africa 83
  see also Ice Age
clothes 167, 214, 222
Clovis Cultural Complex 185, 186, 187, 188-96, 190
cockle and mussel shells 92
Coelodonta antiquitatis 87
Colby site, Wyoming, North America 184, 187, 192, 193, 196, 196
Colocasia esculenta 178
Commarque, Dordogne, France 106
Coobol Creek, Australia 157
Cosquer, Henri 118
Cosquer Cave, Cape Morgiou, France 118-21, 118-21
Courtin, Jean 119
Cro-Magnon people 48, 80, 84, 124
  culture of 88
  development of imagery 98
  emphasis on female genitals 100
  Homo sapiens in 50
  skull 85
  tools 85
crocodile 169
Crocuta crocuta spelaea 87
crying 26
cultural tradition
  among apes 53
  in Southeast Asia 128-9, 128-9
  see also burials; ceremonial life; ritual behavior; social organization
cuscus, northern common 175, 175, 183
Cuvier, Georges 33

Dali, China 48, 66
dancing 115, 116
Dar es Soltan, Morocco, Africa 80
Darling River, Australia 156, 160
Dart, Raymond 37, 37, 60
Darwin, Charles 34
Darwin Crater, Australia, glass from 166, 167
dating techniques 74-5
  interdisciplinary approach to 198
  see also cation-ratio method; radiocarbon dating; thermoluminescence
dead
  interacting with 17, 18, 24, 72
  see also burials
Debert site, Nova Scotia, North America 187, 192
decoration, pigments used for 164
deer
  depicted in cave art 106, 120
  giant 87
  red 120
defense, aggression for 26, 27
Denali culture 212
Denbigh Flint Complex 212, 212, 220, 223
Dent site, Colorado, North America 187, 188
Des Rideaux, Lespugue, Haute Garonne, France 102
Descent of Man 34
Devon Island, Arctic Circle 217
Die Kelders Cave, Africa 78
Dillehay, Tom 191
diprotodon 162, 168, 168
Dmanisi, Georgia 63
DNA analysis 34, 178, 178
Dolní Věstonice, Moravia, Czech Republic 88, 88, 89, 105, 132
  Venus figurines 100, 103
Domebo site, Oklahoma, North America 187, 192
domestication
  dogs in the Arctic 219
  translocating animals 175
Dordogne, France 77, 84, 90, 103, 104, 106, 107, 112, 115
  sites 48
  see also Font-de-Gaume; Gorge d'Enfer; La Ferrassie; La Madeleine; Lascaux; Le Moustier; Les Eyzies; Regourdou; Rouffignac; Solvieux; Vézère River
Dorset culture 221, 222, 223
  camp 226-7
Drachenloch cave, Switzerland 70
Dry Creek, Alaska 137, 187
Dryopithecus 36, 36, 42, 42-3, 43
Duke of York Islands, Bismarck Sea 6-7
"dynamic figure" style 158, 159
Dyuktai tradition 133, 137

Early Man Shelter, Cape York, Australia 162, 162
Ebbou, Ardèche Valley, France 121
Ehringsdorf, Germany 48
El Castillo, Santander Province, Spain 108
El Inga, South America 187
electron spin resonance (ESR) analysis 49, 75
Eliye Springs, Kenya, Africa 67
elk, Irish 87
Ellesmere Island 217, 219, 223, 227
Equus Cave, Africa 78
Equus ferus 86
erectines *see Homo erectus*
Escale, France 24
Eskimos *see* Inuit
estrus periods 57

Europe
  Acheulean tradition in 64
  animals of Ice Age 86-7
  archaeological sites in 58
  climate zones in 83
  erectine sites in 63
  Homo erectus in 49
  Homo sapiens in 49
  Ice Age in 82, 84-5
  late glacial sites in northern 143
  migration of modern humans 78
  Neanderthal sites 66
  Neanderthals in 71
  origins of modern humans 84-95
  settling of northern 140-3
  Upper Paleolithic settlement and burial sites 84
  vegetation zones 83, 83
"Eve" theory 80, 144
evolution
  of Australian fauna 149
  of the Great Apes 36
  of *Homo sapiens* 55-73
  human origins 33-53
  of human sexual dimorphism 41
  our earliest ancestors 42-3
  primate 42-3
  of sex roles 30
  theories of 78-81, 80, 84
extinctions 86-7
  in Australia 162, 168-9
  in Near Oceania 179
  in North America 186, 204, 206
  of protohominid species 62
Eyasi, Africa 48

faunal dating 75
Federmesser cultures 140
Fell's Cave, South America 187
Fenn cache, North America 193
Fergusson Island 180
fertility 111
Finja, Sweden 89, 142
fires 17, 18, 23, 23-4, 46
  Arctic fuel 209, 214, 217
  in Australia 165, 168
  heat-treated rocks 176-7
  at Zhoukoudian 65
"First Family" 37, 38-9, 39, 50
fishing 81, 93
  Arctic 212
  depicted in cave art 106
  Jomon culture 137
  Near Oceania 172
  Norton 224
  salmon 105, 106
  Terra Amata 64
  see also middens
fission-track dating 75
Florisbad, Africa 78
Folsom Cultural Complex 185, 187, 188-9, 196-202
Folsom site, New Mexico, North America 186, 187, 188, 199, 202-3
Font-de-Gaume, Dordogne, France 107, 112
food supply 62
  in the Arctic 212, 214, 217
  distribution within the group 57-8
  Magdalenian 93
  mammoth kill site 193
  in Near Oceania 172-4
  organic residue analysis of 178
  in Paleoindian cultures 204
  reindeer 93
  sharing 205
  sharing between the sexes 61
  Upper Paleolithic 104
  vegetables and small game 59
Fosna culture 143
Fossey, Dian 53
foxes, Arctic 211, 217

Gabillou, Dordogne, France 108
Gaffey, Pru 183
"galip" nuts 180, 180
Gallerie Noir, Niaux Cave, France 109
Gardiner, Allen and Beatrice 51
Gargas, France 109
genetic research 80
  tracing human origins 144
Gimbutas, Marija 102, 103
glaciation *see* Ice Age
goanna 168
Gombe Reserve, Tanzania, Africa 24
Gongwangling, China 48, 48, 63
Goodall, Jane 24, 26, 53
Gorge d'Enfer, Dordogne, France 77, 106
gorillas 23, 36, 53
  evolution of 34-6, 43
  sexual dimorphism 30
  skeletal structure 18
  skull shape 49
  using tools 51
Gosden, Christopher 183
Goshen Cultural Complex 185, 187, 189, 202-3
graves *see* burials
Gravettian tradition 88, 89, 107
  Venus figurines 101, 103
Great Rift Valley, Kenya, Africa 62
Greater Australia 127, 130
Greenberg, Joseph 145, 190
Greenland 212, 217
Grimaldi, Italy 89, 103
  burial sites 99
grinding 154
Grose Gorge, Australia 154
Groswater Dorset Complex 222
Grotte de Placard, France 28
Grotte des Enfants, Balzi Rossi, Italy 95, 95
grouse, willow 86
Groves, Colin 50
Gulo gulo 86

habilines *see Homo habilis*
Hadar, Ethiopia, Africa 2-3, 37, 37, 38-9, 48, 50
Hagop Bilo, Sabah, Borneo 126, 129
Hahnöfersand, near Hamburg, Germany 48, 85, 89
Hall of Bulls, Lascaux, France 108
Halmahera Island, Indonesia 175
Hamburg culture 140, 140
hand-axe technology *see* Acheulean tradition
Hanson site, Wyoming, North America 187, 202
Hassi el Abiod, Mali, Africa 80
Hathnora, India 48, 66
Haua Fteah Cave, Cyrenaica, Libya, Africa 80
hearths 160, 183, 183
  in the Arctic 212, 221, 227
Heidelberg, Germany 49
Hell Gap, Wyoming, North America 187, 189, 189, 199
herding 91-3
Hexian, China 48
Hiscock, Peter 160
Hoa-Binh, Vietnam 126
Hoabinhian culture 126, 128, 129
Hohlensteinstadel, Germany 22
Holocene 83, 143
  climatic conditions 186
  obsidian tools 181
hominids 17, 20, 21, 42
  aggression 23
  burying their dead 24, 28
  as hunters 60-1
  nonhuman 57
  sexual dimorphism 41
  signaling 22
  in Southeast Asia 151

Homo
earliest specimen of 44
erectus 48, *48, 50, 51, 52, 54-5, 58, 62,* 62-6, 71, 78, 151
chopping-tool industries 64
heidelbergensis 49
migration of *59*
olduvaiensis 49
pekinensis 48
Peking Man *48,* 65, *65*
sexual dimorphism 41
skull *63*
ergaster 47, *47, 50, 51,* 78
habilis 44, 44-5, *50, 51, 52,* 55-62, *56, 58,* 60-1
sexual dimorphism 41
skull *57*
heidelbergensis 49, *49,* 62, 67, 71, 78, 84
hand-axe tradition 64
neanderthalensis 67, 68
rudolfensis 45, *45, 50, 51*
sapiens 49, *50, 51, 52,* 78, 82
earliest representatives of 49
evolution of 45-50, *49*
sexual dimorphism 41
sapiens sapiens 80, 84
ability to communicate through symbols 102
Aurignacian tradition 77
in Australia and New Guinea 125, 151, 157
as descendants of Neanderthals 66-7
development of imagery 98
in Europe 85, 123
migration into Europe 77-95
Paleoindian communities 204
tool technology 98
Hope, Jeanette 160
Hopefield, South Africa 71
horses *86,* 186
depicted in cave art 106, 109, *109, 113,* 114, *119,* 120
extinction of 206
hunting 133
Przewalski *92*
signs of domestication of 92
Upper Paleolithic *91,* 92, *92*
Hortus, France 24
Howells, William 80
Hudson Bay, North America 217
Huffman, Michael 53
human origins 33-53, *43*
The Hunters or the Hunted? 60
hunting 81, 91-3, *93*
in the Arctic 210, 217
bison, in Folsom times 199-202
caribou 222, 224, 227
by earliest hominids 60-1
by early *Homo* 58-9
erectines and big-game hunting 64
mammoth, in Clovis times 195-6
Neanderthals 71
in northern Europe 143
Norton 224
Paleoindian *184-5,* 204
Pleistocene period, Tasmania 166
on sea-ice 222, 225
seal 225
subantarctic 166-7
Upper Paleolithic 133
walruses and baleen whales 224
Huxley, Thomas 34
hyena, cave *87*

Iberian Peninsula 104, *104*
ibex, depicted in cave art 106, *119,* 120
Ice Age 57, 82, *82,* 140
animals of Europe 86-7
climatic fluctuations through time *72*

Neanderthals 71
Younger Dryas 83
Illich-Svitych, Vladislav 145
Independence I culture 217, *221*
Indonesia *131*
initiation rites 115-16
intelligence 35
comparing humans and apes 51-3
sequences of actions 18, 24
storing knowledge 28
in use of tools 56
see also memory; persistence
interglacials 82
Inuit 212, *221*
ancestors 225
Ipiutak culture *220,* 224, *224*
Isaac, Glyn 61
Isernia La Pineta, Italy 63
Isturitz, France *99*

Java, Indonesia 48, *54-5,* 63
Jebel Irhoud, Morocco, Africa 48, 49, *49,* 67
Jenjiawo, China 48, 63
Jinniushan, China *48,* 66
Johanson, Don 37, *50*
Jomon culture 137
Judds Cavern, Tasmania, Australia 167

Kabwe, Zambia, Africa 48, *50,* 67, 71, 78
Kakadu National Park, Arnhem Land, Australia *157, 158*
Kangaroo Island, Australia 155
kangaroos
extinct 162, *162*
gray 169
Kanzi *51*
Kapova Cave, Ural Mountains, Russia 104
Kebara Cave, Mount Carmel, Israel *24-5,* 67, 70, *70,* 73
Kedung, Indonesia *48*
Kenyapithecus 34, 42, *43*
kestrel *86*
Kibish Formation, Omo River, Ethiopia, Africa 49
kill sites 105, 207
bison *198,* 198-202, *201, 202,* 203
in North America 189-92, *196*
Paleoindian *187*
Kilu Cave, Solomon Islands 178, 179, 180
Kimberley region, Western Australia 154, *159*
Kimswick site, Missouri, North America *187,* 192
Klasies River Mouth Cave, South Africa 48, 49, 78, 80
Klein, Richard 78, 124
Knife River flint sources, North Dakota, North America 195
Knud Peninsula, Ellesmere Island *223,* 227
koalas 169
Kobuk River, Alaska 212
Koehler, Wolfgang 51
Komsa culture *142-3,* 143
Koobi Fora, Lake Turkana, Kenya, Africa 44, 45, *45,* 47, 48, 57, *57,* 60-1, 75
Koonalda Cave, South Australia 163, *165*
Kostenki, Russia *4-5,* 89, *89,* 105
Venus figurines 100, *107*
Kostenki–Bershevo culture 132
Kow Swamp, Australia 157
Krapina, Croatia 24, 72
Kromdraai, South Africa 45, *50,* 75
Kurupka, Chukchi Peninsula, Siberia 137
La Chapelle-aux-Saints, France 24, 67, 70

Neanderthal burials 72
La Ferrassie, Dordogne, France *1,* 28, *29,* 48, *85, 100,* 103, *107*
Neanderthal burials 72
La Gravette, France 88
La Madeleine, Dordogne, France 89, 91, *98,* 234
burial sites 99
La Marche, France 92
La Pasiega, France 92
La Pileta, Spain 108
Lachlan River, Australia 161
Laetoli, Tanzania, Africa *19,* 37, *37,* 48, *50*
Lagopus lagopus 86
Lake Eyre, Australia 148
Lake Menindee, Australia 161
Lake Mungo, Australia *147,* 156, *161*
burials 161
Lake Turkana, Kenya, Africa 19, *57,* 62
erectine sites 63
see also Koobi Fora; Turkana Newcomer
Lalinde, Dordogne, France *100*
Lamb site, New York, North America 192
Laming, Annette 114
Lancefield Swamp, Australia 162
land bridges 82, *125,* 127
Asia and Alaska *137,* 186, 212
Australia and New Guinea 150
Australia and Tasmania 151, 166
Lang Rong Rien, Thailand 126
Lange-Ferguson site, South Dakota, North America *187,* 192
language 145
comparing humans and apes 51-3
evolution of 22
linked to genetic origins 144-5, *144-5*
origins of 46
reanalysis of American Indian 190
speech 17
teaching chimpanzees *51,* 51-2
to transmit moral values 18
Upper Paleolithic 99
Lantian, China 63
Lascaux, Dordogne, France 28, 91, *107,* 109, *109,* 111, 112, *116,* 116-17
Hall of Bulls *108*
Late Stone Age 81
Laugerie-Basse, Dordogne, France 92, *93*
Laussel, Dordogne, France *12*
Laussel, Dordogne, France *12*
Lawn Hill station, Queensland, Australia 160
Le Mas d'Azil, France *89,* 91, *99*
Le Moustier, Dordogne, France 67, 71, *72*
Neanderthal burials 72
Le Portel, France *107*
Le Tuc d'Audoubert, France 115
footprints *114*
Leakey, Louis *21*
Leakey, Mary *19, 21,* 37
Leakey, Richard *21, 51*
Leang Burung, Indonesia 126, *128*
Lehner site, North America *187,* 192, 196
lemming, collared 186
Leroi-Gourhan, André *107,* 111-14, 115
Les Combarelles, Dordogne, France 106, *107*
Les Eyzies, Dordogne, France 84, 91, 104
Les Trois Frères, Ariège, France *107,* 114, *114*
Lespugue, France 103
Venus figurines 100, *107*
Levalloisian technology 71, 98, *128, 129*
Libby, Willard 94
Lindenmeier site, Colorado, North

America *187,* 196, 204
dating Folsom deposits 198
lions
American 186, 206
cave *86,* 120
depicted in cave art 106, 120
marsupial 168, *168*
Lipscomb Bison Quarry, Texas, North America 199
Liujiang, China 48, *124,* 125
Llano *see* Clovis Cultural Complex
Lomekwi, West Turkana, Africa *50*
Lothagam, Africa 48
Lou Island, Admiralty Islands 182
"Lucy" 30, *38-9,* 39, *39, 50*
Lufengpithecus 36
Lumley, Henry de 64

Maba, China 48
Macaca fuscata 53, *53*
McCullogh, Dr Karen *227*
McJunkin, George 186
Magalania prisca 169
Magdalenian phase *85,* 89, 91-3, 95, 99, *107,* 140
stylized female figures *100*
vulva images *108*
Maka, Africa 48
Makapansgat, South Africa 37, 48, *50,* 60, 75
Malakunanja II, Arnhem Land, Australia 153, *153, 156,* 160
Malangangerr site, Arnhem Land, Australia 154
Mal'ta Afontova, near Lake Baikal, Siberia *132,* 133, 137
mammals 175
mammoth-bone huts *see* shelters
mammoth steppe 86
mammoths *107, 110,* 186, *186,* 188, 212
depicted in cave art 106, 109
extinction of 204, 206
hunting 194, 195-6
kill sites in North America *187,* 189
in Siberian cultural tradition 125
woolly *86, 113*
Mammuthus primigenius 86
Manus Island, Admiralty Islands 171
Marshack, Alexander *28*
marsupials 174, 175
Martin, Paul S. 206
mastodon 186, 192, *206,* 212
extinction of 206
Matanuska Glacier, Alaska *140-1*
Matembek, New Britain 180, 181
Matenkupkum Cave, New Ireland 183, *183*
Mauer, Austria 48
Meadowcroft Rockshelter, Pennsylvania, North America *187,* 190-1, *190-1*
Mechta el Arbi, Algeria, Africa 80
Megaloceros giganteus 87
Meiendorf, northern Europe *89,* 140
memory
burying the dead 28
complex sequences of actions 18, 24
Mer Islands, Torres Strait *130*
Mezhirich, Dnepr River, Ukraine *93,* 95, 116, *132,* 134-5, *134-5*
microliths 81
middens 160-1, *161*
Middle Paleolithic period 77, 81
tool technology 78, 80
Middle Park, Rocky Mountains, North America 203
Middle Stone Age 81
migration
of *Homo erectus* 62
of *Homo sapiens sapiens* into Europe 77-95

Mill Iron site, Montana, North America
    187, 202, *203*
Mississippi Valley, North America 192
Mojokerto, Indonesia *48*
molecular clock 34
Monte Circeo, Italy *48*, 70, *70*, 73
Monte Verde site, Chile *187*, *190*,
    191, *191*
Montmaurin, France *48*
Mopir, New Britain 180
moral values 17, 18
Mount Carmel, Israel 67, 80, *124*
    see also Kebara Cave; Skhul Cave
Mousterian tradition 67, 71, *71*,
    77, *89*
Movius, Hallam 128
"Mrs Ples" *40*
Mungo I, Australia 161
Mungo III, Australia 161
Murray River Valley, Australia 156
Murray Springs site, North America
    187, 192
musical instruments 28, 115
    bird bone flute *28*
mussel shells 92

Naco site, North America 192
Nariokotome, Africa 47, *48*
Natron, Africa *48*
Nawamoyn site, Arnhem Land,
    Australia 154
Ndutu, Africa *48*
Neanderthal, near Düsseldorf, Germany
    48, *50*, 66
Neanderthals *21*, *49*, 66-73, 68, *68-9*,
    80, 85
    burying their dead 24, *24-5*, 28
    cave bear cult 46
    and language 145
    no evidence of image-making 98
    precursors of 66
    skull *1*, *85*, 88
    tool technology of 78, 98
    see also Mousterian tradition
Near Oceania 171-83
    Pleistocene sites *172*
neutron activation analysis 180
New Britain 171, 182, 183
    animal species on 174
New Guinea 149, 150, 171, 175
    animal species in 174
    modern humans in 124, 125, 151
    people in ancient 156
New Ireland 171, 175
    first settlers 183
    Pleistocene sites *172*
    stone artifacts 180-2
Ngaloba, Tanzania, Africa *49*, 67
Ngandong, Java, Indonesia *48*, 71,
    72, 126
Ngorongoro crater, Tanzania, Africa
    20, *20*, *16-17*
Nguom Cave, Bac Thai Province,
    North Vietnam *129*
Niah Cave, Sarawak, East Malaysia
    126, *126*
Niaux cave, France 91, *107*, 109, 112
    footprints 115, *115*
    Gallerie Noir *109*
"Noah's Ark" model *49*, *80*
Nombe, New Guinea Highlands
    154, 162
Nordland, Norway *142-3*, 143
North America *122-3*, 185-207
    modern humans in 124, *132-3*, 212
    Paleoindian sites *187*
    vegetation zones 83
North Platte River, Colorado,
    North America 188
Norton Complex *220*, 224
Nullarbor Plain, Australia *165*
Nunamira Cave, Florentine Valley, .

Australia 166, *166*, 167, *167*
Nutcracker 44, 45, 60

obsidian tools *180-1*, 180-2, 183, *183*
    from Idaho, North America 193
oceanic polar front *82*
Okvik culture *220*, 224
Olary region, South Australia 163, *163*
Old Bering Sea culture *209*, *220*,
    224, *225*
Old Man of La Chapelle-aux-Saints,
    France 67
Oldowan industry *17*, *21*, 56, *56*, *57*
Olduvai Gorge, Tanzania, Africa
    endpapers, 20, *20*, *21*, 44, *44*, 46,
    48, *50*, 56, *56-7*, 58, 60-1, 75
    erectine sites 63
Olorgesailie, Kenya, Africa 64
Olsen-Chubbuck site, Colorado,
    North America *204*
Omo Valley, Ethiopia, Africa 44, *48*,
    49, 67
optical dating 152
orang-utans *32-3*, 53
    evolution of 33-6, *43*
    skull shape *49*
    using tools 51
organic residue analysis 178, *178*, 182
The Origin of Species 34
Ouranopithecus 36, 42
    macedonensis 36
Ovibos moschatus 87
oxen, musk 87, *206*, *215*, 217

Pachamachay, South America *187*
Pacific Islands *see* Near Oceania
Pacific Ocean 171-83
pademelon, dusky *174*
Paleoarctic tradition 212
Paleolithic *see* Middle Paleolithic
    period; Upper Paleolithic period
paleomagnetism 75, *75*
Pamwak site, Manus Island, Admiralty
    Islands 180, 182
Pan
    paniscus 53
    troglodytes 53
Panakiwuk, New Ireland 181
Panaramitee-style art 163, *163*
Panthera leo spelaea 86
Paranthropus 33, 44, 45, 55
    aethiopicus 51
    boisei 44, *44*, *50*, 51
    crassidens 45, *45*, *50*
    robustus 45, *50*, 51, *52*
    walkeri 45, *50*
Pavo Real site, Texas, North
    America 192
Peary Land, Arctic Circle 217
Pech-Merle cave, France 91, *107*,
    112-13, *112-13*
Pedra Furada, South America *187*
Pei Wenzhong 65
Peking Man *48*, 65
permafrost 211
persistence 17, 23
Petralona, Greece *48*, *50*, 66, 67
    skull 84
Phalanger orientalis *175*, 183
phalangers 174
Piette, Edouard 92
Pikimachay, South America *187*
pine, bristlecone 94
Pinus longaeva 94
Placard, Charente, France *85*
Plainview culture 189
plant gathering 81
Pleistocene 82, 83
    art in early Australia 162-5
    in Australia 160, *160*
    in Greater Australia 154, 155
    in Near Oceania *172*

in North America 185, 186-207
    in Southeast Asia 128
    in Southwest Tasmania *166*
Poggenwisch, Germany 140
Point Barrow, Arctic Circle 225
Point Hope, Arctic Circle 224
Pongo pygmaeus see orang-utan
population
    Magdalenian period 93-5
Port Refuge, Devon Island, Arctic
    Circle 217
possums 174
potassium-argon dating 74, *74*
pottery 126, 223
    dating 152
    first 137
    Norton 224
Potts, Richard 57, 61
power structure 46
Pre-Dorset culture 218, *219*,
    219-22, *221*
primates 17, 18
    aggressive signaling 23
    intergroup aggression 26
    sexual signaling 18
    skeletal structure *18*
    using tools 19
    see also apes; chimpanzees; gorillas
Proconsul 34, *43*
    nyanzae 34
pronghorn 196, *198*
protein sequencing 34
Przewalski horse *109*
ptarmigan 217, *217*
Pteropus temincki ennisae 174
Punuk Cultural Complex *220*, 225, *225*
Punuk Island, Bering Sea 224
Pushkari, Ukraine *89*
Puturak, Chukchi Peninsula,
    Siberia 137

Qafzeh Cave, Israel *48*, *49*, 67, *67*
Qeqertasussuk, Disco Bay, Arctic
    Circle 219, *219*
Quadan people of Upper Egypt 81
Quinkana fortirostrum 169

Rabat, Africa *48*
radiocarbon dating 74, 94
    in the Arctic 212
    Dorset camp *227*
    limits of 151
    Meadowcroft Rockshelter 190
    Monte Verde site, Chile 191
    Pre-Dorset sites 222
    rock engravings 163
    shell middens 161
    Sungir 138
    uses of 152
Rain Ravine, Greece 36
Rangifer tarandus 87
rat, Norwegian 26
Ratcatchers Lake, Australia 161
rats 172, 179, 183
    king *179*
regional continuity theory *49*, 80, *80*
Regourdou, Dordogne, France 73
reindeer 87, 91, *93*, *122-3*
    depicted in cave art 106
    hunters 140-3
religious beliefs
    first signs of 66
    Neanderthal 70-1, 72-3
replacement theory *49*, 80, *80*
reptiles 172, 174, 179, 183
rhinoceros, woolly 87, *107*, *110*
    depicted in cave art 106, 109
"Rhodesia Man" 71, 78
Richey-Roberts Clovis cache, Washington
    State, North America *187*
Rissen, Germany 140

ritual behavior 46, 106-16
    Clovis 193-5
    Dorset 227
    early Arctic cultures 220
    first signs of 66
    Ipiutak 224
    among Neanderthals 70-1, 72
    origins in Southeast Asia 124-5
    Paleoindian cultures 205
    at Zhoukoudian 65
Roberts Jr, Frank H.H. 186
rock engravings 158, *158*, 162-3, *163*
rock painting
    in Australia 158, 163, *164*, *165*
    Bushmen fighting 26, *26*
    see also art, cave
rock shelters 71, 89, 91, 93, 98,
    104, *115*
    Arnhem Land escarpment 153
    Near Oceania 172
Rocky Mountains, North America
    196, 199
rodents 175
Rouffignac, Dordogne France 106, *107*,
    109, *110*, 112

sabertooth cat 206, *206*
Saccopastore, Italy *48*, 68
Sahara Desert, Africa 63, *78*, *79*, 80, *81*
Sahul 127-30, *130*, 149
Saiga tartarica 87
St Acheul, France 64, *64*
St Césaire, France *48*, 68, 85, 88, *89*
St Christophe, Dordogne, France 93
St Lawrence Island, North America 224
St Michel d'Arudy, France 92, *92*
Saldanha, South Africa *48*, 71
Salé, Morocco, Africa *48*
Sambungmacan, Indonesia *48*
Samburu Hills, Kenya, Africa 36
San Luis Valley, Colorado, North
    America 202, *202-3*, 204
San Pedro Valley, Arizona, North
    America 189
Sangiran, Indonesia *48*
Sarcophilus harrisii 162, 168
Sarqaq *218*, 218-19, *219*, *221*
Sautuola, Don Marcelino de 97, 98
Savage-Rumbaugh, Sue 51
Savignano, Italy *103*
Scandinavia 140-3
scavenging
    by earliest hominids 60-1
    by early *Homo* 58-9
Schledermann, Dr Peter 227, *227*
sea level, changes in 82, 127-30
    Australia 168
    Greater Australia *149*, 150, 155-6, *160*
    migration from Southeast Asia 151
    North America 186
    rising 143
sea travel 171, *172*
    to Australia and New Guinea 125
seals 120, 210, 211, 214, 217
    for food and clothing *215*
    hunting 225
sediments, dating 152
Segebro, Sweden *89*, 142, *143*
self-awareness, comparing humans
    and apes 51-3
sequoia, giant 94
Sequoiadendron giganteum 94
Serengeti Plain, Tanzania, Africa,
    20, *20*
settlements 19
    Arctic 212
    Dorset 223, 226-7
    in Europe 84
    Homo habilis 61
    mammoth bone dwellings 89, *89*
    pit dwellings 132
    Pre-Dorset 222

reconstruction of mammoth bone
hut *93*
seasonal 71, 142-3
Upper Paleolithic sites *88*
see also rock shelters; shelters
sexual behavior 17, 53
evolution of human 18-19, 57
sex roles in prehistory 30-1, 46
sexual dimorphism 30, *30*, 41
among baboons 57
evolution of *Homo sapiens* 55
shamanism 114-15
shamans 98, *108*, *114*
communal hunting 201, 205
depicted in cave art 106
Ipiutak 224
Shanidar Cave, Iraq 46, *48*, 68, 70,
72, *73*
shelters 46
Arctic 212
Choris 223
Dorset 223
Independence I 218
mammoth-bone 95, 132, 134-5
Norton 224
Pleistocene sites in Australia 160
see also rock shelters
Shroud of Turin 94
Shugnou, central Asia 133
Siberia *122-3*
Siberian cultural tradition 125
signaling 18, 22, 23, 57-8
Simon, William 192
Simon Clovis cache, Idaho, North
America *187*, 192, *195*
Sinap, Turkey 36
Sireuil, Dordogne, France *103*
Sivapithecus 36, *36*, 42, *43*
Siwalik Hills, Pakistan 36
skeletal structure *18*
Skhul Cave, Mount Carmel, Israel *48*,
49, *49*, 67, *67*
skin color 62
sloths
giant 186
ground 206, *207*
social organization
among apes 53
in the Arctic 218
chimpanzees *35*, 58
communal hunting 200-1
comparing humans and apes 52
Cro-Magnon women 100
development in modern humans 58,
78, 88
Dorset 227
evolution of sexual signals 57-8
Homo habilis 61
Magdalenian 91, 93-5
in Paleoindian cultures 204-5
personal status 95, 100
ritual systems 102
settling northern Europe 142
totemism 111
Upper Paleolithic 98
Solo, Java, Indonesia 72
Solomon Islands *170-1*, 171, 175
animal species on 179
Kavachi volcano erupting *182*
Pleistocene sites 172
Solutré, France 88, *89*, *91*, *92*, 105
Solutrean tradition *85*, 88, *89*, *91*, *107*
Solvieux, Dordogne, France 104
Son Vi, Vietnam 126
Sonviian tradition 126
"sorcerer" male figure *107*, 114, *114*
South Africa *see* Africa; Klasies River
Mouth Cave; Kromdraai;
Markapansgat; Saldanha;
Sterkfontein; Swartkrans; Taung
Southeast Asia
Acheulean tradition in 64

erectine sites in 63
Homo sapiens in 50
migration to Australia from 151
modern humans in 125, *126-7*
Upper Paleolithic 128-9
Upper Paleolithic sites *125*, *130*
Southern Forests Archaeological
Project, Tasmania, Australia 166
Southwest Asia 68, 123
Neanderthal sites *66*, 71
Neanderthals in 71
speech *see* language
Spirit Cave, Thailand 126
steatopygia *102*
Steinheim, Germany *48*, *50*, 66, 84
Stellmoor, Germany 140
Sterkfontein, South Africa *32*, 37, 40,
45, *48*, *50*, 75
Sthenurus 162
Stoneking, Mark 80
Straus, William 67
Suess, Hans E. 94
Sun Mother and the Creation 148
Sungir, Russia *89*, 95, 99, 105,
132, 138-9
suslik 87
Swanscombe, England *48*, 66, 84
Swartkrans, South Africa 45, *45*, *50*, 60,
61, 75
symbolism
fertility 102-3, 116
sexual 111, 116
in Upper Paleolithic art 110

Tabarin, Africa *48*
Tabon Cave, Palawan, Philippines
126, *129*
Tabun Cave, Israel *48*, 67, 68
Tagua-Tagua, South America *187*
Taima-taima, South America *187*
Talasea, New Britain 180
taro 178
Tasmania, Australia 149
evidence of human occupation 155, 160
Homo sapiens sapiens in 126
Ice Age hunters 166-7
late Pleistocene sites in *166*
Tasmanian devil 168, 169
Tasmanian wolves 58, 59
Tata, Hungary 28, *28*
tattooing 116
Taung, South Africa *48*, *50*, 75
Taung child 37, *37*, 40, 60
teeth 55
temperatures 85
changing 83
see also climate; Ice Age
Terra Amata, France 23, 46, 64
territorial boundaries 19, 205
Teshik-Tash, Uzbekistan *48*, 70, 72
thermoluminescence dating 49, 74,
151, 152, *152*
for Malakunanja II *153*
threat display 26, *26*
Thule culture *221*, 223, 225
sites *210*
Thunderbird site, Virginia, North
America *187*, 192
thylacine *164*, 168, 169, *169*
Thylacinus cynocephalus 165, 168,
169, *169*
Thylacoleo carnifex 162, *162*, 168, *168*
Thylogale brunii 174
Tighenif, Algeria, Africa *48*, 49
Tihodaine, Algeria, Africa 80
Tingkayu Plain, Sabah, East Malaysia
126, *128*
Tinterhert, Tassili n'Ajjer, Algeria,
Africa *81*
Tjonger, Holland 140
Toad River Canyon, Canada
178, *178*

tools 17, 18, 19, *20*, *21*, 30, *143*
Aboriginal flint *165*
at African sites 78
from antler, bone, or ivory 60, 78,
81, *89*, 125, *167*
Arctic 210, 212
Arctic Small Tool Tradition 212,
213, 217
Aterian culture 80
blade technology *10-11*, *89*, 98
from Bobongara *151*, 151-3, 154
bone-points of wallaby 167
burins 77, *89*, 98
chopping 17, *21*, 56, *64*
Clovis *184*, 186, 189, *192*, 192-5
comparing humans and apes 51-3
Cro-Magnon 85-95
defining the use of 56
Denbigh 212, *212*
Dorset 222
Dyukhtai 133
flake *21*, *89*, *128*
Folsom 196-8, 199
geometric microliths 125
from Greater Australia 154
grinding pits *157*
grinding stones 81, *156*
ground-edge 154
Hamburg culture 140, *140*
hand axe *55*, 64, *64*
heat-treated *176-7*, 182
iron 224
language necessary to make 46
Mal'ta Afontova 133
microlithic blade technique 125,
137
microscopic analysis of wear
patterns on 182
Mousterian 71, *71*
Near Oceania 180-2, *183*
Norton 224
Oldowan 17, *21*
organic residue analysis 178, *178*
points 77, 81, *89*
Pre-Dorset 219, *219*
precursors of microlithic technology
143
Sarqaq 218, *219*
Siberian stone 125
sickles made of bone, antler, or
wood 81
in Southeast Asia 124, 128-9, *128-9*
stone *18*, 19, *21*, 45, 55, 56-7, *57*, 58,
71, *167*
Sungir, stone 139
thumbnail scrapers *167*, 167
tortoise cores 71
see also weapons
Torralba, Spain 46, 64
totemism 111
tree line 211
Trinil, Indonesia *48*
Turkana Newcomer 47, *47*, *50*, 62,
78, *80*
see also Lake Turkana, East Africa
"Twiggy" 44

Ubeidiya, Southwest Asia 63
Ul'khum, Chukchi Peninsula,
Siberia 137
Upper Paleolithic period 77, 128-9
Asia *125*
burials and settlements in Europe
4-5, 84
cave art 97-121, *104*
cultural traditions of Europe *89*
grinding stones 81
Southeast Asia *130*
tool technology 78, 80, 85-95
Upper Pleistocene *see* Pleistocene
uranium-lead dating 74
uranium-thorium dating 49

Uromys rex 179
Ursus spelaeus 86
Usselo, Belgium 140

Vail site, Maine, North America
187, 192
van den Berghe, Pierre 58
van Lawick, Hugo 24
Venus figurines *12*, 31, *31*, 88, *89*, 100,
101, 102-3, *102-3*, *107*
from southern Siberia *123*, *133*
vervet monkeys 22, *22*
Vézère River, Dordogne, France 72, 84,
90, 91, 93, *98*, 104, *104*, *105*
see also Gorge d'Enfer; La Madeleine;
Laugerie-Basse; Le Moustier
Vogelherd, Germany 22
Vries, H.L. de 94

Waal, Frans de 53
Wajak, Java, Indonesia *48*, 126
Walker, Alan 45
walking upright 17, *39*, *40*
earliest evidence for *19*
evolution of *Homo sapiens* 55
Laetoli footprints 37, *37*
sexual signaling 18
skeletal structure *18*
wallabies 169, 172, 174
Wallacea 130, *130*, 149, *149*
Wallanae River, Indonesia 126
walrus 211, *215*
war as organized aggression 26-7
Washoe 51
weapons
Arctic Small Tool Tradition 212, 217
barbed harpoons of bone *85*
bow and arrow 81
Clovis 186, 189, *189*, 192-5, *194*,
195-6, *196*, 205
Denbigh 212, *220*
Dorset 222, *222*
Fishtail points *187*
fluted projectile points 188, 189,
192, *195*
Folsom projectile points *197*, 199
Goshen projectile points 203, *203*
Pre-Dorset 219, *221*
Sarqaq 218, *218*
spear-throwers 98, *99*, 195
see also tools
Wehlen, Germany 140
Wenatchee, Washington, North
America 193, *205*
West Turkana, Kenya, Africa 45, *45*
whale, killer *214-15*
White, Tim 37, *50*
Willandra Lake, Australia 156
Willaumez Peninsula, New Britain
180-1
Willendorf, Austria 31, *89*, 100, *102*,
103, *107*
Williamson site, Virginia, North
America 192
Wilson, Allan 80
wolverine *86*
wolves *86*
Arctic 211
dire 206
wombats 169
Wonambi 168
Wood, Bernard 47, *51*

Xirochori, Greece 36

Yanomami Indians 93
Yayo, Africa *48*
Younger Dryas 83

Zhoukoudian, China 46, *48*, 63, *63*,
64, 65
Zuttiyeh, Israel *48*